THE HOUR OF DECISION

Rudolf Steiner
(1923)

THE HOUR OF DECISION

Human Responsibility for World Evolution through Our Spiritual Connection with the Earth and the World of the Stars

Eighteen lectures held in Stuttgart, Dornach, and The Hague from January 1 to April 1, 1921

Translation by
Dorit Winter and Clifford Venho

RUDOLF STEINER

SteinerBooks

CW 203

SteinerBooks | Anthroposophic Press
834 Main Street, P.O. Box 358
Spencertown, New York 12165
www.steinerbooks.org

Original translation from German by Dorit Winter and Clifford Venho

This book is volume 203 in the Collected Works (CW) of Rudolf Steiner, published by SteinerBooks, 2025. It is a translation of *Die Verantwortung des Menschen für die Weltentwickelung durch seinen geistigen Zusammenhang mit dem Erdplaneten und der Sternenwelt*, 3rd edition, published by Rudolf Steiner Verlag, Dornach, Switzerland, 2022.

ISBN: 978-1-62148-323-6
eBook ISBN: 978-1-62148-324-3

Printed in the United States of America by Versa Press

CONTENTS

Lecture Fifteen

DORNACH, MARCH 13, 1921

Lecture Sixteen

DORNACH, MARCH 27, 1921

Lecture Seventeen

DORNACH, MARCH 28, 1921

INTRODUCTION

Clifford Venho

These lectures offer a unique glimpse into Rudolf Steiner's activity during the challenging post-war years. As Steiner's work struck ever wider and deeper into the broader culture, challenging the status quo in every field of social, cultural, and economic life—with initiatives such as the movement for social threefolding and the founding of the first Waldorf School—unprecedented opposition to anthroposophy arose from all sides, most vehemently from certain academic and clerical circles. The response of the members of the Anthroposophical Society to the opposition, though well intentioned, was often woefully naïve and inadequate. This opposition, together with the lack of wakefulness on the part of the membership of the Anthroposophical Society, would lead, less than two years after these lectures, to the burning of the first Goetheanum on New Years' Eve 1922/23. Already in the lecture of January 30, 1921, reading the signs of the times, Steiner warned:

> If things continue like this, then Ahriman will get his due; for that is the spirit who greedily creeps around the modern centers of learning, wanting to keep them as they are; for that is how he finds his due. The ahrimanic spirit, this cold, ossified, bald Ahriman—if I may express myself pictorially—creeps around our modern centers of learning; he wants them to stay as they are. He will certainly lend a hand if it comes to something like the destruction of this Goetheanum.

The lectures were not intended as a self-contained lecture cycle but were rather spread out over the first months of 1921, some in Stuttgart, one in The Hague, and the rest in Dornach—hence their wide-ranging nature. And yet, a red thread runs through them: a picture of humanity at the hour of decision. The word *decision,* as if written in golden letters, stands at the heart of these lectures. It appears nearly twenty times in the course of the lectures, as in: "the hour of decision," "this age of decision," "a decision that comes from the depths of human nature," etc. And while Steiner speaks of many decisions facing us today in all aspects of life, at the core of this age of decision lie the three paths open to humanity: the path of Lucifer, the path of Ahriman, and the path of Christ.

Rudolf Steiner first describes the luciferic path as that of a nebulous mysticism in which one luxuriates in the glow of supersensible ideas which are no more than abstractions, in which one flees the "evil world" and seeks the solitude of the heights far above the banality of the workaday world. On this regressive path, Earth evolution would be drawn back into a "caricature of Old Moon." Wherever the lure of an ancient, decadent wisdom entices human souls, there hovers Lucifer.

The ahrimanic path is that of "bald-headed" materialism. In extreme intellectualism, in a science devoid of spirit, in our modern centers of learning, there lurks Ahriman. At one time, the human being was part and parcel of an ancient humanity's conception of nature, where knowledge of nature meant knowledge of the human being. This evolved into the modern conception of nature, where the human being has been erased, where our view of nature is free of any traces of the human being. This modern scientific worldview was the necessary foundation for the development of modern technology, but unchecked, it leads to the mechanization of humanity.

Regarding the third path, Rudolf Steiner says in the lecture of January 29, 1921:

> The third possibility is to look for the balance, the equilibrium between the two. One cannot speak of the equilibrium with as much certainty as is the case with one or the other extreme. The equilibrium must be sought by having both in the appropriate way, shall we say, on the right and on the left, without being too strongly attracted by one or the other but passing through both in the balance of life, letting the one be regulated by the other, letting the one be ordered by the other.

In a later lecture, Steiner deepens this picture of the three paths, describing how humanity, having lost the image of man that should be at the heart of its knowledge of nature, developed to the point where the human being became a "zero." He became devoid of spiritual content, of any connection with his own true image as a spiritual being. And in this space of the zero, there arose the impulse for freedom. In other words, the path of Ahriman, of a natural science devoid of the image of man, led the human being into the arms of Lucifer, into an external demand for freedom in the social sphere. The working together of these adversaries becomes clear also in the fact that an impersonal intellectual culture, in which people take no real interest in knowledge but merely store it up on library shelves, whether physical or digital, an intellectual culture in which it is seen as the highest achievement to be able to say: "I think how everyone else thinks," or in other words, where "one is proud of avoiding any departure from what has been formulated in a certain way once and for all"—an intellectual culture in which one lives as in a cloud-like existence, with the abstract ideas hovering like an atmosphere over the earth—there the luciferic sprits are waiting for these abstract ideas untouched by the human heart. This impersonal intellectual culture turns humanity into automatons.

In response to this situation, Steiner speaks of two holy commandments that can be heard today in the spiritual world as remedies to the luciferic and ahrimanic temptations. The one is: "External science must be supplemented by the science of the knowledge of the human being." That is, science must be humanized through a spiritual understanding of the human being as a threefold being of body, soul, and spirit, with a concrete understanding of the interaction of all three members. Steiner provided many specific insights in this field—foremost among them, the view of the life of thinking, feeling, and willing in connection with the activity of the nerve-sense, rhythmic, and metabolic systems, first described, after painstaking, decades-long research, in *The Riddles of the Soul*. In a sense, his entire undertaking on behalf of spiritual science was an endeavor to bring before humanity a "science of the knowledge of the human being." Of his foundational work *An Outline of Occult Science*, for example, he says: "You will not find a world devoid of humanity anywhere there. You will find what you yourself are, from one stage to the next, portrayed in world evolution itself" (Dornach, January 30, 1921). As a remedy to cold, dehumanized, impersonal science, Steiner presents another way:

> The other way is this—that one is interested in all the details, that the mind catches fire and enlivens science, that it melts science down into living concepts, that everything we comprehend, everything we grasp is received by the inner life of soul. In this way, one can really imbue everything which science gives with inner fire; in this way, by comprehending the individual sciences, one can gradually penetrate into the whole existence of the world; in this way, one can form something which becomes an intrinsically personal matter for every human being who pursues it. (Dornach, April 1, 1921)

In this way, a path toward spiritualizing external science through a true knowledge of the human being has been opened to humanity.

Souls today come to Earth longing for spiritual nourishment of this kind. But the soul is in danger of a soul death through a science devoid of spirit. It is up to human beings to provide the nourishment by which the eternal in man can be sustained in this age of decision. It is not enough to say, "I am an eternal being, and the eternal core of my being will be preserved under all circumstances." Only through the science of the spirit, through perceiving the spirit in all material phenomena, can the soul receive what it needs to carry vitality into the following incarnation: "The continuation of souls, their health, yes, the continuation of soul life itself, the staving off of the soul death of humanity depends on the spiritualization of our natural science!" (Stuttgart, January 16, 1921).

The second holy commandment that resounds in the spiritual world is: "You shall not let the impulse of freedom continue without cosmic feeling!" As described earlier, as a result of having been "hollowed out by modern science," we experience ourselves as free, as separate from the world of nature. Out of this inner feeling arises the demand for freedom in an external sense, as a being who has become "zero." This leads to the "luciferization" of social life, whereby freedom is demanded without having grasped the true nature of the human being as a cosmic being—as we find him described in *An Outline of Occult Science*. The antidote is a "feeling of human connection to the world." By developing a true feeling for our place in the cosmos, we nurture healthy social forces.

Thus, the two holy commandments, which act as a remedy for the extremes of the ahrimanic and luciferic paths, arise from the true Christ mystery:

> These two things—knowledge of the human being and feeling for the entire cosmos—these are what give the human being equilibrium. But this he can find if, in the most modern sense, he can really grasp the Christ mystery, grasp it as anthroposophical spiritual knowledge can give it to him. For there we speak of Christ as a cosmic being that has descended to the earth from cosmic infinitude. We learn to feel cosmically, and need only imbue this cosmic feeling with content. This we can do only through anthroposophical spiritual science, otherwise the concept of Christ remains empty for us. *The concept of Christ turns into mere phrase if we do not grasp the cosmos itself as human.* (Dornach, January 30, 1921 [emphasis added])

Thus Rudolf Steiner paints a picture of humanity at the great hour of decision. Over one hundred years have passed since these lectures were given, and yet we still stand, perhaps more intensely than ever, under the sign of this decisive hour. Which path will humanity follow?

> The task lies along such lines. It really does not consist of a few people feeling good about knowing this or that; rather, it consists—the task of this spiritual science when it is taken seriously—of intervening in the evolution of humanity in such a way that world events form themselves in the right way from out of humanity. (Dornach, April 1, 1921)

THE HOUR OF DECISION

Rudolf Steiner

Lecture One

STUTTGART, JANUARY 1, 1921

LET US START today with a reflection on the festive season, that time of year which every year again renews the memory and commemoration of the Mystery of Golgotha, as well as the direct perception of the Mystery of Golgotha.

We actually have three such festivals within the development of Christianity: the Christmas festival, the Easter festival, and the Whitsun festival. And one can say of these three festivals that each in its own way brings the human being into a relationship with that within which Christian development sees the meaning of all of earth events. These three festivals also differ with regard to the human soul forces.

Christmas is more connected to feeling. It is also the festival which is, in a certain sense, the most popular because understanding it demands the deepening of perception, the deepening of feeling, and because it is the one which is most widely accessible to the human being.

Easter, which requires the human being to raise himself up to an understanding of the actual Mystery of Golgotha, to the penetration of a suprasensory being into human evolution, makes the greatest demands on human understanding. It is a festival which, to some extent, raises human understanding to the highest level. It is, of course, also celebrated broadly, but it cannot be popular in the same way as Christmas.

The third festival, Whitsun, establishes a special relationship between the human will and the suprasensory world, the world, namely, to which the Christ-being as such belongs. The transfer of will impulses, which are then in turn transmitted to the world, is brought to human consciousness by the true meaning of Whitsun.

Thus, in a threefold way, what one could call the Christian mystery becomes clear through these annual festivals. One can become aware, in a variety of ways, of how the Christmas mystery approaches the human being, and we have, in the course of many years, considered the Christmas thought from the most diverse points of view, especially with regard to the Christmas festival.

This time we want to remember something that can become clear to anyone who considers the Christmas mystery from the perspective of the Gospels. In the Gospels we are presented with a twofold annunciation of the birth of Christ Jesus. One annunciation is offered to the poor shepherds out in the fields, those to whom—one might say, as in a dream or some other way—an Angel announces the birth of Christ Jesus. Here we have to do with an awareness of this event that awakens through inner soul forces, which are constituted in a particular manner through the surroundings of the birth place of Christ Jesus. And a second annunciation is represented in the Gospels: this is the one which goes forth to the three kings or the three Magi from the Orient. They follow—so we are told—the language of a star, which announces to them that Christ Jesus has come into the world.

Thus we are referred to two way in which an earlier humanity came to higher knowledge. It is also a matter of something which today is no longer considered in the right way. Today, one often imagines that people simply have a perception, a way of thinking, and that this perception, this thinking—in short, the unfolding of inner soul forces—has been essentially the same through all the centuries and millennia as it is today, albeit that it was more primitive in earlier times. We know, from our anthroposophical spiritual science, how the soul constitution of humanity has changed in the course of time, how in ancient times, approximately during the seventh and eighth millennia of the post-Atlantean period or earlier, humanity saw its own life as well as the surrounding world very differently; and how then this soul constitution changed again and again and became what we now know as the intellectual analysis of the world and the purely sense-perceptible conception of external things. This development goes from a somewhat older, instinctive clairvoyance through our present-day soul constitution in order once again to become a kind of clairvoyance in the future, a seeing of the world which, however, ought then to be combined with the full consciousness of humanity.

At the time when the Mystery of Golgotha took place on earth, the old clairvoyance, which was instinctive, was to a large extent already, if I may put it like this, paralyzed. True, human beings had a soul constitution that differed from today's, but they also no longer had the old clairvoyance; nor did they have the old forms of analyzing the world more precisely through all manner of wisdom. Both the old teachings about wisdom and the ancient instinctive clairvoyance had dimmed by the time the Mystery of Golgotha approached humanity. Nevertheless, remnants were still present, and it is precisely through the Gospels that we are clearly informed, if we understand them correctly, that such remnants were still present. Such remnants were present in individual, chosen personalities. Such chosen personalities may have been the humble shepherds in the field, who, through their pious hearts, possessed a certain power of clairvoyance which came over them in a dreamlike way; they might also have been the kind of personalities who are introduced to us as being at the top of the social ladder, such as the three Magi from the Orient, who from ancient times preserved the ability to see into the course of world events through a certain wisdom teaching. And so, the humble shepherds could see approaching them, in a kind of dreamlike experience, in a kind of inner perception, what took place through the event of the birth of Chris Jesus. On the other hand, the three Magi from the Orient were able to develop a science that, by following cosmic phenomena, phenomena in the heavens, enabled them to recognize the significance of what took place on the earth beyond the ordinary course of life.

Thus, we are referred to two quite specific yet different kinds of knowledge. Let us first consider what was still present for the three Magi from the Orient as a last remnant of an ancient wisdom teaching. We are clearly shown how these Magi could decipher the path of the stars. Through this portrayal we are referred to an ancient astronomy, an ancient way of observing the secrets of the world of stars which also revealed the secrets of human events. This ancient astronomy was unlike our astronomy. Our astronomy is, indeed, in a certain way, also prophetic; it can predict the path of solar and lunar eclipses, and the like. But our astronomy is only mathematical and mechanical. Our astronomy speaks only of the relationships between space and time insofar as one can express them mathematically. But what takes place in relation to the inner life of the human being apart from space and time, yet still in space and time, but with a higher meaning, this the ancient astronomy, the ancient star wisdom, saw in the path of the stars. If we bring the science of a more ancient humanity to consciousness, we find that this star wisdom is essentially what gives this old science its content in the first place. Human beings investigated the stars to determine what happened on the earth. But for them the world of stars was not that abstract, machine-like being it has become for today's humanity. For them the world of the stars was full of life. They perceived being in every single one of the planets. In a way, they spoke to every one of the planets with an inner soul language, just as today we speak from human to human through outer language. They understood that they experienced something inwardly, in the soul, which in a way reflected and reproduced what took place out there in the magnitude of space through the path of the stars. It was a living, spiritually imbued view of the universe. And the human being felt himself placed spiritually, in a soulful manner, into this universe. Wisdom about this universe was also cultivated in schools which one could call mystery schools, in which the pupils were prepared in a careful, intimate, inward way to be able to understand the course of the stars in a way that made human life on earth comprehensible.

What was the nature of these preparations? These preparations, specifically for the knowledge of the starry sky and its effects, were such that the human being, even then, in the time of instinctive clairvoyance, was educated for a life that was more awake than normal outer life. The broad masses of people had a sort of instinctive clairvoyance. This corresponded to a soul state which was less awake than our normal soul state. During ancient times of human development, one could not think in a state of such wakefulness as one can today. One could not arrive at mathematics or geometry in the same sense as today. All of human life between birth and death was more a matter of dreaming; but for that very reason, because it was a life of dreaming, it perceived the environment in a more living way than our completely wakeful life. And the strange thing is that individual pupils of the mysteries, amid the last remnants of which stood such men as the three Magi in those ancient days—one could say approximately into the second millennium, even the first millennium before the Mystery of Golgotha—were introduced to knowledge that was very similar to our geometry or mathematical knowledge.

For outer humanity, Euclid† was the first to present geometry. But this was merely a transmission of geometry to wider humanity. What Euclid presented as geometry had already been alive in the mysteries for thousands of years; but it was only communicated to selected pupils of the mysteries. It had a different effect on them than it did later on. It seems strange and paradoxical, but it is like this: what in our day is already learned by children, our geometry, our arithmetic, this was learned in the mystery schools by individuals who had been specially chosen from among the masses as being particularly gifted and who were accepted into the mysteries.

Today one can often hear that mysterious things were taught in the mysteries. According to their purely abstract content, these mysterious things are the same things that are taught to children today. They are not different at all, and the mysteriousness does not lie in how these things are unknown to people today, but in the different way in which the matter has been brought to humanity. It is, of course, very different if the content of geometry is brought to children simply by appealing to their understanding in an age when people live in their waking consciousness from the moment of awakening until falling asleep, or whether, in an age when the old, instinctive clairvoyance in which consciousness was dream-like, these things were brought to specially selected human beings with a more mature consciousness. Today, humanity does not always have correct ideas about these things.

You see, there is a poem to Varuna† in oriental literature. It tells of Varuna appearing in the air that blows through the forests as wind, of Varuna appearing in the thunder that peals from the clouds, of Varuna appearing in the human heart when it stirs itself to action, of Varuna appearing in the heavens when the sun crosses the heavens, of Varuna contained in the mountains as Soma juice.[†] Today you will usually find in books that people actually do not know what Soma juice is. In their erudition, people today state that they do not know what Soma juice is, even though there are people who drink it by the liter and know it very well from a certain perspective. But there is a difference between knowing things from the perspective of the mysteries and knowing them from the perspective of awake consciousness in profane feeling. And today you can read about the philosopher's stone,[†] which was cultivated during a particular period when one considered the being of substance to be rather different than one does today. And again, the historians describing alchemy will tell you that they do not know the philosopher's stone. I have always indicated in lectures here and there that this philosopher's stone is well known to most people. They just don't know its essence and don't know why it is called what it is. Most people know it very well, for they actually use it by the kilo.

Occasionally, things really are quite different from what today's abstract, theoretical, alien, and unreal view of things is able to imagine. Nor is there a real view of what it means to take up our geometrical, our arithmetical science in a mature state, with a completely different soul constitution than that of today's humanity. In my book *Christianity as a Mystical Fact*, I indicated this special quality of the mysteries. But such important things are usually not properly understood; one usually does not take them earnestly enough. What one needs to understand is that what constituted the mysteries in ancient times was the manner, the way in which things were brought to human beings. And that is really how it was with purely mathematical considerations, for which Novalis[†] still retained a fully human, feeling content when he experienced mathematics as a great poem, which most people today certainly do not. So it was this feeling aspect, but grasped as the pouring out of mathematical forms in the world, into which the pupil of the ancient mysteries was led. And then, when the mathematical understanding of the world approached the pupil of the ancient mysteries, he became a human being with a worldview such as is described as that of the Magi from the Orient. Then the mathematics of the universe, which in our day has become something entirely abstract, revealed *beingness* in the universe because what was revealed was supplemented by something else which approached him. And so, what corresponded to the external knowledge of an ancient culture, which had been preserved in its last remnants for the Magi, having come to them from the Orient, was the cause for the one annunciation: the annunciation through the wisdom teaching, through external science.

On the other hand, the inner experience of the mysteries of humanity could develop in people who were particularly predisposed to it, such as those who are represented by the shepherds of the field. There, the inner forces in the human being had to reach a particular stage. Then, what happened in the world of humanity became immediate vision, imaginative, instinctive-imaginative pictorial perception. Thus, through inner vision, there announced itself to the humble shepherds in the field that which was summarized for them in the annunciation: "The God is revealed in the heavenly heights, and through him there can be peace among all men of good will."

Thus the world mysteries spoke both to the innermost aspect of the humble shepherds in the field and to the outermost reaches to which human wisdom could rise at that time; world mysteries spoke both to the shepherds and to the Magi from the Orient. And the great mystery of earthly life was announced from two sides.

What did the Magi from the Orient experience? What was especially developed in such pupils when mathematics was brought into their soul constitution, which was already especially mature? You see, Kant says of mathematical knowledge that it is *a priori*. What he means by *a priori* is that it is acquired before any outer, empirical experience. This is an empty phrase. This *a priori* means nothing. It only makes sense when, out of spiritual science, one can indicate that mathematics arises out of us, that it is something which comes out of the inner life of the human being into human consciousness. And whence does it come? Well, it comes from experiences we had in the spiritual world before conception or birth. There we lived in the great, wide cosmos. There we experienced what we could experience before we had our physical eyes and physical ears. There we experienced *a priori* with respect to life on earth. Whatever was experienced there *a priori* rises up for our consciousness unconsciously out of the inner life. People do not know, unless like Novalis they have a presentiment, that when they do mathematics, there arise experiences from before birth or conception. For anyone who is able to look at these things in the right way, mathematical cognition alone is evidence that one existed in a spiritual world before conception. For those for whom this is not evidence of a prenatal life, for them the other fact exists—namely, that they just don't think thoroughly enough about the phenomena of life, that they have no idea of the actual origin of mathematics.

Pupils in the ancient mysteries who had the sort of wisdom which had been preserved as final remnants in the Magi from the Orient, received a clear impression of it: If we gaze at the stars in such a way that we penetrate them with mathematical lines, with our calculation, then we distribute across the outer widths of space that within which we lived before our birth. And a pupil of the holy mysteries said to himself: "Now I am living here on the earth, looking out into space through my eyes, noticing what is spatial around me. Before my birth or conception, I also lived within this appearance of cosmic space. There, I myself counted from star to star what I now replicate here through mathematics; there, I myself hurried from star to star with inner forces; there, I lived in what I now construct." In that way, everything human beings experienced before birth or conception became present for them. Therefore, they also took it up as something holy. Therefore, they also knew that it was the spiritual world which they became aware of; it was the world in which they lived before they trod the earth. This knowledge about the world which a human being experiences before he treads upon the earth was present as a last remnant for the Magi from the Orient; through this they recognized the approach of the Christ-being.

From where did the Christ-being come? It came from that world in which we live between death and a new birth, and it united with the life we live through between birth and death. The science that deals with the world in which we live between death and a new birth can, therefore, reveal something like the Mystery of Golgotha. Thus, by means of this science, the Mystery of Golgotha, the Christmas Mystery was announced to the Magi.

In that the human being lives here on the earth and develops what his understanding reveals to him about his surroundings, develops the impulses for his actions, for his social life, he unconsciously experiences something else in himself. He is unaware of it, but just as he experiences the aftereffects of his prenatal life, he also experiences that which then strides through the gates of death and becomes the content of life after death. These are the forces that are already present in a germinal form between birth and death and only blossom fully in the life after death. These forces worked with great intensity in the old instinctive clairvoyance; and they still worked as the last remnants in the poor shepherds in the field because of their great piety. We live in these forces especially between falling asleep and waking up, when our soul is outside the body and lives in the outer space. Then it lives in such a way as it will only once again live, now consciously, when it discards the outer physical body after death. These forces, which under certain conditions can penetrate daily life from the world of dreams or the world of sleep, were very active in the old instinctive clairvoyance. The poor shepherds experienced these forces; and through them there was revealed, from a different side than for the three Magi, what could be announced as the Mystery of Golgotha.

What does one experience through those forces which especially belong to the human being between death and a new birth when they are kindled in the life between birth and death, as they were for the Magi from the Orient? One experiences what happens beyond the earthly. One is carried away from the earth into the world of stars, in which one lives between death and a new birth. That was the world into which the Magi from the Orient were introduced, away from the earth into the heavens.

What does one experience through those forces that arise inwardly, especially in the world of dreams, which generally arise out of the inner world of the human being? There one experiences what takes place in the inner regions of the earth. There it is the telluric forces which are mainly at work, those forces which we have on account of our body, on account of living in our body. They are especially at work in what we experience between falling asleep and waking up. Then, too, we are in the outer world, but mainly in that outer world which belongs to the earth.

You will say: It contradicts the truth to say that we are outside our body. – That is not a contradiction. One only ever notices what is outside of oneself; one does not notice whatever one is living in. Only those who are especially ignorant about certain areas and only want to develop empty phrases are capable of gliding over such things easily with their phrases and of saying something like: It is not a matter of establishing a spiritual science based on knowledge attained outside of the human being, for the important thing is precisely that the human being attain knowledge from within in addition to the external knowledge of nature. – Yes, with such a gush of wordiness one can establish schools of wisdom in Darmstadt,[†] but one will still remain a mere phraseologist even if one does establish schools of wisdom. For if one understands the matter in the right way, one can even say: Yes, one must describe the world from within in order to attain the suprasensory, but one must of course first enter into the inner world, and then what remains external has to be seen from outside of the body, and one must then look back at the body. Keyserling's speeches about looking at things from the point of view of the soul do not really seek to enter into the inner aspect of the human being; instead, they use mere empty words. Therefore, when we are in the state between going to sleep and awakening, we look back and perceive, so to speak, our body. Thus we perceive that which connects our body with the earthly; for it is, after all, of the earth. The poor shepherds in the field actually received the revelation of the earth from their bodies, in that they perceived, while in their dream-like state, what took place through the voice of the Angel.

And it corresponds completely to the Mystery of Golgotha that the revelation came from two sides: that of the Magi from the heavenly revelation, that of the shepherds from the earthly revelation. For a heavenly being, a being that until then had not belonged to the earth, is arriving. So it is through heavenly wisdom that one must be able to recognize its arrival. Then one learns to recognize that something descends from heaven. – If one has the wisdom of the shepherds, then one gets to know the earth; one feels one's way into the weaving life of the earth, which perceives the arrival of the heavenly being. It is the same Annunciation, from the other side. In a wondrous way, there flowed into a unified event what was communicated to human beings from two sides.

And if one now looks at the way humanity took up the event of Golgotha, then one has to say: In this and other respects only remnants of the old wisdom were still present. I have already indicated how the Mystery of Golgotha was understood with the remnants of the old wisdom, with a certain Gnosis, in the first centuries AD. Then one tried to penetrate the event of Golgotha more and more with merely intellectual analysis. And in the nineteenth century, naturalism gradually arrived in this area of confession. Nothing of the suprasensory content of the event of Golgotha was grasped anymore. Christ became the wise man from Nazareth, conceived of in a purely naturalistic manner. A new, spiritual comprehension of the Mystery of Golgotha became necessary. One ought not to confuse the fact of the Mystery of Golgotha[†] with the way human beings relate to this fact in their intellect.

Now, the soul constitution of the shepherds in the field and of the Magi from the Orient existed in its final remnants at the time of the Mystery of Golgotha. As humanity developed, all this changed. Things change and suffer metamorphoses.

What happened to the wisdom of the Magi from the Orient? It became our mathematics, our astronomy. The Magi possessed supra-earthly knowledge, which was essentially a grand memory of prenatal life. For us, this has shrunk and become deadened in our mathematical, mechanical understanding of the heavens, where we apply nothing but the laws of mathematics and mechanics to the outer phenomena. What rises up within us when we look at what has remained to us as mathematical astronomy, that is the present-day metamorphosis of what the Magi possessed.

And when we look at our outer sensory knowledge—mere perception through the eyes, through the ears—then it is the externalized inner knowledge of the shepherds in the field. What still gave the shepherds in the field the inner mysteries of earth existence allows us to look at the outer world coldly through our natural-scientific observations. Our natural-scientific observation is the daughter of the wisdom of the shepherds. But the daughter looks nothing like the mother. And our mathematics, which became astronomy, is the daughter of the wisdom of the Magi. Humanity had to go through this. When our natural scientists sit in the clinics and laboratories with their dry research, they really do not have much in common with the shepherds, but it is a direct metamorphosis of the wisdom of the shepherds. And our mathematicians are in the direct stream of inheritance of the Magi from the Orient. What was external has become internal, what was internal has become external. And thereby we have, first of all, fundamentally strayed from understanding the Mystery of Golgotha; we should be conscious of that. Yes, we have really strayed from this understanding. But perhaps many of those who have strayed furthest from this understanding are those who call themselves official preachers and prophets of Christianity.

With the cognitive powers, the powers of perception, and the powers of faith which are at work in human beings today, the event of Golgotha can no longer be comprehended in its true being. It must indeed be found in an entirely new way. The wisdom of the Magi has become our dry mathematics, through whose pictures alone the heavens are still seen; it has become internal. The inner must be re-enlivened. It must, so to speak, build up again from within that which is external.

Try now to understand the content of a book like my *Occult Science* from this perspective. The Magi grasped the wide world of the stars; they saw spirituality in this world of stars because they could see into prenatal human experience. This became abstract in our mathematics. But the same powers which develop our mathematics can be brought to life again, can be intensified again by means of imaginative vision. Then we give birth, from within, to a world which we can again see as the outer world, although we create it from within, which appears to us as Saturn, Sun, Moon, Earth, Jupiter, Venus, Vulcan. We see the heavens with inner vision, as the Magi from the Orient perceived the secrets of the Mystery of Golgotha through outer observation. What was external has become internal, has reached the abstraction of mathematics; so the internal must again be expanded to the outer universe, in that inner contemplation leads us to a new astronomy, to an inwardly experienced astronomy.

Only through such a turning toward a new understanding of the Christ do we today fulfill, in a certain sense, the meaning of the Christmas festival. Does the Christmas festival still have a special meaning for most people today? It is a very nice custom—though not very old, hardly one hundred and fifty years old—to make the Christmas tree into the symbol of the Christmas festival. After all, the Christmas tree began only in the nineteenth century.† What is it? One can make an effort to find the meaning of the Christmas tree. It is just when one makes that effort and learns how the Christmas tree gradually arose out of the small branch which Ruprecht, the servant of St. Nicholas, carried in his arms on December 6, it is just when one follows the story of the Christmas tree that one comes to see that the Christmas tree is directly connected to the Tree of Paradise. Human consciousness tends toward the Tree of Paradise, toward Adam and Eve. What does this mean? It is the one aspect of how, in our time, the Mystery of Golgotha is announced again.

People turn from the Mystery of Golgotha back to the creation of the world, to the origin of the world. They do not grasp the meaning of the salvation of the world and turn back again to the God of world creation. This is expressed by the gradual disappearance of the actual symbol of Christmas, the symbol of the cradle, which was present so marvelously in the Christmas Plays of earlier centuries, in which the Christmas tree is actually the Tree of Paradise. The old Yahweh religion again took the place of the Christ religion, and the Christmas tree is the symbol for the emergence of the Yahweh religion. However, this Yahweh religion appears multiplied amongst mankind. For Yahweh was rightfully revered as the One at a time when his people felt themselves to be the one people, unable to see beyond their own borders and expecting that one day they would completely fill the earth.

In our time, people talk about Christ Jesus and worship only Yahweh. For in the individual nationalities, as was especially clear during the war, there was talk about Christ; but it was only the original God, the God Yahweh, the one living in heredity and in nature. The Christmas tree on the one hand, on the other hand, the national gods who did not rise to Christianity; and this was how people turned back from understanding the Mystery of Golgotha to a much earlier understanding. In the assertion of the principle of nationality, in the proclamation† that the individual nations follow their gods, there is a regression to the old Yahweh religion. The Christ is most denied by those who want to worship him in any kind of national form.

You see, what has to be taken into account is that in every kind of annunciation, in the annunciation of the shepherds and in the annunciation of the Magi, something quite universally human is given; for the earth is common to all people. And insofar as the shepherds received the earthly annunciation, they received an annunciation that cannot be distinguished or differentiated by nationality. And insofar as the Magi received the great sun annunciation, the heavenly annunciation, they too received something universally human. For if the sun had shone first on the territory of one folk, then it also shone on the territory of the others. The heavens are common to all, the earth is common to all. With Christianity, what is universally human becomes active in humanity. This is expressed in the depiction of Christmas when it is presented as a two-fold annunciation. Such things, which used to be completely understandable for a different soul constitution, become understandable again today through spiritual science.

And how is spiritual science treated? Indeed, it is treated very strangely especially by those who call themselves official representatives of Christianity. No doubt some of you have seen that Group in Dornach, with the Christ figure in the middle, which is to stand at the east end of the Goetheanum in Dornach. You know that when I explain this Christ figure, I explain how above there is an ideal countenance of the human being, how it appears to me as the real countenance of the Christ. Those who have seen the figure will recall that it is a purely human, idealized face. The figure has recently developed a bit further, but as long as it was on view, it consisted of a block of wood from the middle downward, as the workers had built it. For the lower part especially will have to express the striding will.

This figure is surrounded at the top by two luciferic figures, which are separated from the Christ figure, and below by two ahrimanic figures. Now there is a certain missionary preacher by the name of Frohnmeyer.† He has published a little book about theosophy. And it also deals, very superficially, with anthroposophy. It says—and not as though someone had somehow told this man about it, but rather as if he himself had been there and looked at it himself—it says in this booklet: a Christ is to be placed in Dornach who bears luciferic traits above and animalistic features below.

I have often heard it said that you can sometimes check your state of mind when you come home in the evening in a very special way by lying down on the bed and putting your top hat on the bedspread. If the hat appears as a single hat, then you are sober; if it appears to be doubled, then you are definitely drunk. Well, whoever sees the Christ figure in Dornach as having luciferic traits above and animalistic features below, such a one was certainly in the condition of a man who sees two hats after having put one on the bedspread.

This matter has a very serious background, for it was written by someone who was a Christion missionary preacher. It appears in a publication in which there are other things of similarly untruthful content. Some time ago, this man was named a doctor of theology by a theological faculty. This man teaches in a theological faculty, where he is listed as a lecturer. You can imagine what kind of truth might permeate the teachings of a person who has this kind of relationship to truth and who claims to have seen what he describes.

That is how things stand today regarding the truthfulness of those who want to represent Christianity officially. I ask you: Do not these Christian, that is, anti-Christian representatives—anti-Christian because of their untruthful, mendacious minds—prove the need for a renewal of Christianity? Are these people not the living proof that Christianity needs renewal? Perhaps that is also the most understandable reason why one has the fiercest enemies in such people: for it is then exposed what kind of Christians these people are! Of course, they don't want that. They want to continue fishing in murky waters, want to announce their slander and untruths everywhere, and then they want to stand there as the shining light of Christianity.

This is what we should inscribe in our hearts today: When we think of the Mystery of Christmas, we actually need to look at a birth. We should not just chatter about the Christmas festival, nor should we just chatter about how we feel about it; instead, we should look at something which must be born anew in our time. True Christianity must, truly, be born anew. We need a universal Christmas festival. Spiritual science strives to be able to prepare in the right way a universal Christmas festival for humanity.

Lecture Two

STUTTGART, JANUARY 6, 1921

TODAY, EVERYTHING DEPENDS on introducing into life, in a really living way, the findings and soul impulses that want to flow through spiritual science. It must be emphasized again and again that in view of the great tasks of the present, it is not enough to inform oneself theoretically about the truths which underlie human life and world existence, and which can be gained from anthroposophical spiritual science; rather, it is a matter of observing the interconnections in real life and of understanding life itself on a spiritual-scientific basis. For centuries, humanity has become accustomed to seeing only a part of reality. And it is precisely in this way that, bit by bit, those states of consciousness that then led to the current catastrophic life were prepared. People today live without understanding life, without any of the understanding for life needed for the present phase of human development.

As students of anthroposophical spiritual science, we will certainly advance easily to the conviction of repeated earth lives, to the idea of causation in an earlier life—in spite of the full existence of freedom—for what happens to a person or what a person undertakes in a present life. However, when it is a matter of grasping actual life, we all too easily submit to ideas which have been produced in the last centuries and which, of course, are not actually sufficient to grasp human life; they are entirely suitable for grasping certain facts of natural events but are dull when it comes to the complexity of human life. And one might say: What most lags behind the demands of life today is, actually, the life of science. And yet this scientific life in turn exerts a great influence on the thinking of the broad masses of people. When I speak of the effect of this scientific life, I do not have in mind those who have some sort of relationship to science. I have in mind the whole broad mass of humanity, which, regarding the most important questions of life, submits to those who through outer institutions seem called upon to judge one thing or another. Then one acts according to such judgments. But nothing of a real understanding of human life is contained in such judgements. What must be carried into this human life is what can flow out of anthroposophical spiritual science. It must, above all, be carried into those branches of public discourse which provide the basis for the understanding of life.

If, today, someone approaches spiritual science, he begins to grasp what underlies repeated earth lives. But if he then wants to inform himself about what is going on in the present, and if he then approaches history, among other things—and by history I mean that which belongs to the education of the broad masses—then in that very history there prevails that way of thinking which is suitable for explaining only natural things and natural facts. Humanity has moved more and more toward expunging anything spiritual from history. And if, today, someone wants to explain realities that arise from historical life in any domain, then he has little choice but to inform himself about what earlier generations experienced; the second-to-last generation, the third-to-last generation, and so forth back through past centuries. How, to cite a concrete example, does a German today learn history? He focuses on the very people who lived there in Central Europe, to whom he himself belongs. He lets himself be told about events that took place among those people; he traces these events back to the fathers, the grandfathers, the great-grandfathers, to earlier generations. He then goes on, backwards, perhaps all the way to the time of the Middle Ages. He is always conscious that he is dealing with a developing humanity, which he can trace back to the migration of people and so on, and he wants to explain what is happening to people of the present time from what happened in relation to these previous generations. He becomes acquainted with the ongoing stream of historical development as it takes place in successive generations. Actually, people only have the concept of inheritance in relation to human beings; they think that the sons inherited certain things from their fathers, whether those are their own characteristics or have been passed down to them from their fathers and so forth. Thus, people go back in time from the present generation to the previous one, and so forth.

If we now consider all this from the perspective of spiritual science, does it represent the full reality? Isn't it the case that souls comprising a single generation in present human bodies were not necessarily incarnated in Central Europe in their earlier earth lives, that they were perhaps incarnated elsewhere under quite different circumstances? They carry the forces which they brought with them from earlier incarnations into their present bodies. These forces work just like that which ran down with the blood through the generations; they work in conjunction with these outer, physically inherited attributes. Can one succumb to the illusion that one understands the present age with regard to its people, with regard to its events, if one considers only a part of reality and not the entire reality, if one does not say: "In people of the present time, there live souls in which the forces that prevail definitely do not lead us back through the generations, but perhaps instead lead us into very different regions, where these souls lived in a former life?" One does not understand what is happening on the earth if one does not seriously consider in a concrete sense what lies in the recognition of the fact of repeated earth lives. One cannot honestly acknowledge repeated earth lives abstractly, on the one hand, and, on the other, view history as it is practiced today. By so doing, one simply separates outer life, in which one adheres completely to tradition, from that which one actually recognizes as essential. The desire must arise more and more to really see within life itself those things which one has recognized as true based on their spiritual foundations.

Because this is so, I am not going to wait to talk about certain research which is perhaps experienced by some people today as very paradoxical, but which must be proclaimed today because humanity demands an understanding of the *whole* reality, and because everything which does not lead toward an understanding of the whole reality simply belongs to a declining life. It is, of course, the case that most people today, when confronted with the full seriousness of spiritual-scientific truths, shrink back. Things seem too bold to them. For them, what spiritual science says is too much of a stretch from what they are used to thinking and feeling. Therefore, they may take a sip of this spiritual science, but they do not attain the full seriousness of its grasp because they do not have the courage really to carry these things into life, let alone into the observation of concrete life.

Before presenting the following argument, I must emphasize something again to which I have often drawn attention before. I have often said: whoever wants to find something through spiritual research in spiritual worlds must beware of mere combinations of concepts or associative ideas. For what one thus imagines is usually the opposite of the truth, or at least something which differs very much from the truth. It is precisely the deeper truths which at first seem paradoxical. They can only be found through real lived experience.

So let us take this question seriously: When we observe contemporary conditions from the perspective of true spiritual science, what is the situation of the people of this civilization which fell into such a catastrophe?[†] I expressly note that what I have already indicated here and there in detail, and what I also want to discuss now, is absolutely as I have already described it. But, of course, one can characterize what for this field is a far-reaching reality only by always giving further details.

I have often pointed out[†] how there are many souls living today who, in a former life during the first centuries AD, were incarnated more in the south of Europe and who are now incarnated more in Central Europe. This is definitely true, although it pertains only to a certain number of souls. Today I want to place before you what pertains to large portions of the current population of the earth. Here we arrive at the question (and what I will provide as an answer to this question is indeed based on real, intensive spiritual research): Where, then, were the souls of a large portion, virtually the majority, of the Western and Central European population, all the way into Russia, in an former earth life? If one examines this question conscientiously with the help of available spiritual research methods, then it turns out that one is dealing with souls who had gone through a relatively shorter life between the last death and this birth. One is led to the west. One is led on one's path of research to where, after the discovery of America, a large portion of the European peoples settled this America and exterminated, or at least extremely suppressed, the native peoples. One is led into the centuries of the conquests of America, to those souls that were in the bodies of the Indians over whom these conquests had poured. One will understand what I have to say only if one judges these exterminated Indians correctly. Certainly, they were not educated people in the sense that we now understand education, but there was something in these souls which I would like to call a universal pantheistic religious feeling. It was especially among these Indians, not necessarily the decadent peoples but those who formed the leading element there, that one found a religious feeling, oriented toward a spiritual, even monotheistic being with a unified spirit, felt intensively and vitally in the manifestations of nature and also in the deeds of human beings. One must take this mood of soul into account, and one must make one's way through many a prejudice, as through an undergrowth, to grasp the fact that in these souls something is visible that is different from what one sees in the Indian when one sees him only in accordance with outer, naturalistic methods as if half animal. And the souls of this exterminated, conquered Indian population live today in the greater part of Western and Central European peoples, all the way into Russia. We do not comprehend reality if we do not come to understand this apparent paradox.

These were souls who in their earlier incarnation did not benefit from Christianity. That is why, for the greater part of the European population, Christianity is not something that was already in their souls before this present birth or conception. They acquired it for the most part with the sounds of language. It is something which was acquired externally. How Christianity actually lives in today's European souls will be understood by those who know that in the majority of these souls, in a former life on earth, there were no Christian impulses at all; instead, there were impulses for a sort of pantheistic religious feeling toward the great universal spirit. However, a lot got mixed into this population by the souls that came up more from the south and had been incarnated in more southern regions of Europe in the first centuries AD, and that had lived in regions of north Africa and were then mostly reincarnated as I just described. These are the two kinds of souls that primarily constitute the Western and Central European population, all the way into Russia, as already mentioned. We should be clear that we ought to study the ways and means that a soul expresses itself in the present, what its aspirations are, how it thinks. To understand all this, we have to realize that a large portion of the present population can only be understood if we do not merely consider the common practice of following the generations back historically, but rather if we know that in those bodies which go back through blood relationships to fathers, grandfathers, great grandfathers, and so forth, back into the time of Charlemagne and further, that in those bodies souls are active—endowing them with their whole soul configuration—souls which lived in far distant America and were conquered by the Europeans.

We find another truth that can result from such spiritual research. We can look back to that population which was present in Europe more or less at the time of the great migrations, precisely that European population which had accepted Christianity from the south in the form that was then still different from what it is today, for it was still thoroughly permeated with elemental, original soul forces, because an imponderable power was at work within all of life. It was not yet permeated with abstract intellectual theology; it was something which affected, above all, the basic feelings of the soul. These souls, which were present in the Europe of that time and took up Christianity in this way, then, after a life between death and a new birth—which took longer than it did for others precisely because of the special kind of soul formation that entered these people—these souls are today for the most part incarnated over in Asia. In particular, among these souls who were Christianized in the time mentioned, there were many who are incarnated in Japanese bodies today. Whoever wants to understand this peculiar life in Asia, which today really does offer many riddles, has to be clear that in Asia today there live many souls who in their previous earth life took up Christian feelings in a particular form, who carried these Christian feelings into contemporary oriental bodies, who were surrounded from childhood on, already through their language, by what has remained in a decadent form from more ancient oriental culture. I would put it like this: something truly Christian lived in the dissemination of Christianity to which such souls were subjected in former times, as opposed to what they heard, what resounded in their hearts and minds from the decadent world of oriental religion and culture. This can be traced right up to the educated, the most highly educated of all, and one actually gains an understanding only if one does trace it in this way. One gains clarity about the actual significance of a personality like Rabindranath Tagore† if one is clear that this, too, is a soul which in a former earth life was a European Christian, a soul which, out of this European Christianity, pours a certain warmth of feeling through all that it produces. By contrast, everything that one encounters with Tagore in his coquettish nature, in this cultural coquetry, flows out of decadent Orientalism. There is, indeed, a strange hermaphroditism in the personality of just this Tagore. On the one hand, if one has a natural, healthy feeling, one always becomes aware that all the oriental coquetry of today is present; but, then again, one is drawn by a tremendous warmth of soul.

Today, it really does not work simply to nibble at the surface of what is theoretically presented as the view of repeated earth lives. Today, life in its concrete reality wants to be regarded this way, even if this is still uncomfortable for people. For, fundamentally, people today shy away from acquiring self-knowledge. They make no effort to see in real life what they propound as an abstraction. In a way, the human being is embarrassed to look in this way into his own nature. He does not want to be represented in the world as he truly is. That is why he disapproves of actually examining the realities in this realm. The degree of confusion, of riddles in contemporary life, becomes understandable when one takes into account the kinds of things I have been presenting to you.

But let us take a different population. It is precisely when the spiritual researcher has undertaken such investigations, leading to the results I have just described, that he is driven to the question: What actually happened to the population from a somewhat earlier period over in Asia? For in matters of spiritual research, it is the case that, pushed by life, by some sort of riddle that arises, you somehow come upon what you can research. First, it is life that leads you to start the research at a particular place; then your vision is ignited by that. A question leads you to a different area, and then you can only say: In the end, it turns out to make sense that you are driven by one question, by one result, to the next. You become, in a manner of speaking, aware that if you want to investigate what happened to the souls of the Indians, what happened to other souls of the former European population, then you must ask the question and it will be answered for you: What has become of those souls who, with their particular upbringing of that time in the Middle East, in the East altogether, were in Africa when Christianity arose, that is, at the time of the Mystery of Golgotha? I don't mean those souls who took up the teachings of the Mystery of Golgotha, but rather the souls who did not take them up, who propagated the old oriental, Asian culture. One doesn't always have an accurate concept of the continued existence of this old oriental, Asian culture—which today is decadent—during the time when the Mystery of Golgotha took place. For many people, it was a spiritualized, a very spiritualized culture. For many people, this included the capacity to have very clear ideas about certain relationships in the spiritual world. What was, of course, not present among those of whom I am now speaking was any notion of what becomes of a person who allows himself to be permeated by Christianity. But there was a very strong understanding of spiritual relationships, permeated with pictorial ideas. A worldview with a high degree of spirituality belonged to these people, a worldview that caused them to consider, in many respects, the spiritual world as the only true world, a world worth striving for, and caused them to flee, in a certain way, the outer, sense-perceptible reality. These were people who speculated a lot, but their speculations were in part still nourished by old, instinctive, clairvoyant forces—speculations about the progress of the world through various levels of spiritual development from earlier, ancient times. These were people who spoke of eons following one upon the other and becoming ever more coarse, ever more materialistic, until at last, the condition of the current formation of the outer, physical world came into being. In short, these were people who gazed earnestly and deeply into the spiritual. Through their special soul configuration, these souls were preparing themselves for a longer life between death and a new birth; they needed a long time before the urge to descend into a new body awoke in them. And a number of these souls, very many of them, are incarnated today in the American population. This American population, which in many respects tends to take up practical, material life, was engendered in its entire constitution because these souls had formerly lived in such a spiritual awareness of the world, as I have described it, but then plunged into a very, very dense corporeality, and, fundamentally, they now seek to live out in a refined treatment of this material world what they had earlier as a fine spirituality. One understands the particular way in which the American spirit deals so very practically and scientifically with the things of the world if one knows how this reflects an earlier orientation toward the spiritual world, which is now carried into material life without being aware that one wants to grasp the spiritual in the material. It is the material counter-image of the spirituality which these souls experienced in their former life on earth.

You will see how fruitful it is when you try to understand what you encounter in this or that fact, in this or that behavior of the present generation by taking such things into consideration, and when, at the same time, you develop the consciousness: only now do I grasp the full reality, whereas when I am told the history of the generations, I merely stand before an abstraction—even if it is an outwardly perceptible abstraction.

It is really necessary for you to realize how little the great majority of mankind today is inclined to seek self-knowledge in such a way, how little people find the courage for going beyond the outer, historical, physical, sensory observation. It is, of course, precisely in what flows into our young souls by way of education that it becomes clear how people today are torn out of the full reality of life, for they are everywhere actually taught only a piece of reality. Of course, when one asks modern people to take spiritual life, as expressed in the soul's repeated earthly lives, seriously, and to refrain from what is merely external, it is something from which they recoil, as if it could burn them. In this regard, one experiences the most unbelievable things from the scientific leaders of today. Of course, the time has not yet come to disclose in public lectures the sorts of things I have just mentioned. But today one does certainly have to go quite far in public lectures. For example, recently in Zürich I spoke more or less about what I also presented on Thursday in a public lecture[†] here; and so, in order to make myself understood about the sphere in which the spiritual researcher carries out special inner soul exercises to cultivate his methods, I said: This flows into a sphere that must be permeated by the inner will of the person, with inner clarity such as can otherwise only be found in the pursuit of mathematical derivations, in the pursuit of mathematical truths. A scientist from Zürich[†] heard this lecture; truly he was not the worst, rather one who actually is among the more talented. But among some other really quite obtuse things with which he then criticized this lecture in an extensive feature article in the literary supplement of the *Neue Zürcher Zeitung*, he says that I invoked the idea that the inner methods of research belonging to anthroposophical knowledge are to be built up in a clear soul process that is modelled on the clear soul process of mathematical judgment. In addition, this scholar, who is, indeed, a young scholar, meaning a "beacon of hope" for the future—and there is really no end to the astonishment with which one reads the work of such a person who wants to be taken seriously—this scholar said: Mathematical certainty actually relates only to the fact that one connects the mathematical entities with each other. If there is a point, a line, and an angle, one can connect the point and line and angle, then truth, or certainty, results. But the point and the line are themselves uncertain, just as atoms and molecules are uncertain.

This man thinks he is saying something terribly clever, but it is only characteristic of how distorted the thinking of the contemporary scientist actually is. For if someone with normal, healthy senses states that in the course of the soul exercises in anthroposophical research there is mathematical clarity, then what can be discussed about the certainty of linear relations or the uncertainty of single points is of no concern to him. What such a philosophically oriented private scholar thinks about the certainty of points and lines is completely irrelevant. Let what such a person wants to imagine be certain or uncertain. But one lives in a particular soul mood if one considers the Pythagorean theorem clearly. That process is what the anthroposophical method follows, regardless of any arguments about whether the triangle of the Pythagorean theorem is certain in itself or whether its one square is certain in itself.

Thus, one needs be quite clear that one really cannot build a bridge to such a scholar, because such "minds" are entirely deformed by what has been bred into the present. But on the other hand, it is really urgently necessary that a sense of reality enters into our entire life. Without this sense of reality, we will not make any progress. That is why anyone who wants to be sincere about the truth and insights of anthroposophically oriented spiritual science must not shy away from bringing things which he may well grasp abstractly, like the teaching of repeated earth lives, into concrete life. At the same time, it remains quite true that it is precisely the dogmas—i.e., the abstract dogmatic forms of the truth—which should be developed as late as possible. For example, it remains quite true that something like our Waldorf school[†] should not be a worldview-school. Therefore, in that case, it is much less a matter of having the abstract idea of repeated earth lives grasped by young souls. But without touching on such abstract thoughts, simply by having such insights as I have been presenting today in one's own background, historical life will be illuminated and comprehended in the lessons. Then something quite different will live in the hearts and minds of these souls, who, perhaps without any theory or dogma about repeated earth lives, will receive such a historical description, will simply live into it because one finds ways of describing contemporary life, as one understands it oneself, by finding the confluence of a quite foreign soul life with what flows in the blood lines directly out of the past through the succession of generations.

Today it is important not just to talk about the spirit but really to carry the understanding of the spirit so far as to discover the working of this spirit in concrete, material existence. Our sciences have everywhere taken on an abstract form, even when they merely splash around in external busyness. Then, whatever is developed in external busyness, even if it is a vivid abstraction, nevertheless remains an abstraction if one has no spiritual grounding for it. And whoever objects: Then you just have to believe those who see spiritual life; after all, you cannot simply attain initiation science as easily as something else!—such a person would, on the basis of such an objection, basically be in agreement with the preacher and professor Traub,[†] who says that you need not have experienced things yourself if they basically do not affect you (such as, for example, the birth of Alexander the Great) but that you would have to experience for yourself, or would have to be able to experience for yourself, what you recognize as directly affecting you, because you do not want to accept it merely as someone else's experience. For people who possess this sort of logic, I would like to recommend that they check when it was that they recorded the fairly obvious date of their own birth in their diary, or whether there is some other fact which is obvious in their personal life but of which they cannot become conscious other than through their good faith in others! So much for the rejection of the so-called principle of authority. But one ought to try once to find the path which, precisely through healthy common sense, leads to the understanding of what spiritual science offers. One simply ought to consider these things thoroughly and with intense earnestness, and one will see that even for such seemingly paradoxical and remote truths as I have stated today, access is indeed possible to unhindered, uninhibited healthy common sense. Mind you, if one obstructs one's own healthy common sense with such walls as get built when one views history merely as a system, whether in the physical sense, according to the blood of inherited human characteristics, or in the ongoing stream of developing events, as long as one obstructs one's own understanding of reality through such prejudices, one will simply be unable to approach this reality. But the moment one surrenders to healthy common sense in the right way, if one just begins to want to understand, then one will see what lives in souls of the present. If one is only interested in understanding it, then one cannot understand it as merely originating in the blood through inheritance or through what streams from one generation to the next. Admittedly, it is a question of finding the courage to approach these matters. But once one finds this courage, one will surely get beyond the mere abstractions and reach the concrete understanding of the truths.

Lecture Three

STUTTGART, JANUARY 9, 1921

LAST TIME I drew attention to the way in which conditions in today's civilized regions of the earth are to be understood as the result of the incarnation of souls. I drew attention to how anthroposophical truths must be seen in outer realities, how we must take seriously those things which hold us back, which hinder us—for example, the current understanding of the historical development of humanity as merely a sort of continuation of externally perceptible powers from one generation to the next. One must be absolutely clear that what flows as blood through the generations does not explain the events of the present. These events can only be explained if one is aware that the souls come from quite different regions than those where the physical ancestors of present humanity, in one territory or another, have lived. We attempted to shed some light on this. Today I would again like to discuss this whole situation, which we characterized for our earth existence, from another side.

I will indeed have to refer to some aspects that have already been developed in previous lectures from different points of view. In our time, however, it is primarily a matter of gaining more and more inner impulses in order to be equal to the tasks of the present. This cannot happen if only a few people, in all earnestness, have a sense for the great tasks of the present. We now live at a time when many people must realize what has to happen. And that is why work must be done so that as many people as possible penetrate what must be known, wanted, perceived in our time, so that humanity might come to something of an ascent. For in our time, not wanting to ascend means wanting to descend.

Now, still another realization arises in relation to the incarnation of souls into contemporary bodies, in addition to what I said last time.

In earlier lectures, I already indicated that spiritual-scientific research clearly perceives that many souls which ought now to descend from spiritual worlds into physical bodies regard this incarnation with a sort of aversion, a sort of antipathy. In our time—and this is the basis of our current conditions on Earth—there is a kind of antipathy in human souls coming down again into physical bodies. Of course, it is self-evident that by suggesting this, one is speaking of soul experiences which preceded the incarnation into physical bodies and which do not belong to today's ordinary memories, so that what one characterizes in this manner is unconscious for many people today. But it can become conscious if what is born out of spiritual research is measured against the contemporary phenomena. Measuring these findings which come from spiritual research against contemporary events is something we should, in general, take very, very seriously.

Fundamentally, the present time does not approach human beings as past eras approached them. As you know, I am really averse to using the phrase "transitional period"—after all, one always lives in a transitional period. It's just a matter of what is transitioning. And it is less a matter of spreading this phrase than it is of recognizing what is entering the present from the past, needing to be overcome, and what must be prepared for the future. And, in that regard, one simply must say: This twentieth century in which we live, in its relationship to evolving humanity, is such that, by living partly in this twentieth century, those souls dwelling in physical bodies will experience something very special in this life on the earth. The experiences are to be meaningful and, in a certain way, decisive. Just try to compare what can be experienced today with human experiences of earlier times, and you will realize that it may be that some people are speaking offhandedly when they say: What has happened so far in the twentieth century bears no comparison with earlier events of history as it has been recorded in human annals. But it is just in penetrating more deeply into contemporary events that one has to notice that this is so, that certainly humanity is to experience things in our time which cannot be compared with things of an earlier time.

I could single out many things from current events to underscore what I just said. But I will mention only a few. It is precisely from the perspective of the region of the earth where we live—viewing things more from a spiritual point of view for the moment—that we can say: It is fundamentally almost frightening to discuss how in this Central European region changes have taken place with such monstrous speed, changes which have been taking place since approximately the middle of the nineteenth century and on into our twentieth century. Usually, however, one does not pay attention to all that happens. Anyone who has a feeling for this can compare how the people of Central Europe thought seventy or eighty years ago with how they think today, but especially how they felt back then and how they feel today. It is a very clear external difference. There has been an extraordinary change in the soul constitution of Central European humanity. And, to this, something else must be added. Certainly, people, at least most people, sleep through the most important events, they do not notice them. But these events exist nevertheless. Today there are well-meaning works by people in more western regions of the earth, by Englishmen, by Americans, which are full of outer compassion for the material situation of Central European humanity. That is true. But what underlies precisely this spiritual stream should be followed with the greatest alertness in Central Europe. For this Central Europe, which today more than ever finds itself placed at the decisive position between the Orient and the Occident—whereby I understand by Occident more those regions in which an Anglo-American element predominates—this seems above all, if one considers the present external circumstances, to be deprived of its particular spiritual nature. I really ask you not to misunderstand what I am now saying. One can certainly have full understanding for the material needs, and it is not so difficult to have that today in this time of misery and need; but it is the spiritual need which must, above all, be taken into account today.

Just try to summarize—without listening to what is said because of prejudice, perhaps said because of prejudice in your own soul—what current events hold in store for the destiny of Central Europe in spiritual terms. Doesn't everything, everything tend to exterminate this Central European spirituality from the earth? If one were to take this fact into account impartially, one would really feel smoldering in oneself the impulse to do whatever one could for the progress of this truly Central European spirituality. If no significant developments of strength occur, then both the East of the earth and the West of the earth will unite over Central Europe, at first probably in terrible enmity, but then, supplanting this enmity, in some sort of stream which actually cannot be wanted by Central Europe, and which will then want to propagate itself as world culture, as world civilization. And what I am now saying is connected to the antipathy that today's incarnating souls have for living in today's physical bodies. Not only those souls of whom I recently told you that most of them came from the former Central Europe and then moved to the East in their current incarnation, not only those souls had little desire to incarnate, to be in these bodies, but also those souls who are in western areas, in America, in large parts of England, who, as you know, used to live in oriental bodies a relatively long time ago; they, too, did not view their incarnation with full sympathy, as had been the case in earlier times of earth evolution. Neither the souls of the East nor those of the West live, if the word is permitted, in a completely normal way in these bodies. This can be clearly noticed when one approaches today's civilization by means of spiritual-scientific research.

We have, then, above all, these people of the East. We now know which souls they are. And through the various depictions of spiritual-scientific cultural history, we also know in which bodies these souls live. The souls of the East certainly do not all have a common interest, but a certain interest predominates all the way into Eastern European regions. These souls, the leading souls, they all unconsciously experience the consequence of their antipathy toward incarnation in that they do not completely align themselves with the setting of earthly events, they do not become fully absorbed in the facts of these earthly events. Among souls of the East, there is an inborn aversion, particularly among the most important people of the East, for becoming acquainted with what has become external culture in Central Europe and the West, for what has become external natural science, external technology, and so forth. And one can say: Entirely in contrast to precisely what had been the best soul constitution of earlier times in

Central Europe, we see today how also numerous souls in Central Europe, in consequence of the circumstances of their incarnation which I described last time, are seized by this aversion for penetrating contemporary facts, contemporary conditions. Let us simply take an unbiased look at our own time. How many people are there today who want inwardly to place themselves, in an entirely false way, back into the spiritual view of the Orient, who feel a certain mystical urge not to take part in what is happening today in the outer world, who would like to flee into a mystical, rapturous contemplation of life, who want to bring into our completely different way of life what was once justified for the oriental life of earlier times but has now become decadent?

That is the one thing that is so harmful in our time: unworldly mysticism. This unworldly mysticism is present in various forms. It is present among those who are infatuated with any sort of spiritual view based on an oriental pattern. But it is also present in a way which is not noticed as much but should be. For today, all over the civilized earth, from East to West, we live in a very strange relationship to something which is inwardly related to our entire civilization, indeed, to life altogether: we live in a strange relationship to language. The further we go toward the Orient, the more the striving to prevent language itself from properly descending onto the physical plane is present; to let language, speech, be permeated from a certain direction of the soul, not to be absorbed by the words, but instead having a brimming, overflowing feeling which does not make an effort to expand fully into the words. One would like to say that there is a striving not to adapt language to the conditions of the physical plane, but instead to retain it, in a way, in the human being, so as to bring to expression in language states of intoxication, experiences of intoxication. One has to acquire an eye for how there are many people presently who find it downright despicable when someone makes an effort to make language as malleable as possible. They then find it too intellectual; they then find it too settled into the physical plane. They want to keep language in semi-darkness, in a twilight state. To them, only what keeps language in a twilight state is poetic; they love to be infatuated by the element of speech. Such souls do not find it sympathetic when one strives to have every word, every sentence correspond to some kind of fully experienced reality. Such souls would like to speak without living with what language is meant for—with the realities. This not-wanting-to-live-with-realities is something that is very characteristic for a large part of our present humanity. And this is, more or less, the characteristic of language itself, the more one moves eastward.

The Western languages, by contrast, have a different characteristic. They already seek to meet reality through language, to dive down into reality through language, but they do not form the language themselves; they let language blur, so that although they do dive down into the realities, they do so without sufficient malleability in the language, with language that does not embrace things lovingly enough. This is connected to other Western tendencies. The particular way of looking at things, which does not actually reach up to the human being, has come from the West. First of all, we have Darwinism,[†] which most certainly contains admirable things when it comes to understanding the animal kingdom. One really need look less at the fanatical followers of Darwinism than at Darwinism itself. There is a great deal there which penetrates the animal kingdom admirably, and one can then say: The human being stands at the apex of the animal kingdom. But that does little toward an understanding of the human being himself. We see this in the West in the social realm as well. In the West, we see strange perspectives which actually exclude the human being from consideration. We see how within the national economy of the West, the human being as such does not play a special role. What does play a role is whatever clings to the person externally, materially. The private property that a person has is actually seen as the individuality within the national economy, not the person himself. Nor does one speak in the West about that freedom which springs from the entire human being; instead, one speaks—with conviction—only about economic freedom. Since the time of Adam Smith,[†] and earlier, people speak of economic freedom, of what the human being can toss into the scales of civilization because he owns something which he can enjoy in the world, and because of the fact that this possession gives him economic independence, and so forth. But one does not speak about what the human being actually is, about what springs from the inner aspect of the human being with the character of freedom.

But all these things indicate far deeper phenomena. Those souls incarnating today with a certain antipathy into oriental bodies because other circumstances force them to do so, they actually often strive to prevent the cognitive capacities of these bodies from comprehending the present-day earth. They seek, in a way, to keep the consciousness of the human being outside of present-day earth. In the most eminent sense, there is something luciferic in this soul constitution, and this luciferic element wafts across from the East.

In the West, however, there is something in the souls that is ahrimanic in the most eminent sense. They do not want to take hold of the bodies in such a way that they can look out into the world through these bodies with open senses; instead, they sink into these bodies in such a way that they do not encompass these bodies in the full sense, do not spiritualize them. They live in these bodies without completely penetrating them. The result is the unavoidable consequence which will occur if one lives in the human body and has no open sense for what exists all about in the world. If one has an open sense, one discovers not only the outer physical, sense-perceptible reality, but one discovers the underlying spirituality of this physical, sense-perceptible reality. One will not discover this underlying spirituality if one is inserted into the body without penetrating this body fully to its periphery. That is the soul mood of the West. One might say that due to these conditions, it really is the case that some bodies of people in the West are constituted in such a way that as the bodies grow, their souls in them do not fully come into their own. But because the human souls in these bodies do not fully come into their own in these bodies, the bodies can become sheaths, repositories, for entirely different beings which then move into them, beings which sleep through precisely that which lies in the peculiarities of the human soul itself.

And through all these things, one mood spreads from the East, another from the West. The mood that is spreading from the East intends to keep the human being in old ways of feeling, old ways of experiencing, which ascend to a spirituality more instinctively, and not to let the human being descend toward the earth far enough to connect himself with the situation here on the earth. In the West, on the other hand, the prevailing stream fails to take the present into account in such a way that one can perceive the ever-progressing spirituality in all existence, but rather that one stops at what the human being has become, for one dwells in him without penetrating him because one does not actually love him enough to want to fully penetrate him. The Western goal is to conserve the present-day condition of humanity with its materialistic ways of thinking, its materialistic activity. The Eastern goal is to prevent the human being from interacting with the materialistic conditions of the earth, so that the human being does not fully absorb the present. From both sides there is actually the desire to prevent the human being from completely grasping the present. And a tremendous fear, which is unconsciously gripping humanity, also supports this. Anyone who impartially observers the present time and the great decisions it harbors has to confront these decisions with a certain kind of courage.

There are two ways to avoid facing the decisions of the present. One way is to become a rapturous mystic or theosophist and superficially repeat "ex Oriente lux." Then one can establish an inner sense of well-being by fleeing, in a way, from the events of the present. One can rise above them, can even consider oneself to be an exceptional human being in this mysticism or theosophy, and can scorn everything taking place all around as "the evil world," the world of matter, which is inferior.

This is the harmful aspect of this extreme. The other extreme is also harmful; it comes to light more in the Western stream, which then, in its ultimate consequence, produces the materialistic human being in whom the fear of facing the decisions of the present takes on the other character, so that he says: "The human being is the product of what happens in him physically, physiologically, and to talk about anything that has been given to the human being as his own decision is nonsense and something one need not take into account. It is necessary to cultivate what once developed physically in humanity. To speak of a special spirituality is superstitious." On this side, one flees spirituality, while on the other side, one flees materiality.

Thus, today we have two extremes of human soul constitutions: on the one side, materialism, which is ahrimanic, on the other side, mysticism, which is luciferic. On the one hand, we have the great worldview moving from the West to the East, which develops only a mechanistic natural science based on matter, which pervades, so to speak, our education. On the other hand, we have the movement from the East to the West, which today really does not take hold of fewer spirits, and which will take hold of ever more spirits. And one would wish that anthroposophy will not be destroyed by becoming subject to just the mystical zealotry emanating from these spirits. We have, after all, this other stream, which wants to draw only from an unworldly sphere; in particular, we have this stream in the theosophical worldview which wants to bring in from the East things which have long since faded away, which are not at all suitable for humanity today.

These are the two extremes which, possibly in spite of terrible enmity caused by outer conditions and internal opposition, would actually like to reach out to each other from both sides. And because these streams exist, and because this is the case, one might say in trivial terms—although it is, in all honesty, not meant trivially, but rather tragically—that this is the reason why the people of Central Europe are doing so badly spiritually.

This is what one should pay attention to with the wakeful inner eyes of the soul. For if we were to express the matter somewhat radically, we would say: In this Central Europe, the greater synthesis, the congruence, the higher harmony of these two extremes, which is the only source from which the progress of mankind can emerge, was prepared. For in Central Europe, there was a culmination of spiritual streams that arose from truly significant foundations—lastly from that which, as if dimming at that time and overrun by the other, first appeared as an intellectual spirituality in German idealism, in the worldviews of Fichte, Schelling, Hegel,[†] whereby that of Schelling was even, in the end, close to gradually giving birth to something[†] which could have arrived at a real anthroposophical spiritual science; but the times were not yet ripe for this.

But it really does seem as if all the world had conspired to prevent what was being prepared from happening in any way. I should like to say: from the Orient and the Occident, Lucifer and Ahriman are conspiring to prevent this synthesis. For here, in this central region of the earth, there actually were people who, even if they did sometimes get stuck along the way because of the circumstance of their time, strove toward spirituality; but, at the same time, they strove toward a devoted knowledge of nature. What a wonderful pendulum swing there is, for example, in Goethe between his being continually attracted to view the world as spiritual and, then again, to view the world in the breadth of external natural appearances. How avidly Goethe sought harmony between what the spirit told him and what nature revealed to him.

And how we see this Goethean sense, which was already rooted in all of Central Europe, how we see it overrun! On the one hand, we continually see the influence of the West. We have seen it in our external science, which, if I may use the expression, is completely "decayed" and which, in its methods, completely rejects anything spiritual. Even if it sometimes believes it has taken up something spiritual, it is still averse to incorporating anything spiritual in its methods, especially in scientific research. And what, on the other hand, have we had to experience in the past decades among those who want to work their way out of this antagonistic mood which clips their wings? Within that part of European civilization which gave rise to something like Schiller's *Letters on the Aesthetic Education of Man*,[†] a wonderful unfolding of soul and spirit activity could have resulted; instead, countless people adhered to the mystical chatter particularly of Americans like Ralph Waldo Trine[†] and the like, adhered to the mystical chatter which in comparison to the spiritual substance in Central Europe was extremely inferior, a soul-egoistic striving for inner satisfaction, not a truly spiritual upswing. There we see the whole scope of what I might call: the tendency to flood Central Europe's original impulse with what comes from the West. Of course—from an anthroposophical perspective this is quite self-evident—no criticism is meant toward anyone. People must be respected equally all over the world. But is that which lives in people the same as that which runs through human souls as a culture, an atmosphere of civilization? Is it in any way right for someone to say: Look, there is one who is turning against the Western spiritual streams and thereby reproaches Western people? – No, he does not reproach people; instead, he wants to indicate what lives as a spiritual atmosphere in the West.

And, on the other hand, do we not see how, in Central Europe, many people are utterly filled with a longing to incorporate any fragment of ancient wisdom from the Orient into spiritual life? This sort of absorption of Oriental spiritual wisdom truly hurts the soul of one who is knowledgeable. Even if one takes something which is relatively easy to assimilate, like the *Bhagavad Gita*,† one must be clear that what a Central European can receive from the *Bhagavad Gita* today can, at most, be something which he forges for himself, but which is definitely not Oriental spiritual wisdom. For that doesn't exist anymore, not even in the Orient. People gush when they can meditate on some passage in the *Bhagavad Gita*, but, fundamentally, they don't get anything serious out of it; instead, they merely have something which creates a certain kind of inner satisfaction. They do not have the courage to take hold of the balancing spiritual atmosphere which could now be inhaled in the central regions of the earth. It must be said: Precisely through the infiltration of so-called Eastern theosophy, there has been, for a long time now, a damaging counter-current within Central Europe. This judgment is not based on the use of Oriental nomenclature, or Oriental concepts, or on the idea that one should not attempt to understand the Orient. That is self-evident. Entirely different things are involved—things which I tried to characterize in my remarks.

In contrast to all this, it has to be pointed out that such devotion—be it to the overt materialism of the West as it comes to light in this stream, or the veiled materialism of the West as it appears through Trine or Christian Science,† which is also nothing but materialism, only from the other side—means spiritual regression. Both the devotion to it, as well as the devotion to all manner of mysticism, that is what definitely brings regression in the spiritual sphere. Progress can be brought by what has been basically well prepared, but already exists today, as, in a manner of speaking, a layer under the foundation of Central Europe; and over it the confluence of Orient and Occident has already been layered. For, in truth, as has been indicated here many times, and as can be seen in my publications and lecture cycles: The external Bible, the external New Testament, these have, basically, experienced the same destiny as other Oriental writings. They no longer exist in their true form. And if one tries to come to the true form, then it can only happen through spiritual science, which in turn brings the vitality that is necessary to penetrate into these things. However, if one brings this living quality into the Bible, into the New Testament, then those who are official representatives, the Traubs† and so on, are the very first to place it in the world as phantasy, or something monstrous, something damnable.

Here in Central Europe, there would basically be those people who really wanted to raise themselves to spirituality, on the one hand, and who, on the other hand, would also have a sense for grasping the whole breadth of the external, natural world of appearance. This is what is necessary today. Only out of this spirit can humanity progress. That is why it is just as necessary in the sphere of cognition that people today deepen their relationship to natural phenomena as it is necessary, on the other hand, for them to deepen their relationship to what spiritual science can bring. Neither the one nor the other contains the full truth; only the harmony of both in the human soul provides the whole truth. The same goes for the practical sphere. Neither the one-sided practice of religion, which wants to flee from the world—or at least wants to experience the world as it actually is just now and therefore wants to live in all sorts of religious elevations, which are unworldly—neither the religious practice, on the one hand, nor the external routine which prevails in our public life can provide progress. Only he who, on the one hand, lovingly embraces what the outside world demands of us in the way of practical measures and who, on the other hand, is inclined to combine what the outside world demands of us with what can be acquired through spiritual-scientific education, which enables one to become skillful in a way that is not merely an external training but is illuminated by an inner, spiritual way of acting that is also rooted in the constitution of the soul, only such a one will progress in the external, practical life. Only in this way can one get at what the present time sets as a task. This, above all things, is what we must realize.

There are so many people today fighting against what is meant here by spiritual science because this spiritual science speaks quite unabashedly about spiritual facts, because this spiritual science speaks of souls finding their way out of the spiritual world into earthly lives with this or that mood—with sympathy or antipathy—just as one speaks in physics of anodes and cathodes. This spiritual science is rejected from many sides because it looks at natural phenomena as well as at spiritual facts. This spiritual science is rejected by those who want to look only at external nature because they cannot actually imagine anything by it, because they perhaps find only words in it. But this spiritual science is also rejected by all those who want to dwell in vague mysticism, in old, conventional religious practices, who have not found the connection to newer modes of life. This spiritual science is also rejected by those who have no content whatsoever in their concepts, who, instead, merely slip and slide forward in the sound and content of words like so many philosophers of the present day, even those who found "Schools of Wisdom"[†] today. But that is exactly what we do not need. We do not need a word-wisdom that rejects penetrating into the facts of nature. Nor do we need a vague, gushing mysticism. And we cannot make use of spiritless penetration into natural phenomena. What we need is a synthesis, a connection of both, for only that corresponds to reality. And from this perspective, we have to take into account that our language, human language, if one simply advances from east to west, and basically also in Central Europe, has taken on just those forms which give this language its malleability, which allow this language to be something which one feels in the innermost aspect of one's humanity with the whole mood and constitution of the soul. On the other hand, it is just this language of Central Europe that wants to be something that now also flows out into the outer events, that is not retained egotistically within the human being. This is something which might be noticed in the kind of language used by Goethe or Hegel. There it is clearly evident as a tendency. And the tendencies that are evident there, these can be developed a great deal further, all the way to the very thing we want to achieve through spiritual-scientific intentions.

It should certainly come as no surprise that spiritual science is slandered, unconsciously slandered—I might say objectively slandered—by those infected by what comes from the Orient as well as what comes from the Occident. But, on the other hand, spiritual science must ever and again clarify the essence of its being. And that is why it was clearly my duty to speak to you about these things today; and it would actually be incumbent upon those within the anthroposophical movement to try to work out very clearly what this spiritual science intends, to work out very clearly how, within anthroposophical spiritual science, one does not avoid speaking about spiritual realities, about the suprasensory world, as a complete reality, in the same way as one speaks of the physical world; to work out also how important it is for this spiritual science to make the soul so strong, by means of a spiritual-scientific education, that the human being retains an open, free judgement about things which today are practical necessities. What everyone within the spiritual-scientific movement ought to really make quite clear to himself is that our practical enterprises flow out of precisely our spiritual view with a certain inner consequence. For it is then incumbent upon him to place this spiritual science into the right light, in view of the world's errors, to show what it actually wants. Today one cannot find too many opportunities, for one still allows countless other opportunities which would make it possible to present this spiritual science in the right light to pass unused.

It may seem to you that I am illuminating some things from far too many aspects. But today it is not a matter of having to experience ever more facts of interest from out of spiritual worlds, but that we should stamp the impulses that can come out of these suprasensory worlds into the sensible world in the right way.

Today it is necessary that the awake soul is really aware of the danger which threatens the development of humanity from both sides: the one which wants to enthrall humanity in luciferic gushing, as well as the one which wants to push it down entirely into ahrimanic materialism. For false mysticism, false intellectuality, unworldliness, which strive toward rapture instead of toward full external clarity and inner light, this false Oriental mood is actually striving toward an inner untruth. It becomes an inner untruth, just as the Occidental mood, which wants to press the human being down into materialistic views and materialistic behavior, leads to external lies.

That is the danger threatening humanity today: on the one hand, the decline into inner untruth through false mysticism and through the conservation of old religious practices, and, on the other hand, into the external falsehood—the clichés of our time are already the beginning of external falsehood—through diving down into mere materialism. These two dangers ought actually to be recognized with wakeful souls by just those seeking an understanding of anthroposophical spiritual science. This is what I wanted to inscribe in your souls today as a thought that should not only be a thought that is heard and taken theoretically, but as a thought which really wants to become warm in the soul, so that this warmth has impulses for life as a consequence. For spiritual science is not what it wants to be if it does not warm the soul and thereby, by means of this detour toward warmth of soul, really create impulses for life. If we do this to the best of our ability, every one of us, then something will arise out of the unity of thus tuned souls that is very, very necessary for the present.

And now, my dear friends, I would like to interject a comment which is very painful for me, but which I must make. I have said once before, but must say again today, that I cannot now accommodate the many wishes there have been for private conversations and so forth; I cannot now carry out my personal life as I used to, because insofar as these tasks now take up the entire day and sometimes also a part of the night, the friends should really realize that there is no spare time for private conversations. It seems that this has been very, very poorly understood. But, on the other hand, there is a good way to eliminate what I have to admit is a harmful situation: that would be for all of us, as much as our strength allows, to work together on the tasks of the anthroposophical movement. For, the reason why individuals are currently so overworked is simply the consequence of our having so few people who are really energetically engaged. This, too, will be easily misunderstood, for usually it is understood to mean that everyone tries to contribute in ways that are personally pleasing. But one really has to expose this misunderstanding if one wants to emphasize the truth: that we have too many co-workers. In those positions which we were able to create, we do not have too few, but too many, according to some considerations, too many. But it is not a matter of having everyone push toward what was created; instead, a possibility needs to be brought about to work with real energy toward having more and more created. Only if we understand the situation in this way will we be able to make progress in the right way.

As I said, it is exceptionally painful for me, but it is nevertheless absolutely essential that I must reject so many private requests. And, my dear friends, many things which are personal matters can really be solved by different means, until a more favorable time comes. There is a widespread conservatism amongst us that tries to force conditions which were once quite good, but which cannot now exist anymore until we manage to meet the absolutely necessary tasks with real energy from morning to night and into the night as long as the time is given us. We really must understand each other in these matters, otherwise our movement will absolutely not flourish. There is far too little awareness that mutual help, mutual consultation is necessary in view of how our movement has spread. Just imagine if every time I could be here in Stuttgart, I really intended to have private conversations with everyone sitting here; how then would the tasks which are just now facing us be solved? Perhaps there are those who will say they do not understand these things properly, but there will also be those here who certainly do understand why I must say these things.

Lecture Four

STUTTGART, JANUARY 16, 1921

Our considerations during my time here† have concerned the full earnestness about life that can arise out of anthroposophy in the face of the great tasks of our time. When one says, "in the face of the great tasks of our time," one need not always think of what hovers, as it were, over people, to be controlled by a few authoritative individuals over the heads of others; instead, one must be clear that what happens these days between people in everyday life contains in itself, streaming through them in a certain way, what belongs to the great tasks of our time. This should naturally be the first consequence of the anthroposophical worldview that flows through our souls. For this anthroposophical worldview leads us to recognize that spirit lives in everything, not just in abstract heights but in the life which surrounds us and in which we stand every day. And it is just this which we must learn to apply to the great tasks of life and to the small, everyday experiences and actions.

If we consider life today, especially from this perspective, we can ask ourselves: What components of this life, especially with respect to spirituality, surround us? What do we live in spiritually, as human beings in this era today? We have remnants of old denominations that gather their followers in congregations and teach them—in some manner or other that is traditional, that has been handed down—what is regarded as belief in the eternal nature of the human being. This belief is taught to people in various forms, various nuances, by means of the various denominations. Then people live with this belief and also think they are satisfying the needs of their souls through this belief. In addition to this belief, we have today, as popular as the individual denominations themselves are among their followers, that which comes from the science that is practiced today in our educational institutions. This science has gradually developed to consider only sense-perceptible, physical material—at most, to penetrate it with a few inadequate spiritual ideas, which, however, are also already more or less disappearing. There is an ever-growing tendency for science to look at only what can be found through sense-perceptible observation and, at most, arranged by means of the intellect.

No matter where we look in the civilized world today, we will see that people draw from one of these two sources: on the one hand, from what they are taught as so-called serious, exact knowledge which they accept on authority; for everyone takes science on authority unless they happen to work in a field of science themselves; and it is in this way that the great mass of people accepts this knowledge. And, in addition, one is instructed by popular magazines on how to think about astronomy, physics, chemical facts, about biology, zoology, mineralogy, botany, history, and so forth, and then says: All this must be true, for it originates with the very people who are authorized for these things through the usual means; beside this, one takes up the other aspect which flows from the different denominations. One does not bridge these two, for usually the people are taught by means of their confessions that they are to keep knowledge and belief apart, that they must under no circumstances allow knowledge and belief to merge. An awakening to a conscious awareness of these facts takes place in the rarest of cases. One makes an effort to recognize what is conveyed to people as exact truth through the habitual channels by the scientific authorities. But one does not follow up so as to check how in reality the working methods function that give rise to such science.

On the other hand, one hardly ever investigates the beliefs that have been propagated through the ages and traditionally brought to the people by today's representatives of these beliefs. Only in the rarest of cases is there an attempt to gain full consciousness about what is actually going on here. And when it does occur, then one hardly ever sees the matter in the right light. For, assuming that someone or other, let's say within the Catholic or Protestant faith, rises up in protest against what is called dogma, then, usually this dogma is seen as "nonsense" so that one polemicizes against this dogma and thereby discards the traditional belief but is not able to replace it with anything else.

Such a dogma—I will mention a central dogma in a moment—is, for example, that of the Trinity, the triune personality of the divine being. Anyone who receives such a dogma in the way it is formulated by today's denominations can somewhat easily polemicize against such a dogma if he starts out from the perspective of today's scientific thinking. For he will be able to reveal very easily in this sense what is "nonsense" about such a dogma. However, anyone who researches the origin of such a dogma will find that dogmas of the common denominations took hold of humanity over long periods of time, and that at the source, the point of origin of these dogmas, there exists what I have often characterized as the instinctive clairvoyance, the atavistic clairvoyance, the seeing into the spiritual world of the early period of development in humanity. It was from this clairvoyance that such dogmas emerged; and I might say: something like the dogma of the Trinity originated in deep, thorough insights into the structure of world being. At one time this dogma of the Trinity was a deeply recognized truth. It represented a deep insight into interrelatedness within reality. But this is what was present in that earlier era, in which human soul capacities, the cognitive forces which, as already stated, were a kind of instinctive clairvoyance, suited such a dogma. The dogma then propagated itself. It no longer suits today's cultivation of human soul forces. As a rule, many earth lives have elapsed for each human being who was present at the emergence of this dogma. The souls have had varied experiences during those earth lives. In the external world, this dogma has persisted; it was propagated from generation to generation. Today it has taken on a form which can no longer be understood by means of the words through which it is communicated. And now these souls have reincarnated; the dogma is presented to them ecclesiastically.

There is no inner human relationship between what is presented to human souls by religion and what these souls strive to experience and to know inwardly in themselves. What is so bad in the present time is not that the dogmas are wrong, but what matters is that the dogmas exist in a form which can no longer grasp the truth; they no longer correspond to contemporary conditions; the dogmas no longer meet what human souls need. So that we can say: today these dogmas are preached by actually being exhaled into the empty wind. And those who confess them, confess them without inner soul-truth, for they mostly do not understand the dogmas. But to accept what one doesn't understand is an inner untruth. And, basically, it is from these inner untruths that in our time so much harm is caused by the untruth in the world.

The extent to which untruth has taken hold of humanity in recent years is really unmeasurable. But, basically, it is not surprising that this is so, for the simple reason that if souls live in this untruthfulness which I just described, it really is no wonder that they have no sense for truthfulness in their external life. This, above all, should be considered by those who today believe they must agree with traditional beliefs. It is indeed a serious matter with which one must concern oneself in this realm.

One could say that the souls, which in the meantime have gone through various earth lives, have outgrown these dogmas since these beliefs were formed. Just as one must take the things I have developed for you in both of my last lectures seriously, so also must one take the view of repeated earth lives in this realm seriously, very seriously.

But let us look from the same perspective at what mankind has been given by external science. A type of knowledge is formed there which originates only in sense-perceptible, physical observation. This is to be united with what lives in us as human soul; the soul is to take up, to fill itself with merely sense-perceptible, physically observable material.

Observe the living human being immersed in life. He carries within himself the soul which has passed through earth lives, which does not find in the outer religious denominations anything it can relate to. Yet, at least for certain realms of life, it does relate to today's recognized science. The question must be raised: What happens to the human soul when it relates to this recognized science, which is based only on sense-perceptible, physical observation? The souls which today are incarnating into physical organisms, these souls, in earlier incarnations, actually absorbed things which had an entirely different relationship to nature, to the environment, to the world, than what is absorbed today in this science. One can find relatively few souls who are incarnated now who in their previous life were not incarnated in such a way that they, for example, related to what was told to them about natural phenomena as a kind of knowledge, or let us say, some sort of idea about spirituality. A natural science bare of spirit, as has been promoted in the past three to four hundred years, did not, after all, exist before. What was given to humanity as natural science in those earlier eras, eras which are relatively recent, was such that in presenting a sense-perceptible finding, one still retained in this sense-perceptible finding something which saturated it with spirituality. That is indeed why so many people of the present time, who are not particularly interested in their own time, find nothing in con temporary sense-perceptible natural science to satisfy them; they leave it aside and do not busy themselves with it; instead, they unearth all sorts of old tomes and then research what Basilius Valentinus,[†] or some other of his kind, has handed down to people by way of natural science. It is true that a good deal of spirituality yet remained in the ideas that people had about nature in those days, but usually the deep respect which those who deal with these things today have rests only on the fact that they do not understand them, and that they consider what is not understood to be very deep.

Important in this realm is that the human souls now incarnated in contemporary bodies also no longer have any real relationship to that old knowledge and are grafted with what permeates the rest of life, with what everyone is fed today in school—that is, they absorb in one way or another the knowledge stemming from sensory, physical observation. But what is actually present if one regards the situation inwardly?

Today we enter our bodies with what our souls experienced in earlier lives, but we enter our bodies in a particular way so that we no longer have a relationship to what our souls experienced in earlier earth lives. Throughout the different earth lives—and this had to happen because it was the prerequisite for the development of freedom—souls have been formed in such a way that they were, in a certain way, hollowed out by what they acquired earlier, so that they no longer have any relationship to what they absorbed earlier, so that they are, in a certain way, empty with regard to what actually lives in the world. In this regard we no longer bring anything over from earlier earth experiences. We certainly do bring over the results of our moral qualities, but, fundamentally, we do not bring over anything from the earlier experiences, from the earlier earth lives, that could lead to a kind of inborn knowledge of the world's mysteries. Souls today do not come into bodies as they did, for example, into Greeks bodies. In Greek life, the soul which had passed through birth still entered into the physical body with a force nurtured by ancient wisdom, so that it could refresh this physical body with spiritual-soul life forces. That is no longer the case today. In most cases today, the soul enters into the body in such a way that it is like a consuming of the body. And for souls born today, it is the case to an ever-greater degree that they have something that consumes the body, that they lame the body, that they, as it were, pervade the body with death forces. If development were to progress in this sense, then we would most certainly enter into the undermining, into the decline of life on earth. People would become ever weaker in their wills. People would show, more and more, that they cannot raise themselves up to grasp active impulses. People would, in a way, go through life merely as automatic recorders of life. How sad that in the present time we have to see how rare it is that human beings allow themselves to be inwardly fired up by a living idea. How much do we find that people today suffer, one might say, from soul sclerosis, that they toss about dead ideas, that they toss about in their heads only what they can take up through traditions, thus becoming automatons.

It really is like this: if one goes through the world today with an unbiased mind and observes people standing in life today, then one actually cannot, fundamentally, tell them apart, one from the other, by the dozens. One really cannot tell them apart. One talks with A, with B, with C; all of them tell you the same thing. Of course, each one believes he is saying something personal, but you cannot really tell them apart at all; they all say the same thing. You actually meet just one kind of person, in various samples, and sometimes you ask yourself: "Am I not deceived? Isn't the one I'm talking to today the same as the one I talked to yesterday?" But this corresponds absolutely with the results of observing successive earth lives in relation to this current, particular earth life. Souls simply no longer bring with them what they had earlier, what went from earth life to earth life and kept reappearing, albeit with waning force, and which was present as inborn knowledge. This just doesn't exist anymore. And then, when what can only be observed outwardly as physical, sense-perceptible natural science is connected to such souls, then these souls are filled with knowledge of what is fleeting, a knowledge that expresses only ideas about what is external and fleeting. The nineteenth century did, after all, add the "Law of Conservation of Energy" to the already older "Law of Conservation of Mass"[†] so as to deceive itself in the terrible illusion about this fact. It invented these laws in order to delude itself into believing that in nature nothing is preserved, and that instead, everything is transient, that also matter and force are transient. Nothing but human automatons will remain of the soul when incarnations repeat themselves in future, if these empty souls get filled only with sense-perceptible observations of natural-scientific material. For it does not exert a vitalizing, fructifying force on the soul.

Today, souls coming from earlier earth lives are born yearning for fructification by something so as to make progress, in turn, in following earth lives. But taking up knowledge of what is merely transitory only provides death of the soul, only murders the soul. This is what must be seen clearly today, that if it continues as it is, there will be only incomprehension for the old dogmas, that then only paralysis, death could set in through a natural science devoid of spirit, and the soul would have to suffer a second death, a soul death. It absolutely depends on the human being and on humanity to keep souls alive. Human beings today may not allow themselves to give in to comfortable passivity by saying: "I am an eternal being, and the eternal core of my being will be preserved under all circumstances." This does not correspond to the real consequences. This eternal core of being is indeed present in the human being, but it is precisely in this age of decision that it must be fructified if it is not to die off. And there is no other means of keeping the soul alive than to break away from the mere physical, sense-perceptible observation of nature and to establish a true spiritual knowledge, to show, also in relation to the facts of nature, how spirit lives in everything that can be observed as sense-perceptible. It is a matter of not validating anything which merely registers as sense-perceptible matter, but instead of promoting the idea that all physical, sense-perceptible matter is saturated with concepts of spirituality, which is of course living in it, and which should not be allowed to be driven out. For when souls coming from earlier earth lives take up this spiritually penetrated natural science, they are fructified, and thereby able to carry their vitality over into following earth lives. The continuation of souls, their health, yes, the continuation of soul life itself, the staving off of the soul death of humanity depends on the spiritualization of our natural science!

It is out of these facts and not out of some arbitrary prejudice that we are striving today for this spiritualization of natural science. And when humanity opposes this spiritualization of natural science in many ways, then this humanity, for the very reason that it is ignorant of the actual meaning of the facts, is actually incited by spiritual beings whom we know well; the less the soul has carried over from earlier incarnations, the more can these beings make themselves felt in human nature. Out of the entire structure of our contemporary life, which consists of natural science devoid of spirit and religious confessions devoid of meaning, there arises, again and again, in the most absurd ways, the opposition to the will for a spiritualization of natural science. The necessity of a deep inner understanding of such facts, and—if I may use the word—an orientation toward such facts, cannot be emphasized often enough. We cannot take the current rejection of spiritualized knowledge seriously enough, whether it sprouts up in the manner I heard mentioned this afternoon—I do not know to what extent it is true—namely, that the lectures given as recently as last week[†] were boycotted following a decision by a group of students wearing colors, or whether it will assume some other form. Today, one really can collect large stacks of documents opposed to spiritual science. And what is making itself felt in really dark, underhanded ways will in a relatively short, possibly very short time become really noticeable to those who love to sleep through these things. Nowadays, it is certainly still more comfortable to be inattentive to such things than to be attentive to them. But we are just no longer at the point where we can make our way back to being ignored by the world. That is no longer possible. And that is why there is nothing to do but move forward. But this moving forward is bound to be an active participation in the ever-worsening discussions—one really cannot call them discussions anymore, but let us just call them that—"discussions" of our time. Only if we succeed in representing spiritual science with greater strength, which can only happen if everyone does his part, and we do not shy away from uncompromisingly and in an unvarnished way characterizing furtive yet manifest hostility toward spiritual science, only then can there be hope of getting through. This is much less a matter of merely catching and defending what appears, when taken literally, to be opposition to spiritual science. That certainly is necessary in some cases, but it is not enough. For, ultimately, this is merely a secondary manifestation whenever malicious opposition to spiritual science arises, either because something is foolishly misunderstood or there is malicious misunderstanding. That is certainly something secondary, which does, of course, now and then have to be put in the right light. It is naturally secondary when—I already mentioned this recently in a public lecture[†]—such people as Frohnmeyer make claims about the main figure in the sculptural group in Dornach, which can be experienced as the Christ-figure, by saying: In Dornach a "Statue of the Ideal Human" can be found, "above with 'luciferic' traits and below with animalistic characteristics." It is certainly necessary to point out something like this—not only to defend spiritual science but because of a much deeper, more profound reason. Whoever is capable of putting such a terrible untruth into the world has a damaging effect on humanity in all he writes and says, instead of having the educational effect he is supposed to have. And what is significant is not that someone utters such a colossal lie; what is significant is that one can see in the capacity of a person to lie so strongly a symptom for the path on which certain leaders of humanity walk today. In the attacks on spiritual science, one can recognize how the sense for truth is configured today. And it is into this broader sphere that the work in this spiritual realm must be carried. That is what matters. One must not shrink back from seeking out this deficient sense for truth in all areas. And humanity must learn to understand that its work toward the future will be possible only with a real sense for truth, when souls are to find their way out of the incarnation of this era into the incarnation of the next. Today, it is not a matter of something formal but absolutely of the real life of the soul through its successive earth lives. If one looks for it, one will find the connection between that inner untruthfulness of thinking, as characterized earlier—outwardly in confessions offered the soul without creating any inner relationship to truth—and the untruthfulness in the outer world. For, ultimately, it is really a remarkable phenomenon that such untruths arise so strongly particularly among those—and by this I don't mean that they aren't present among fellows in other faculties—who are actually the teachers of humanity, who should be the great keepers of the seals of religious truths.

That is the first duty of anyone today who wants to have any kind of relationship to spiritual life—to seek out the untruthfulness that has become embedded in historical culture. The extent to which this historical-cultural untruthfulness is ingrained is extraordinary. This is characteristic of our age. From politics, where it first grew its evil swamp plants, it ultimately penetrated into various other areas. And the condition has already occurred that people can hardly distinguish between truth and untruth with regard to certain phenomena of life. You see, a certain phenomenon of life—untruthfulness—which we encounter at every turn in daily life, plays a role in both this daily life as well as in the great affairs of life. Ultimately, untruthfulness today has sprouted from the same tendency, regardless of whether it appears among the enlightened gentlemen—though certainly enlightened by a peculiar light—who were gathered in Geneva,[†] or among the various bourgeois and proletarian kaffeeklatsches. What lived as spirit in Geneva, and in the bourgeois and proletarian kaffeeklatsches, is beloved as untruthfulness, and let me say parenthetically—those present must not take this amiss, parenthetically I may well be allowed to say it—that it is also not completely eradicated within the Anthroposophical Society. This untruthfulness is a contemporary cultural-historical phenomenon, and one has to deal with it. Above all, it should not be excused in any realm; instead, it must be characterized and placed before contemporaries. Again and again, we experience how, when the urgent necessity to point out such things arises, people take offence, even people in the anthroposophical movement, because these things are uncomfortable for them, because they have to live within the untruthfulness and therefore the characterization of untruthfulness is extremely uncomfortable for them in this or that case.

These things, which I mentioned today, and which are meant to be taken in connection with what I said in the two previous considerations about the reincarnation of souls throughout the civilized world today, as well as about the desire present in a part of humanity to hinder the decisive element that wants to approach humanity today, can provide a concept of the great seriousness of the tasks of our time.

These tasks of our time are thoroughly imbued with the deepest seriousness. And, therefore, because it is so necessary for us to start from this point of view, especially given our foundation, I spoke last time at the end about how painful it is for me that today so much time is taken up without there also being the possibility of continuing the earlier anthroposophical work as it was before the necessity arose—for it is indeed a necessity—to work on the things which have often been discussed here and which absolutely must be present today. If we want to find a right relationship to these things, then this is necessary, necessary precisely out of the spirit of the great tasks of our time.

We really must make the following clearer and clearer to ourselves today: Our friends have frequently settled into the anthroposophical movement as it has basically existed since the beginning of this century. This anthroposophical movement is something that really is not a reality only on the physical plane but is a continuous preoccupation in the spiritual world, an immediate preoccupation. Obviously, outer practical measures are also a preoccupation in the spiritual world, but not in the same sense as the anthroposophical movement itself. And it is about this that I must say a few words today. The anthroposophical movement, in its spiritual aspects, goes on regardless of whether the people who represent it here are industrious or lazy, whether the people who represent it make the effort to move things forward or not move things forward, it goes forward faster or slower, but it remains present in its spiritual reality. Because it has become necessary to bring about practical things which have sprung directly out of the challenges of our time, these things are different. These things must be done in a timely manner since it is impossible to manage these things if they are not completed in a timely manner. If, then, things in practical life are done at a slow trot, the result can be that they simply come too late. However, within the anthroposophical movement, one has become used to what can move along slowly or quickly. And it has now become customary to carry this practice, which one has got used to, into the type of thing where this practice will not work. And this is mainly what underlies what I recently wanted to characterize when I indicated that a possibility must again be created to foster the anthroposophical movement from which, ultimately, everything flows. How long have I had to indicate that it is really not possible to have personal conversations now. Yes, my dear friends, at the end of last week, we—the few people who really can work on practical aspects—had days that lasted until three o'clock in the morning. And yet, people continue to be indignant if it is not possible to accommodate their desire for personal conversations. But I would like to know where the time for that is supposed to come from. This has to be understood. From this, a laxity must not flow into the anthroposophical life itself; on the contrary, strengthening of the anthroposophical life should be the result. For you may be sure, if this strengthening of anthroposophical life occurs, then the other necessities in the practical realm of life will also occur of their own accord. But this strengthening must, above all, take place. This strengthening must occur in such a way that we try to eradicate everything dreamlike from our souls. Whatever wants to brood on some island of life, whatever does not want to pay attention to what is going on in life today, that is what so paralyzes the pursuit of the real tasks of life. These tasks are paralyzed when, on the one hand, people simply remain blind, remain sleepy in the presence of what is taking place in outer life, and look for their well-being, which is more the desire of their souls, in involvement with all sorts of life-estranging, mystical problems on their islands of life.

I am touching here upon something of extraordinary importance, something about the great tasks of our time which directly applies to the ideas of our movement. Every single one of us would have to collaborate on the strengthening of this anthroposophical movement. One can collaborate on the strengthening of this anthroposophical movement if one develops a free and open eye for the major symptoms of decline in our cultural life. It is not acceptable for anthroposophists not to care about these major symptoms of decline. It is not acceptable for you not to turn toward what permeates today's civilization with a force that is driving it into the abyss. Although there is no wish to hear this, on the one hand, and, on the other hand, it is continually forgotten, I have to continually point out that these things will not get better on their own. And today's contemplative brooding, which for many is a kind of transcendental exhibition, is what causes us extraordinary damage. Instead of having the will stirred up and saying to oneself, "I want to do something," one broods over whether the conditions here or there are such that one can do something.

My dear friends, if one had thought about the anthroposophical movement in this way from the beginning of the century, it would never be what it is today. For the clever people who appeared at that time said that in Munich one had to work in such and such a way; and the even cleverer ones then distinguished between Schwabing and Munich, hearing the grass growing everywhere, telling them how to work in the specified place. Then those came along who found very particular conditions in Hannover or in Frankfurt. That was something one found everywhere. If one had somehow listened to all that, one wouldn't have moved forward by a single step. It was, even back then, a bad thing, but today, when it is often a matter of practical life, it is an even worse thing. For today it is not a matter of having us ferret out such grass growing, but rather of harnessing our will so that we can really do something, so that we can really work. Of course, it is immensely easy to say, "In the transcendental atmosphere that I sense in this or that place, one cannot do this or that"; it is much easier than simply wanting to do something. One ought to rely as little as possible on outer aspects today, and as much as possible to activate inner aspects. That is what really cannot be emphasized often enough.

And in addition to that, anthroposophical seriousness must absolutely be maintained, but the strength must be mustered to enter into outer things with real interest. We really must know what is happening in the world—and a lot of things are happening. But it is astonishing how little, even in our circles, one is concerned with what is happening.

I want to emphasize a saddening fact. This fact has many causes, but there is not enough time today to describe them all for you one by one. But the fact is that subscriptions for our journal for threefolding have increased almost not at all since May. And yet we are a society of thousands upon thousands of members. It is really quite sad that such a fact must be recorded. But such facts exist, and this is but one of them. Believe me, it is really true: the opponents are quite a different crew; they are on the job everywhere. And their machinations spread. I am not saying these things thoughtlessly, and particularly not without thought about what we must be aware of today if we don't gather up all the strength we have in us, if we don't add up every single, individual strength. That is what we need. We must have so much anthroposophy in us that we can go to work, otherwise we will be too late. And I do not see that what needs to be done is being done from another direction, for then I would certainly not fall into the trap of saying that we will be too late.

Some wonderful things are already in the offing, especially the participation by a number of students in our endeavors. It is precisely from this area that the most fruitful things can arise if one approaches matters with a genuine, true understanding; but we must also be clear about how one must approach this matter. It is certainly not possible with unclear mysticism. It is a matter of meeting all of this with inner diligence.

This and many other things could be said today, but I think you can find the other things yourselves if you follow the trains of thought which have been set in motion and develop them further yourselves. But that they do develop further is what I would like to express at the end of this last lecture as a preliminary wish. And now times are such that I cannot mention such a wish with the expectation that it be fulfilled in future years, but that I can see it in only weeks, when I can be here again. For, fundamentally, things are such that we really need the time, that really every week which we don't use can be lost.

Therefore, my dear friends, I would like to say two things to you at the end of this lecture: First, I want to express the wish that what I said today is understood by the time we see each other again. Second, that results in accordance with this wish can be pointed out. With that in mind, I bid you farewell.

Lecture Five

DORNACH, JANUARY 21, 1921

Our considerations before I left,[†] and already in the weeks prior to that, were all focused on showing how what we call spiritual science can pass into real life, can reach into it, and how what we call the world has a certain inner connection to what we experience inwardly in the human being. And as you review the considerations we have just made about these matters, I ask you now to thoroughly deliberate on the question of what it would mean for the total development of humanity if the most urgent, most meaningful results of anthroposophically oriented spiritual science were to penetrate into the lives of people working with one another in the social sphere. One would know that the human being, by coming to consciousness in his physical body, preserves something in this physical body which points to the time before birth, or conception, that he was there in a condition in which he bore the desire for life between birth and death, that he bore within himself the sense that the soul which had lived for a long time only in the spiritual world needs to look at the world through the physical senses, and also needs to be active in the physical body, in order to progress.

This conscious observation of the pre-existence of the soul would not remain a mere theoretical view if it were understood correctly. Instead, it would take hold of feeling and willing and thereby become an immediate life force.

We can certainly see this in people today. They all show us something of a lack of initiative on a large scale. This lack of initiative on a large scale, which has such a paralyzing effect on all the forces that are necessary to bring descending life back to an ascent again, this paralysis can only be improved by the human being becoming conscious of belonging to the spiritual world. This, however, cannot enter the soul through theoretical considerations but only through the living contemplation of what the human being was before he descended into the physical world. If you take that which looks beyond the time that the human being experiences here between birth and death not as the object of some vague belief but instead as the object of clear knowledge, then it does not have such an abstract effect on the human being as today's religious confessions; instead, it will have the concrete effect of a direct force in the human being. Human beings work in such a way that what lies in their work reaches beyond death. But when the human being takes up such ideas, life is poured into all that the human being can know.

Just consider for a moment that today our knowledge of nature is broad. As regards external knowledge, we have to say that humanity has made incredible progress. The recent bloody years have shown that this progress was unable to improve humanity with respect to morality. And, actually, such people as Wallace,[†] whom I mentioned frequently earlier whenever I wanted to emphasize just that, were right when they said: We have experienced incredible progress as regards knowledge of the outer world, but as regards a moral condition, humanity is as it was in ancient times; it has not progressed at all.

This progress must really be made today in this historical period, for people cannot remain the way they are now in their soul state. But how is this to happen? How can the more theoretical view of the world be enlivened? Take a seemingly crude example. We use hard coal for human life. We know that this hard coal constitutes the remnants of ancient forests and is therefore fundamentally a plant substance. But how does plant substance, the entire world of plants, relate to the human being as such? If the amount of carbon dioxide in the air were calculated over a few millennia, it would be an enormously large amount because we exhale carbonic dioxide, because we deposit carbonic dioxide in the air with every breath. In the course of thousands of years, this carbon dioxide would cause humanity to perish; it would extinguish life. But the plants absorb the carbon dioxide, excrete the carbon, make their own body from what they absorb of the cast-off products of the human being; and the plants that once covered the earth, they in turn create what are now our coal seams, our coal deposits.

As you see, it is a remarkable journey. First of all, the qualitative aspect comes into consideration; for, of course, our coal didn't arise from our breathing but from other beings; yet this must be considered qualitatively. What we somehow excrete creates the foundation of what we then use from the earth. That is the extent to which one can think in accordance with the results of natural science.

Spiritual science leads us further. Let me remind you of how I told you that the human being discards his physical body by entering spiritual worlds with his soul-spirit. But I also told you that the physical body that is discarded signifies the earth's rebuilding.

Just as we give coal to the plant world when we exhale, so we give our body to the whole earth. And what we see around us is absolutely the product of beings like ourselves, such beings who were our predecessors during the Moon, Sun, and Saturn periods,[†] the first three pre-earthly embodiments of our planetary system. What they bequeathed to the earth is today's earth substance. And when future worlds arise, then what we discard as our physical bodies will live in them. It is a thought which, if one follows it, is incredibly far-reaching. For from our knowledge of nature, which otherwise remains incomplete, we gain a connection between the human being and the whole environment. It is extraordinarily important for us to gain this. For if we take as foundational all we have considered, then we must say: In our whole being, not just in our thinking but in our whole being, into the outermost aspect of our physicality, there lives what we turn into our moral ideals. The dualistic way of looking at things, which cannot bridge the natural view of the world with the moral world order, also cannot imagine how what we have in our moral ideals is connected with the activity of our muscles. If one looks at the world as we have in our recent considerations, then one sees how what we think in our moral ideals is incorporated into our bodily processes. One sees the spiritual and the bodily processes interwoven into a unity.

This way of looking at things ought to become universal. If it were included in the education of our children, then there would be people who grew up not having, on the one hand, in the sense of the Kant-Laplace theory, a world which arose out of nebular conditions, from which stars and sun and planets split off, from which then, by means of a splicing of amoral matter, human beings were formed, which then turned themselves back into purely natural substance; instead, what springs up in us as moral ideal would be at one with what existed at the origin of world evolution as purely natural being. And we human beings would recognize ourselves as called upon to implant in natural existence the moral ideals we experience. In future worlds, we would recognize as laws of nature what we now experience morally.

If children were to grow up under the influence of such a view, they would place themselves into the world in such a way that they would experience themselves as a part of the cosmos and thus have feelings for life stemming from those forces which they would absorb together with a knowledge of the cosmos. Yes, by being educated to act, they would know that what they do would be imprinted into the whole world. If this feeling existed, how differently human beings would live than they do today, when it is possible for someone to ask: What am I, actually, in this world? seeing himself standing alone, arising out of undetermined forces of nature, interspersed with moral ideals as though with soap bubbles. Such a person can be paralyzed with respect to his feelings for life. When he looks up to the world of stars, he sees the stars moving through space, but he has no relationship to that; for, after all, they are themselves merely naturally arising worlds, disintegrating into themselves, without meaning and without inner spirituality.

We must consider what, as a life force, could become the spiritual view of humanity. We have to indicate this again and again, for this is what contemporary people understand least of all. They say that this spiritual view is unworldly. But it is the contemporary view that is unworldly. Why? It works with the dogmas of the past, which in the past made good sense because they arose out of a certain instinctive clairvoyance. This instinctive clairvoyance has disappeared; people no longer have a relationship to it. The dogmas that have been preserved are no longer understood. It is not that the dogmas are wrong, but rather that today's humanity has no relationship to them. And apart from what has been preserved as dogmas, humanity today has a natural science without spirit. Anthroposophy wants to provide a spirit-filled natural science, one which enlivens the human being; and what trickles in as knowledge about spirit in nature will transform itself in the human being into social forces just as nourishment transforms itself physically in the human being. If one wanted to enter into things seriously, one would experience how spiritual knowledge would be taken up as nourishment by the soul, would be digested—if I may use this expression—by the soul to become a socially effective force. We will gain social impulses in no other way than by taking up spiritual knowledge from surrounding nature. Anyone who thinks that social reforms can be derived from any other impulse is thinking about things of the world more or less like someone who thinks about a human being and, in order to nourish him well, forbids him to eat. Anyone who speaks about social forms today but not about spiritual knowledge wants to do the same with respect to the social order of humanity as someone who wants to nourish the human being by prescribing a starvation diet. This is a profound absurdity in the contemporary views of humanity, one which it cannot see through at all.

What we bring in from the spiritual world when we enter into this life between birth and death is definitely merely like an image. And, fundamentally, our soul life is a life of images, and this life of images was animated in earlier times by what was already present as a spiritual element in the view of nature. In ancient times, there was no view of nature without a view of spirit. People today read up on older views of nature; they read nothing there about a natural science devoid of spirit. Anyone delving back into the thirteenth, fourteenth century and reading about what was then said about nature—even if he might sneer at the childishness, the superstitiousness—will find that the essential thing was that everything that was described was described as being permeated by spirit. Today we try as hard as possible to see natural phenomena without spirit. Yes, seeing everything devoid of spirit is considered the highest form of observation.

But what we take up from nature without spirit can definitely no longer vitalize the life of the images. We get stuck there and do not want to confess to being an image, a mere picture, an image of a bygone life which does not want to be fructified by the present life. For this present life should fructify the bygone life so that it can, in turn, be carried up through the portal of death into spiritual worlds. Only by being seen in this living way can spiritual science give the human being what it should be giving him.

Take, for example, the dogmas in the old theological books. There are many people today who simply fight against these dogmas because they consider them to be absurd. In no way are they absurd, not even a dogma like that of the trinity; it even has the very deepest meaning. By means of the ancient instinctive art of clairvoyance, it was read from nature itself. And for thousands of years of human evolution, this dogma gave an incredible amount to humanity. The external churches preserved such dogmas. Today they barely exist as anything more than a certain formulation. People today have no need to develop a relationship to the content of an old clairvoyance. What remains has no bearing on people by virtue of their present nature, whereas it once was living nourishment for the soul. Apart from these dogmas, we have external natural science, a natural science devoid of the spirit, which kills our soul if it is not spiritualized.

These are the two basic evils that spiritual science, as it is meant here, has in mind. It wants to provide the soul once more with something that can enliven this soul, can inject strength into this soul, so that the soul immediately feels itself to be a member of the entire cosmos, and in its social activity feels how the responsibility that comes from our small activity as a single human being has cosmic significance for the entire development of the future. We must look beyond the narrow circle we create through our spiritless education. For this constriction has been carried out by humanity itself, which wants to carry it out ever more. That is why spiritual science has such a difficult time of it, because, fundamentally, it wants to be that which does not lie merely in words, or in thoughts, or in ideas, but first flows as a lifeblood of spirit and soul through the thoughts, through the ideas, through the words and trickles directly into the human soul. That, too, is why in representing spiritual science, it is much more a matter of *how* one speaks than of *what* one says. Today we see the great conflict between materialism and spiritualism. This great conflict stems only from the fact that people do not want to recognize that there is a profound basis for the saying: Between two opposing assertions, there in the middle lies the truth.

Is it true that God is in us? It is true that God is in us. Is it true that we are in God? It is true that we are in God. The two assertions are opposites. Both are true: God is in us; we are in God. The two assertions are opposites. The real truth, the whole truth lies in the middle. And the essence of all disputes in the world is that people always lean toward a one-sidedness that is true but is just a one-sided truth, whereas the real truth lies between two opposite assertions.† One must know both if one wants to get to the truth. For example, as world evolution is now, one has to have the most earnest will to get to know material existence; one really cannot be allowed to lapse into the obsession of those who say: "We want to busy ourselves with spirit; we don't want to become acquainted with matter." Getting to know matter as much as possible, that is the one side of human knowledge and the striving of human will; the other side is getting to know spirit. For what we should actually strive for exists between these two, and both sides are wrong—those who say the world is only matter and those who say the world is only spirit. For, what is matter? Matter, the way the human being knows it, is what has remained behind once spirit has become spirit again. Your own human form is nothing but what was once divine thought, was once the effect of divine thoughts (see Plate 1 in the appendix, left side). Think of how water, when it freezes, attains form; in this way, this divine thought attains form and becomes the human sheath. And a new thought, a new divine thought shows itself in man's inner being, which again goes forth, and this divine thought here (left) was again transformed from a form which in more ancient times was a thought. What we observe as matter is really nothing but solidified spirit, and what we observe as human spirit is youthful form, is form grasped in its process of becoming. Spirit and matter are different only as pertains to their age in the world. And the mistake in this respect is not that we turn toward matter or that we turn toward spirit, but rather that we want to preserve in the present that which we should receive in life, which we should fructify so that it may become the future.

If we take what we have brought into the present from our preexistence—that is, what we have as soul-spiritual life—and permeate it only with dry, external, spiritless natural science, then we harden it; we do not allow it to be seed-like; we do not let it sprout into future worlds; we ahrimanize it.

And if we want to grasp that which is form—which is divinity that has grown old and crystalized into forms—by means of a nebulous mysticism into which we dream all sorts of things, then we do not support ourselves with the physical support which the divinity has given us, but, instead, we luciferize matter. What is nebulous mysticism? The human being ought to look into himself; he ought, from out of the cosmos, to recognize within his physical organism what he is in this life between birth and death. Instead, he fantasizes that he himself has a divinity within him. He *does* have that within him; but he does not acquire it through mystical fantasizing. He luciferizes what he should see in the later form of the bodily sheath. These are false views of matter and spirit, which cause people to argue with each other; for matter and spirit are the same, only at different stages.

This is what is especially necessary for the present to understand. Otherwise, it will not be able to grasp social life. Today one really must make the effort of penetrating with one's thoughts into true reality. This is something people don't want to do. They want to remain on the surface.

A few days ago, I heard a lovely little story[†] about something that took place recently in Zürich. One of our friends spoke at a university celebration about the scientific significance of anthroposophy. A man inclined toward socialism responded that one really ought not to educate people today with such mystical fantasy, but rather with exact science, for even Goethe already said: "No creative spirit penetrates into Nature's interior."

What this Swiss delegate put forth is based on a merely superficial view of things Goethe said. For in quoting this statement by Haller, Goethe says: "I have been hearing this repeated for sixty years and have been cursing it. . . ." This is how spiritual life is dealt with today;

this is the way one knows things, and yet this makes one an authority to a certain extent after all. This is altogether the way one strives for knowledge of the world today. Whether there is someone who believes that Goethe uttered this saying, which he "cursed" for sixty years, or whether some economist makes the following statement, it ultimately all amounts to the same thing. A very learned economist,[†] a national economist, wrote a book about free or fixed pricing. So he had to do a lot of research about how, let me say, the national economy could be made into something more social. Included among the various things he discusses, there is also this. He says: Even Georg Brandes said that the people are guided in their social, economic activities not through reason but through instinct. That is why one ought to enlighten the people. One must bring enlightenment to the people.

Now Georg Brandes is not a deep thinker; but one can reply: So and so many economists work at so and so many universities; they are enlightened. But when they practice economics with each other, then instinct works among them just as it does among others, not at all differently. For as things have been structured today, particularly by means of a highly developed intelligence, instinct is what has remained in social life. The instincts are active. But now one must go further. Now one must ask oneself: How does one bring light into this activity of the instinct? For this alone can have a social significance. It is simply nonsense to believe that a majority of people can be guided by these instincts. They cannot. These instincts simply stem from the coexistence of people. Something has to arise which transforms these instincts, which can enter into these instincts. Reason cannot enter into these instincts. Let us remember the old instinctive vision; it developed into our intellectualism. But this intellectualism lives only in the inner spiritual existence of the human being. On the other hand, the external social forces are saturated with instincts. Something which is related to the old instinctive vision but has an impact on spirituality must now penetrate into this instinct: imagination must penetrate it. We have then: old instinctive vision—intellect—imagination (see Plate 2 in the appendix). Only imagination, as we call it in spiritual science, has the power to bring light into the instinctive life.

What enables us to understand things in a purely external way, scientifically, to create botany, zoology, mathematics, can be fed by the intellect, but that is not the case with what constitutes human interaction. What we call imagination must enter in. Imagination must saturate social life. That is what matters. Human instincts lived in all social life, from ancient times until today. Fundamentally, it is only in the second third, or in the last third of the nineteenth century that humanity finished its entrance into an age which no longer wants old instincts. You can prove quite precisely that at the turn of the eighteenth to the nineteenth century, old instincts still existed in social life. The uncertainty of these instincts only began at the time when the intellect developed most brilliantly. Social life then remained as tradition.

Just think for a moment of what enormous effort people had to make in the nineteenth century to still have any kind of moral views. They had to preserve, in the most abstract ways, what remained from olden times. And it was out of absolute necessity that the old moral ideas were propagated as fossils. Today we need a rebirth of morality, for only that can bring about what is social. But that cannot emerge from the intellect; rather, it can only come from moral intuition. Phantasy, moral phantasy must raise itself to the spiritual world so as to fructify itself in the spiritual world. That is what matters today, otherwise humanity will begin to descend into the loss of moral impulses.

The abstract confessions which tend only toward belief cannot find strength for life through this belief. Belief alone does indeed provide something for soul-egoism; but with soul-egoism one might just be able, if necessary, to live as a single human being. If one wants to engage in activity, which of course means to be active socially, then it is necessary for soul-spiritual lifeblood to permeate us. But this can come only from concrete spiritual life. This consciousness of the life force of the anthroposophical worldview is what must flow through the anthroposophical movement.

Pantheism is a favorite objection[†] that also gets raised against something like anthroposophically oriented spiritual science. Contemporary confessions consider pantheism to be heretical, a confusion about how the divine lives in the things that surround us. But why do the contemporary confessions call our anthroposophically oriented spiritual science heretical? Because those confessions are completely permeated by materialism! Indeed, if a Jesuit looks at the surrounding world only as matter, then it is blasphemy to say that this matter is God. But is anthroposophically oriented spiritual science to blame for how Jesuit X can regard the surrounding world as only matter? It is not matter, it is spirit, and what Jesuit X recognizes as matter in the surrounding world is shown to be illusion by anthroposophically oriented spiritual science. One does not explain the world which one considers to be illusion as divine being, of course not. However, explaining what surrounds one as divine while at the same time recognizing external sense-perceptible existence as illusion is quite different than seeing what surrounds one as crude matter and then wanting to explain this crude matter as divine.

You see how far apart are the things that the other means and that are really there within our anthroposophical spiritual science. But we must not tire of actually asserting these things before the world. Otherwise, what can occur is something that recently appeared in a Swiss newspaper[†] as an objection against my method of achieving spiritual knowledge. What was more or less said there was that I claim one can see the spirit; but that won't work because spirit is not sensory and only what is sensory can be seen. One cannot touch the spirit; therefore, no one can see the spirit.

You see how it really is a dismal method that appears there, grounded in nothing other than that the person in question says he cannot see the spirit and therefore no one can say anything about the spirit; one can know nothing about the spirit for one cannot touch the spirit. And an entire newspaper section deals with variations of such a train of thought. That people haven't the consciousness required to read to the end, or even to become acquainted with things, is what has such a terribly devastating effect today. "No creative spirit penetrates into Nature's interior," are the first two lines in Goethe. One stops with them and does not notice that immediately following Goethe says: "I've cursed this for sixty years."

What we have to take notice of everywhere is superficiality; one cannot draw attention to this often enough. We have to track down this terrible tendency for superficiality everywhere. Today it expresses itself mainly in the social realm, in economic thinking, where it has such a terribly harmful effect. There one prefers not to delve down into things, prefers not to delve down into what lies in the nature of things.

For example, it was reported today that people in a particular field say—and it is certainly said frequently—that the "essentials of the social question"† are so difficult to grasp. I suppose, if someone says, "Something is difficult to grasp," then he wants something easy, something which is easy to grasp. But if one cannot make use in social life of something which is easily grasped, if one simply bungles it, when it is necessary to grasp something that is a bit more difficult, for which one has to make a bit of an effort because thinking something difficult is what is necessary for thinking about social life today, if the immense damage of recent times had been caused by people wanting to penetrate social life with thoughts that were easy to grasp and had thereby ruined it, then the expression that things were difficult in this realm would be downright frivolous! And that is basically what it is.

It is a matter of not even harboring this inwardly frivolous thought, that this matter is difficult. For if the thoughts were given as they are wanted, then they would lead to nothing but bungling. In order to work properly, it will be necessary to really overcome this apparent difficulty and to get involved with this matter. That is the point. One ought to deal with the concerns of this serious time in this serious manner.

We will discuss this further tomorrow.

Lecture Six

DORNACH, JANUARY 22, 1921

On the basis of the things we discussed here recently, I would now like to mention details which might be useful to you as members of the anthroposophical movement so that you can defend this anthroposophical movement, and all that must now develop out of it, against attacks from this or that quarter. In recent times, one sees certain attacks arising everywhere—there are certainly plenty of attacks, but today I only want to characterize a particular kind—certain attacks which are directed against our practical undertakings, against what must arise out of the anthroposophical movement as life practices. Indeed, it is widely said: "These people create a Kommende Tag; these people create a Futurum. What do they want with that? They really don't want to do anything with these institutions other than to arrange practical things for those who profess the anthroposophical worldview." So, to some extent, economic institutions were also founded solely to provide a kind of power, even if for now it is just economic power, to those who profess the anthroposophical worldview.

If one were to look more closely at what underlies such undertakings, how they emerge from the whole spirit of the anthroposophical movement, then such an accusation would not be able to arise. But, on the other hand, it is undeniable that even people within the anthroposophical movement often contribute amply to the surfacing of such misunderstandings. However, it is completely impossible that the entire fabric of what is here being called anthroposophy, which wants to present itself to the world, could somehow warrant such a judgement. Certainly, this becomes clear only to someone who takes into consideration the whole spirit of this anthroposophical movement.

This anthroposophical movement definitely counts on all the forces that exist in the development of humanity. How often has it been stressed that the development of humanity proceeds through particular turning points and that these turning points must be observed. I would like to begin by drawing attention to one such important turning point, and thereby show how little justification there can be for the judgement that we want to bring a particular doctrine, a particular dogma to people.

I might say that a kind of anomaly, a kind of outgrowth of fanaticism, can manifest among one or the other anthroposophist who wants to advocate a particular doctrine; this anomaly might even be evident in many; but this is not in the spirit of the anthroposophical movement. For if, in the spirit of this movement, we look back on the development of humanity, we find that in those ancient times when instinctive vision was widespread in humanity, the whole human constitution of the soul was different, that human beings had an entirely different way of relating to the world.

What was the actual intention of those sites from ancient times of human development which we often characterize as mysteries? Let us leave out all the details and take hold of the meaning of these mysteries.

Those who were found to be suitable and mature enough to be admitted into the mysteries partook once during their time on earth—that is, in the time between birth and death—in a certain teaching, which was given to them by the leaders of the mysteries and which came from what these leaders could impart about suprasensory worlds. No such leader of the mysteries made a secret of the fact that, in his opinion, instruction within the mysteries did not emanate merely from human beings, but that through the particular cultic rites that were carried out in the mysteries, superhuman, divine-spiritual beings were present during the mystery rites and that with the help of these, let us say, attending gods, the teaching and everything connected to it was carried out. The essential aspect of this is therefore that the arrangement of the mysteries was such that they attracted, so to speak, divine-spiritual beings who, through the mouths of those who were the leaders of the mysteries, provided the teaching for the students of the mysteries.

In more ancient times, everything within humanity was arranged socially in such a way that the entire arrangement was accepted as a social arrangement, not only by the leaders or students of the mysteries but absolutely also by those who were outside of the mysteries and could not take part in the life of the mysteries. It was absolutely the case—just think of Egypt—that those who were rulers of the state received their directives from the mysteries. The mysteries were seen as the natural sites of leadership for everything to do with social life.

Today, one can indeed provide esoteric schooling which can proceed in forms similar to those of the old mysteries, but they have a different meaning. That is just it, that with respect to such things, a significant turning point in human evolution occurred between our time and the ancient time. In the old days, the human being depended absolutely on these teachings that were given him through the mysteries, teachings through which he did, so to speak, approach the divine-spiritual beings themselves, so as to receive these teachings between birth and death. Now things have changed. We now live after that turning point in human evolution when things changed. What the human being used to learn between birth and death through the mysteries, he now learns before he descends into a physical body through conception or birth. He learns it according to his karma, according to his preparation in an earlier earth life. So what the human being experiences between the great midnight hour of existence and birth is something that includes this teaching.

You will find what has to be said about these things in other contexts also indicated in a cycle I gave in Vienna in 1914[†] about life between death and a new birth. But I would now like to characterize in more detail what I merely indicated there in broad strokes.

Thus today the human being experiences something similar to the ancient mystery teaching before he descends from pre-existence into the physical body. That is a fact which must be taken into account by someone standing in reality through spiritual science. Today one can no longer think in the way one thought in ancient times about the human being who is born. In ancient times, one regarded the human being in such a way that one said: The human being descends to the earth and is called upon to be initiated through the mysteries into what he really is as a human being. That is not how things are today. What I said pertained to human beings who had passed through fewer earth lives than today's human beings who in their earlier earth lives have absorbed a great deal into their souls, which then has led to their being able to go through a certain amount of instruction from the divine-spiritual beings in their prenatal condition.

One needs to presuppose something like this when facing a child. Today it is no longer our task to pour, so to speak, into the child what had to be poured into him in olden times. Today it is our task to say to ourselves: "This child *has* been taught; he has merely laid a physical body, which has already been instructed, around his soul; that which was his pre-birth instruction from the gods must make its way through the sheaths around that soul; it must be brought out." That is how we should think pedagogically today. If we think in terms of real anthroposophically oriented spiritual science, it will be clear to us that we can, basically, do nothing else through all our teaching than remove the hindrances that are placed in front of the emergence of what the child brings with him into the world from prenatal life. It is for that reason that in our Waldorf education such endlessly great importance is attached to the fact that the teacher really regards the child before him as something of a riddle that he has to solve, in which the teacher must seek that which the child is concealing within himself.

Furthermore, the teacher must absolutely not lay chief importance on anything which he has undertaken to funnel into the child. The teacher must never proceed dogmatically in any way but has to regard the child himself as his teacher, to watch how the child, through his particular behavior, reveals the very way in which those sheaths are to be penetrated, so that from out of the child himself divine instruction can emerge. Then Waldorf pedagogy and didactics do indeed consist of removing those sheaths which surround the child, so that the child can come to himself and discover within himself his own divine instruction. That is why we say: It is not at all necessary for us to stuff something we have thought up as a theory, no matter now nicely it is described in books, into the child. We will leave that to those who are grounded in old traditional religious beliefs and want to turn the children into Catholics or Protestants or Jews. But that is not how it is. Nor do we want to stuff anthroposophical pedagogy into the children; we only use what we know from anthroposophy to help us become skillful in calling into existence the living spirit, which lives in the child from its pre-existence.

Through anthroposophy we want to acquire dexterity in teaching, not a number of dogmas which we teach the children. We want to become more skillful; we want to develop an art of education so as to make of the child, in the way that has been characterized, what he is to become. We are clear about the fact that all other knowledge, which today is brought to the human being from the most diverse sides, may indeed instruct the head but cannot make a person an educational artist because it does not affect the whole human being, but only the head. Anthroposophy takes hold of the whole human being and makes him a master of that "artistic grasp," as I might call it, which has to be carried out with the group of pupils in the way just described. Therefore, we use anthroposophy to become skillful teachers but not to teach it to the child. For we are clear about this: The spirit is alive; it is not a sum of concepts or ideas, and it appears in each child in an individual way if we are able to bring to consciousness what each child carries to earth through birth. We would impoverish this earth if we wanted to teach the child a compilation of concepts. Instead, we enrich the earth if we nurture and care for what the gods have given the child, which the child brings down to the earth. Then what is living spirit appears in so and so many human individualities, not what anthroposophy brings to human individualities in order to make them apparently uniform. Thus, bringing the living spirit into life is what is important. That is why we are not at all interested in bringing some sort of anthroposophical dogmatism to the children.

That is one practical outcome that has emerged from anthroposophical spiritual science. This particular form of instruction, the educational art, is certainly different from anything people have imagined up to now because they cannot think of anything other than: "I believe in a certain dogma; therefore it's best if I teach this dogma to the children." That does not interest us at all, such bringing of dogma to children, because we know that the child brings a message when it comes into existence through birth, and that one would ruin this message if one were to bring a dogma toward the child. The spirit does not need to be cultivated abstractly. If one is able to release it through anthroposophy, to enable it to exist, then it is present as living spirit, not a sum of doctrines. These doctrines exist only as the means to awaken the living spirit in humanity and to keep it in continuous development. That is why it is unfair when the belief is spread about that we want to push anthroposophy dogmatically in our Waldorf school or in any other pedagogical endeavor. We want neither to push anthroposophy dogmatically nor somehow to impose anthroposophy onto individual sciences. On the contrary, we want to bring out the individuality of each science.

We are quite clear that it is a question of creating something in the world, expressly with anthroposophy, which eradicates all dogma, which expressly brings individuality into the world everywhere in all spheres. From this perspective, this attack that rages at us from all corners† had to be rejected when it was a matter of pushing anthroposophy as doctrine into a scientific or pedagogical realm.

As far as our practical economic activities are concerned, it has become apparent in the last weeks, and indeed with remarkable unanimity, both over in Germany as well as in Switzerland, and also in other places, that on the occasion of the latest publication of the Kommende Tag and Futurum,† people were saying: "All sorts of anthroposophists are to be united there, so that they can now also have economic institutions and the like; other people are permitted, at best, to be involved, but they are not given any particularly meaningful voice in the administration, and so forth." If we wanted something like that, it would contradict the very principle on which we stand: that we really look at the development of humanity in all details and act accordingly; not that we want something that is absolutely right but that we ask ourselves: What must happen *today*? And then we must draw attention to the second turning point in the evolution of humanity. Economic institutions arise today out of a certain principle of inertia in people everywhere. Formerly, they arose from a small circle in small territories; now, because the states have become the economic enterprises, because entrepreneurial empires have taken the place of individual enterprises, they have expanded to gigantic proportions and become these enterprises which today spring only from inertia. Today one speaks of "national economy"; this is a case of forging two things into one. Every particular group spirit binding a folk together is, I may say, outwardly embodied in blood. However, world conditions have long become such that today's economy can have absolutely nothing to do with the kind of group-bonding expressed in the blood if healthy conditions are to prevail. Today it is something that in the most eminent sense expresses pathological economic conditions when, let us say, there is a dispute about the Rhine border because one wants to have a different economic community on the other side of the Rhine than on this side of the Rhine, that is, out of popular requirements. These popular requirements originated in entirely different forces; they have nothing to do with today's world economy. These things actually turned into a particular crisis only in the course of the last third of the nineteenth century. It was only then that the turning point in the evolution of humanity actually became so apparent.

As we have just explained, in ancient times the human being entered physical existence without, so to speak, instruction from the gods; he had to be instructed through the mysteries. Today he enters having already been instructed, and what is in his soul need only be brought to consciousness in him. In ancient times, with regard to social and economic coexistence, humanity was simply organized in such a way that the human being was born into the social context, into the group. He was born into a group according to the forces that had worked on him before birth. It wasn't only the principle of physical heredity which was the basis of, for example, the oldest forms of human inequality, the caste system. In the most ancient caste divisions, it was absolutely the case that the leaders of the social order followed the old way according to how the human being was pre-destined before his birth or conception for a particular group of people. In those days, when the human being had experienced even fewer earth incarnations in his previous existence, he was born, by virtue of these few incarnations, into a group in a very specific way, and only within this group could he develop socially. In ancient India, whoever belonged to a particular caste would have perished if he had been meant to be born into a different caste because of his earlier incarnation and what he had experienced in the spiritual world before birth. It was not merely blood inheritance which was the basis of these castes, but something also which was a spiritual pre-determination. Humanity outgrew that. Between that time and our own time, there is, in this respect, another turning point. People today still bear within themselves marks of a group nature, but that is simply an illusory semblance. People are born into nations; they are also born into a particular class stratification; but to the extent that they then grow up in a particular era, it becomes evident relatively early in childhood that such a determination from prenatal existence no longer exists. Today people are taught by the gods in their prenatal existence. The stamp of a particular group is no longer impressed upon them. That is something which remains as a last residue in physical heredity. To belong to a nationality today with one's consciousness is, so to speak, a piece of hereditary sin, is something that should no longer play a role in people's souls.

In contrast to that, it is a particular factor of our time that the human being, while growing up, grows out of all grouping. But within economic life, he cannot remain without grouping, because in relation to the economic life, the individual is never decisive. Spiritual life arises out of the innermost part of the human being, whereby he is able not merely to achieve a kind of harmonizing of his capacities but, by means of a particular kind of schooling, to expand and retain them. But today economic judgment can never come from a single person. I have given you examples[†] of how economic judgment must err if it comes from a single person. I would like to draw your attention again to an example from the second half of the nineteenth century.

I have told you that in a certain period, around the middle of the second half of the nineteenth century, discussion about the gold standard arose everywhere in parliaments and other institutions. Those who advocated the need for a gold standard put forward arguments among really quite clever people. I don't say that ironically, but rather because the people who, at the time, spoke as practitioners and theoreticians about the gold standard in parliaments and other institutions, really were very clever people, and what was said about the gold standard in individual countries actually belongs to some of the best parliamentary implementations. And almost everywhere one thing was pointed out. Through great perspicacity, it was pointed out that the gold standard would get free trade going and sweep away all protective tariffs. And if one now reads the things that were said at that time about the effect of a gold standard on free trade,[†] one can rejoice about how clever people were at the time. But what then happened was the exact opposite of what the cleverest people said: Everywhere, as a result of the gold standard, protective tariffs arose. The cleverness in economic life, which came from the individual personalities, has not helped people at all. One could prove this in the most varied realms, for it is simply so that although the human being is competent as an individual when it comes to nature or other matters of knowledge concerning the human being, when it comes to economic matters, he is never competent as a single individual. One cannot have judgment about concrete economic things as a single individual. An economic judgement can only arise when people join together, associate with each other, and one supports the other, when reciprocity prevails in the association. It is not possible for the single individual to arrive at such an economic judgment which can then pass over into economic activity. It is the opposite of what happens when the human being has a scientific judgment. In the case of a scientific judgment, the human being ought to give a comprehensive judgment out of his whole being; in concrete economic judgment and action, it is a matter of having one person know part of something, the second something else, the third something else again; the producer knows something in one realm, the consumer knows something in this same realm. These must merge; a group judgment, a collective judgment must arise. In other words, the old group formations are done with; group formations must arise out of economic life through human beings themselves. These must be the associations of economic life.

It follows from the concept of a necessary force in development that the associative life must take hold of human beings; this associative life must replace the old group connections which today only reproduce themselves in humanity like an original sin.

If we consider this, then we will also say to ourselves: With regard to knowledge, human beings descended to earth in ancient times uninstructed; they received knowledge in the mysteries. Today they descend already instructed and we have to arrange our education in such a way that we retrieve what human beings learned from the gods. With regard to economic institutions, human beings used to be pre-determined; in a way, the gods had stamped them. They were born into some kind of caste, some kind of group. That is over. Human beings are born without being stamped; they are placed into humanity as single individuals. They have to form groups themselves out of their spirituality.

It really is not a matter of grouping together people who profess anthroposophy; whether or not they profess anthroposophy will depend on what the gods taught them before they were born, whether through their earlier incarnations they were ripe for this divine instruction and now descend in such a way that we can bring anthroposophy out of them. It is in many more people today than one believes, and a large number are merely too lazy to extract out of themselves what is in them; it is also the case that school instruction is not set up in such a way that the sheaths are loosened and people really come to their consciousness. As regards the practical, especially the economic realm, it would be downright senseless to unite people because they are anthroposophists; rather, anthroposophy is understood again so as to gain insight into the way in which people, out of their consciousness, have to search for the groupings, according to their earlier incarnations. It is a question of giving people the opportunity to undertake the forming of groups—in other words, to carry out what is entirely anchored in the history of human evolution. So there, too, it is not a matter of grouping people together according to a particular dogma, but of giving the opportunity to people who are called upon to find themselves as groups according to their previous incarnations. A great many riddles are contained in these things as soon as one goes from the abstract to the concrete, and, I might say, a great many mysterious things. For whether people belong to the one group or the other is really not a very simple matter.

The longing that people have for great simplicity really shows up in a strange way. I have just been handed a small announcement about a lecture which the laudable Frohnmeyer gave yet again on "Theosophy and Anthroposophy," and there it says: "The purely personal comparison with Christianity which was made at the end is reminiscent of the well-known fact, 'that these people are unfortunately annoyed by how the great is so simple.'" He evidently thinks that anthroposophists are annoyed by the fact that the great is so simple, as the lazy reverend Frohnmeyer would like it to be, because he doesn't want to exert himself, to acquaint himself with greatness in its particulars. One just always has to translate things into the right language! That is what we have as a task right now: to translate things into the right language.

Of course, it is not a matter of hurling at everyone the teachings about the instruction received by people before birth, or the teachings about how in the past people were born into a group whereas now they are not being born into groups; but we ourselves can let ourselves be saturated by these truths and through the very manner of our proceedings will then find the possibility of showing people we are as far from introducing dogmas into schools as we are from grouping people who profess a certain dogma into economic groups, into economic associations.

This was also observed at our Stuttgart Waldorf School, where you can see that we have no interest at all in teaching anthroposophy to the children. We want to use a method of instruction which one can only attain through anthroposophy. And that is something purely objective. But for children or parents of children who want to have Catholic instruction, a Catholic priest visits the Waldorf School; and for those who are to have Protestant religious instruction, a Protestant priest visits the school. We do not create any obstacles for these people. Only in our time, when so many parents, especially parents from the proletariat, no longer think of sending their children to Catholic or Protestant religious education, it was necessary to ask these people whether they would like to have free religious lessons born out of anthroposophical education. The result is that those who would otherwise have been educated without religion, who had no religious instruction whatsoever, come in large numbers to the so-called anthroposophical religious instruction, which, however, does not teach anthroposophy but only arises out of anthroposophy. That these children participate more eagerly in their religious instruction than those with the Catholic or Protestant priests is not our fault but presumably the fault of the Catholic or Protestant priests. Nor is it our fault that things came to such a pass that gradually a number of children went over to the other religious instruction, and things went so far that, I believe, the Protestant religious instructor said: "Soon I won't have anyone in my class anymore because they have all run off." But that was already the case last year. Did we have any intention of bringing some kind of dogma to the children? We have no interest in that whatsoever. We know that if our method succeeds in removing the sheath—as I have explained—then the children will have the best instruction—namely, that which they received in the spiritual world before their descent to earth.

Mind you, it is very much in the interest of certain religious confessions to tarnish this instruction, not to let this instruction spread. For whoever can compare, for example, the strange relationship between the papal encyclicals[†] today with what is going on in the spiritual world certainly knows that the divine-religious instruction which children enjoy before they descend into the world is absolutely not what one would like to give them in certain religious confessions in the world today.

This is particularly noticeable in the Catholic Church because the Catholic Church, through its cultic rituals, through its ceremonies, in contrast to the Protestant Church, still has a suprasensory influence; but this suprasensory influence can manifest itself in the most diverse ways, and one can indeed say: Something can be an error because it deviates in a certain way from the truth; something can also be an error in that it is the opposite of the truth.

And as far as the practical things are concerned, the things we discuss in our meetings—meetings which sometimes last until 2:30 in the morning, sometimes even longer—are things which I obviously cannot reveal here; for what is discussed in such meetings, is valid only in those meetings. But I can assure you that at the meetings held in this manner over concerns about Futurum and Kommende Tag, anthroposophy is not negotiated; rather, the things that are negotiated are of quite a different nature. There are things which definitely should be negotiated in the most practical way: how to cultivate this or that area, what to do with this or that, and so on. Then, whether something is somehow anthroposophical, theoretically anthroposophical, is of no account. Instead, what is discussed there, should take hold of economic life as skillfully as when one has thoughts which becomes flexible, which are brought into reality in the way they can be when the spirit is taken hold of in a living way through anthroposophy.

Then one merely has to show people that neither the statutes of Kommende Tag nor those of Futurum contain anthroposophical doctrines, but that only economic affairs are involved, and that it is only a matter of recognizing that these economic affairs are better than the economic affairs of other similar contemporary undertakings. But this is one of the aspects that must be defended because, as I said, it is one of the attacks; and these attacks now rage at us from all sides and will accumulate in a terrible way in the near future if we don't succeed in clarifying our concerns clearly and energetically to the world. Everything points toward that. For what I recently had to say in Stuttgart is true: What has not yet been learned within the anthroposophical movement is to be attentive to the realities, to remain livingly united so as to bring to the world's attention the things which matter. The opponents, as I recently said in Stuttgart,[†] are "men of a different stripe!" They are organizing themselves and they will show their organization. We will definitely succumb if we don't realize that these opponents are of a different stripe, and that now, after all, just as much effort can be made on behalf of the good as efforts are now being made on behalf of the bad.

In this way I wanted to bring to your attention just this one point, with regard to which you will definitely hear formulated attacks because of our practical undertakings. If you open your eyes, and, of course, that is essential—I mean, figuratively—then you can hear them, and then there will also be much to defend today in this regard. I wanted to say this to you today, which, let me say, may inspire your souls in this direction, in case it is necessary to cultivate defense. And this "inspiring of your souls" can arise if we know what it meant that in ancient times the human being descended to the earth without having been instructed by the gods, that he now is instructed before birth in his prenatal condition, and that all of life must then be arranged accordingly; and, on the other hand, what it means that in earlier times the human being was predetermined by the will of the gods to be born into castes, classes, folks, tribes, and so on. After the turning point that lies in the past, however, the human being is called upon to form groups on the earth himself through economic necessities. This happens in economic associations. It is precisely the proper recognition of earth evolution and of the spiritual evolution of humanity—and of the connection between these two—that shows how what we call "threefolding" is not merely a political program but the result of what flows out of a real recognition of human evolution, what arises out of a real recognition in the present and for the immediate future.

We will shall speak further about this tomorrow.

Lecture Seven

DORNACH, JANUARY 23, 1921

Today I would like to add to the observations we considered here recently about cosmic and human truths, truths which, as we mentioned again yesterday, are connected with the nature of humanity's evolution in our time. It may be necessary today to insert a seemingly personal remark here or there in order to supplement what has been said from this or that side. You know that I very rarely do that, but when I do so, it is always only to elucidate, as will be the case today, something strictly factual.

We live in a time which demands something very specific from the human being. It demands from the human being, let me say, a decision that comes from the innermost depths of human nature. It must absolutely be noted and understood that we really are only at the beginning of the era of human freedom. And this rumbling in intellectual, moral, and social realms is nothing other than the expression of the fact that through deep forces that run in the depths of human development, humanity is to be brought into the realm of freedom.

We need only look, without bias, at what happens in our own life or the lives of various peoples, and we will tell ourselves that there are numerous factors which determine an individual person, or an entire people, or a community of people, or groups of people from without, or even—but without freedom—from within. This "being carried by circumstances" is what, fundamentally, was the force of humanity's development. But the human being must emerge from this developmental force more and more. And the future of the earth will consist in the human being increasingly cultivating that which today one must characterize by saying: For the first time, the human being really faces significant decisions.

This "being faced with significant decisions," which must be met out of the innermost part of the human breast, of the human heart, of the human soul, this is also expressed in the outer course of events. In fact, far too little attention is paid to the great changes which took place in all areas of political, social, spiritual, and scientific life in the second half of the nineteenth century.

You see, today one can notice symptoms everywhere which reveal this change in ways big and small. Let us take a very obvious example. You know that among the many enemies opposed to the anthroposophical movement, the clerics of this country [Switzerland] are included; they clearly show that Jesuit power supports them and that Jesuit power is again something which has significance in this country. One need only observe what is happening in various realms today and one will see that many people are intertwined with what they call the outer religion-oriented education, and so forth. Therefore, it could be of particular interest, precisely for this country, to take a look at a remarkable document which, because I found it so interesting, I had photographed. This document originates in Switzerland† and was written in Switzerland in 1847. I will read it aloud:

> Dedicated to the Swiss Confederate Army and their brave leaders as a permanent monument in memory of November 24, 1847, when the rule of the Jesuits in Switzerland came to an end.
>
> The Almighty has awarded victory to a just cause. Those days from November 12 to November 30, 1847, are unforgettable for every Swiss soldier—those days during which in consequence of statute resolutions of the Twentieth Day of the Haying Month [July 20] and the Fourth Day of the Winter Month [December 4], 1847, the seven armed Catholic members of a defense alliance, Lucerne, Uri, Schwyz, Unterwalden, Zug, Freiburg, and Wallis, were threatened from all sides by an impressive and belligerent army of 100,000 men under the commander-in-chief, General Wilhelm Heinrich Dufour of Geneva, and had to capitulate one after the other; these days belong to the most memorable events in Swiss history. With relatively

> very few dead and wounded, the clever and experienced General succeeded, by means of his strategies, in overcoming the tyranny and power of a hypocritical clergy full of fanaticism, and the inhabitants blinded by their Catholicism, who as enemies faced the Swiss Confederate Army, including a militia of over 80,000 strong, which was entirely overcome within a few days, to dissolve the defense alliance and drive the Jesuits out of Switzerland.

And the concluding sentence, which, in my opinion, is especially interesting, reads: "God's protective fatherly hand reigned over the army."

You see under whose protection the expulsion of the Jesuits back then was undertaken, and how one appealed to God's protective fatherly hand always to reign over the Swiss peoples as it had reigned when General Dufour succeeded in cleansing Switzerland of the Jesuits. That was how it once was! In 1847.

But these are not the only things that have undergone essential changes in the course of the last half century; there have also been other changes. And these changes have a very particular character. They are of such a character that whoever does not want to depend solely on the external success of events as they have played out during this time must necessarily become confused. The best way to become confused and to be unable to escape certain tangled webs is to let only the external events of the last half, or last two thirds, of the past century work upon you. If someone wants to find his way today, an orienting direction, an impulse that comes entirely from within, is indeed necessary. And the best aspirations of recent times have been flung into this chaos that is based on the confusion caused by the fact that one wants to depend only on external events. Of course, it should be acknowledged that in recent times, in many realms of life, particularly in the realm of technology and the relationship between technology and science, great and significant progress has been achieved and triumphantly celebrated and that such recent praise is by all means justified. But even if you take the best scientific results of recent culture, the best technical achievements, if you take everything that can be considered good as it has emerged from this tangled knot of recent culture, in which you can find much that is useful, much that is enlightening, much that can bring progress, especially material progress to people; but you will never find, neither in the realm of science nor in the realm of technology, nor in any other realm including the realms—I must emphasize this again and again—which have brought good, you will never find anything that can radiate from the external world into the human soul in such a way that the human being might receive an impulse of direction from such things originating in the external world. That is why spiritual science had to insert itself precisely in this age, for from it should arise that which cannot be taken from the external world but can only be taken from spiritual worlds, and taken in such a way that when it flows into the external world, it absolutely represents an impulse which has nothing to do with all that can be taken from the external world. The impulse that is to be given by anthroposophically oriented spiritual science is an impulse to be carried from spiritual worlds into the external world. Along these lines, one is thoroughly misunderstood these days, and enlightenment in a particular direction was the basis for my explanations yesterday. For I wanted to indicate how one should not say that we deceive people through our impulse of renewing education, which, by the way, is indeed born of spiritual vision, or that we deceive people through our practical measures with something that is merely a theoretical worldview. Yesterday I said how far from reality such claims lie. But one also ought not to say the opposite, and this again is related to a proper perception of anthroposophically oriented spiritual science: It should not be said, as people usually imagine today, that this or that outer activity comes from a theory, from a program; one ought not to imagine that what we establish—whether in a realm like that of education, or a realm like the practical economic life—originates in some kind of program in the way that one imagines today that things like this originate in programs.

For example, a few days ago, someone said to me: "Fundamentally, this particular view of the 'threefolding of the social organism' would not have come about if this threefolding had not sprung out of anthroposophy." I had to correct such a statement thoroughly, for it really is so—and here I must insert several personal things which are meant quite objectively and yet are very much related to this matter—that what meets you and others today as "threefolding," insofar as it was conceived by me, absolutely did *not* arise from an abstract thought or from thinking about how social life is to be arranged so that something of a utopian character would emerge from it, as can be found in various contemporary views. It did not arise in this way. In a way, my own spiritual vision has been the one stream which naturally merged with the other streams, and in particular, with the economic stream, which is an economic view that arose on the foundations of its own life.

Years ago, I explained how this particular view of mine about the economic life of recent times arose from economic necessity. I had to reply to this when I was told that this threefolding was extracted out of anthroposophy, as it were, the way one extracts something in an abstract-logical way out of some sort of program, which one then sets up as activities. After all, I spent my boyhood years as the son of a minor railroad official, at a time when, during the 60s and 70s, the railroads had—let me put it like this—only developed out of a semi-embryonic life. Basically, it was only later that this became the great method of transportation. I participated in all the measures which still existed under the influence of the first leading railway constructions. Thus I stood under the direct influence of the burgeoning transportation system. This view later united with something else which then led to having to imagine the economic life as I did then imagine it as the "threefolding of the social organism."

Let us consider: well into the 70s of the previous century, the most essential basic element of recent development was the transformation of transportation and traffic. What developed during this time was global transportation. In those days, I lived in the very midst of this recent phase of global transportation, under the direct daily, hourly influence of the details that developed through this global transportation. And then in the last third of the nineteenth century, actually only in the last quarter, came the great turnabout which led from global transportation to global economy.

Global economy differs from global transportation. It was international transportation that brought on the international economy. International transportation is merely the last phase of development of national economy. Whatever is prepared in an individual country, essentially, of course, is balanced out amongst the various countries through world-wide transportation; but a certain individualism of production remains in the separate countries for each country. This then changed under the influence of the transportation itself. The world changed from international transportation and traffic to an international economy. And an international economy exists only if raw materials are, to a great extent, purchased in one country and then freighted to another country to be industrially processed there. So it is not just through the traffic, but rather through the economy itself that a state or country is dependent on another so that the economy itself spreads, to a certain extent, across the various countries. This spreading of an international economy, this sort of merging of the world into a common international economy, took place primarily in the last decade of the nineteenth century. And it happened, I might say, in a way that has been most clearly demonstrated in the supply of Indian and American cotton to the European textile industry.

It was precisely the cotton industry which exemplified most characteristically the transformation from international traffic to an international economy. And during the time when one could still see exactly how this happened, I was, for a period of eight years, an educator[†] in a home through which only cotton from India and America was shipped to Europe, in which only cotton agents and manufacturers traded in things made from cotton; and there one lived entirely in the interests which encompass all that comes just from these things. I lived entirely within all of this because I never saw these external things as negligible or somehow said one needs to return to a mystical twilight in the face of these external things; I was definitely deeply interested in all of this, especially when dispatches arrived which had to be decoded. A dispatch arrived which said "Drahtzieher" [mastermind]. This "Drahtzieher" had to be looked up in the code book and its meaning was: Such and such a source offers so and so many bales of cotton for this and that price. All this was extracted from the word "Drahtzieher," and could then potentially become a very significant business venture.

At this time, during which I was extremely interested in the samples of American and Indian cotton as they arrived and were heaped up in high piles in the office, each with its own specifications, its own wrappers on which were written all manner of interesting things, while I carefully studied all this—do excuse this personal remark, but it is connected in a way with the matter at hand—I also studied, at the same time, Goethe's "Fairytale of the Green Snake and the Beautiful Lily,"[†] which ran completely parallel. And, fundamentally, what flowed toward me at that time out of my study of the "Green Snake and the Beautiful Lily" then led, after three times seven years, after twenty-one years, to my first Mystery Drama, *The Portal of Initiation*.[†]

I only wanted to mention these examples to which I could add many others. But to the man who told me that what I thought about the economic life flowed from—as he of course assumed—an abstract anthroposophy, I had to respond that I actually was thoroughly acquainted with the transportation business, had written waybills—how I had made ink splotches on them, in addition to the marks I was supposed to write on the waybills—that I had experienced the cotton industry and the cotton trade, and that it was from these things, which are connected with the nerve of modern life, that my economic views arose. These are not simply theories but really drawn from life. And I do have this feeling: that one can produce these things from life if one has the good will to really look at life. However, one must then also look at the parts of life which some scorn if one wants to arrive at what really arises out of life practice, what can really prove to be practical for life. And it was precisely out of everything that arose from practical life, from all that resulted from immersion in practical life itself, also out of the tangled knots of practical life, that one could come up with these things. For among those people who opposed me at that time, there were some who still had the aftereffects of the great crisis of the year 1873[†] in their life's destiny.

Mind you, it was just at this time that the curious connections between worldview and external economic life—those connections which are just what are to be overcome by our way of thinking about spiritual life, on the one hand, and about the economic life, on the other hand—showed up. At that time, the director of the railway where my father was employed was a man named Bontoux.[†] This Bontoux was, let me say, a little demigod for the surroundings in which I lived at that time. Mrs. Bontoux, who, I don't know why, was always called "the Baroness," was considered to be an extraordinarily pious woman, and from a certain perspective these really were extraordinarily pious people.

Bontoux then left the post of General Director of the Southern Railway, and joined a consortium, a large undertaking with tentacles that stretched from France to Siberia, and in his "piety" succeeded in doing a huge amount of business in the service not of secular powers but of those pious powers in whose service he had otherwise also placed himself when he held his prayerbook. Then the whole thing came crashing down, giving rise to the famous Paris Bourse crash[†] from which a certain ecclesiastical community had pulled its hand away in a timely manner, leaving Bontoux to rush in alone. But, at that time, a certain presence of ideas based on a worldview, let us say in financial undertakings, was clearly noticeable, and there one could get a very good lesson in what to avoid. Mind you, some people can't imagine that one learned the right lesson, and that this led to having to think about the relationship between anthroposophy and Kommende Tag and Futurum differently from the way Bontoux thought about the relationship between the Catholic Church and the Serbian Bank.

These things are all observed from life itself. And that one can observe life itself, that one does not approach life with theoretical dogmas, that is the very thing that should come from a correctly understood anthroposophy. For anthroposophy distinguishes itself from other worldviews in that it can be (or at least this is how it should distinguish itself) selfless—meaning that it does not trumpet its dogmas all over the place, but instead that it does actually provide guidance for getting to know life in all its fullness and breadth. For only in this way can it meet the most important, the most fundamentally important demands of contemporary humanity.

Whoever saw with open eyes what could be experienced by really looking into what was happening saw confusion everywhere, saw that even among good people this confusion existed, and that one would be lost if one just swam along with what the external world offered. Into this had to flow the impulse from spirit lands which, let me say, was called upon to provide direction from a completely different source, for this direction cannot be received from external sources even in cases where goodness lives in externalities.

This is precisely what expresses the mission of anthroposophically oriented spiritual science. But just consider what kind of impulse lies in this age, when external events everywhere—whether in the scientific or cultural life, or in the external practical life—turn into an inextricable tangle. Consider how necessary it is at this time to find something precisely out of spiritual sources which can provide direction in the world today.

But consider also how, on the other hand, a different inducement emerged out of these things for people. For one thing, if a person gives himself up to the stream of unresolvable knots, he will be tempted to avoid taking his own guidance in hand and instead will surrender to the confusing externalities, letting himself be carried by the stream of confusing externalities. One could see this, and it was very painful to see, how people under this influence became more and more dependent, how, on the one hand, they had the urge to have their own opinion but then formed their own opinion only according to what crowded in on them from the knotted, chaotic external life. People want to be independent because it is just a fact that the demand for freedom lives in the subconscious. People also imagine themselves to be independent, but they give themselves over to the stream which runs in the way I have just characterized, because today being independent—that means being free—means a strong shaking up of the inner life, and they don't want this shaking up. In this way, they enter particularly into the realm of ahrimanic influence, into something which aims for spirituality with all manner of pretty and prettily coined words, but which has its roots in nothing other than personal egoism and the urge to let this personal egoism be carried by social life.

It is the most important characteristic of the present that people are, fundamentally, stuffed full of egoism, and that when they speak of social requirements, they actually mean: "What is the most preferable way for this egoism to be carried by society." Fundamentally, people speak about social life and mean egotistical life. They want the kind of social life that allows egoism to thrive best. But the "threefold social organism" could not speak in this way. It could not speak about a paradise. It had to leave that to the Lenins and Trotskys and so on. It can only speak about what is possible organically in the social body, about what is viable, about what can happen, about what can be realized. This is what we must achieve. For if we want to succumb to illusions and seek illusions, we will most certainly make no progress.

We must get into the habit of not looking at the whole of life on the basis of some abstract principle, but instead of being absorbed in life, of looking at the details of life with full participation, regardless of whether they seem to belong to entirely spiritual things or to entirely material things. A tremendous shift came about when the economy of the whole world became a single entity, and humanity could not understand this, could not bear it. One merely proclaimed it; one did not understand it inwardly. To be sure, much has been published about world economy but this was all mere chatter, for the talk about world economy, this looking at world economy, was not always digested. And so it came about that people were at first driven into the world economy but didn't understand how to order life accordingly, and they now live in a world which raises one barrier after another, which wants to conserve impossible national economies in the worst way by means of all manner of barriers, custom duty, and passport barriers, who therefore want to preserve something which fundamentally has long ceased to exist. What we now experience is nothing but the incomprehension of what emerged because life in the last third of the nineteenth century and the first two decades of the twentieth century basically offered confusing knots to which one ought not to have surrendered outwardly. From this surrender to the chaos, to the many confusing knots, there ultimately arose that which expresses itself so often in the hostilities toward anthroposophy. These hostilities now take on the most unbelievable dimensions, in both scope and intensity. And one can say: Out of what is surrendered to the external world in the indicated negative sense—I have, of course, already established the positive sense of how one can surrender to the world, in that, for example, one can also live with bales of cotton—out of all this there arise today all the things which can appear in these strange ways. For can one not, in fact, if one takes the things just purely physically, see in the whole manner and means of how these things are expressed which spirit ensouls them, if one can even speak of "ensouling." [He reads aloud]:

> About Steiner's Goetheanum in Dornach† it was said, "We did not regret the visit, and we advise anyone who wants to form their own judgment about Dr. Steiner to see this temple, this image of his spirit, to see it with their own eyes. Who does this man think he is, and who does he think others are that he dares to let every convulsion, every feverish dream of his brain flow into concrete, be carved into wood, ground into glass and painted on the walls?"

And, finally, a strange little group recently joined the various people, chauvinists, extreme socialists, in particular the leadership of the socialists, and so forth; certainly, this is not news, for one could also already become acquainted with the efforts of this little group† in the years 1912, 1913. What I just read to you is followed by some rather odd sentences: "These are merely very small samples of hostile attacks"—and now the author expresses his opinion about the origin of these hostile attacks—"under the Uranus-influence. We see that there is no lack of scorn and mockery. But the hate-filled warning of an opponent gives special food for thought."

I would then like to read them aloud. But this little group who have allied themselves with the various other opponents are astrologers, and behind them lies a very special sort of nefariousness—of which, admittedly, many of them are unconscious—because much can be done with these things, and because they contain something particularly provocative. But if one now relates these things to each other, they are very strange. For example, there is one attack which includes these words: "We consider it very necessary to keep a watchful eye on Rudolf Steiner. The man who wanted to become Minister of Culture in Württemberg during the revolution by seeking support from Judaism, communists, and cranky heads stuffed with idealism, will certainly not let his participation from the political theater of our fatherland disappear."

So here there is talk about fellowship with Judaism and communism. Let us contrast that with a different attack. It's good to compare these things, for in the comparison, particulars may emerge: "All previous founders of religions, like Christ, Buddha, and all wise men and prophets"—I don't believe I ever made the slightest claim to such a title, but it seems the enemies do that—"never valued external, earthly treasures, palaces, and temples. On the contrary, they remained without significant possessions and guided people to higher spirituality, taught them to pray in quiet little rooms without external trappings! They achieved their spiritual ideas and wise teachings without needing the material help of rich councilors of commerce."†

Thus you see, on the one hand, the association with communism and Judaism, and, on the other hand, the association with rich councilors of commerce. All that is missing now is association with particularly influential generals!† It really must be stressed, since these things really must be said, and, as it seems to me, no one else is saying them: I know that neither those who are portrayed here as communists nor those who are portrayed as councilors of commerce—even if generals were also mentioned—would be offended when I say that there really ought to be a thorough investigation of whether I ever used either one of these "communists" or "councilors of commerce" or "generals" for my own purpose. I could have done without any of them, and one would first need to investigate whether I went to them or whether they came to me. This is what ought to be determined, this is something that requires serious attention. And something else. If now, on the one hand, one really speaks in this way: Rudolf Steiner can only find support among Jews, communists, and so forth—on the other hand, previous religious leaders implemented their spiritual ideas and wise teachings without needing the material aid of rich councilors of commerce—then one can say this sounds a lot like the slander of 1908, which arose among the Jesuits when they claimed that I was a particularly dangerous Freemason,† while, on the other hand, there arose the slander that I myself was a Jesuit. This is how "accurately" one is known by people. But one really ought to ponder whether perhaps the most important thing also exists in the communist, in the Jew, as well as in the rich councilor of commerce: namely, the human being. What matters today is the human being, and what must be sought is the human being in every form. For the old party templates, like communists, the old folk affiliations, like Judaism, and ultimately also the old titles, like councilor of commerce, mean extraordinarily little today when, with all available force, we must enter into what is universally human.

However, it does seem that those who are spiritually connected with all sorts of things except what wants to bring a true spiritual impulse to muddled humanity today are especially ahrimanically possessed. And so one can really listen calmly when the following is said:

> The planetary influences of Saturn and Uranus may have an evil effect on the personal human being, bring him serious worries or hostilities, but that is how the human being will be forced to master and overcome the life of his lower I, so as to ultimately make it mature for serving mankind. The celestial influences of 1921 will therefore either shatter Dr. Rudolf Steiner or force him toward heightened spiritual efforts, by deepening and concentration—as they would for all people with a similar basic horoscope—or, if the astral influences cannot be utilized spiritually—they will cause serious material damage, painful losses, or bodily illnesses. Some who were born at the end of February during critical years could also run into personal danger as is seen more clearly in individual basic horoscopes.

Well, it is not at all necessary to conclude from the influences of Uranus and Saturn that it is essential to master the life of the I and so forth; for I have tried to reveal to you, for example, the sources from which the threefold social organism and something like the *Portal of Initiation* have sprung; and I myself can look calmly at all that is coming as influences from Saturn and Uranus. These are not the things that worry me. What worries me are completely different things. And as long as the following holds true, a certain amount of worry can well exist. For the things that are tied to this ought to be seen in a different light.

A particularly hateful opponent is quoted here who says the following: "Spiritual sparks of fire, hissing like lightning at the wooden mouse trap [meaning the Goetheanum], are present in sufficient numbers, and Steiner will need to be very clever to act 'conciliatorily,' lest one day a real spark of fire should bring the glory of Dornach to an inglorious end."

Here is a clear indication of something which the world would like to see happen here on the Dornach hill!

Then the little group musters itself and looks for the cause of such threatening talk in the workings of Uranus being close to the sun, and so forth. So the attacks are not only extensive, but they are also infused with a remarkable intensity. And, above all, as far as I myself am concerned, I would like to say: Where the influences of Uranus express themselves in this way, they certainly show themselves to originate from a side lacking in goodness! There they already show by their own appearance whose spirit child they are.

But, on the other hand, we must be really clear: When "physical sparks of fire" are longed for in relation to "spiritual sparks of fire" of which it is said they are "numerous enough," then growing concern is required among those who perhaps hold in inner love what has been achieved outwardly here and what is associated with it. It is really necessary to take some care[†] in preserving the work which was carried out by the combined work and sacrifice of many. For those people who look at this work hatefully with their ideals or even their willful intention of striding toward a nefarious deed—they really are plentiful today!

You might say I shouldn't have read this aloud here. Oh no, my dear friends, that is by no means the case! That it gets to be known in the wider world will be ensured by those others. But that you, too, get to know this, that perhaps you will feel differently about such things, at least the majority of you, that is something I must at least try to ensure. For, otherwise, because of the habits which have now been established in the broadest circles of this very room, it could remain hidden from our friends. For, unfortunately, so much does remain hidden. But the intensity of hatefulness manifesting against anthroposophically oriented spiritual science ought to flash just a little into the consciousness of our friends.

Nor was it merely a joke when yesterday I had to say: the opponents are, in many respects, men of a different stripe; and they will prove themselves to be men of a different stripe if we don't also try to be vigilant, to be guardians of what has been brought about by great sacrifice and work.

For even if, as is the case now, evil succeeds in finding so many guardians, it should also be possible that what we after all must regard as the good also finds its guardians! Be faithful guardians of the spiritual treasure about which we had to say today, based on certain relationships: It was not brought into the world through some sort of subjective idea; it was brought into this world through observation of life, out of contemplation of those demands which are the most important demands facing humanity in our time, and which become ever more important the more we approach the imminent future. Be attentive to all those who want to destroy this work which is so necessary for humanity! For this intention to destroy is very, very strong in many. Be strong yourselves, for what lives in that spiritual movement which also gave rise to this building here did not arise out of chaos; it is an impulse which was brought into the chaos. And if one approaches it, one feels: it provides strength; it provides life. Be guardians, true guardians of what you seem to have chosen as your very own by having placed yourselves into this anthroposophically oriented spiritual-scientific movement.

Lecture Eight

DORNACH, JANUARY 29, 1921

Based on our various considerations, you can see that, although perhaps not outwardly apparent, there does exist an inner connection between a being—namely, the principle being inhabiting a cosmic planetary body at a particular time—and that cosmic body itself. One can consider from various angles the connection between the human being and all of earth life—as we might also say—and all that belongs to it. Today we want to take a look at this from a single perspective so that we can then again form ideas for ourselves about the actual nature of man.

As we know, the human being completes his earth life in successive incarnations. These successive incarnations bring him into a more intimate relationship with the actual planet Earth than the periods between death and a new birth. During the intervals which the human being spends between death and a new birth, he consists of a more spiritual nature. In such times, he is more removed from the earth itself than in the times between birth and death.

Whether one is more distanced from the earth or has a more intimate relationship to the earth—either way it entails also having a certain relationship to other beings. For what we call outer, sense-perceptible, observable regions of the earth are, ultimately, merely the expression of certain relationships between spiritual beings. Even though a physical view of our earth may, at first, look the way geologists imagine it to be—that it is only a rocky structure, so to speak, surrounded by a sheath of air—this is basically only the outer semblance. What actually appears there as this rocky structure is only the corporeality for certain spiritual beings. And, again, what appears to us beyond the earth, what appears to us in this way as being beyond the earth, shining down upon the earth as the world of stars, this too, as it appears to us, is only the outer sensory expression for a certain relationship among spiritual beings, among hierarchies. By means of what appears to us as the heavy earth—which is closest to us through the fact that, in a way, it is the solid ground on which we develop our life between birth and death—chiefly by means of what appears to us as the sense-perceptible outer earth, we develop our life between birth and death. Through everything that shines toward us out of the cosmos, through what gleams for us as the world of stars with which we appear to have so little connection, with this we have more of a connection between death and a new birth. One can even say that it is more than a picture, that it is a reality of profound significance to say: The human being descends out of the starry worlds to physical birth so as to fulfill his existence between birth and death. Only, we ought not to imagine that the form which is the semblance of the universe, the semblance of the cosmos when we, here on the earth, speak of the world of stars, that this is also the view for our suprasensory vision between death and a new birth. For there, the world of stars which appears as external reality for the human being living on earth reveals itself in its inner being, in its spiritual being. We deal with the inner aspect of what, for our earthly existence, is external. Basically, we have to say to ourselves: Both when we look down to the earth and when we look up to the cosmos, we are—when we look with our senses—always dealing with a kind of semblance, and we arrive at the truth only when we return to the beings who, with their different degrees of cosmic self-consciousness, are the basis of this semblance.

Thus, whether one is looking up or down, it is semblance. Truth, beingness—these lie behind this semblance. But that this semblance appears to us above and below, this is related to the possible threat of losing our path toward full humanity in our life between birth and death, on the one hand, and between death and a new birth, on the other. Just as here on earth between birth and death we may become too familiar with this earth and can, in a way, develop in ourselves the urge, the instinct, to become too familiar with the powers of the earth, so also can we develop the urge between death and a new birth to become too familiar with cosmic powers beyond the earth. For here on the earth, we stand too near the external pictorial expression, the beings sheathed in sensory material; we stand here somewhat estranged from inner spirituality. When we develop between death and a new birth, we stand fully within spirituality, we experience this spirituality as part of ourselves, and then there is the threat of possibly drowning in this spirituality, of dissolving in this spirituality. Here on the earth, we are subject to the possibility of hardening in physical existence; between death and a new birth, we are subject to the possibility of drowning in spirituality.

These two possibilities derive from the fact that in addition to those powers already cited when one speaks of the normal order of the hierarchies, there are other beings. Just as the elemental beings are to be found in the three kingdoms of nature, as the human being finds himself, as the higher hierarchies find themselves—of which one says, when one speaks in the sense of true spiritual science, that they are there according to their "cosmic ages"—there are others which unfold their being in an untimely manner. These are the luciferic and ahrimanic beings† of which we have often spoken, and about which you will already have formed the idea that the luciferic beings are essentially those which actually, as they now exist, should have lived in an earlier cosmic age. On the other hand, the ahrimanic beings, as they now live, should have lived in a later cosmic age. The luciferic beings are delayed cosmic beings; the ahrimanic beings are premature cosmic beings. The luciferic beings refused to participate in the age which was prescribed for them; they were unable to join because they refused to participate fully in that development. Thus they reveal themselves now when they manifest themselves, as having remained behind at an earlier stage of development.

The ahrimanic beings—if we want to express it this way—cannot wait to become what they are predisposed to become at a later stage of cosmic evolution. They want to be that way already now. That is why they harden in their current existence and show themselves to us now in a form which they actually ought to reach only at a later point in the evolution of cosmic life.

When we look out into the vastness of the cosmos and see, I might say, the ensemble of stars, what view do we have? Why do we have this view? We have this special view, the view of the Milky Way, the view of the whole ensemble of stars, because it is the revelation of the luciferic being of the world. Whatever surrounds us as somehow luminous, radiant, is the revelation of the luciferic being of the world; it is now as it is because it remained behind at an earlier stage of its existence. And when we tread on the ground of the earth, the rigid earth, then this rigid earth has its rigidity, its hardness, because in it the ahrimanic beings are, in a way, massed together—those beings who should actually attain at a later time in their development the stage which they are now acquiring artificially.

Therefore, it is also possible that by devoting ourselves to the sense world through gazing toward the heavens, we make ourselves more and more luciferic. Thus, when we have this inclination between birth and death to surrender to the view of the heavens, this does not signify anything immediate or direct; it means that something that we brought back from our time in the spiritual world before birth or conception, when we lived with the stars, has remained with us as an instinct. There we entered into too strong a relationship with cosmic worlds. There we became too much like these cosmic worlds, and therefore from these worlds we have retained the tendency, which does not appear as a particularly strong tendency in mankind, to become especially absorbed in the sensory sight of the starry worlds. We develop this tendency when we, through our karma—which we always draw towards us between birth and death—oversleep the time between death and a new birth, when we develop too little tendency to have full consciousness there.

In contrast, the surrender to earthly life is what we develop directly here between birth and death. That is the actual ahrimanic possibility in human life. The luciferic possibility is therefore actually connected with what we acquire through our relationship to the world of spirit semblance; and the ahrimanic relationship which we acquire is based on our developing too strong an inclination to our surroundings in the outer sensory world. If we grow too strongly into this earthly element, if we, so to speak, grow up too strongly in this earthly element, so that we cannot guide our soul constitution toward the suprasensory within this earthly growing-up, then ahrimanic relationships appear.

Now, all of this has a deeper meaning for the entire development of the human being. Because between death and a new birth we can drown, so to speak, in the spiritual world, and because of what we then become if we do not find the proper balance here between the spiritual and the material world, thereby developing too strong a relationship with what is not of the earth, and if these things accrue ever more and we do not find the appropriate balance between the spiritual and the material in this incarnation, then we can eventually arrive—in certain cases already in the next incarnation, and in our age such things are actually being decided—at an earthly existence in which we cannot age, so to speak. That is the one possibility which can face us as a particular danger: the inability to age. We can be reborn and the luciferic powers can, as it were, hold us back at the stage of childhood; they can impose something on us so that we do not mature. People who excessively indulge in a kind of rapture, a nebulous mysticism, who have a certain aversion to tautly contoured thinking, who spurn wanting to have clear concepts about the world, also those people who spurn developing inner diligence of soul, inner liveliness of soul, such people, who more or less dream along, are then prone to the danger of being unable to age in the next incarnation, to remain childish in the worst sense of the word.

It is a luciferic impact which will enter humanity in this way. As a result, these people would not be fully immersed in earthly life in the next incarnation. They would, as it were, not emerge sufficiently from the spiritual world to enter into earthly life. The luciferic powers, which once entered into a connection with our earth, endeavor to kindle the kind of instincts in people which makes it possible for them to arrive at a stage where they will remain children, where they do not age. The luciferic powers really want to bring about a time when there are no old people walking the earth, but rather people who live their lives in a kind of youthful delusion. In this way, these luciferic powers would cause the earth to become more and more *one* body as a whole planet and also to have a common soul in which the individual souls blur. What Lucifer seeks for the evolution of humanity is a common soul nature and a common physicality; he wants to make something like a big organic being out of the earth, with a collective soul in which the separate souls lose their individuality.

You may recall that I have often stated how everything in Earth evolution depends not on the mineral kingdom, not on the plant kingdom, not on the animal kingdoms—all of which are basically waste products of evolution—but that what everything depends on actually takes place within the confines of the human skin; and that within the organization of the human being forces exist which are the forces of evolution for our planet; then you will grasp that what the earth ultimately becomes cannot be seen if we make physical concepts for ourselves; these physical concepts have only a narrowly limited interest for us. We will only get an idea of what can become of the earth once we get to know the human being. However, the human being can enter into a connection, an affinity of forces with the luciferic power, which has connected itself with the earth, and then the earth can have, in a way, too few individualized beings; it can become more of a being of collectivity, an indeterminate total being with a shared soul nature. This is what the luciferic beings strive for. If you take the picture which some nebulous mystics create of a desired future condition, which they always represent as wanting to merge into the All—which they represent as at best wanting to disappear into some sort of pantheistic whole—then you will, in this way, certainly perceive something of how the luciferic tendency lives in some human souls.

The other aspect is that ahrimanic beings have also entered into a connection with our earth. They have the opposite tendency. They work, above all, through such forces as attract our organism to themselves between birth and death, completely infusing our organism with spirituality—meaning, they make us ever more intellectual, permeate us ever more with the intellect. For our awake intelligence depends on the connection between the soul and the physical body, and when hypertrophy sets in, if it becomes too strong, then we become too similar to the physical, then we also lose the balance. Then there arises the tendency which prevents the human being from alternating in the right way in the future between earth life and spiritual life between death and a new birth.

This is what lies in Ahriman's striving—to prevent the human being in the following earth period from passing through earthly life and spiritual life in the right way. Ahriman wants to prevent the human being from undergoing future incarnations. He wants to make the human being experience already now, in this incarnation, everything he can experience on the earth. This can only happen intellectually, not in a completely human way. However, there is, indeed, the possibility that the human being becomes so clever that in his cleverness, he can form ideas of everything that can still exist on the earth. It is, after all, also an ideal that, in their cleverness, some people have to really get into their minds an idea of everything that can still exist on the earth. But one cannot get an idea of the experiences which one can have in future lives; in this life, one can only grasp the images, the intellectual images, which then harden in the physical body. And then one acquires a deep aversion toward participating in future incarnations. Then one really sees a kind of bliss in not wanting to appear on the earth anymore.

Ahriman is especially able to generate such aberrations among decadent Eastern cultures—I have often explained to you how Eastern culture has fallen into decadence.† Although Easterners are more dominated inwardly by luciferic powers, Ahriman is able to approach their being and, precisely because they have been taken up by luciferic powers, implant in them the tendency to want to conclude their earthly life in a particular incarnation, not to want to appear in a physical body anymore. Then even certain teachers of humanity who serve Ahriman can place before humanity the ideal of ending their relationship to Earth existence in a certain incarnation, before the Earth itself has reached its goal, and not to have to enter into physical existence anymore.

Among all those things which appeared in certain theosophical teachings that have been slavishly borrowed from today's decadent East, there appears something which never has been taken up in any way by our anthroposophical view: that it is indeed a special degree of perfection for the human being if he no longer needs to appear in earthly life. This is an ahrimanic disposition. Fundamentally, something terrible is produced through this ahrimanic impulse. As a result of this ahrimanic impulse, the earth could get to the point where instead of being a large, unified organism with a unified soulfulness, which is what Lucifer intends it to be, the earth could get to the point where it becomes overly individualized. Human beings would, at some time, arrive at a level of ahrimanic development in which they would, indeed, die; but the terrible result would be that those who have died would become as earth-like as possible, would stick to the earth as much as possible, so that the earth itself would become merely the expression of the single, individual humans. In a certain sense, the earth would become like a colony of single, individual human souls.

This is something Ahriman is striving for with the earth: to make the earth well and truly the expression of this intellectualism, to intellectualize it completely. Today humanity must absolutely understand that the destiny of the earth depends on human will itself. The earth will be what humanity makes of it. The earth will *not* be what physical forces make of it. Physical forces will fall away, will have no meaning for earth's future. The earth will be what humanity makes of this earth.

We live, so to speak, at a decisive hour of the earth's evolution, in which people can say one of three things to themselves. One is to live in nebulous mysticism, in reverie, captivated and influenced by physical sensuality, that is, in brooding—and a life of sensuality is also only a brooding—in a sleepy state, in which one does not participate in life in clear concepts. That is one inclination people can follow.

The second thing that can become a tendency for people is to permeate themselves completely with intellect and reason, to gather together, as it were, everything that only reason can gather together, to despise everywhere what pours forth products of poetry and fantasy over earthly existence, to look everywhere only at the mechanical, at what is pedantically intellectual.

People today are faced with the decision to either become spiritual sensualists who completely sink into their own existence—for whether one sinks into one's own existence through nebulous mysticism or desolate sensuality is the same thing, for these are basically only two sides of one and the same thing—or to think about everything soberly, to schematize everything, to classify and categorize everything. These are the two possibilities.

The third possibility is to look for the balance, the equilibrium between the two. One cannot speak of the equilibrium with as much certainty as is the case with one or the other extreme. The equilibrium must be sought by having both in the appropriate way, shall we say, on the right and on the left, without being too strongly attracted by one or the other but passing through both in the balance of life, letting the one be regulated by the other, letting the one be ordered by the other.

This cosmic hour of decision is before the human soul today. Man can decide either to follow the luciferic temptations and not allow the Earth to be completed, to let the Earth be the way Old Moon[†] was, to make the Earth, I would say, a caricature of Old Moon, to let it become something like a big organism which has an individualized dreaming soul, in which the human souls are contained as in a common Nirvana;[†] *or* to over-intellectualize, over-individualize, to give up the commonality of the Earth, not to want to have anything in common but to sclerotize, to ossify the body by pouring too much intellect into this body. The human being can decide whether he turns the body into a sponge through nebulous mysticism and sensuality or into a stone through over-intellectuality, too much independence. And today's humanity gives the appearance of not wanting the balance between the two but of wanting the one or the other.

On the one hand, we see more and more how Western instincts unfold toward intellectualism and independence, toward pedantry; all of which wants to judge everything in such a way that the human being thrusts himself too strongly into intellectualism and corporeality. On the other hand, we see how the other danger threatens from the East, that human beings ignite and burn their bodies. We see it in the views of the decadent East and we see it in the development of Eastern Europe, in the terrible social aspirations arising there, which are merely the other aspect. The hour of decision has already come upon humanity. Humanity must now decide to find the equilibrium. And one can recognize the task placed before humanity today only out of the depths of spiritual-scientific knowledge. One must acquire those concepts which can make one aware of the possibilities that exist so that humanity can develop toward the one side or the other side. On the one hand, we have the merging with Nirvana, which has already become a "holy teaching of the Orient" but is far removed from the ancient interpretation of Nirvana, which was actually a striving for equilibrium based on the old clairvoyance. What the decadent Oriental now imagines Nirvana to be is the luciferized world. On the other hand, what emanates ever more from the other side, from Western strivings, the strivings which develop out of modern civilization insofar as this modern civilization is not imbued with spiritual-scientific knowledge, is the mechanization of the world, the ever-increasing striving to make processes of human existence mechanical. Ahrimanization on the one hand, luciferization on the other.

If what I described last time[†] from a certain point of view as the chaotic, undirected life of recent times were to continue, then doubtlessly the ahrimanization of humanity would occur. This ahrimanization can only be held back if the idea of the spiritual world can be brought into the over-intellectualized, over-individualized, entirely egotistically permeated life of human beings. We need this view of the spiritual world everywhere. What we need above all is for these spiritual impulses to enter the individual sciences; otherwise, the result will be that the individual sciences, bit by bit, reign over humanity like an abstract authority, and that humanity will be entirely ahrimanized by these individual sciences, which will clasp them with authoritative force. It is especially important today, when the social riddles of life strike as they do into human development, to raise one's gaze to the relationship between human being and his planetary life.

Within the old confessions, ideas about the connection between the human being and the spiritual world have atrophied in diverse ways. For example, Protestantism threatens to atrophy into mere abstract understanding; Catholicism has atrophied into an external principle of power. These are only other expressions for the temptations approaching the human being. What is essential, however, is for the human being to find an inner direction, to attain an inner impulse which allows him to have a clear view of what connects him to his planet, and through his planet to the entire cosmos. Human beings must again attain the feeling: geology is not Earth science. The picture of a mass of rock upon which there are oceans of water surrounded by air—that is not the Earth; and what surrounds us as the Milky Way and suns—that is not the universe. The universe is ahrimanic beings below, luciferic beings above, which appear through the external appearance of our senses, and beings of the normal hierarchies toward which the human being can raise himself if he penetrates both of these sensory appearances to reach the truth; for the actual beings do not appear in the outer sensory appearance; they merely reveal themselves through this outer sensory appearance.

This is what contemporary human beings must realize: I can look at the Earth. If I am able to interpret what appears to me as an outflow of spiritual beings on the Earth, then I perceive what lives in Cherubim, Seraphim, Thrones. But if I am not able to perceive what lives on the Earth spiritually, if I succumb to the illusion of what appears to me on Earth through the senses, then I am merely a geologist, then I cannot raise myself up to being a geosophist, then my being will be ahrimanized. And if I gaze up at the world of stars and only have ideas about what I see through my senses, then I am being luciferized. If I am able to construe spirituality through what appears to me in external appearance, if I am able to say to myself: Yes, the stars appear to me, the Milky Way appears to me, suns appear to me, they announce Kyriotetes, Exusiai, Dynamis—Beings of Wisdom, Power, Might—then I will find equilibrium.

It is not a matter of talking about cosmic beings as being better than earthly beings, but rather that we everywhere penetrate through sensory appearance to true beingness, to that beingness with which we, as human beings, are actually connected. Sensory appearance as such does not deceive us. If we interpret sensory appearance rightly, then the spiritual beings are present, then we have them. Sensory appearance as such is not deceptive; only our view of what appears to the senses can deceive us—namely, through our excessive relationship to the earthly between birth and death, on the one hand, and, on the other hand, to our excessive relationship with the world beyond the earth, which we pass through during our passage between death and a new birth.

Contemporary humanity perceives hardly anything of such ideas if it looks only at what has gradually developed in our civilization. That this was once different has been completely forgotten. Today, people do read what was written about nature in the twelfth and thirteenth centuries—indeed, almost greedily—but they do not read it with enough common sense. Were they to read it with enough common sense, they would see that the age in which one thinks as one does today is actually only a few hundred years old and that people still thought differently about the external things of the world in the eleventh, twelfth, thirteenth centuries, even in the fourteenth century, that they did not see stone in the stone, nor earth in the earth, but rather the body of divine spirituality. And in the stars, they did not at all see what one sees today, but rather the revelation of divine spirituality. Only in recent centuries did things develop to the point where now the human being possesses only geology and cosmology, but not geosophy or cosmosophy. Cosmology would luciferize him, and geology would ahrimanize him, were he not rescued through the equilibrium brought by geosophy and cosmosophy. Anthroposophy consists of the individual Sophias—cosmosophy, geosophy, and so forth. We understand the human being properly only if we know how to connect him spiritually with the universe. Then we will not seek him only in his relationship to the light, which would indulge the luciferic powers, nor only seek him one-sidedly in his relationship to gravity, which would indulge the ahrimanic powers, but, instead, try to pour into his will the impulse that enables him to take up within himself the equilibrium between light and gravity, between the tendency to the earthly and the tendency to the luciferic. Man must achieve this balance, and he can achieve it only by once more adding the suprasensory to his concepts of the sensory world.

And, now, still something very paradoxical: Let your soul consider what has just been said, what the human being must know so that he can make a decision in this age; assume that the human being actually would have to speak about the possible ahrimanization or luciferization of the world. Place before your soul the fact that this is an important matter for humanity, and then consider what you read today in conventional literature, what you hear issuing forth from lecture halls and other educational establishments, and contemplate the great divide; then you will see what is necessary in order for human beings to rise from today's life, today's decadent life, to what is urgently necessary. Serious work in the spiritual realm—that is what is urgently necessary. This one can do only if one decides to take seriously such concepts as we have spoken about again today.

Tomorrow we will speak more about this.

Lecture Nine

DORNACH, JANUARY 30, 1921

THE IDEAS WE'VE developed from various sides about man's inclination towards the luciferic nature, on the one hand, and the ahrimanic nature, on the other, have led to the recognition of the necessity for the human being to find the balance between these two tendencies, tendencies which signify detours from the path to an equilibrium, as it were, between the luciferic and the ahrimanic. Now the question can certainly arise—and it is a difficult question of knowledge and conscience especially for modern mankind: How does one find this equilibrium, this state of balance, so that one need not succumb to the danger of the luciferic, on the one hand, and the ahrimanic, on the other?

This question is answered in different ways for the different ages of human evolution; and any answer to this question requires recognizing whatever is drawing the human being in that epoch specifically in one or the other direction. In general, we have learned to understand what draws the human being into a luciferic or an ahrimanic direction; but for our particular epoch, this must once more be given special attention.

Since the beginning of the fifth post-Atlantean epoch—in other words, since the fifteenth century—both the intellectual as well as the social life of civilized humanity have changed significantly when compared to earlier times. Intellectual life gradually became such that the human being himself was actually excluded from a contemplation of the world. The human being observes nature, and it is within natural science that the greatest progress has been made by humanity in recent times. But that is just what is characteristic—that actual knowledge of the human being did not progress by means of this natural science; instead, consideration of the true nature of the human being was, in a certain sense, cast out of the realm of human knowledge. The human being is well informed about everything else in the world, but he does not know himself. The human being has become acquainted with zoology and believes he understands how the beings of the animal kingdom developed from the lowest to the highest, and then one ranks the human being, so to speak, accordingly. One takes everything one has learned about the animals and then applies it to the human being. One does not arrive at anything new to explain human nature; instead, one searches within the animal world for the elements that are to explain human nature and merely says: "The human being is the highest level." One really doesn't say anything special about the human being; instead, one says he is simply the highest level. This one does with regard to all details concerning the human being, and does so with an instinctive matter-of-factness. The result is that a true knowledge of the human being simply does not exist.

This particular kind of knowledge is present not only in the individual sciences; it has already become something which absolutely dominates the widest circles on earth. It is something which the human being imbibes every day with his morning paper, so to speak. And if he doesn't imbibe it with his morning paper, then in some other way; for it is, after all, something which is already inoculated into the children at school. This modern scientificity has become something which is becoming more and more a matter of common knowledge, filling up the human being with ideas and concepts which constitute his state of soul. Thereby he arrives at a certain consciousness about the world, but he himself is not contained in this consciousness. That is the one thing.

The other thing is modern social life. You need only study this social life as it was before the fifteenth century. The world was, in a sense, full of pronouncements which were a time-honored social wisdom that people had in common with each other. By oneself, one did not know whether something was good or evil. Nor did one have any doubt about that, for one grew up within a social order which conveyed good and evil, whether as tradition or as pronouncements tinged more by religion. And it was out of this common substance of pronouncements—in other words, out of something which wafted, so to speak, authoritatively through the social order—that the human being determined when he had to do this or that.

Much of what used to be grounded far more intensely in the social order of humanity we now have only in language; and since our language has become mere rhetoric in many respects, we are left with mere phrases. Just think in how many instances and how extensively people are used to using the word, the little word, "one"—"one" thinks like this, "one" does this, "one" says this and so on—even though in most cases today this is mere rhetoric, without any meaning whatsoever. The little word "one," the pronoun "one," really only has meaning in a language that still belongs to a folk in which the individual has not yet become as strong an individuality as he is in our time, where an individual's utterance expresses, with some justification, a common pronouncement. That aspect of modern science which is gradually filling souls and which has led to man's forgetting himself in his conception of the world, leads to the ahrimanization of the human being in our time. And that which in his social life leads man out of bondage—for example, out of the bondage of the old guild system and into the modern, free economy—this leads to the luciferization of the human being. Yet both are essential. Both had to arise in the evolution of humanity. For in the earlier knowledge that the human being gained, the human being is always involved. For example, in earlier times, one could not obtain knowledge of nature without also obtaining knowledge of the human being. One could not obtain knowledge about Mars without at the same time obtaining knowledge about the significance of Mars for human life. One could not obtain knowledge about gold, without obtaining certain insights into the human being.

Everything that was human at that time was cast out. In that way, one arrived at a pure view of nature, freed of any view of the human being. This view of nature then had to become the foundation for modern technology.

This modern technology only provides what has led to the great triumphs of recent times if it contains only that which the human being can survey with his pure intellect. Observe any machine, or observe any institution of modern technological life insofar as we exclude anything that is actually social, then you will see: everything is arranged in such a way that the human being is excluded from what is actually undertaken. Thus modern technology also had to resort to the means—although one is not conscious of it—of utilizing only the corpse of nature.

When we construct a machine, we tear apart the material from which the machine is constructed, just as nature tears apart the human being to make a corpse out of his still living organism. In our mechanisms, we everywhere have corpses of natural existence. But the human being was not born out of this corpse of nature, which constitutes our mechanical world, which we have gradually developed as technology. The human being was born out of living nature, a nature that is alive down to the realm of the minerals. To this nature, we have, with our modern technology, added a different nature, a corpse of nature. We have, so to speak, after all the geological strata were formed in the Earth (blue and orange, Plate 3 in the appendix), dumped a topmost geological layer (green) onto it all, a layer consisting of our machines, which no longer contain anything of living nature. By adding modern technology to what was there before, we work in the death of nature.

This makes a shattering impression on the human being if he considers it to its full extent, if he contemplates how detached the modern human being has made life—not merely through external mechanical technology but also through technological thinking.

Just consider something like the conclusion of the war which took place between China and Japan[†] toward the end of the nineteenth century. What took place after the peace agreement, in consequence of the peace agreement? The Chinese minister made out a check for a tremendous sum in the millions. He had this check taken to a bank. Some minor clerk took this check, and this check simply became the reason that this incredible sum of millions was, in purely banking terms, transmitted to the Japanese envoy in China. Something took place there in a corpse-like, naturally external, shall we say, shadowy, corpse-like manner. And nothing else was affected by this, apart from the fact that this credit of millions, which until then the Chinese Empire had kept in the Bank of England, was transferred to Japan through the writing of this check, the transmission of this check. If one had wanted to pay this sum of millions in reparation in the old way—I will assume the easiest form would have been payment in cash—instead of payment with the help of a check from China to Japan by way of credit, what would that have meant for all this cash in the form of Chinese money as it is now, or was relatively recently, to be sent from China to Japan? So where one is still dealing with realities, even the mildest form shows what became of modern life relatively quickly in the last third of the nineteenth century. All of human thinking was taken hold of by such things and quite naturally found its way in. Intellectualism, which is what ahrimanizes humanity, became a matter of course.

On the other hand, it is simply the case that in his social life, the human being also had to experience what was experienced. Just as he would not have come to pure knowledge of nature without intellectualism, so he would not have come to consciousness of his freedom without having had his experience of social life. The human being was hollowed out by modern science. He no longer knows anything about himself. He cannot grasp the being of man. But, on the other hand, there arose the highest human tension, the highest challenge to this humanity of his, to act out of the primal impulses of this being itself, in that the human being was to act as a free being.

If one wants a symbol for what actually took place there, then one can only say: The human being lost the fullness of his nature ever more and became completely zero in his own view. For, modern natural science, as it exists, contains nothing of the human being. Bit by bit, the human being became zero. And in this zero, the impulse of freedom ought now to radiate forth (see right-hand side of Plate 4 in the appendix).

This is the contradictory nature of the modern human being. He is supposed to be free—meaning, he should find the impulses of his being, the impulses of his actions, in himself—but if he wants to go there with his cognition, which is to give rise to his actions, then he finds zero, finds himself as an inwardly hollow being. It is a necessity that this had to happen; but it is equally necessary for modern humanity to find its way out of this again. For within this freedom, one luciferizes oneself if one does not achieve the equilibrium; and within modern science, one ahrimanizes oneself if one does not achieve the equilibrium, does not achieve the balance.

How does one achieve the balance? Here one has to indicate something which one could call "the golden rule of modern anthroposophically oriented spiritual science."† Science is good. Science had to arise in recent development. But this science needs supplementation. It needs knowledge of the human being. And this knowledge of the human being can only be gotten through spiritual science. There is no knowledge of the human being involved if one dissects the human being and then takes the brain and the liver and the stomach and the heart, for then one gets, although merely in a different form, what one also gets in the animal world. All this is really worthless for knowing the human being as such. Only what one gains about the human being through spiritual science has value for knowledge of the human being. As soon as one knows that the I of the human being is rooted in the will, that with his will-filled I he actually represents his earthly spirituality and with it grasps metabolism as such in the earthly realm, as soon as one knows this, one has a first point of reference for the study of this metabolism in the human being and then its specification throughout the human organism. Spirituality gives rise to an understanding of the bodily nature of man. If one learns to recognize how the rhythmical system expresses itself in the formation of the course of respiration, the coursing of the blood, then one breaks with the superstition that the heart is a pump which somehow propels the blood like water through the organism. Then one learns to recognize that spirituality intervenes in the circulation of the blood, that this is where rhythm intervenes in metabolism, affecting the circulation of the blood, and then, in the course of human development, already during the development of the embryo, the heart is sculpted out of the blood's circulation so that the heart is formed out of the circulation of the blood, meaning out of spirituality. If one then learns to recognize how the life of thought in the nerve-sense system in turn wears down the process of metabolism, then one learns to recognize the nerve as something that is a residue of the life of thought. Then one penetrates the human being in a way that one cannot with the animal, because things are very different in the animal.

This is approximately how the materialist thinks about these things: here is a nerve (red) and this nerve effects a thought of some kind (see left-hand side of Plate 4 in the appendix). No, that is not how it is in reality; in reality the life of thought is carried on, and while it is carried on, it destroys the organic matter, makes, in a way, a channel of debris in the expansion of the nerve (lighter color). This is the deposit made by the life of thought, something which is an excretion from the organism. And the nerve is the organ of excretion for the life of thought.

In the materialistic age, a materialistic comparison was used—namely, that the brain secretes thoughts[†] the way the liver secretes bile. This is nonsense, for the opposite is true: the brain is precipitated by the thoughts—of course, it is always precipitated anew because it is continually being replenished by the metabolic organism. A person today, who is quite scientific, won't know at all what to make of this at first, for he will say that all of this is also the case with the animal, which also has a brain, such and such organs, and so forth. But it is precisely in this way that the human being reveals his lack of self-knowledge; for to speak of the human being and the animal in this way is comparable to a legislator demanding that all the razorblades be taken from the barbershops and given to the taverns because he associates knives only with eating and concludes that a tool with a particular form must have only one purpose. The important point is to recognize that an organ in the human being serves an entirely different purpose than it does in the animal and that the whole way of observing things that I have now described in its most basic elements simply does not have the same meaning for animals. It is precisely the knowledge of what man has as material organs out of the spiritual realm that is so tremendously important, for it is this concrete self-knowledge that matters. All gibberish and chatter about some kind of mysticism, which today is based on the idea that man must grasp himself inwardly, all this dreaming is nothing; for it does not lead to real self-knowledge of the human being but to an inner feeling of well-being. With unflagging diligence, the human being must take note of how his individual organs sculpt themselves out of the spirit. Real science must be built up out of spirituality. One must, so to speak, reproduce sculpturally, out of the spirit, the human being as he stands before us. That is the one thing.

Thus, one can say: While today's humanity lives as it does, allowing science to be presented authoritatively by various institutions, there exists a holy commandment in the spiritual world: External science must be supplemented by the science of the knowledge of the human being. And humanity must grow unhappy if it receives only external science.

In ancient times, the mysteries existed to prevent people from getting hold of what was harmful for them. However, this is not compatible with the spirit of modern humanity, so this humanity must obtain in its conscious representatives what in earlier times was taken care of by external authorities. Humanity has to receive the light of real, true, concrete self-knowledge of the human being through those personalities who, through their studies, prevent the individual sciences from casting their shadows, insofar as this shadow-casting would darken humanity. Sciences without human self-knowledge are damaging, for they ahrimanize humanity. Sciences with the counter-image of human self-knowledge are a benefit for humanity, for they really lead humanity to the goal which it should reach in the near future. There should not be any science that does not move into a relationship with the human being. No science should exist which cannot be pursued into the innermost essence of the human being, where, if one follows it, this science will receive its true meaning.

Thus, through this real, concrete self-knowledge, one arrives at the equilibrium, at the balance which the sciences have unbalanced for us. The contemporary human being is usually not at all interested in what kind of being he is in the world. True, if he wants to be especially profound, he succumbs to some sort of prattle claiming he is a little god or something similar, whereby, however, there is again no real conception of this god; but how a single human form is fashioned out of the entire universe is of little interest to him.

Social life becomes luciferized if it leads only to the demand for freedom within what has become zero. If the human being achieves real self-knowledge, he will not be zero to himself, for then he will know how within his skin the entire world context creates a reflection, how each human being carries the result of the whole world within his skin. In social life, the impulse for freedom is carried into equilibrium when we get to know the spiritual that underlies the world, when we get beyond the mere materialistic worldview, which is the very thing that has become characteristic for the emergence of knowledge in recent centuries.

The human being has been lost. The external world has become devoid of humanity. In external astronomy, we observe the sun, the planets, the fixed stars, the comets; we see them as some kind of objective bodies moving through space. We look for laws governing their movements. There is nothing of the human being in that. Read my *Occult Science* and try to place before your soul what appears there as a description of world evolution. As soon as you read there about Old Saturn, you will not be reading about something that today's astronomy portrays; rather, you will immediately be reading about what appears as the first predisposition of the human being. In that portrayal of Saturn, everything which was present during Saturn evolution as the first predisposition of humanity is completely present. And with this history of world evolution, you will also track all of human evolution. You will not find a world devoid of humanity anywhere there. You will find what you yourself are, from one stage to the next, portrayed in world evolution itself.

What is the consequence? If you go through what modern science gives you about some kind of nebular conditions[†] which contract and so forth, from which our current world is supposed to have originated, but within which the human being cannot be found, you have, in reality, nothing human; it all remains intellectual. You get to know something which might interest your head, but it will not grip your entirety as a human being. Your entirety as a human being can only be gripped by knowledge that contains the entire human being. And, fundamentally, it is only the lethargy of the modern human being which is not at all used to developing feelings and will impulses when he takes up anything into himself. It is lethargy when, while reading about the evolution of Saturn, Sun, Moon, and so forth, all the way to Earth, and then again to the perspectives for the future, the human being does not find his feelings to be stimulated, does not feel—although everything is given in clear concepts: There you stand within the world, there you exist together with this entire world, there you know yourself to be at one with this entire world!

This being-at-one with the world is what distinguishes this knowledge of the world coming out of anthroposophical spiritual science from today's usual worldview. Just let today's humanity, which lacks this, be filled with this consciousness of belonging to the whole world, then those social moods which can lead humanity forward will arise. Whereas, by contrast, what has arisen—which could certainly lead to the demand for freedom but does not give human beings a sense of responsibility—has only caused people to bring about the very chaos in which we now live. Luciferization can only be prevented by having humanity recognize its place in the universe, by having humanity penetrate not only the physical world, the sense realm of the world, but also the spirituality in the world; so that humanity feels itself as spirit in the spirit of the world. True social feeling arises from this feeling of human connection to the world; from this, too, streams what is necessary for the human being to fructify social life.

Once again one can say: The sense for freedom brought about for human beings by modern social life leads first of all to luciferization. At present, people may not perceive this. But in the spiritual world, within which we always exist, there is a holy commandment which speaks to the human being: You shall not let the impulse of freedom continue without cosmic feeling! Just as knowledge of the human being must join the external sciences, so cosmic feeling must join the developments within contemporary social life.

These two things—knowledge of the human being and feeling for the entire cosmos—these are what give the human being equilibrium. But this he can find if, in the most modern sense, he can really grasp the Christ mystery, grasp it as anthroposophical spiritual knowledge can give it to him. For there we speak of Christ as a cosmic being that has descended to earth from cosmic infinitude. We learn to feel cosmically, and need only imbue this cosmic feeling with content. This we can do only through anthroposophical spiritual science, otherwise the concept of Christ remains empty for us. The concept of Christ turns into mere phrase if we do not grasp the cosmos itself as human.

From the description of the cosmos in which the sun is as described by contemporary astronomy, in which spectral analysis is valid as described by contemporary physics, the Christ could not have descended to the earth! Anyone who clings to this description of the cosmos as knowledge cannot make sense of any sort of true, real Christ-being. Such a Christ remains empty, or he becomes "Harnack-like"[†] or something similar. If, at present, one wants to get to know and feel the Christ as a cosmic being, then one needs the evolutionary history which seeks the human being throughout Saturn, Sun, and Moon. Knowledge of what enables the Christ to arise out of the cosmos will spring up wherever there is something human in the cosmos. And if one then gets to know the human being to the scope of his materiality, which is wrought within his skin out of the spiritual, then one gets to know him so as to know the Mystery of Golgotha as the incarnation of the cosmic Christ in the individual human being. For the human being described by today's science—from mathematics up through psychology—there is no possibility of imagining that the Christ somehow embodied himself in him. To understand this, the human being must come to true self-knowledge. Today there is no form of Christianity that the modern human being can unite with his soul constitution, except through that self-knowledge which is given by spiritual science and the cosmic knowledge of man which is given by spiritual science.

These relationships are recognizable throughout our anthroposophical literature. And it is simply the case that these relationships ought to be compared everywhere with what is necessary now for the progress of humanity. People frequently want to reserve what they've received through their past education and life habits for Sunday; but then they would like to see the rest of their lives as separate from this knowledge; they do not want to touch it. Sundays at the altar are for deeper soul needs; for external human needs there is the state. Both are accepted on the basis of tradition without there being any thought about where we will end up if this traditional acceptance continues.

I have repeatedly drawn attention from various sides to the seriousness of our times. Today I wanted to indicate how the entire path of scientific life ought not, fundamentally, to be carried further without having all the individual sciences illuminated by self-knowledge, and how social development ought not to be observed without including in this social development a sense for the cosmos, as can be gained only from a worldview that perceives the human being himself within the elements of this worldview. That is the peculiarity—namely, that when we carry out anthroposophically oriented spiritual science, we see the whole world in the individual human being, and that when we consider the world, we find the human being everywhere within it.

Such things certainly remind us of the ancient inspirations and imaginations which humanity once had; but they are not renewed externally—rather, they are extracted out of the consciousness to which mankind is called today by the spiritual world. After all, not only things which the human being sees around him in the physical world are taking place. The human being is as much in the spiritual world as, with his physical organization, he is in the physical world. And in this spiritual world within which he exists, something is taking place, something is happening. The human being, by being like this or like that, has significance for the spiritual world.

Just suppose someone were to observe only what happens here in the physical world around him. At most he might take into account something regarding a traditional religious confession, which, however, has no relevance to this world because it deals only with some sort of abstraction; and this person then accepted today's traditional science. He can develop this science which is devoid of humanity, he can fill his soul with this science just as millions upon millions of people have more or less, consciously or unconsciously, filled their souls with this science. Thereby, however, people then also exist in the world of the spirit; for there is significance for the spiritual world, too, when we fill ourselves with this science. And what is the significance for the spiritual world? If things continue like this, then Ahriman will get his due; for that is the spirit who greedily creeps around the modern centers of learning, wanting to keep them as they are; for that is how he finds his due. The ahrimanic spirit, this cold, ossified, bald Ahriman—if I may express myself pictorially—creeps around our modern centers of learning; he wants them to stay as they are. He will certainly lend a hand if it comes to something like the destruction of this Goetheanum.

On the other hand, social life, in which people fulfill their earthly requirements without regard for cosmic feeling, by only talking about these earthly requirements without being penetrated, warmed through, fired through by cosmic consciousness, this is where the luciferic being finds his due. There we see how Lucifer exists. Here I cannot make use of this image, which is an image, but one that really is born out of the proper idea of what is ahrimanic, the image of an ossified, creeping, bald Ahriman who creeps around the centers of learning, wanting them to remain as they are. This would not be an appropriate image for the luciferic beings. But a different image is appropriate: Out of egoism, out of a non-existence of cosmic feeling, let goodwill and well-intentioned social desires express themselves everywhere, then the luciferic being is let loose from what speaks there. With these social demands, which are aroused in the world devoid of cosmic feeling, the human being spews forth from himself what then turns into lovely Lucifer. He lives within human beings themselves, in their stomachs spoiled by bad social instincts—taken spiritually, of course—in their spoiled lungs, that is where the luciferic source exists. He struggles to free himself; the human being spews him forth out of his whole being, and in this way, our spiritual air is filled with luciferic beings, filled with social instincts devoid of the feeling of connection between human beings and the cosmos. On the one hand, bleak Ahriman, skinny, skeletal, gaunt, creeping about our abstract education; on the other hand, something which first squirms slime-like out of the human being himself, taking on the semblance of beauty, thereby beguiling the human being—these are images, but they are realities of our time. And only through self-knowledge and only through a feeling for the connection between the human being and the cosmos does the human being find the balance between ossification and the semblance of beauty, between the being of bones and the being of slime, between what creeps around him and what wants to free itself out of him. And he must find this equilibrium, this balance. What has become of the culture, of the civilization of modern times is, essentially, nothing other than what one could call the marriage between the bony and the slimy elements. Man lives in this life in such a way that civilization enters into Spenglerism, into decline. For, fundamentally, Spengler[†] could only depict the world as he did because he stood before a world that had arisen out of the marriage of boniness with sliminess. But man must find the equilibrium.

These are serious times, for the human being must become human. He must learn to dismiss both the boniness and the sliminess and must become human, become human in such a way that the intellect is warmed through by the heart, the heart is infused by intellect. Then he will find the equilibrium. And, in fact, the human being will then decay neither—speaking spiritually—into slimy mysticism nor into bald-headed science; instead, he will open himself up to what is human, and to what I might be permitted to call, having characterized it, anthroposophical. That exists right in the middle, the truly human, the anthroposophical; it truly exists in the middle between these two polarities into which civilization has gradually entered. In truth, when the Anthropos, the human being, really reveals his being, he is, in truth, neither ossified nor slimy; instead, he is the one who holds the equilibrium between the intellect and the heart. This is what must be sought.

You will understand what must be grasped today by the deepest human and cosmic being if you contemplate the two images I placed before you today. They are meant to be taken as images, but images which point to true realities.

We will speak further about this.

Lecture Ten

DORNACH, FEBRUARY 5, 1921

IN THE NOVEMBER issue of the Catholic *Hochland*,† an essay entitled "Drei Welten" [Three worlds] appeared under the name Hsi-Lung. It is written about the civilization of the present and its impulses from a Chinese perspective. How this article is rooted in Chinese civilization and what that means is not so much a matter of interest for us here; what should interest us much more is that it appears within our own European world and considers contemporary civilization from a particular point of view. First of all, by means of the organization into three worlds, it deals with three significant modern cultural impulses, as the author sees them. The first cultural impulse which he distinguishes is the modern occidental civilization, which he then contrasts with the second cultural impulse—the Eastern, Asiatic culture. We will speak later about the third impulse. He considers modern European civilization from an Asian perspective, from a perspective in which the human being is rooted in ideas that originate in an ancient civilization. They express themselves in a certain way in the feeling-world of people who live in what exists, up to the present day, as Asian culture derived from an ancient, grand, mighty wisdom, which has, however, fallen into decadence.

In these feelings, and with enormous intensity, lives much of what could be called a penetrating criticism of precisely this modern European civilization. An Asian person of today—as can be seen in Rabindranath Tagore†—talks about European civilization from the perspective of an ancient culture, and from this perspective, he criticizes in all manner of negations what this European civilization has to offer. We need only look at the kind of sentences which appear in this article to see immediately the critical spirit giving rise to what can flow over from Asia toward European civilization:

> Yes, modern European scholarship has itself taken on something of the servile spirit, of the arrogance of the technical age. It spills into the wide expanse as hair-splitting specialization, beclouded and swamped by thousands of quotations or armored with statistics and petty experiments. No depth, no wisdom, no life! Measured by its own standards, its results can be valued highly; but a different evaluation is not allowed anymore, and whoever longs for one runs the risk of being considered backward and medieval. The same goes for the economic realm. Wherever the machine displaced life, competing industry filled the gaps with new needs, and ways and means to satisfy these needs, and, entirely disinherited, the organization of society thus dragged on for a while. And so, the widespread masses also finally seemed docile. Yes, the age of global trade, of factories that never rest, of standing armies, of cinematographs, machine guns, sky scrapers, gramophones, and world riddles proudly proclaimed: All this is subservient to me! Resentfully, however, the outraged elements and human atoms announced an uncanny echo, which still today expresses itself in war and revolution. It resounds through all the restlessness: "and amounts to annihilation."

A harsh criticism of what has arisen in recent human development within modern European civilization! Let us just try—and it should be tangible—to place before ourselves the actual characteristics of this European civilization. Actually, it is rooted in what has arisen—as we have often characterized—in the last three to four centuries, during which, on the one hand, natural-scientific knowledge was, in a manner of speaking, liberated from the historical tradition of the religious life of earlier epochs in Europe. And this modern civilization is further rooted in everything connected to these natural-scientific findings by way of modern technology. Everything which resulted there developed, shall I say, out of human foundations as a kind of opposition to historical tradition. Personalities who stand at the starting point of this modern civilization are almost characteristic of our European life.

Let us consider, for example, a personality like Copernicus,[†] to whom much of what has just been characterized as the direction of European civilization can be attributed. He is a Catholic priest. Therefore, he at first lives with the ideas with which he was educated as a Catholic priest. But he lives in an age in which there arises in his soul, side by side with his education, what then became the modern mechanical view of the heavens, from which also sprang—or at least they both sprang from the same source—the entire mechanical worldview of modern times, including the mechanical world order in politics and economic life.

All this now lives in such a way that it takes hold ever more of the broadest circles of Western civilization, so that it seems to the Easterner as if it had only a physical body but no soul. Everywhere, the soul is missing. And it seems to the Easterner as if the European soullessness, because of this absorption in purely mechanical thought, would also affect everything else he perceives in the European, when this European encounters the Easterner. The Easterner, in his entire way of feeling and what he calls his wisdom, feels entirely misunderstood by the European.

A few more characteristic aspects may be added—namely, the expression of how Japan took on something of Western European civilization, but how Japan, according to the Eastern view, runs a certain risk: "Of course, the people of Japan are now in danger of confusing their deeply founded patriotism and chivalry with European piracy and the spirit of exploitation. But, nevertheless, the ferment that helps to conserve the ancient works and unite East Asia and the south into a kind of unity will not soon become ineffective: namely, Buddhism."

Thus, what the Asian sees in what he encounters from the Europeans is practical piracy and the spirit of exploitation. And the Asian sees this to be a matter of having had this piracy and sense of exploitation arrive with the mechanical worldview, with everything which arrived in contrast to the older tradition. This Asian thinks that the European has gradually forgotten to bring his soul into anything at all he considers to be culture or civilization. The Asian has the idea that the European has no knowledge at all anymore about what the soul might be. Characteristic is the following: "And what did Europe itself do?"—he means in recent times. "Where do its most sacred goods remain? Buried, forgotten, pushed aside, or piled up in museums, with labels."

Thus, what is, indeed, essentially there, the Asian sees only in, shall I say, sharp contours. Everything which once was life, which worked upon human beings when they received the spirit from the relevant architecture and from murals, by hearing this same spirit sounding toward them from architecture and painting, all this—according to the Asian—is, fundamentally, stored in museums, as far as modern European civilization is concerned, piled up and labeled, so that it is seen only as antiquities. And the Asian strongly perceives that what was soul for an earlier civilization is also, fundamentally, labeled in this way, and that the European actually no longer knows what soul in the world, in the sense of the Asian, actually is. Thus the Asian sees chiefly soullessness in the European.

A scene is presented there which does, in a certain way, express what the Asian thinks: "And the peoples of the East, of this second world? Did they even possess sacred goods? How could they have dared to act independently, let alone spiritually, having been crushed dozens of times by allied European barrages? In the end, this was, after all, something which could have become dangerous for European civilization!—Is it even worth getting to know it?"

Thus, the Asian writer is asking whether, if one wants to be human in the full sense of the word, if one observes the world not just from the perspective of physical mechanics but from the perspective of having a soul, whether there is any value at all in having much interest in that which is, above all, of special interest to the European. He continues:

> One afternoon, the almost seventy-year-old empress dowager rested in sight of the looming walls of the summer place on the "Hill of Ten Thousand Blessings." She had had a yellow silk throne set up at her favorite spot, on the artful marble ship in the large lake. Amidst the consummate splendor, the ruined sculptures, paintings, and stained glass of the pavilion were doubly conspicuous. Turning to a new lady-in-waiting, Tzu-hsi, she said, "This was the

> work of European soldiers (1900), and I am not willing to have it all restored and to forget their lesson." She was thinking of all the bitter experiences, and how already some forty years earlier, a loyal State Councilor described the spirit of the Europeans to her: "They finalized some twenty treaties with China, containing at least ten thousand written characters. Is there a single word in any of them about honoring the elders, cultivating virtue, a single word about observing the ceremonies, duties, integrity and proper sense of shame, the four principles of our peoples? No, and again no! All they talk about is: material advantage" (Wu-ko-tau to Tzu-hsi, 1873). The empress also could not possibly honor the obverse advantages of European expansion, the Christian missions, for as head of state she had throughout her life gotten to know only the material advantages which the European powers derived from protecting the missionaries. She had a keen eye for all the spiritual ineptness and pretentiousness of the Europeans who rushed to her, and toward the end of her life, she well appreciated the technical aids like railroads, mines, army and navy, but really only as means. Much maligned, she was a complete and great human being. Every day, the early hours belonged to the lecturing ministers, the great council, exhibition questions, and the reports of the viceroys, examiners, and censors, whose frank, frequently uncomfortable judgement was nevertheless often heard by her. . .

Well, that, I might say, is Asian criticism. It would always be uttered in such a tone if we were to hear it from the lips of a personality who today lives within the ancient cultural wisdom that has remained in Asia. Of course, every Asian contrasts European civilization with the second world, the one he has himself, whereby he has little awareness of how this world, which in its origins certainly provided an incomparable font of inspirational, intuitive, and imaginative wisdom, has fallen into decadence. The Asian as such, the Asian who is, in our sense, educated, speaks in a way that indicates a feeling: Earth is the home of humanity; on this Earth, there once lived beings of a higher order than the beings we call human and they founded a civilization; humans adopted this civilization. Humans lived within it. And the Asian believes that he still lives within this divine civilization. The earth has, in a way, inherited this ancient trove of wisdom, which speaks to the entire human being, not only to the intellect, like the mechanical European civilization. And this Asian is not interested in what could become of the earth, apart from its being the bearer of what it received of the ancient heritage.

Within today's civilization, the European has, fundamentally, lost any understanding for the feeling of such a point of view, such a way of thinking and imagining; that has to be conceded. Today's European reads his Homer, reads about Achilles,† appreciates them in a certain way, but one can say that right from the start he doesn't really take them seriously. And he cannot take them seriously insofar as he has grown up in today's civilization. How can the European take seriously what resounds from ancient European ages when, for example, he reads and understands with his contemporary ideas the words of Homer: "Sing, O Muse, of the wrath of Achilles, son of Peleus."† Homer, himself, does not narrate; he says that the Muse narrates—in other words, that a spiritual being within him narrates. That is not taken seriously by the European. He takes it as mere rhetoric. He takes it as something that, well, is merely said. Fundamentally, he does not have a real feeling for how the Greek knew himself to be ensouled by divine beings who really spoke within his soul; he did not believe that his mouth proclaimed what his intellect, his reason, formed; rather, his mouth proclaimed what a divine being spoke within himself. Does anyone today feel deeply and profoundly that the Greek who sang in this way felt himself to be a sheath for this divine being?

How did this Greek actually feel? Well, he felt that in this divine being he also saw that which once founded a civilization on earth for those beings whom we call human (though they were not human in the modern sense), that which remained within humanity, which, as divine spiritual being, can inspire humanity; so that it should not be understood as if there were merely human voices in one's own inner human realm. And do we even notice the deep contrast facing us when we compare the Greek epic with Greek drama, when we compare Homer with Aeschylus?† Homer sings by letting the Muse sing; he sings as an epic poet, as a narrative poet. This is absolutely connected with the perspective of the ancient Greek—namely, that ancient beings who descended to earth from spiritual worlds are still active in human beings today and sing of what once was, of that from which the earth emerged, and from which everything we live in has arisen.

When, in this way, one narrates what contemporary civilization has brought forth, then one must surrender to those divine beings who once descended from higher spiritual worlds and who now can ensoul human beings. This is how the Greek saw the essence of the epic—that it was spoken by beings who came to this earth from previous incarnations of the earth. In addition, the Greek recognized that something is already living within the human being which will be properly cultivated only in the future, which today is still sub-human. The Greek felt this to be Dionysian. He expressed this by ascribing to such divine figures, even if but subtly in the case of Dionysus, somewhat animalistic features. The Greek perceived what was thrust up out of the bedrock of human impulsiveness, human emotions, human will forces, as something which was still chaotic and unordered in the human being; but in future worlds, into which the earth would reincarnate, it would find calm expression akin to what the human being today can describe in calm contemplation, in calm observation. And the Dionysian element, which still thrusts itself up in spiritual-animalistic form out of the human being, to this the Greek ascribed drama. That is why in Aeschylus we still see a glimmering of how, in an archetypal drama of Greece, we initially see only one main character, the god Dionysus, around whom the choir developed and became conspicuous and sang about this Dionysus. When the Greek looked inward, he said to himself: "In me lives something which is higher than the human in me, something which came over to the earth from ancient worlds. If I give myself over to it, then I give myself over to something superhuman, and I say, 'Sing, O Muse, of the wrath of Achilles, son of Peleus.'" Thus the Greek turned toward the divine-spiritual past, out of which the human being arose. Thus the Greek became an epic poet. When the Greek turned toward the future, he saw how in the future, when the earth had been replaced by other worlds, the human being would, only then, become human; he saw this in the Dionysian animal-spiritual form, in the dramatic turmoil, the dramatic movement. He looked at the human being from the outside and did not speak of the Muse but instead of Dionysus, and there he became dramatic.

And, in terms of poetry, the Greek saw the actual human element only in lyric poetry. He saw the superhuman in the epic. The subhuman, self-dramatizing, which he created out of his own strength as a seed for the future, this he saw in drama. What was humanly rhythmical, billowing up and down in human nature, this the Greek saw as lyric.

Thus the Greek placed himself as soul into the spiritual-physical world; thus he experienced himself in relation to the spiritual-physical world. And the invocation of the Muse has to be taken seriously if one really wants to represent the thought life of the Greek. And one also has to take seriously the fact that the archetypal drama actually did not represent merely human events, but the working of Dionysus in the human being. For one must point out that the Greek said something like this: If you do not see the human being inwardly but only observe him outwardly, then he meets you in a Dionysian form. Apollo and Dionysus—Apollo the leader of the muses, the one who preserves what lives on in the earth as the past, and Dionysus, the burrowing, desolate seed, which will only be clarified in the future—these are the two great polarities. And Greek lyricism stands in the middle.

One really must look back to such conditions in the archetypal culture of Europe, to this feeling oneself as a human being in the cosmos in relation to the gods of the past, the gods of the future, if one wants to have a proper perception of what it has become today; one really must contrast this antiquity of European culture with what exists today as a mechanical worldview, which today is the very thing that the Asian criticizes so sharply. And one must have a feeling for how a modern man like Goethe, who, after all, did not exist in the mechanical world in which we exist today, but rather still lived in the age in which this mechanical world developed its first impulses, how Goethe longed, with every fiber of his soul, to escape this European life, to return to what European civilization had once been. This is what lay in Goethe's feeling when in the

80s of the eighteenth century he longed for Italy so that he might glimpse, within the decadence, what still was present as the source of European civilization.

One must realize that the Asian indeed lives in the decadence of this ancient culture of wisdom, but one must also realize that although this culture of his, this civilization of his is given to decadence, he nevertheless has a keen feeling for what developed within Europe out of what this Europe once was. Hence his sharp criticism, which works with such intense shadows, which he contrasts with the lights that, in his view, are still to be seen in the Orient, which may be outwardly dirty and all manner of other things, but which, in his estimation, has soul, and which, when he looks at this soul, feels no compelling need at all for an interest that wells up from an admiration for trains, steamships, cinematographs, gramophones, Haeckelian riddles of the universe,[†] and so forth. Such thinking about world riddles is entirely foreign to the Asian, for it is based on a combination of what only the senses perceive, whereas he knows that it was a reality that humanity received from higher spirits what enlivened the soul and made the human being truly human.

Today one has become extraordinarily petty in this respect, believing one is grand and regarding what once lived in earlier primeval European culture as belonging merely to a historical age whereas the one and only thing that counts as grand is what these European peoples brought forth in the nineteenth century. Today, living in the age of great decisions, people ought to get past this pettiness; they ought to be able to raise themselves up to realize that there is significance in having people over in Asia who, in their souls, still have something of a living consciousness concerning spirit and soul, and who look at everything the European calls grand with a sharp, withering, caustic criticism. One ought to realize that this means something. One ought to say to oneself: What lives there in the Asian souls will one day be precisely the thing to lead to the European catastrophe, for it has a strong impulsiveness for the souls, mainly because it exists in contrast to the European soul constitution, which has been deserted in the mechanistic era and which cannot rise up here to build something of soul and spirit. Those Europeans who feel the barrenness of

European mechanistic life would much prefer to take what is necessary for their spirituality from the decadent Orient than to look up to something that is being built up. That is why they do not want to hear what is distinctly resounding from Asia already now, and which always sounds like this: "And what is Europe itself doing? What became of its holy treasures? Buried, forgotten, pushed aside or piled up in museums, with labels. As far as the eye can see, it sees outside only vulgarity. And when a European community is established again out of the tangle of hate and deceit, waste of power and misery, it will no doubt continue to fabricate, strike, colonize, militarize, to continue to win the entire world but lose its soul."

And then reference is made to something that a European is prone to say. A European, however, can only achieve, shall I say, a lame criticism. Here we hear more: "Or should we expect a new salvation from America? A judge as competent as Kühnemann[†] comes to the conclusion (*Germany and America*, chapter 13): 'Before 1914, no one knew what America really is. But now we know: America means no progress and no teaching for the moral world. There is no model for new thoughts of a more elevated humanity. On the contrary! Nowhere does the sin clinging to the neo-European culture appear so terribly naked and uninhibited as here: the blind selfishness of greed for money, without conscience, as the all-dominating thought. Nowhere does it wear its mantle of ugliness and hypocrisy more openly and woundingly, mouthing service to humanity where a cold sense for advantage thinks and acts.'"

This is what the Asian cited. But it is nevertheless—if one feels it, then one has to say so—something which fundamentally arises from a petty understanding. For it is—let me say it somewhat sharply—a professorial, European nagging which is entirely justified, yes, justified ten times over; but the source of this Kühnemannian criticism of America is not the same as the source of the Asian criticism of modern European civilization. The source of Asian criticism of modern European civilization, well, that is something which speaks as once the Muse spoke for Homer. This is something which also provides a force similar to what the Greek dramatist once had when, observing the human being externally, he dramatized his Dionysian emotions.

When the Asian criticizes European civilization, he does, in a way, speak out of the cosmos.

This is what the European ought to say to himself today as well. He should look with great intensity at this contrast which we must perceive today when we compare what lives in our literature, in our writing, in our so-called education, with an age which believed it had to announce from divine souls the earthly-cosmic relationships.

And now we look at various people who are beginning, but only just beginning, to perceive in the spirit of European civilization something of what actually exists within this civilization. In the same issue of *Die Tat*—which is compiled with respect to what is desired there, which most people today don't even see yet, but which small and indeed mostly demonic "cliques" practice—in this issue, which is compiled so masterfully, you will also find a discussion of a book by Hans Ehrenberg.† The article discussing this book is called, "Wege und Irrwege nach Rom" [True and false paths to Rome]. We see how in his book, entitled, *Die Heimkehr des Ketzers. Eine Wegweisung* [The homecoming of a heretic: A guide] by Hans Ehrenberg, a contemporary university lecturer, this Ehrenberg is, in a certain way, a representative personality, possessing all the professorial characteristics. I myself was able to become acquainted with this in him. We see how he does, in a way, become averse to the bleak wasteland in modern science and modern culture. He sharply rejects everything which appeared within the past three to four hundred years in European life, in the life of the entire modern civilization. And he would like a religious spirit, a truly religious spirit to re-enter modern feeling, modern civilization. To this end he wants to point the way to Rome. And he brings to our attention that there is, besides the Petrine Establishment, a Johannine Establishment,† and that the following words are ascribed to John: "Children, love one another."† It is very characteristic that the one who criticizes this in this issue of the journal opposes, "Children, love one another" with a different Johannine phrase. He counters Ehrenberg with: "I know of a different Johannine word: If there come any unto you† and bring not this doctrine, receive him not into your house, neither bid him God speed!"

There you have a knowledgeable man, steeped in Catholicism, speaking entirely out of the Roman spirit, whereas Ehrenberg is a dilettante in the Roman spirit. For the one who adds to the Johannine words, "Children, love one another," he knows—if I may express myself allegorically—that a human being needs muscles and bones, that he needs not only muscles and tendons and ligaments but also bones. Without allegory, realistically speaking, this means that the human being needs a doctrine, a content, a life of ideas which carries him; and that on the basis of this life of thought, from out of this life of thought, something of muscles, tendons, and ligaments are attached to the bones, as love of the soul-spirit of the human being must be attached to the bone structure: the doctrine, the content. This is what is characteristic of modern people such as Hans Ehrenberg, that they come and say: science contains nothing, science dries us up, science is unredeemed, science leaves our soul cold and empty. We must foster love. But this would then mean: In the human organization, we must renounce a healthy fostering of the bones, for there is no reason to have bones; the human being will become much softer, much more cuddly, if he has rickets. So that, on the one hand, we have mechanization and, on the other hand, we see something that does, with some justification, want to escape from mechanization, but strives for a rachitic structure. For love remains a mere catchphrase if it exists in this way without the context of a spiritual doctrine. It only arose there out of the desperation of one who, because he does not have the courage for a skeletal system for the culture of our time, wants to remain stuck in the rickets of civilization.

In this kind of European who yearns for cultural rickets, the Asian, in whom something of the bony strength of ancient oriental wisdom still lives, can naturally not see anything leading to the future. So the Asian looks at Europe, in which, on the one hand, mechanistic culture announces itself—which the Asian designates as piracy and exploitive spirit—and in which, on the other hand, something exists that seeks to cling to things with its muscles but does not want to connect to the sturdy bones.

In surveying this, the Asian then arrives at a remarkable perspective, a perspective which, however, is propagated with real passion within certain European circles, for these circles know what they want; that must definitely be noted. And I would like to quote now what the whole thing is leading to. This essay, "Three Worlds," which is written from an Asian, Chinese, standpoint, characterizes, as I just explained to you, the world of recent European civilization, the world of ancient Asian culture, and then it presents the "third world."

And he characterizes these three things as follows, shouting, as it were, toward Europe that which the Asian must think, that which still lives outside of Europe as viable for the future. If Europe doesn't want to die, what must it do? That is just about what the Asian asks. And his answer is:

> In truth, the synthesis must be a third thing, a third world. And this third world arises above and between the other two, indeed in the midst of them, without denying them their worth, even if it is only that they are educational factors. The very oldest is the spiritual world inspired by supra-nature, maintaining itself throughout the centuries in the small kingdoms of chosen peoples in the midst of overpowering cultures and their widespread vassalage—then, in the form of Christian leaven, transforming the ancient world and growing into a towering tree under which the peoples live. The world of the Catholic Church is what educated the magnificent medieval human being—the one and only harmonious European. It is the Catholic Church which, in spite of making enemies, maintained itself and, even in the tumult of modern disintegration, did not grow mute but, indeed, resounded as the only noble and human element in our time, like the deep ringing of bells above the noise and indecency of the metropolis. Where else is the much-implored Judge of world history, where else the conscience of the world, where else the protector of morality? This world alone saw everything come and go; it alone is the world of authority. In the face of the world of the East, it will powerfully resume the conquest of St. Francis Xavier[†] and his disciples. In defiance of modernity, it demonstrates that more strength and self-control now belong to humility than to the consciousness of mastery. It can array the beggar in royal dignity. It is the religion of splendor and renunciation, of the harmony

> of affirmation and negation, of freedom in devotion and unity in dogma, of the "perennial philosophy," of strict rites, ceremonies, and discipline, and then again of generous understanding, adaptability, social welfare, artfulness, and deep soulfulness. And this world should be anxious about how it can assert itself and should seek to compromise with modernity? And even children of this church are fearful and ask at every "Non possumus!" (we cannot!) of the authorities: How are we to survive? Oh, ye of little faith, have trust: "I have overcome the world," not: "I have agreed with the world," but rather the harmony is to be sought higher up, beyond the first and second world in the supranatural, in the true supra-humanity of the Son of God and his Kingdom.
>
> The less muddy the tones, the purer and more freeing will the finale of a song be after all its dissonances. O felix culpa! That is why it is good to clearly work out the thesis, antithesis, and synthesis. That will give rise to full and rich humanity. After all, in life everything is interwoven, and all three worlds exist together.

Thus, the one and only hope for Europe, from an Asian, Chinese standpoint, is the Catholic Church, and we find in a journal which, as mentioned, is put together in exemplary fashion, coming from people who know the contemporary impulses very well—we find, propagated in this journal, this perspective which interests us much more than the provenance of this article as such. Here we find it said that there are presently three worlds: the world of the modern European civilization, which lacks soul, and the old Asian culture, which Europe cannot simply accept, for the two do not understand each other; but it is said that a third lives in Europe—eternal Rome, the Catholic Church. And it must be built. And today we see many, many Europeans absolutely tending toward this goal.

What is hidden behind all this, what lives in all of it, is not seen by a great number of people because a great number of people do not participate in what actually weaves and works within today's modern world. On the one hand, one does not see what the admittedly empty soul life of modern mechanistic civilization demands; on the other hand, one does not see the mighty force of destruction pouring out of what the Asian is bringing to attention, and one does not see the tremendous force with which Rome is working in the present chaotic time, and with what promissory forces the work is undertaken. One does not want to see it because it is inconvenient, because it requires one to take up a particular perspective in which one must work with diligence and energy, spiritually, soulfully, and physically, if one wants to achieve clarity in this realm.

Lecture Eleven

DORNACH, FEBRUARY 6, 1921

YESTERDAY I DREW your attention to how modern European civilization appears according to the judgment of the Orient. And then, in conclusion, I pointed to the third of the three worlds—in addition to this modern European civilization and to the older Asian culture—namely, Roman Catholicism. We ought not to ignore such a judgement carelessly—no thinking person should do so—for what is involved here has extraordinarily deep significance for the currents of contemporary civilization. We will come closest to what actually exists there if I remind you once again of what I said from a certain point of view in the public lecture last Tuesday in Basel† about our current civilization. I would like to mention it again briefly here, in accordance with the customs we follow for such contemplations in anthroposophical circles. In the older cultures, and in the age I yesterday indicated as that of the Greeks, there was an absolutely full awareness of what one calls the threshold and the guardian of the threshold; and indications about this existed everywhere in these ancient cultures. It was believed that based on the preconditions of human knowledge, one could indeed know something about the world and about the human being, but that without preparation, one was not permitted to penetrate beyond what was called the threshold of the spiritual world.

One suspected that there were things beyond the threshold, meaning beyond a particular boundary of knowledge, which were not to be taken up without preparation by the human soul constitution because the people feared that if they entered these realms of knowledge without preparation, they would have to lose their self-consciousness—the degree of self-consciousness which they then had; they would, in a way, enter a state of soul-powerlessness. That is why a certain discipline of will, a certain cultivation of will, was required of those who wanted to become pupils of wisdom, pupils of the mysteries. By cultivating this discipline of the will, self-consciousness was strengthened so much that those involved were able to cross the threshold and pass by the guardian. And then they entered a realm which, had they been in their ordinary soul constitution, would have caused this powerlessness, would have removed their self-consciousness.

Now, one must definitely point out that as a result of the entire course of humanity's development, there is today a general, popular human consciousness of what in those ancient times was assumed to be beyond the threshold. In that public lecture, I pointed out how, for example, the ancients, in their schools of initiation, followed the so-called heliocentric worldview, placing the sun absolutely in the center of our planetary system. But this teaching was guarded, and only individuals like Aristarchus of Samos,[†] who, to a certain extent, did not want to guard it, made some aspects public. One feared that such teachings would affect the soul in such a way that the human being would lose the ground beneath his feet. Therefore, it was precisely that which in those ancient times one did not want the unprepared human soul to approach, which today is known by every human being. For what can be said about the heliocentric worldview could be said in relation to many realms which today are simply general knowledge. Today's popular ideas, influenced by contemporary natural science, were considered to be beyond the threshold. That is why the religious denominational traditions, which have retained the ancient verdicts, always avoided the dissemination of this modern natural-scientific perspective. Hence Galileo's trial; hence the fact that until 1827 it was prohibited among Catholic believers to acknowledge or to disseminate the teaching of Copernicus. They had retained an old opinion about these things, and were, of course, unable thereby to stop the course of humanity's development. Humanity entered from a different side into that region which had been designated as beyond the threshold.

Why was it possible for humanity to stride into this realm without falling into a powerlessness of soul, as the ancients, with their soul constitution, undoubtedly would have? Humanity was able to stride into this realm because they—you see this in my *Riddles of Philosophy*—had arrived, through a particular development of the conceptual world, at a kind of self-consciousness which precluded that powerlessness of soul. Now human beings can acknowledge not only the Copernican worldview but also other ideas tending in that direction without succumbing to the feeling of powerlessness. Let us then take a very precise look at this.

For the ancients, today's popular view was, basically until the fourteenth century, beyond the threshold; it was viewed as being beyond the threshold, and the Guardian of the Threshold was the designation for that power—it is more than a personification, it is a real being—which one had to pass if one wanted to enter that realm which is the realm of the modern natural-scientific worldview. Modern people no longer lose their soul consciousness; they do not experience powerlessness in their souls. But they do lose something once they have entered the realm which the ancients regarded as being beyond the threshold. Today's people have not exactly lost their self-consciousness, but they have, for the moment, lost consciousness of the world. They have acquired knowledge about countless details of sense-perceptible existence; through intellectual analysis, they have discovered all sorts of laws about connections in this sense-perceptible existence, but within this broad realm of individual sciences, which today have certainly become popular, they have not reached an understanding of the spiritual content, the spiritual background of what surrounds the human being in the sense world and what is summarized in the concepts of modern natural science. By approaching the developmental phase of modern times, the human being has, in a way, crossed into the realm beyond the threshold without an awareness of how the world is everywhere permeated by spirit. He did not have to lose himself, but he had to lose the spirit of the world. And this spirit of the world—it has been lost.

The particular religious confession that insisted on not crossing this threshold, on remaining on this side of this threshold, attempted, as you know, in the year 869 at the Eighth Ecumenical Council in Constantinople, to close off, to obstruct the paths into the realm in which humanity generally exists today by eliminating the spiritual as such from the series of powers belonging to the human being. It became dogma to acknowledge only body and soul as members of the human being and to say of the spiritual that the soul possesses some spiritual characteristics. But referring to the human being as consisting of body, soul, and spirit was forbidden. Thus it was a resistance against the admission of spiritual knowledge. This caused the human being to enter the realm beyond the threshold without consciousness of the spiritual world. In this way, the human being entered this realm, which the ancients entered only with preparation that had been conferred upon those pupils of the mysteries who had endured a strict disciplining of the will. But it was entered into in such a way that although the human being did not lose his self-awareness, he did lose his awareness of the world. That is why what matters today is the threshold which I have often indicated in my writings, which modern humanity must get to know, the threshold which has to be crossed by crossing the limit of outer sense-perception and intellectual analysis into the realm of the spirit, which one can discover through the opened realm of sense.

This is the basis of the presentations given in anthroposophical spiritual science, and this is the radical difference from what has appeared as theosophical teaching. Theosophical teachings are really just rehashings of old things. When they talk about the Guardian of the Threshold, they talk just as the ancients talked about the Guardian of the Threshold. Read up on how reference is made to the Guardian of the Threshold in my book *Knowledge of the Higher Worlds* and you will find a completely modern account created directly out of a contemporary consciousness. If those who today presume to judge anthroposophical spiritual science would just note such things, they would not fall into slander by mixing anthroposophy with the rehashing of ancient Gnostic teachings or the like.

Such things have to be looked at very carefully, for they also show us how modern civilization has developed in its deeper foundations, and one will then be able to approach with the right preparation an opinion such as the one I described to you yesterday in my conclusion; it tends, from the oriental perspective, to recognize Catholicism as that power within the crumbling modern civilization which truly still has something spiritual in it. On the one hand, one really must understand something like this, but at the same time, on the other hand, one must see through the dangers coming from precisely the efforts characterized by such notions. In fact, one must be clear about the following: If Roman Catholicism is understood in its totality today—of course, not as it is understood by individual priests who are on the whole very poorly educated, but if it is taken as a theological system, as the content of a comprehensive worldview—then Catholicism is such a content-rich system of a comprehensive worldview. That is what is so grandiose about the Catholic teaching as it arose in the form of medieval Scholasticism—that it is a worldview-edifice, closed off in all directions, logical in its details, and ontologically worked through. It is a worldview-edifice that retained from ancient days the idea of the Father, the Son, and the Holy Spirit, a worldview-edifice which therefore contains certain world-encompassing dogmatic teachings about the trinity, a worldview-edifice which, in the Augustinian-Thomist worldview, has even managed to bring forth a view of the human social order. It is an edifice that is closed off in all directions, and to penetrate it requires, above all, careful study. To understand the Catholic system, the Catholic religious teaching, if one wants to call it that, one must be able to operate with the most incisive concepts; one must have clear and explicit transitions between concepts; one must be able to operate with concepts which modern philosophers find extremely uncomfortable, and which Protestant theologians in particular find uncomfortable. This is what actually should be known: that whatever the human being longs to penetrate with his knowledge—even if it is merely a revealed knowledge, a knowledge of faith for higher realms—there are related teachings in Catholicism, that Catholicism will never make the mistake which I characterized yesterday as a worldview that has succumbed to rickets; for Catholicism has a solid, strong-boned belief structure which proceeds from the principles of nature and works its way up, which builds itself up from below, to arrive at a comprehensive worldview which the human being can then unite with his soul, even if the higher realms are recognized as merely revealed truths. But what

Catholicism contains is the fact that fundamentally it is nothing other than the last remnant of the worldview which was built entirely on not crossing the threshold into the realm in which modern humanity actually exists.

That is the great contrast between Catholicism and modern civilization. Catholicism has, in the course of time, extended itself in manifold ways through Councils, through other dogmatic stipulations. However, it is but a reverberation of old teachings insofar as it draws together what the ancient human being grasped without having been prepared to cross the threshold. And so Catholicism stands there like an architecturally magnificent building which, however, towers over us from ancient times in which there was not yet any reckoning with what must now enter into the whole of evolution through modern natural science, through the modern world of concepts, and through what has already entered and must enter through the social concepts we adopt.

You see, if Catholicism were to be the only teaching to spread through humanity, then the Earth's development might as well stop today. Seen from a true perspective, it is like this: human souls have already absorbed what they can absorb through Catholicism as a system, through the foundations of Catholicism, in their previous lives. Were Catholicism to exist as the only general teaching, then the Earth could already now reach its end, for Catholicism reckons only with what was, so to speak, the achievement of human development by the fourteenth or fifteenth century. Then arose the times during which modern natural science had to insert itself, times in which the human being, by giving himself over outwardly to the world, only absorbed whatever was unable to lead him to spirituality. Those times came when the human being, in a way, by giving himself over to the shrewdest insights, really did face a field of corpses. For what we encompass with our natural-scientific concepts is and remains dead, and remains a field of corpses, regardless of whether we acquire our physiological, anatomical perceptions in the dissection room, or whether we conduct experiments in our chemistry labs. By obtaining our knowledge in the dissection room, we obtain it from a human body without a soul. By experimenting in a chemistry lab, we experiment with natural forces in a way that is void of spirit. On all sides, we face a world which, compared to the fundamental vitality of the world, is a field of corpses. And this is also true of the demands facing modern humanity. This modern humanity is now given the task that it becomes all the more alienated from the spirit the more it looks around, indeed, the more exactly it looks around, the more it arms itself with the telescope, the microscope, the X-ray machine, the spectroscope, and so on, the more it penetrates into the environment and wants to examine it through meticulous statistics. Our modern science is definitely aimed at not letting the human being find anything of the spirit. He must add spirituality from within to whatever he can gain from without. He must have a new spiritual science. He must, so to speak, stride across the field of corpses which present themselves to him as only death, which in the physical or spiritual museums show him at most the shadows of what was once spiritual. He must stride through these shadows and must, while striding through the field of corpses of modern science, have the capacity within himself to carry into this field of corpses that which offers a new revelation, a new spiritual science, which can truly spring forth from the human being anthroposophically. Only by doing this will the human being achieve his full power. He cannot lose his self-awareness; but by striding toward what was beyond the threshold for the ancients, he must not only retain his self-awareness, he must intensify it through knowledge of the spiritual world, which can arise out of this self-awareness, so that he may find the full world, the true reality, in the external world of the senses.

That, however, is what faces the human being of present-day civilization only now. But humanity must become conscious of standing before this threshold that must be crossed. Humanity must become conscious of the fact that the results of modern knowledge may not be somehow denounced or extinguished, that one may not, out of a desire for comfort, reject what the modern view of nature provides, but that one must carry a new knowledge of the spirit into this modern view of nature; for, thereby, it adds to earlier Earth evolution what must yet come so that Earth evolution can achieve its goal. Catholicism can never bring people further than where they already are. With respect to knowledge of the world, human beings have made progress in the last three to four hundred years. But people may not continue like this within modern civilization. They must carry spiritual life into this civilization.

That is the thing that oriental judgment still fails to recognize in modern civilization. Oriental judgment sees only the field of corpses in modern civilization, which is the result of what I showed you yesterday as a critique from the oriental point of view. Oriental judgment does not yet know—because it only knows inherited divine teachings—that it is precisely by facing the field of corpses in modern civilization that the human being can find a strength in himself to develop the genuinely human, the spirit wholly connected to the human, which again spreads light across the entire cosmos.

This is where spirits differ sharply. We look at what Catholicism brought. In recent times it brought Jesuitism, not Christianism. It brought the dogmatic view within Jesuitism which designates Jesus as emperor,[†] as conqueror, as someone who, fundamentally, I might say, includes spiritual characteristics in his soul in the way the soul includes spiritual characteristics in keeping with the ruling of the Council of Constantinople in 869. Basically, the newer consciousness has not yet become aware of the Christ. Christ as a supra-earthly, suprasensory being ought to be recognized by anthroposophical spiritual science, he ought to be recognized as that which has connected itself with Earth evolution from spheres beyond the earth because this Earth evolution requires something which simply hasn't been there before. Fundamentally, Catholicism doesn't yet deal at all with Christ, it deals with Jesus. And modern Protestant belief has definitely followed suit in this regard. A true Christology has not yet been created outside of anthroposophical spiritual science. And this true Christology is related to the human being's ability to find the spirit out of his own spiritual consciousness, to find it in spite of striding across a field of corpses with the natural science which everywhere shows him, and must show him, spiritlessness. This is what oriental consciousness does not see. It does not yet see that this is the very means—the scientific, technical, and so forth, including in recent times also artistic interaction with the outer world—by which the human being loses his consciousness of the world. By losing this consciousness of the world, the human being is challenged all the more to find such a spiritual consciousness of the world out of his own inner strength.

In fact, this consciousness of the world exists. It is there as seed. It emanates from Goetheanism, out of what was attempted at the turn from the eighteenth to the nineteenth century; it emanates from what was sought there. And by continuing further and further, one can find a straight line from Goetheanism to modern spiritual science. It is only a matter of becoming capable of grasping and recognizing the living spirit, as in modern spiritual science it is not an ideology which is provided, not just ideas about the spirit are provided, but rather ideas are provided which the spirit itself sends forth into the world. This is what must be seen clearly: that in the modern, abstract teachings, one has everywhere only ideas *about* things, but in spiritual science, ideas are provided which spring forth from the spirit itself, which are once more, in a way, archetypal spiritual revelation; that the world thus expresses itself through its own spirit as spiritual science; and that we once again have the living spirit.

Now, however, we have to be clear that much of the pettiness of our contemporary civilization must be overcome if we are to face the great things in this way. Today human beings tend toward Catholicism in huge hordes, in huge areas, and Catholicism has an inner feeling of conquest by having all signs indicate that it can trample the new spiritual striving to death, that it may extinguish anything which somehow existed as the beginning of such spiritual striving, that it can, so to speak, thereby extinguish everything new which is to be added to the old in Earth evolution. This will-to-extinguish is definitely present.

Now however, a terrible agnosticism of the soul arose in modern times within human minds; it was, in fact, related to the rachitic way of striving for a worldview. People want to receive into their souls an awareness that this soul exists in relation to a spiritual world; but they don't want to spur their will, they don't want to lose their "freedom" in order to reach something which certainly requires inner activity: the grasping of spirit through spiritual science. They want to unite their souls passively with spirituality; they don't want to undergo the difficulties which one certainly must undergo while actively grasping spirituality. I would say: today the lazy minds who nevertheless develop longings for eternity seek the way back to old worldviews because they do not feel the strength to take up God in their souls actively. These days people everywhere are keen to form their judgements hastily, to see only what is offered to them on a silver platter. They want to make political and social judgments based on what is easily accessible and are then so puffed with soul egotism that they don't even notice when they encounter a contrary judgement that seeks to arise on the basis of broader knowledge. This is precisely what is so painfully disturbing in our decadent civilization today. To support this view, I would like to provide an example that is far removed from our recent considerations. You see, a lot has been collected here, not in order to spread dogmatic views about the recent catastrophic years of modern civilization, but rather to deliver the foundation for forming independent judgments. The attempt has always been made to bring these judgements into the most broad-minded but thereby also truest direction.

Now, consider how many people today are satisfied when they have just a few opinions, or this or that view offered them by general journalism. For example, people talk about the origin of this war, which has claimed so many lives in the last years; they listen to the statesmen talking and the like, and they accept these things because the feeling has died out—in the modern worldview's field of corpses such things can die out—that in a certain place the truth emerges more strongly than in another place, that one has to distinguish between the one and the other place. Because, you see, for the assessment of the European situation, it seems to me more important than many things that people have allowed to be imposed on them in recent times, for example, the following, which has now come out—in this place opinion has long since been moved in this direction, and things as they have now come out are only new proofs of it—that among others also the French ambassador Paléologue,[†] who was at the Russian court in 1914, wrote his memoirs with a really senile kind of loquaciousness. Indeed, all of them wrote memoirs, it's just that one is a bit more dishonest, the other a bit more loquacious; and this French ambassador reported with great loquaciousness what he experienced in Petersburg. There, in the presence of the President of the French Republic, Poincaré,[†] great festivals were celebrated. On the evening before such a festival, the two demonic people, Anastasia and Militza, the daughters of King Nikola of Montenegro, spoke with the French ambassador. These two evil women spilled their hearts to the French ambassador. It was on July 22, 1914. The French ambassador provided a literal report[†] of what they said to him: "Are you aware that we are living through historical, yes, holy days? . . . Tomorrow, during the inspection of the troops, the military band will play only the 'Marche Lorraine' and 'Sambre et Meuse.' Today I received a telegram of the agreed upon version from my father. He notifies me that war will start before the end of the month. Oh, what a hero my father is!" . . . "Nothing will remain of Austria. . . . They will take back Alsace and Lothringen [Lorraine]. . . . Our armies will unite in Berlin. . . ."

Such things must also be observed if one wants to judge the current situation. There can be no excuse that one was unaware of such things, especially no excuse amongst those under whose eyes the work was done to create not a dogmatic judgement, but rather to create the basis upon which to build a judgement. But I simply want to present an example of that. In Paléologue's memoirs you can find other interesting facts, for he prattles on about the most remarkable things with a kind of senility. I am not mentioning this to speak about the cause of the war, but I mentioned it to represent something that modern humanity really must acquire. One hears so much in the world. One must acquire a feeling: This is where something of the truth is to be found, there nothing of the truth is to be found. The world does not express itself in such a way that it can satisfy one with a ready-made judgment. The world expresses itself in such a way that one must have a feeling for the place where the actual truth is to be found. The external sense world is indeed a *maya*, and it is a *maya* to the extent that even in the moral-ethical-political realm, under certain circumstances, the judgments of two such evil women as Anastasia and Militza have had greater importance than the judgments of the envoys and ministers. For, after all, what the ministers prophesied in 1914 did not come to pass; but when Anastasia and Militza said: There will be a war before the end of the month, what a hero our father is! Nothing will be left of Austria; they will take back Alsace-Lorraine—then these demonic women were certainly prophets, for what they said did happen, rather than what the ministers and generals said. The world is certainly a complicated structure, and only someone with good will toward truth and the research of truth comprehends how complicated everything which faces us as world actually is, appearing first as *maya*. In science, we have learned to look only superficially at truth. But this has carried over in a bitter way into all of modern life. This is something which must be taken into account thoroughly, especially on our soil. For if we do not rouse ourselves to wake up and transcend the mire of judgments in which mankind finds itself today, we will not be able to find such points of view, beyond all pettiness, as are necessary to distinguish the modern Guardian of the Threshold from the ancient Guardian of the Threshold, in order to know what is really beneficial for mankind. We must be clear that the sluggish minds, which nevertheless long for the eternal, and are, in addition, egoistic souls, would like to rush, in great droves, toward anything well-tried; and that they avoid rousing their souls so as to collaborate on taking divine spirituality directly into the human will. The difficult hour of decision is now, when it must be revealed whether there is the strength within modern civilization to find the spirit in the field of corpses belonging to modern natural science. If that can be, then no matter how many try, in their passiveness, to find the eternal in what already exists, and no matter how many oriental critics there are, they will only find decadence in European civilization, but not its fruits, nor what is nascent in it, which, however, is what needs work.

The decision is all the more significant because the old oriental culture still retains spirituality and does in actual fact find a kindred spirituality in Roman Catholicism. If modern civilization does not attain spirituality, then orientalism and Romanism will definitely inundate the world. If modern civilization wants to attain spirituality out of itself, then it will not be able to resist this spirituality, for this spirituality in fact corresponds to the final stages of development of our Earth evolution. But the great hour of decision is upon us. Only he who sees what is essential in this hour of decision and is determined to take these things with utmost seriousness knows what is going on today.

For this, however, it is certainly necessary that people acquire a thorough, deep, earnest feeling for truth. Anthroposophical spiritual science does not deny the spirituality living in the ancient streams. Anthroposophical spiritual science recognizes the danger of oriental Chinese culture finding itself related to European Chinese culture, and we therefore understand how it is precisely also the intellectuals who run in droves to the European Chinese culture, for there they find, if they wish to remain passive, that which they can unite with their souls as eternal. They find it only in a luciferic way, by remaining behind in those epochs of Earth evolution which actually have already passed. The Earth would be deprived of its development if this were to happen. One really need not be blind to the greatness of the Catholic doctrine of belief; but it is precisely when one is not blind, but rather recognizes it, that one understands its connection with what human souls have already passed through, and understands the need for something new to enter human evolution. But the question can arise: How can it be, then, that the far more honest oriental spiritual striving which has come over from ancient times does not yet see that which is surging up from the whole of modern European civilization, working its way up, and which in its spiritual affinity could actually be comprehended by the oriental?

Indeed, people, including Orientals, cling to what they encounter externally. And what is it that people encounter externally? Anthroposophical spiritual science is certainly becoming ever more widely known; but observe how in many places care is taken as to *how* anthroposophical spiritual science becomes known! This must be mentioned again and again, because it is absolutely necessary for anyone who wants to become acquainted at all with this anthroposophical spiritual science to know this.

Here, for example, is a gazette, *Evangelisches Missionsmagazin,*[†] published by Mrs. Wirz, new issue, Volume 65, February 1921 (Basel, Verlag der Basler Missionsbuchhandlung). Here is a discussion of a book by D. L. J. Frohnmeyer, *Die theosophische Bewegung, ihre Geschichte, Darstellung und Beurteilung* [The theosophical movement, its history, description and assessment], which clearly indicates that this book is to be regarded within the Christian-Evangelical community as an important catechism about the nature of anthroposophy. This little book by Frohnmeyer is presented as that which reveals to humanity, with great conscientiousness, the content of anthroposophy—that is, the view is circulated that if you want to know what anthroposophy is, read Frohnmeyer. Those people know how to do this kind of thing. They present a catechism from which the faithful can learn. And immediately afterward is a discussion of the book, *Die Hetze gegen das Goetheanum* [The agitation against the Goetheanum], in which, among other things, it is quite prettily said: This rebuttal, this agitation is unpleasant because the rebuttals from the anthroposophical side are also not exemplary. In this way, Dr. Steiner wanders into untruths against his better judgment.[†]

Well, I looked up page 20 in this booklet, *Die Hetze gegen das Goetheanum*, to see whether there was anything there that could be characterized in this direction. But this is what it says: "Dr. Boos, in order to take up the gauntlet, wrote: this is a knowing untruth.[†] Of course it is a knowing untruth, for one must know that the Akasha Chronicle cannot be found on any bookshelf, because it cannot be possessed as a physical document. It doesn't exist as such."

There is no definition here; there is nothing here which could violate the "definition" that this is an untruth contrary to better judgement; for anyone writing about the Akasha Chronicle as if it were a physical document has to know that he cannot have it in his library the way that one can have the *Upanishads*[†] or the *Bhagavad Gita*[†] in one's bookcase.

It is just about proven that this must be said against better judgement, and then the reviewer writes that I have given a "definition"! On the entire page there is no definition, instead, it is really demonstrated that this Kully claims, against better judgment, that the

Akasha Chronicle is a physical document. Yet it is said here that I defined known untruths—against better judgement! Naturally, it is, additionally, a horrible view which Heinzelmann represents, for anyone can entrench himself behind all of it by claiming he did not say it against his better judgement but had simply believed it. That this is even possible is again a question that concerns our entire decadent, superficial, and comfortable scientific enterprise. There is no definition on page 20; there is an indication that something was claimed against better judgement. So here again an untruth is spoken against the better judgment of the same person who above said: "There are certainly mistaken particulars about anthroposophy in Frohnmeyer's paper."

Because they were reproached for this matter, they can no longer spread these mendacities; but they are now beginning to justify them by saying that, after all, the Reverend Frohnmeyer adopted these claims from another priest, who is known to be absolutely honest. Well, just how honest he is one can see from the fact that he probably saw the matter clearly and made his claims anyway. This is how people deal with the truth. And those who deal with the truth like this call themselves bearers of theology and are the teachers of our young people! It has never been my intention here to say anything against Frohnmeyer or Heinzelmann or the like because they attacked anthroposophy; for me, what matters is that people who deal this way with the truth, who have this sort of concept of science, are destroyers of youthful minds; what matters for me is to show the direction our science has taken, quite apart from the way attacks are made against anthroposophy. I am completely indifferent to them because I know too well that such a sentence has an entirely different meaning than the one that this Heinzelmann attributes to me. It's said there that Reverend Frohnmeyer is physically close to the present center of anthroposophy and has studied the writings as thoroughly as possible. That there is really little chance of this is so obvious to me that, fundamentally, there is nothing special for me to object to in what Reverend Frohnmeyer says against anthroposophy. For all these people cannot understand the matter. The main thing is that one must rebel decisively against the spirit which has entered into science here. That is what matters, for it is the spirit of untruthfulness; it is the spirit which hides these untruths behind all kinds of cloaks. And this is what cannot be stressed often and sharply enough: as long as truth is handled in this manner in the universities, we will be unable to overcome what we are so deeply entrenched in, for it is these people who so systematically shape judgment. If the authorities distribute Frohnmeyer's writings like catechisms, and if these things are read in the Orient, then naturally the Oriental will first read, in this representation of theosophy, all the wish-wash which is merely a watering down of what he, in his orientalism, naturally knows much better. And as a chapter within this European watering-down of oriental theosophical teachings he finds anthroposophy, categorized according to the concepts of Heinzelmann and Frohnmeyer, and he can then naturally not imagine what it actually signifies. For it is drummed into him that this is a rehashing of old gnostic teachings, and so forth. In short, the Oriental is given a picture that cannot possibly show him how the entire modern European civilization can once again find a vision of the spirit. No wonder, then, that even someone in the Orient who may have the capacity to see such things must see them in a false light.

This is what must be said again and again among us, because it must enter distinctly and intensively into modern consciousness; and the question that must be considered is why such a heap of falsehoods about anthroposophy is being unloaded. Well, because the gentlemen feel uneasy! Just think about how, if faith is taught and pursued in the Frohnmeyer way, then one naturally reckons on there being no verification, no scrutiny. One can only write like this if one is standing before an undiscriminating crowd which follows, herd-like, with a blind feeling for authority and blind faith in what has, after all, been placed over them by higher powers. It is unpleasant for these gentlemen that within the Anthroposophical Society, there is a crowd of people who become capable of judgment about these things, who look into these things.

But then it really must be the case that those who belong to the Anthroposophical Society feel themselves obligated to investigate. What is important for me today is not that a fuss is made over defending against the slander and falsehoods of the opponents; instead, what matters today is that these opponents are made to have their own mirror image reflected back to them, so that what prevails within modern science in terms of truthfulness is characterized. Whoever can hold up a mirror to modern science, on the basis of the facts which can, after all, be found everywhere, will serve us best. Of course, we will never make a go of it if we merely defend ourselves against the slander and falsehoods arising today to oppose us; for such vindications lead to nothing but accusations and refutations; and if one places truth opposite falsehood, then those whom one faces make such a hash of things that one never gets to the end of it. Just think of the tapeworms that have already been created because of how the opponents always twist and turn. The important thing is to bring attention to the kind of spirit, or lack thereof, that lives in modern science, in modern religious establishments, and so forth; and to hold up a mirror to people to reflect their own appearance with truly spiritual characteristics, which one can provide from the perspective of spiritual science, so that a discussion really does finally take place about what must be addressed at the present time. No discussions will arise if we are always just defensive. Of course, this must be done at the decisive moment and it must also be done again and again. However, it is basically of secondary significance. What is important is that we become acquainted with the prevalent lack of spirit and that we characterize this lack of spirit everywhere—we need not say "in its hiding places," for it shows itself in the public streets. That is what matters.

This is, certainly, somewhat more difficult than mere defensiveness. For one can, naturally, proceed to prove truths and falsehoods very easily. But that in itself is not what matters; what matters is to characterize this sort of thing as part of the entire decadence of our time, to emphasize, above all, the decline signified by the prevalence of such a spirit; for which what surfaces as characteristic of anthroposophy is merely an example. We should not care if people grumble, but we should care a lot about what sort of spirit is expressing itself, this spirit of falsehood and lust for defamation which emerges. The example is meant as a symptom to illustrate the larger perspectives of what presently prevails. This is something I ultimately had to say, because the work is becoming ever more difficult. With the spread of anthroposophical teachings, it is the case that one does indeed have to be glad when one gets a newspaper report that doesn't mention anthroposophy. One can find something about it in the most unbelievable nooks and crannies. You might be reading a feuilleton about Carlyle and Nietzsche in the *Neue Zürcher Zeitung*[†] and suddenly you find a sentence which has nothing to do with the rest of the article about how Nietzsche corrupted Goethe just as much as Steiner does. You find such things everywhere. And that is the method for forging opinions.

If we don't, once and for all, commit ourselves to placing this entire spirituality in its completely unbelievable, decadent character before the world, so that the world sees it, we will not make progress. This, then, is what we are increasingly confronted by today, so that the increase of tasks also puts too great a strain—I may say that here—on my capacity for work, and there is much which I would like to get to but can't get to. It is also the case that the number of people who really work actively on what is necessary today is unfortunately much too small. Today it is the case that because of what has arisen in the Anthroposophical Society as necessities, the movement has taken on forms which require the presence of many co-workers. An individual could certainly represent the relevant teaching as an individual; then he would also find the ways and means by which to do everything necessary in order to bring this teaching into the world, insofar as this is possible for an individual. However, since it is a matter here of a Society, obligations arise out of this Society which do not by any means have to be connected with what a single individual wishes. What matters here, in fact, is that once the Society has tackled certain things, it is absolutely necessary that more and more people emerge from this Society who advocate for what matters in a correspondingly vigorous and active way before the world. The number of those who actively work, actively advocate, is, unfortunately, very small, and one must always and again appeal to the same people for various tasks.

Once, when it was a matter of founding something here, I said that everything else did not worry me, except one thing: that in the present time one finds so few people who are really able to cope with any situation. That is what has to be taken into consideration, on the one hand; on the other hand, it is also the case that it is not a matter of assessing original capacities—these have always been there—but they are not extracted from people's souls (*Gemütern*). People do not want to extract activity out of their souls. That is what matters today. They would like to surrender passively to what exists. It is easier to ask oneself, "Which party should I join?" than, "What is the truth of the matter?" For the party exists, the church exists, and so forth, so one can remain passive. However, what matters for the human being today is for him to seek his own way to the truth and actively to work with the truth. If this is not sufficiently understood, then the great decision which the human being faces in modern times will not be understood either, and then we won't make any progress. We can make progress today only by really taking to heart, really finding the ways and means for working within the necessary guiding principles for what must so urgently be placed into the world, without being afraid to penetrate what exists, so as to represent it to the world from the perspective of spiritual science, as if in a mirror.

I am about to go on a trip to Holland, but I must first spend some time in Germany. Before I leave, on the only day that is available—namely, next Tuesday at half past eight, so that I don't disturb the eurythmy practice—I will give a final lecture in which I want to summarize various things I think necessary to tell you at this time.

Lecture Twelve

DORNACH, FEBRUARY 8, 1921†

I HAVE DECIDED to give this additional lecture today because certain important tasks of the anthroposophical movement, or at least the intentions for these important tasks, should be discussed before my lengthy upcoming trip. Today I simply want to indicate certain things aphoristically. We indeed have many reasons for bringing up the historical development of the anthroposophical movement again and again, for this anthroposophical movement depends on being correctly grasped and also handled by those who want to take responsibility for it. We must definitely be mindful of the fact that by its very nature, by its whole being, the anthroposophical movement has grown out of the stage in which it was possible for it to lead a somewhat unnoticed existence. We must not overlook this fact, which is one of the most important in the development of the anthroposophical movement. We really must be clear about how the anthroposophical movement began, and actually also had to begin, for one can only create something out of actual conditions, so that small groups got together and worked as small groups. It cannot be denied that something of the sectarian nature of the old theosophical movement was often carried into these small groups. This was then adopted by some of our members as, I might say, a work habit; but again, what is here meant by the content of anthroposophical spiritual science was, from the beginning, such that it would have been impossible for it to fit into any sectarian behavior. This certainly was strongly in evidence in everything one could experience when the construction of this Goetheanum began here in Dornach. Often, among the groups of members, it was considered possible to place such a building into the world and yet retain old sectarian usages. Such sectarian usages are all too understandable; they are common in some orders and the like, where, in fact, work is mostly done in a way that one could call obscure, where care is taken to avoid coming to terms with what must be considered if a movement is to have a universally human character.

The work habits in certain orders and in the theosophical movement were absolutely not applicable to the content which was making an impact through the anthroposophical movement because, from the beginning, this anthroposophical movement, in spite of addressing the heart and soul of every single person, was, at the same time, fully equal to all scientific demands which can only be made in our time. The latter is a fact which was not taken seriously from many sides, even within the membership. After all, it is part of human nature to want to remain fixed fully in whatever belongs, let us say, to the ancestral or habitual course of life. Within that life there is then, for them, a kind of isolated province. They don't agree with what their religious traditions have given them; they don't agree with what is otherwise offered to them as part of a popular worldview, and so they experience a kind of satisfaction if something can be offered to them which goes beyond both the religious tradition as well as the trite popular worldview provided by the modern materialistic mode of thought. However, one would then like, in a way, to take what one receives—I don't want to say as a "Sunday amusement"—but still, like something which stands for itself, which does not disturb ordinary life. A movement such as anthroposophy, which reckons with all the life forces of the present time, obviously cannot do this. Such a movement takes hold of the entire human being, reaches into all the details of life. And one cannot regard it as something incidental. One may even get into certain conflicts regarding details; such things are unavoidable. Nor is it possible to sustain one's current lifelong habits in various realms by, on the one hand, acquiescing to life's necessities like a good Philistine, while, on the other hand, cultivating anthroposophical reading so that one's heart and soul acquires the anthroposophical life. You see, this would be the most convenient thing, but it does not correspond to the content of what is extracted from the life forces of human development today as anthroposophically oriented spiritual science. Nor can this anthroposophically oriented spiritual science—which requires a view of the world, a view which really touches upon everything concerning the life of man and of the world—be compatible with what is prized among certain circles that actually just want to create little solipsistic, obscure groups out of a sort of lust of the soul, thereby deluding themselves with all manner of illusions while engaging in obscure forms of mysticism and the like. The broad view of the world, of all the conditions of life, which must be the stimulus for anthroposophically oriented spiritual science, is absolutely incompatible with such things. And it is really necessary that this be placed before the souls of our members, that a break must be made with everything reminiscent of any kind of sectarian usages; for, today, anthroposophically oriented spiritual science stands before the world in such a way that it will, first of all, be attacked from all sides, will be slandered from all possible sides. That would certainly not be happening to an obscure movement. And I can tell you a little bit ahead of time about a symptom which one can find if one picks up the February issue of the monthly magazine *Die Tat*[†] [The deed]. I will shortly speak in more detail about it because it is this very issue of *Die Tat* which is symptomatic. However, what is causing entire issues to be devoted to the anthroposophical movement appears with brutal clarity, I might say, in the case of one particularly untalented practitioner.

There you have an article—all the articles in this issue are, from beginning to end, about anthroposophy—which deals with "Anthroposophy and Christianity," written by a particularly untalented practitioner. In this article, you find, if I may put it like this, clumsy fingers pointing at reasons why now, from the outside, so many disputes are taking place with anthroposophically oriented spiritual science. The gentleman says:

> As long as anthroposophy was cultivated esoterically in groups, one could leave it to itself like many another marginal current of spiritual history. But now that it is emerging with the claim of becoming the viable basis of social renewal, and of building the political, cultural, and social life in the public domain based on thinking derived from second and third-hand "Truths," it is time to see through this

> "secret knowledge" which is favored by cultural and spiritual decay and to thrust it back into its proper place, so that the *true* forces of renewal do not have a forerunner that bears false witness to them.
>
> But to our generation, which turns in splendid heaps to anthroposophy, a picture appears in the gripping scene of the first book of Samuel, when Saul, before his death, abandoned by God, turns to fortunetelling.

You see what it is that motivates people to scold anthroposophy in this way. It is what is indicated and expressed with clumsy fingers in the sentence: "But to our generation, which turns in splendid heaps to anthroposophy. . . ." That's it—namely that anthroposophy contains certain sources of effective activity, on account of which one can say that people—excuse me for repeating the expression, it is tasteless enough, because one can't imagine anything as a "splendid heap"—that people turn to anthroposophy in "splendid heaps." But that is the very thing that causes the attacks, and these people would most certainly have left us in peace if we had just worked as we did, say, from 1900 to 1907 or 1909. Back then, I, of course, was not left in peace, but in any case, the attacks, shall I say, came from narrower alleys and were not accompanied by such a will for annihilation as they are now.

But what the inner circle of our movement seems to have particular difficulty understanding is precisely the necessity of working our way out of sectarianism. You see, one can ignore everything else—of course, much could be cited in this direction—but one cannot erect a building like the one in Dornach and continue to cling to certain obscure sectarian habits the way they are often cultivated by the members of the anthroposophical movement. Nor can one do something else. One cannot do what we are doing without a kind of worldly sense, without a broadened worldview. One can, of course, gather in small groups, it doesn't matter whether of six or forty people—that is irrelevant—and somehow proclaim that someone is, let me put it like this, the reincarnation of the Mary Magdalene or even the Christ and so on. If this doesn't go further than the smaller groups, one can do that, and one can indeed indulge in it rather lustfully with such soul sensations. But one cannot appear in public with something like our eurythmy without a kind of worldliness. This presupposes that those who participate in such a movement are neither sanctimonious nor narrow-minded, but rather worldly, that they don't have any sectarian airs that lead them to only feel comfortable in narrow circles; rather, it presupposes that they really want to see the content of such a movement carried into everything which connects them to the world; a movement which consists not merely of a worldview, but which entails everything of a spiritual nature as well as human life as a whole.

That is why there must take place the encounter, for example, with whatever exists in the world today as a spiritual current, or some other kind of current. Sectarianism has the peculiarity that it often speaks snobbishly and with great disdain about everything external yet understands very little of what is external, and so it wants to close itself off, to isolate itself. This just cannot be done by us in the long run. If our movement wants to be taken seriously, it is absolutely necessary that this sort of chatter about one thing or another does not take place; rather, it is necessary that one attain an understanding through a certain—I have to use the words repeatedly—"worldly sense" (*Weltsinn*) for what is occurring, and thereby approaches and illuminates these things from a perspective originating in anthroposophical spiritual science. This is necessary in all realms. Of course, one can say that one person or the other doesn't have the opportunity to do this or that. Of course, one cannot demand of one who does not have the opportunity to do this or that that he do this or that. In recent weeks, in particular, we have been able to experience extensively that certain people in our movement decided at last to act as well. This often gave rise to something quite terrible. And to this one must say: perhaps this or that person should not be asked to do this or that for which he doesn't think himself suitable. But something is entirely possible: namely, to refrain from certain things. For if one does not refrain from doing certain things, they continue to work in the most terrible way.

My dear friends, I don't mean to say something like: "So then we are not expected to participate in any way." No, this is not what I mean; I mean refraining from certain things which, in their gossipy or nonsensical character, one can really ignore. To cite just one example, the following folly did indeed take place: members of our movement participated in gatherings of the opposition.

Such things are, naturally, difficult to discuss because as soon as they are somehow conveyed to the world in a wrong way, it can be said that blind will and blind adherence are demanded. That is certainly not the case; rather, as pertains to the things I mean, it is a matter of gross tactlessness, which then, in the most fearful way, prevents effective work. For if ever and again catchphrases about, for example, what I am doing and saying and not doing are uttered by our members, then we will naturally not make any progress as the anthroposophical movement. I would like to mention one such example, which was also to be found int this issue of *Die Tat*.

You see, it really is only on account of the demand from our members that some lecture cycles were simply printed from notes—because the work necessitated by the anthroposophical movement did not leave the time required to do things the way they ought to be done. The demand for the printing of the lecture cycles originated with the members, but usually something like that arises without one's feeling responsible for such a thing. It is natural that something like that arises from the members, but then one needs to feel responsible for not letting such a thing be distorted. And this now turns up in the sharpest way in the February issue of *Die Tat*, where it says: "I don't want to dwell on Steiner having had a selection of his esoteric lectures, e.g., about the gospels, edited from stenographic notes by his students, *without* taking the responsibility and *concerning himself further* with it (as is expressly stated on the title page)."

These things were not disseminated because I needed them, but because the Anthroposophical Society needed them; but, at the same time, they require the Anthroposophical Society to develop a certain feeling of responsibility, so that what is necessary for its sake, not for mine, should not always reflect back on me, because that prevents me from representing the anthroposophical cause as such in an appropriate manner in the world.

It is absolutely necessary that such things be clearly recognized; otherwise, the Anthroposophical Society will really, in the widest sense, prevent the spread of the anthroposophical cause. Naturally, now that we find ourselves facing very earnest situations, I will have to become much stricter than I have been, having simply had a certain good will for the members. Nevertheless, what needs to be said on this subject *must* be said. And it is just in this context that I would like to mention again that it definitely does not suffice simply to refute this opposition when it arises here or there, as I already said here the day before yesterday. Such refutations—which, mind you, one makes from time to time out of a kind of necessity—are really of no use at all; they really are of no use, for in the present time, among certain categories or groups of people who are active spiritually or otherwise, one is not dealing with people who care at all about any kind of refutation or defense, who give any weight to a defense; instead, one is dealing with people for whom spreading the truth does not matter, for whom what matters is precisely the spreading of untruths.

Thus, it is necessary to point out some matters which relate strongly to a movement as thoroughly spiritual as the anthroposophical movement. One cannot pass by certain events, because they will repeat themselves over and over. You see, I recently received a letter in which someone wrote that he had turned to the well-known Max Dessoir[†]—that Max Dessoir whose moral and intellectual qualities are characterized sufficiently among anthroposophists. Well, the person concerned wrote that he had a conversation with Max Dessoir. Of course, a person like Dessoir is not going to be converted through a conversation; that's something one ought to spare oneself. For, firstly, he doesn't want to understand anything about anthroposophy, and secondly, he is too stupid to understand anything about anthroposophy. So there is no point at all in further discussion with such an individual.

Furthermore, it became evident during the conversation that Max Dessoir will soon write a severe work against me, and then the person concerned declared himself ready to proofread this work first so as to correct any mistakes, to prevent Max Dessoir from making any possible errors! Well, one can hardly believe that such things really are done by us, often by celebrities in our midst. And what is the result? If one complains about such a thing and the person concerned hears of it? He may very well then say: If one does not do such a thing, then it would be said that anthroposophy does not engage in debate with people of science. Indeed, my dear friends, we must not think like this. One should not immediately generalize abstractly; rather, it is a matter of dealing with the individual case concretely, the individual Max Dessoir, whom we have characterized according to his moral and intellectual incapacity; and one really must not honor Max Dessoir by taking him seriously as a scientist; on the basis of a certain inner spiritual purity, one must avoid engaging in a discussion. Such things must, in fact, be understood and really followed and thought through one by one; otherwise, we will really be able to experience that opposing documents are corrected by our members so that these opposing documents are as effective as possible and on no account contain "mistakes," because they have been excised by our members. It is certainly necessary to discuss these things for once, because we face a serious moment for the anthroposophical movement. Much is done to make one say that things arise from our own side that destroy our cause, perhaps sometimes, as in this case too, with the best intentions; but the best of intentions can certainly turn to disaster if it is not penetrated with an earnest thoughtfulness that is imbued with—I have to use the word again—a worldly sense (*Weltsinn*). So incredibly much in our anthroposophical movement today depends on this.

You see, then, today it is not a matter of such a simple defense. But don't now say that I am opposed to defense; of course that must be done, but today what matters is actually to characterize as such the movements that exist. In dealing with a person like Frohnmeyer, one is not just dealing with a mere opponent and attacker of anthroposophy. Much more important is how he does it, and what sort of sense of truth prevails in him. Much more important is knowing that this pastor Frohnmeyer emerges from a very broad mass of people who are just the same. He is simply freer than this mass; he presents this category of people, this group of people, which is very big, to the world. Today one cannot hope that those people who speak in this way will somehow be converted. We do them the greatest service if instead of the truth we place stupidities before them, for then they can more readily achieve their goals. So it is not a matter of simply defending oneself against such people. For then, in addition, one gets into an infinite loop of claim and rebuttal. What matters is characterizing the spiritual base giving rise to such work, and what that means for the whole morass and degeneration of our contemporary spiritual life. Things must be raised to this universal, noble, worldly point of view, because one can easily get stuck at the level of squabbling. But that is not what matters for us; rather, what matters for us is comprehensively characterizing those spiritual aspirations which must today be overcome. Only in this way can one get the better of the Frohnmeyers and Gogartens and Bruhns and Leeses,[†] etc. It really is not so terribly important that someone or other in such a movement happens to have the time to sit down and write a book; just about anyone who has learned anything can do that nowadays; rather, what matters is the spiritual foundation on which these things are presented to the world. One really must be very clear about how people such as Frohmeyer have no choice but to judge anthroposophy as they do. One ought to ignore completely whatever is personal here. For me, it is never a matter of what is personal. I never want to defend myself, or attack a Frohnmeyer or Bruhns or a Heinzelmann or whatever they are all called; rather, I want to characterize the spiritual stream out of which these people arise. Personally, such people might be honorable men in today's literal sense—they are all, all honorable men,[†] I'm just quoting Shakespeare's drama—that is not at all what matters. I don't want to pin anything personal on these people. For example, even Father Kully does not matter; he is also merely the product of a particular stream within the Catholic Church.

These, then, are the things which absolutely must be considered today, given the seriousness in which we stand. This is what we must look at in all circumstances. We must have a spiritual eye for the decadent spiritual movement which is everywhere and must be characterized. For one has to be clear that today the world situation is as follows: in a very large number of people, there lies the disposition for discovering spiritual knowledge for themselves and making everything that comes out of spiritual knowledge part of their lives. Above all, if you could search for and verify those growing up as the youth of today, you would have to say to yourselves: within these young people, dispositions and capacities exist which allow spiritual science to appear as something self-evident. But, on the other hand, the peculiar thing is that enough forces remain to suppress what actually wants to rise to the surface of existence, as is also the case in political life.

Do you believe, for example, that in the defeated or victorious countries there are not numerous personalities today who, if they could somehow become effective, would do something sensible? Indeed, numerous people exist, but one doesn't find them, because those who caused the tragedy, who cling to all the old, degenerate view of the world and of life, are thrown to the surface again and again with an iron fist. As long as one does not recognize that it is completely impossible to accomplish anything with these people who come out of the old streams, even when they belong to the radical parties of today, as long as one is dealing with all those who grew feeble-mindedly out of the old spiritual structures, one will not make progress. We need to be nurtured by truly new forces, and that which holds the reins represses these new forces.

But this is how things also are in the spiritual life more broadly. We actually need to draw a thick line between what seeks to work its way into the world through our youth today and what has occupied the professorships and the like, and gives stamps of approval through exams. That is what makes for such terrible pressure. It must be recognized that what was attracted to occupy the examinations and the seats of learning can absolutely not achieve an enlightened view of what is essential today. The pessimism which declares that the forces don't exist is quite unjustified. Just let something arise which makes it possible to get out of this degeneration. Does it help us at all when we give ever so beautiful university courses here? Certainly, we can thereby inspire individual young people. That has also certainly happened and will happen in many ways. But these young people are enthusiastic for a time, then they grow entirely into their environment, into the examinations and philistinism because they simply have to earn their bread, because they don't find their way at all, because, of course, the development of a really future-proof striving and working is suppressed. These things must be recognized; and we must work in a direction that overcomes them. We cannot do this today, at this serious moment in development, if both humanity and we, in particular, in our anthroposophical movement, don't want to realize that these things exist. And something like this issue of *Die Tat* is indeed characteristic.

You see, one really ought to pay attention to how these things that grow from the foundation of spiritual science are conceived out of the wider reality. For a much broader demonstration of evidence—if it were not important to trace the main lines first—could be found. In my book *Riddles of the Soul*,† I referred to this Dessoir-like ability: Dessoir relates— quite naively, as a very good example of his unique spiritual disposition in his defamatory book, which found great recognition in the world—how it happens that he can be lecturing and be living amidst his thoughts, when he suddenly can't go on. Well, I cited this as something particularly characteristic for this kind of thinking, which just thinks and thinks and then can't continue. Yes, indeed! I found this to be extraordinarily characteristic. [Gap in the shorthand.] There simply are reasons† for not considering him to be a serious scholar, and it is true, isn't it, one is dealing with the kind of world today which gives rise to something like *Die Tat*.

The editor of *Die Tat* is the publisher Eugen Diederichs from Jena. I met him once at a gathering that he held for students in Jena, where the most vocal contributor in the discussion was Max Scheler.† Diedrichs had written to me some time earlier, indicating that he wanted to publish a book of mine. It was 1902 or 1903. The book he wanted, *Christianity as Mystical Fact*, had already been published. He immediately flinched at the word "theosophy." Then the next day he wanted to talk with me. This conversation dealt mostly with a publishing matter, but nothing came of it, for naturally nothing could ever amount to anything with Diederichs, . . . [gap in the shorthand]. He said that mystical writing, Plotinus as well as the writings of other mystics, should be fostered much more because they have a very special effect on people's well-being. It is like drinking sweet wine, or something similar, which then seeps through the human organism. And one couldn't help but observe that he sat there with his rather fat belly, digesting mysticism as he slapped his fat belly with his hands!

Later on, this Mr. Mystic founded *Die Tat*, and this second issue of 1921 now contains all sorts of articles about anthroposophy—first of all, one that is written by someone who is supposed to be hired by certain organizations to combat anthroposophy in particular. What he writes consist of all sorts of infamies and nonsense: I. W. Hauer, "Anthroposophy as a Path to the Spirit." The second article, "Anthroposophy as Monism and as Theosophy," by Walter Johannes Stein is a rebuttal to the first one, for Diederichs wants to show that he is, so he thinks, objective. So naturally he also invites supporters of anthroposophy; but by this means this booklet is especially cunning, for by having the supporters involved, the people who read it are, of course, immediately convinced that Diederichs is an objective man who permits his opponents to express themselves. The difference is that among the articles by supporters is a quite well-written one by a man, Wil Salewski,[†] "The Goetheanum in Dornach near Basel and the Anthroposophical University Course in the Autumn of 1920." Certainly, there are good articles like this in it, but what is written in this very issue by opponents is distinguished by monumental stupidity, by an absolute misunderstanding of what anthroposophy is actually supposed to achieve, what it signifies, and so forth.

But then there is a tragic-comic—one might even say, amusing—discussion which the publisher Eugen Diederichs provides entitled: "Concerning the Special Issue on Anthroposophy." Allow me to read this slime to you:

> This issue represents the attempt at a fruitful discussion by religious men, who stand above any denominationalism, with the anthroposophical field of thought and the leader of this movement, Dr. Rudolf Steiner. The effectiveness of such an attempt depends on the people one has as co-workers. I must confess that, in spite of all my efforts, I have not quite succeeded in attracting Steiner's disciples to stronger collaboration.

I wish they had not taken his bait, so that Diederichs would have been unable to fill his issue of *Die Tat* with the very thing that emanates from our circle.

> One would like to say that perhaps the cause is their inadequate relationship to "humility," in Mennicke's sense, but as editor, I feel the duty to be entirely impartial and can merely state the fact. But I

> do hope that later an anthroposophist of the rank of Reverend Rittelmeyer will contrast his own experience of Christ with the essays of Michel, Gogarten, and Mennicke.
>
> As a private person, I can only confess that so far I have not succeeded in gaining a favorable position regarding anthroposophy.

So it would appear that it doesn't taste like sweet wine that just trickles down.

> Personally, I agree entirely with Mennicke's point of view that anthroposophy is the end point of materialism and rationalism, and thus, in the final analysis, also does not signify a new system. This does not exclude its being able to appear as transitional for a new structure, and therefore it entails all sorts of values, like any eclecticism which builds itself up on the values of the past. Anthroposophy does not seem to me to come from any "immediacy"

—the "immediacy" in this case comes mostly from acid reflux—

> and thus is also not productive—in spite of all the talk about intuition, creativity, and Goetheanistic observation. I know that the theosophists will characterize this assertion as the greatest lack of understanding, but be that as it may, it is uttered from a personal outlook on the mysterious forces of the subconscious.

This "outlook" is what I just described to you! "This is how I see things on the basis of this personal outlook (which is absolutely not meant as an attack on anthroposophy, but merely an avowal)."

So, it is really very pleasant, isn't it, for now those who are smart enough can say in response: "He is not attacking anthroposophy at all." Nor does it even matter whether he is attacking it. Well, then he says:

> So I see danger for the spiritual foundation of the future Germany and consider it urgently necessary that not only the circle of *Die Tat* readers but, above all, young people today examine Rudolf Steiner and the movement that originates with him. For there is such a desire today to retreat to a fortified tower to save oneself from the chaos of contemporary events.

Sometimes governments retreated to a "fortified tower" during times of revolution and riot; a lot could be said about that! But now the publisher concludes: "My co-worker, Ernst Michel, well-known to the readers of this periodical for his essays and books on Goethe, has confronted anthroposophy in this issue from the Catholic feeling for God and the world."

Now, I ask you to listen a little more carefully, for you will become aware of what I have characterized for you already from the most varied backgrounds, and you will soon experience how Catholicism, in a seemingly rejuvenated form, having become a kind of Catholic Dadaism, also creeps into *Die Tat* under Eugen Diederichs: "His essay is the prelude to a special publication of the Young Catholic Movement, which will appear in April, following this issue."

Well, this is what I mean when I say Catholic Dadaist movement. Nor do I say this without cause, for I will shortly tell you more about that article by Ernst Michels, "Anthroposophy and Christianity," and thereby have occasion to acquaint you with a representative of religious Dadaism.

> It is especially satisfying for me to give the predominantly Protestant readership of *Die Tat* the opportunity, in this Catholic issue of the magazine, to measure their Protestant individualism against the Catholic community. I hope that the basic idea of *Die Tat* will receive new support from all these intellectual discussions: Strengthening of the feeling for responsibility toward its own development and thereby also toward the people as a whole.

These are the words of Mr. Eugen Diederichs. Here, then, is talk of a young Catholic movement, for which the prelude is provided by Ernst Michel's essay, "Anthroposophy and Christianity." I have pointed out repeatedly, and in the last two considerations with great energy, what it is that threatens modern spiritual life precisely from this direction. But now this article, "Anthroposophy and Christianity," by Ernst Michel in *Die Tat* is actually religious Dadaism through and through. In it, the oldest offshoots of Roman Catholic Christianity are puffed up for the reader in sultry language. There, in fact, one can make the most extraordinarily interesting discoveries about this religious Dadaism. For example, Ernst Michel finds a basic truth about Christianity:

> It is a basic truth of Christianity that the human being cannot, by himself, overcome the original sin against God, inherited through his blood and essentially removed from the state of sanctification; that he cannot reach a higher level of humanity out of his own strength and disposition; that the breakthroughs from one to another condition are genuine procreative acts of God on the willing creature.

So many words, so many phrases! One could now go through one sentence at a time to find the most childish avowals of a "Catechism Catholicus." The only thing of interest is that Ernst Michel says that it is not up to the individual to discern a final spiritual truth. You did just hear it: in these things it is a matter of "break-throughs," that is, it "breaks through." The human being receives it as grace, meaning it breaks through. One has to give oneself over to that. The human being is not allowed to strive for any sort of highest truth on his own. "There is no spiritual development, there is only unfolding and breakthrough."

But it is really extraordinarily cute to see how this Ernst Michel says, from the standpoint of his most primitive Dadaist catechism: Yes, it is different with the dogmas, these one must believe, they are true! "But in the dogma, the human being or a community do not formulate their fundamental religious experiences conceptually (as an "address of man to God"), but rather God, the head of the Church, speaks as the Holy Ghost directly and immediately through the visible church. . . ."

So the fathers of the Councils who are gathered together, or even the Pope who speaks *ex cathedra*—that is not a human being! And to top it all off, the Dadaist of Religion even invokes Saint Paul, who is also supposed to have said that as an individual, one is not permitted to search for the ultimate truths:

> Here is the place where, without having to fear the danger of Gnostic interpretation, we can quote St. Paul's words to the Corinthians:

> "What we are talking about is God's secret wisdom,[†] which is hidden, which God prescribed before all time for our glory, which no ruler of this world has acknowledged. . . . But God revealed it through the spirit, for the spirit explores all things, even the depths of God. Among humans—who amongst you knows the inside of a human, as the spirit of the human being which is in him? Thus, too, no one has fathomed the inner aspect of God as the spirit of God. But we have not received the spirit of the world, but the spirit which is of God, so that what God has given us can be understood. . ."

and so forth.

Well, you see, if one uses these Pauline words in connection with the path of anthroposophy, then all this can be true. But if one forbids the human being from arriving at truth through the spirit in any way, and then cites these words, then one has to be a religious Dadaist. The same goes for the descriptions of the Christ-experience and so forth. Such heads as these naturally can't take this in. It can enter into worldly heads, but into such heads as these, what anthroposophy has to say about the Christ naturally cannot enter. That is why what is here said about the Christ-problem in relation to anthroposophy is the most hackneyed stuff. So, then, Ernst Michel is also the one who here expresses himself on how one also needs a religious relationship to language, and out of this religious relationship which he has to language, the "splendid heaps" which I quoted earlier arose. A special style of speaking, isn't it?

On the other hand, this Dadaist's article on religious matters rants especially about my style. But that is just what is characteristic: such clumsy, greasy fingers do not reach what is really necessary in order to represent the spiritual truths. For that, a certain discomfort of style is necessary. For that, it is necessary to get beyond the Dadaistic bombast unfolded by Mr. Ernst Michel. It is quite understandable that for Mr. Ernst Michel my Mysteries don't amount to anything. He does not understand anything about it at all. He says, for example:

> The mystery certainly does not lie in the pure *suprasensory*: whoever seeks it there is as much of a materialist as one who seeks it in matter.

> And one has not created a mystery if one slips ghosts of ideas or magical wonders into conceptual attire and lets them prance on the stage according to the scheme: "Reality." Instead, the mystery lies in the creative connection of nature and spirit to the ineffable form. . . .

Well, then, one should imagine this, the "ineffable form," and then say to oneself: "in the unity of matter and form, of force and direction," in the "imprinted form which develops livingly," this is, of course, a quote from Goethe![†] Now comes a sentence—one really needs a Dadaistically religious relationship to language to endure something like this and not regard such things as slime-producing, which, if you have to put them on your tongue, produce slime or something stronger: "Language is the mystery," yes, this is how it appears, this is a sentence: "Language is the mystery, the Son of Man, Jesus Christ, is the mystery. . ." and "the cross . . . is the mystery." You see, one understands quite well that the available anthroposophical literature is by no means made for such a linguistic style, although, of course, in the transcribed lectures which have not been corrected by me, some things could be different. But that doesn't prevent one from pointing out how, when through Diederich's "feeling for responsibility" this sort of stuff is placed before the public, it is really quite rich; and one is therefore called upon to deal with it, is therefore also called upon to characterize it in greater detail. It is strange when such a Dadaist of religion claims that the conversion of inner reality into the sound and rhythm of speech elements is not to be found in my work. He then invokes two people, Nietzsche and Hölderlin, as examples of those in whom such transitions have taken place. That is very characteristic, for such a muckraker of spirituality really has no feeling for how style, when one has to depict difficult spiritual material, is at the same time something by means of which one enters into a condition of life which can prevent the style becoming such as it became for Hölderlin and for Nietzsche, causing that tragic outcome as was caused in Hölderlin and Nietzsche. All of the heinous thoughtlessness of this contemporary clan appears in just such places; it has neither a feeling for the tragedy of a Hölderlin or a Nietzsche, nor for the necessity of an objective style, which is necessary for expressing spiritual truths and spiritual facts. It is necessary today to point this out, so that one is in a position for once to confront muckrakers like Diederichs, and it must be done energetically. One must see from which cesspools, out of which Dadaism, that which wraps itself in the cloak of objectivity as anthroposophical opposition draws its spiritual nourishment today.

These things cannot be expressed in any other way at this earnest present time, because among anthroposophists the opinion should really not arise that such "objectivity" is anything other than a cunning way to grind what lives in anthroposophy into the ground. Naturally, people like Ernst Michel, with his religious Dadaism, or Eugen Diederichs, with his belly-mysticism, do not have the slightest clue about this. That is precisely what has to be taken into account. It is essential at this time to have earnest discussions and not to be drawn into what is put before the world in this way. It has to be said, and it has to be presented to the world in all forms, that it is precisely through spiritual strivings of this sort that our humanity is driven more and more into degeneration, into the swamp, and that it is essential for anthroposophy to remain absolutely committed to its work, which is pure, and bears no resemblance to such swamp flowers.

I am not at all interested if somewhere some praise appears from those quarters, for I pay no attention to either praise or censure from quarters which are incapable—because they lack the will, not the intellect—to approach what, for the sake of humanity's salvation, anthroposophy desires. This religious Dadaism can then, of course, also do no more than come up with sentences like: "The power by means of which the human being raises himself up from the foundation of belief to the mystery is also not primarily knowledge, but *Love* which follows vision and leads ever deeper into vision."

But nothing is meant by this, apart from the lust of the soul, which such people have in mind, and which is not served by anything that arises out of spiritual work, where there must be no place for these religious-sexual Dadaisms that are transformed into the soul-spiritual element, Dadaisms which, even when they appear in all manner of guises, are nothing other than shameless shows of soul lust, like many a thing clothing itself in religiosity that is nothing but a shameless show of lust.

In the face of this, we must be clear ever and again that in our time there lives that which, if it overcomes all such resistance, can lead to a true grasp of the spiritual life creatively active in material life. We must be clear, again and again, that we need the nurturing of these capacities currently present in human beings, that we must dedicate ourselves to this nurturing with every fiber of our soul, and that no nuance of earnestness is strong enough to denote that which must be expended in devoted energy in order to advance on this path. No compromises can be made here. One has to do one's duty. It goes without saying that wherever anthroposophy wants to be heard, there one must allow anthroposophy to be heard; one must do one's duty. However, one must on no account allow oneself to fall prey to illusions. For it is necessary to work uncompromisingly out of the matter itself. Each of us is duty-bound to work on the healing of the anthroposophical movement itself, to enable it to get away from any sort of "Outsiderism"—from any pettiness, any lustful mysticism, so that it truly pushes through to a free, worldly grasp of the mysteries of existence. For only when the mysteries of existence are grasped in this way will it be possible to work on the goals of practical life, which must also be mastered if they are not to become stumbling blocks on humanity's further path of development. It is just in this latter realm that one is misunderstood in every way. Just think of all that occurs to distort these things shamelessly! The well-known *Berliner Tageblatt* fabricates an article[†] about all sorts of trash showing up in Berlin in a remarkably stupid way as divination and prophesy, and in the middle of this anthroposophy and I are mentioned. This article is then spread into the world. It appears in English as well as in Swiss newspapers. The annihilation of the anthroposophical worldview is worked upon in the most infamous, most shameless ways through fake articles. This is what needs to be understood, and some sort of rebuttals won't suffice; instead, one has to characterize the people themselves. It wouldn't be so very difficult to accomplish this, of course, if one characterized the soil from which all this stuff grows and held up a mirror to its own nature. But this is what is necessary and becomes ever more necessary. We cannot simply limit ourselves to setting forth anthroposophical dogma, on the one hand, and, on the other hand, to defending ourselves when attacked; instead, we need an examination of everything presently at work in the dumbing-down and degeneration of humanity. And of that there is a very great deal. This is, so to speak, what we have to say to ourselves every morning, and what is truly stated here without fanaticism. For I have, indeed, not always spoken about these things in this way, and I seldom speak, and seldom spoke earlier about these things; now more often, only because your gaze must be directed toward such mischief flowing from the entire decadence of our time, like this article fabricated in Berlin, which is now making its way through the whole world, where other things, too, are making their way through the world; and one would truly have a tremendous amount to do if one wanted to refute all these things. Then the Frohnmeyers come and say that what they wrote was never refuted. Dr. Boos did refute it; he wrote to the relevant editors, who, however, did not accept the refutation, so that Frohnmeyer afterwards excerpted from the paper what the priest in question, who was there and saw the event, had lied about; but the refutation was simply not accepted. And then, I believe, there was even a correspondence in which there was no mention of this refutation that was received and not accepted. One would really be very busy if one wanted to refute all these things. It is a typical Frohnmeyer- and Heinzelmann-like convenience to say something that certainly doesn't correspond to the truth, to claim that the thing in question was borrowed from here or there, and one just believed it to be true. An author has the duty to examine such things, to investigate his sources.[†]

One cannot deal with these people, who absolutely develop their views out of malice and also out of an overwhelming ignorance, by simply refuting them. Rather, it is a matter of placing the spiritual underpinnings, which can be found everywhere, in the right light.[†]

[Gap in stenography; the conclusion follows:]

It is in the interest of the matter at hand, and not for personal reasons, that I mention having given countless lectures since April 1919 in Stuttgart, containing the most important economic facts and truths, which also contain many characteristics of contemporary spiritual streams which should have been utilized. It is definitely a matter of there having been important material available there. It is "buried." The things are printed, are sent to members of the Threefold Circle, are read there in small groups. What had been intended as something cosmopolitan was again made into something sectarian. It is, in the interest of these matters, painful that things were not taken up but instead handled in this way.

Fundamentally, it is wasted work that is spent on something like this—which was truly drawn from the widest circles!—when it is not taken up, not developed further, not worked on in this sense.

But that is what is necessary, and what we need to do above all else today!

It will not do for us to read these things in a sectarian manner in small groups; instead, these are things which must certainly be worked on further. Everywhere there are seeds asking for further work. And why even work on something like this if it simply lies there as printed matter and no one bothers to take it seriously. But that is what matters: If one continues to work, then one can pursue those things that have been pointed out in particular. That is what is necessary, that one pursues these things further through the work; these are, after all, the seeds that are given on earth. Really energetic work is: lifting our movement out of the sign of sectarianism; whereas if we simply take things in stride as they are and carry them back into sectarianism, we will not progress. Anthroposophically oriented spiritual science does not provide content that is suitable for a sectarian movement; instead, it is definitely the case that it can be positioned as something that can provide impulses for world-wide activity.

But for this to happen, it is necessary that everyone applies his strength. Today we face the necessity of pushing things in a practical direction. We will make no progress if this is not taken up earnestly, if there is no real understanding for how the true spirit can also work in true practice.

Then, however, something must be done that does not bury things in concrete, but rather takes them up so that they continually reveal themselves as living.

This is what I still wanted to say in conclusion: No one, truly no one, need feel personally affected by these things. But at a time when what I recently quoted here can exist, when by means of magazine articles, anthroposophical spiritual science and what it has achieved is so attacked that they conclude with: There are enough spiritual sparks of fire there; now it is necessary that in the near future real physical sparks of fire rain down upon the Dornach hill—at a time when malevolence can be driven from underground to the surface, at such a time it is certain that serious words are absolutely necessary.

That is why I asked you to come here once again today. Don't take it amiss if the opportunity was taken to speak with utter seriousness. I had to bring this to you before my trip, to bring it to your hearts, your understanding, your souls!

Lecture Thirteen

THE HAGUE, FEBRUARY 27, 1921

The times we live in are so serious that it is not appropriate to think in any way about personal circumstances. And so permit me to express, with only a few words, my heartfelt gratitude to your esteemed chairwoman for her kind words, and then to proceed at once to what I believe I need to say to you, since we have not seen one another for some time here in Holland.

Most people today are not conscious of how serious the present conditions are. We may discuss these conditions here from the perspectives attained through a long study of anthroposophical spiritual science. We know that we live in an epoch which began with its special peculiarities in the fifteenth century. It was back then that it began slowly to develop its own idiosyncrasies. And those who can survey this development, by having been initiated into the spiritual circumstances of humanity's development, know that the second half of the nineteenth century signified a particular low point in human development within modern, and especially European, civilization. And this low point, which we can characterize as the arrival of a particular influx of egoism into all the members of civilized humanity—an egoism as had never before existed—this wave of a special development then sent its terrible offshoots into the twentieth century, and these offshoots still have humanity in their grip today.

When I say that a wave of egoism has welled up into the whole of modern civilization, I am not speaking of ordinary egoism in the trivial sense, but rather of egoism in the way we shall look at it in this morning's considerations and in the way in which it clearly appears to one who is initiated into the secrets of humanity's recent development.

We are familiar with the members of human nature. We know that the soul members of human nature have, for a long time, been undergoing a special transformation, a special development. We know that if we go back into ancient times of human development, we are dealing with a particular forming of the human etheric body within the ancient Indian development; that then, however, a particular forming of the astral body begins, and that a kind of middle development then takes place at that time in European development which began approximately in the year 747 BC in southern Europe and concluded in the first third of the fifteenth century, when the epoch of human development in which we still stand today began. 747 years before the Mystery of Golgotha marks the beginning of that phase of human development in which the so-called intellectual or mind soul unfolded. And everything that humanity still appreciates as Greek culture developed because it was precisely at this time that the intellectual or mind soul was at its highest phase of development. As the wonderful Greek culture developed, that which we call the intellectual or mind soul was in the ascendency of its development. Indeed, such high points are always, in some manner, testing times. For their development, the Greeks had to contend with what could be called the youthfulness of the intellectual or mind soul. And out of this youthfulness of an intellect that was not yet permeated by egoism, out of this youthfulness of the human mind arose the Greek civilization which posterity so admired. Latinism, Romanism then took over something of this intellectual-soul character, but it was in a descending, decadent development. One who has a deeper understanding for what lived in Roman culture knows that the intellect already culminated there. At that point, reason reaches a climax. That is why the Romans developed such abstract concepts, developed that which did not yet exist in the entirety of the ancient East, which in the sense in which we know it in Europe did not yet exist for Greece either: the Romans developed concepts of law, legal concepts. Today, the world is viewed in an extraordinarily external way; and one views how we think about law and justice, which actually came from the Roman intellectual soul, as something which already existed in the ancient East, something which already existed for Hammurabi and others like him. But that is not the case. The Decalogue, or the Ten Commandments, as well as what was present in other documents of that time, was fundamentally different from our modern concepts of law. They are something abstract, something that is no longer close to the human soul. And everything that belongs in this manner to the intellectual soul reached its highpoint within European civilization during an age which is actually hardly studied in external history, yet is extraordinarily important and meaningful for anyone who wants to consider human development in the spiritual sense.

The striking year which can be seen as important in a special way for European development is the year 333 after the Mystery of Golgotha. 333 after the Mystery of Golgotha is the middle of the fourth post-Atlantean epoch.[†] It is that moment in time when a fluctuating knowledge of the world and a fluctuating knowledge of humanity co-existed in Europe. There is nothing of the penetrating knowledge of the world as the Greeks still had it; nothing also of a proper grasp of the inner world. Instead, there is a swaying back and forth between longing for great knowledge of the world and the longing for knowledge of the self, for self-knowledge. It was particularly at this time in the fourth post-Atlantean epoch that the souls of the European peoples endured much. At that time, Rome was heading for its downfall. It then left only its language; in a way, it left behind the main part of its valuable cultural material for European humanity. And it was in this way, then, that human beings of the second half of the fourth post-Atlantean epoch continued to live until the fifteenth century, in which our own time began.

We have carried from the previous epoch, in which most of us, in one way or another, had one or more lives on earth—in part through physical inheritance, but especially by having been incarnated before—we have carried this heritage of the fourth post-Atlantean epoch into our fifth post-Atlantean epoch and taken up this heritage.

The heritage of the fourth post-Atlantean epoch lives in all that is part of our present civilization.

We have worked the intellect, thinking, into the consciousness soul. That is significant. At the beginning of the fifth epoch, the consciousness soul, which enables the human being to penetrate to the actual understanding of his I, first took possession of thought, of conceptualization, of the intellect. Humanity became clever, became smart, but clever within the consciousness soul. In human development, this is the elaboration of egoism down to the finest refinement. We should not simply berate this era of egoism; we should not simply criticize it; rather, we should recognize this era of egoism—in spite of the many temptations it causes, in spite of the great soul dangers and also outward dangers it brings to humanity—as the time when I-consciousness arose in its particular intensity. By this means it becomes possible for the human being to take up, within himself, the right feeling for freedom. In our earlier incarnations, in earlier epochs of human development, none of us had this feeling for freedom. To reach the longing for freedom which only the modern human being has, we had to pass through egoism, which offers so many temptations. And one of anthroposophy's most important findings is that we know: we had to absorb something in order to pass an important stage in human development, the stage toward developing freedom. But it is just for this reason that we need to be aware of how this passage for humanity is intertwined with many temptations and dangers, both soul-spiritually as well as physically. And anthroposophically oriented knowledge must bring the possibility of taking up this feeling for freedom, while at the same time ennobling it, of permeating it again with a spiritual knowledge of the world, which, in spite of the existence of the ripe sense of the I, the ripe consciousness of the I, nevertheless allows mankind to solve tasks that are not merely tasks of egoism, but rather tasks for all of human evolution, indeed, of the whole of Earth evolution, of the whole evolution of the world.

In this regard, we are facing a great turning point today in the whole of modern civilization. The time of trials is now. Humanity faces great tasks. But recognizing these tasks is exceptionally difficult, and is made even more difficult by our having gone through the era of great egoism.

We sleep from the time we fall asleep until we wake up. That is right. We are at that time in a condition of dimmed consciousness. Probably most of you know sleep by the negative way it announces itself precisely because consciousness is dimmed. But people do not consider the period when we are awake in the same manner. This time of being awake, this time between waking up and going to sleep, was actually still different for the fourth post-Atlantean epoch. People today think they are awake in the same way that, let us say, people around the time of the Mystery of Golgotha were awake. That is not the case. The entire soul-state was different. In those days, people were awake in a different way. They had a much stronger consciousness of their body. You see, today the human being basically knows extraordinarily little about physical processes. The Greeks, admittedly not the Greeks of the later time but the Greeks of the pre-Socratic or pre-Platonic time, knew an extraordinary amount about the processes of their own body. The truly educated Greek looked, for example, up toward the sun. From the sun he received light. With it he received a feeling of actively absorbing something etheric, that he himself received the light continually in his inner being. And as he thought, he said: "The light of the sun thinks in me; the sun lets its light be drawn in by me; the light which shines on things out there, which allows things out there to become visible, it works in me by being reflected back to itself in a way, so that thoughts spring up in me." For the Greek, the thoughts which were in him were sunlight. At the same time, they were that which lived in him thanks to the working of divine-spiritual beings in the macrocosm. They were that within him which actually lifted him above his ordinary humanity to the divine. The human being experienced himself lifted above the earthly when he felt the sunlight as thought in this way. And when the especially cultivated Greek ate, then, although he viewed the food as something with which he took in an aspect that was not given by the sun directly but something stemming from the earth, he viewed this as a necessity of life, but at the same time he felt himself transformed into the fare which he himself became by means of his mouth, his esophagus, and the other digestive organs. He felt himself to be one with his food, just as he felt himself one with the sunlight. And he felt the weight of the earth as he digested. He felt, in a way, like the snake, which he did not yet value highly, but rather observed somewhat shyly, the snake which wrests itself from the earth, but which, when it has eaten, takes care of digestion in a particularly visible way. That is how the Greek experienced what took place in his body, whether it was perceived as the bright sunlight which thought in him or the food he took up, which he experienced as binding him to the earth. Through the inner connection between his intellect and his own body, he felt himself as a physical human being in a particularly energetic way. You can also deduce this from the following.

When we paint people today in the usual way, as numerous painters of the present generation have done year after year, decade after decade, we are actually lying. We look at people from the outside and believe we can produce something we are experiencing. It really is not true that we can experience that. We could only experience it if we could conjure up in ourselves the way in which the human being felt himself to be at one with all of nature, as was the case for the Greeks. This is something we have to learn all over again in a way that is different from the Greeks. Since the beginning of the fifteenth century, we have attained a soul-constitution which no longer allows us to really penetrate our body; instead, it lives in concepts that are vague because we have mastered thinking for the egoity, for the I. We must be aware of this. And we must become conscious of the fact that we must once again take up spirituality out of anthroposophically oriented spiritual science so that egoity can be filled with something, so that something again enters our life, now in a different manner, which really is in us, which the Greek experienced directly in an elemental way, but which could not last. For ultimately, when the Greek walked, he walked as a necessity of nature, the way that lightning flashes through the clouds or that thunder rolls. He knew nothing of freedom. He knew the human being. He knew even more about the human being than one credits him for today. He knew, for example, to provide words which clearly show that the human being knew something about the connection between the soul-spiritual and the bodily physical nature. The Greek words, or those words which have remained from the Greek, are much more significant today than those which come from our modern therapeutic or pathological view that does not understand anything. Hypochondria, for example, is abdominal cartilage. This is something that the Greeks named out of their full realization of the nature of the cartilage in a certain part of the body due to the activity of the soul-spiritual element in people who are hypochondriacs. These names mean much more than people today suspect, and much more than can be achieved by today's medicine on the basis of its abstract thinking, even if it experiments, dissects, and so forth. We must first take up all these things which are realities, which allow us to penetrate the world again. But that is the task of spiritual-scientific deepening, that we once again arrive at truths, at realities.

Into this fourth post-Atlantean epoch, in which human beings experienced what was in a way physical self-knowledge, what was an understanding of human physical nature, precisely into this period—nearly a third of the way into it—fell the greatest event of Earth evolution, the Mystery of Golgotha. What is the nature of the period in which the Mystery of Golgotha falls? The further we go back, the more we find in ancient times, in the Greek period, in the Egypto-Chaldean period, in the Persian, the Old Indian period, such direct knowledge of the entire nature of the human being. This knowledge of the nature of the entire human being then disappears. Its last remnants exist at the time when the Mystery of Golgotha took place. There still existed something of the instinctive, ancient knowledge of the human being. For example, those personalities who are described for us in the Gospels as the Apostles or the disciples of the Lord still retained something of the old knowledge, but entirely instinctively, not living in their souls with clarity. Others, too, still had something of such knowledge. In those times, such knowledge often fell into decadence, but it did still exist. It was dying out, fading, but enough was left over from ancient days that a large number of people were still able to grasp the Mystery of Golgotha according to the ancient knowledge; in particular, when the Apostle Paul, initiated by divine powers, was placed into the unfolding stream of time and became able to see into the spiritual world. Through all this, temporal conditions were created from which the Mystery of Golgotha could still be understood in a certain primordial, instinctive way. Many people were already at a later stage of development. Namely, the educated Greeks and the educated Romans already had concepts that were far too abstract to grasp the Mystery of Golgotha. But certain people retained the remnants of ancient clairvoyant knowledge and, in particular, of clairvoyant traditions, and they still grasped that a truly otherworldly power, the Christ, had connected himself with an earthly man, Jesus of Nazareth. The year 333 was, in a way, the year in which the last followers of those, within Europe, who really understood the Mystery of Golgotha were present; not that they understood it with our anthroposophical spiritual knowledge—naturally it did not yet exist—but with the remnants of the ancient knowledge which had carried over from Gnosis and the like. A certain spiritual knowledge still existed. An ancient human heritage still lived in human souls. With that they were able to grasp the Mystery of Golgotha.

What has remained of this Mystery of Golgotha? Intellectual traditions. The ancient Gnosis became theology, a mere logical conception of the divine. Theo-logic; a merely logical comprehension, no longer a beholding of the divine.

And after the year 333, the direct perception of the Mystery of Golgotha became ever more decadent, until the beginning of the disastrous ninth century, when, at the Eighth General Ecumenical Council in Constantinople in the year 869, the dogma that the human being does not consist of body and soul and spirit was enacted, demanding that it was the duty of a Christian to recognize that the human being consists only of body and soul, with the soul having a few spiritual characteristics. At that time, the trichotomy, as it was called—the one and only possible knowledge of the human being, that the human being consists of body, soul, and spirit—was dogmatically abolished, and it was commanded that the dogma which states that the human being consists of only body and soul must be recognized as orthodoxy. Modern philosophers often pretend to proceed from knowledge without any prior assumptions and speak of the body, on the one hand, and the soul, on the other. At most, they might speak of the spirit in a very rhetorical way, for they know nothing about it. They would recognize it only if they were to recognize anthroposophical spiritual science. This "assumption-less philosophy," which is taught a lot today, what is it really? It is the result of the dogma of the Eighth Ecumenical Council in 869. And whereas the great philosophers of our time declare that they pursue science without any prior assumptions, they actually shape nothing other than new forms of what the Eighth Ecumenical Council prescribed as dogma for Christianity.

One must see through this. One has to be absolutely clear that allusion to the spirit within the emergence of modern civilization was already deemed dangerous in the second half of the fourth post-Atlantean epoch. Today we are faced with the obligation of reminding humanity once again of the spirit which, for a long period of European civilization, was declared to be the devil. And after the year 333, all that remained was, fundamentally, traditions of the old Christological knowledge. Traditions!

In the artistic realm, what has remained as tradition can be seen more easily. Take a look, for example, at the pictures of Cimabue,[†] there you will see that a world was alive which, as soon as it appears in Giotto,[†] becomes another world. Something lives in Cimabue which also still lives, for example, in Dante, which later human beings do not experience at all. But this standing inside the spiritual world, which was still present in Cimabue, ceases later on. Later on, it is a mendacity to make a gold background. For Cimabue, this was still a matter of course. And have a look at the Russian icons; this is not something that was made from a model, but rather is something in which old traditions still live, traditions coming from a clairvoyance which still existed at the time of the Mystery of Golgotha, enabling humanity to understand the Mystery of Golgotha. Then came the times in which traditions were kept intact by outer means. And then came the nineteenth century, when the ordinary soul-activity, which had yielded such great fruits in natural science and technology was also applied to theology. But what was the result in theology? Christ Jesus, the incarnation of a supra-earthly being, became "the simple man from Nazareth"; indeed, the most excellent human being, but still, not the bearer of a supra-earthly being.

Naturalism is what theology became. The more theologists take Jesus of Nazareth to be human, the less they are inclined to practice Christology, and the more they emphasize it. In theology, too, they really only want to rise to the description of the person, Jesus of Nazareth, not to the grasping of Christ as a supra-earthly being who resided in the person Jesus of Nazareth.

Whoever is somewhat initiated by the spirit into world events has to see some things differently than people who see things according to outer judgments. Central Europe, which today experiences such a tragic destiny, has had to tolerate, among other things which do not need to be discussed here, the fact that Adolf Harnack[†] is seen as a great scholar; the man who brought forth the idea that the Son does not belong in the Gospel, only the Father, and that the Gospel is to be understood in such a way that one speaks only of the man, Jesus of Nazareth, and about what this man taught about God the Father. Through Harnackian theology, looking up to the spirituality of Christ was to be eliminated. In truth, Harnackian theology in Central Europe meant abjuring Christianity, disowning Christianity, it meant the erecting of a worldview which expressly declares: We don't want to know anything anymore about the spirituality of the Christ. This is what has so significantly come over modern humanity, that the most incorrect perspectives are applied to the most vital concepts.

And so humanity today knows what sleep is from going to sleep until waking up, but in general it is not attentive to the other kind of sleep, from waking up to going to sleep, when we go about our daily life and give ourselves over to illusions and dreams about the most important things. Modern humanity doesn't sleep only at night when lying in bed—that would even be the better sort of sleep—modern humanity sleeps in the realm of its egoism when it locks itself into its inner being, when it does not become acquainted with the human body, when it really does not want to strive toward spiritual self-knowledge. That is a different kind of sleep from the kind that is experienced between falling asleep and waking up. To understand this, we must, mind you, really take a look at the nature of going to sleep and the nature of sleep from the time of falling asleep until the time of awakening. What is going on there in the human being?

Why does the modern human being consider sleep to be the same for today's human being as it was for the ancient Greek? The Greek was not awake in the way that human beings are awake today, nor most certainly was that the case for the Egyptian, nor did he sleep in the same way. We have to become acquainted with the particular soul-constitution of each age. When the human soul, that is, the I and the astral body, detach themselves in sleep from the physical body and the etheric body which remain lying in bed, where then is the I and the astral body during sleep?

Such external descriptions, that there is a cloud which arises externally above the physical body—which is certainly a fact for the external, for the most external clairvoyance—are not enough. One must look at what is internal. One must look at what the soul actually experiences between falling sleep and waking up. In the human being today, the soul, between falling asleep and waking up, has those experiences which will again be lived through by souls not yet incarnated on earth. So let us take an event which came to me just now, this minute, before I started this lecture: A little girl was born to an anthroposophist. A year ago, she was in the spiritual world, and since then she has tried to descend into the physical world. So she was in the spiritual world all the decades by which we are older than this girl who was born. While we were asleep, we also actually lived, from the time we fell asleep until we awoke, in the world in which this girl lived before the time of conception, respectively birth. That is also our external world. The not-yet-incarnated souls experience something; in the fifth post-Atlantean epoch, we live with them in sleep and in all the events that are similar to those which such souls experience in the spiritual world.

On the other hand, when asleep while awake, from waking up until going to sleep, we live in the inheritances of the old earthly life. We live in quite cramped closeness, egoistically, inwardly, with what has remained behind from ancient India, Persia, Egypt, because we carry it, of course, into our incarnation. We live with this during the day, sleeping through the present—for the present has many spiritually perceptible events—but cramping ourselves with ideas which we have from prior incarnations and onto which we hold obstinately in our language, for language often contains old wisdom that has been crystalized for us. We do not want this ancient wisdom to somehow affect our souls. For example, nowadays we talk about a *Messer* (knife) and *Schere* (scissors), and in contemplating how the scissors cut, we usually don't consider that the word underlying *Scheren* (scissors) is the basis of the word you see posted on every beauty parlor. As for the word *Messer* (knife), a moral thought is the basis; for *Messer* is related to measure, to measurement. The *Messer* (knife) was what one used in order to cut or measure the portion. Things which have been crystallized in words are ancient spiritual life. Today we use the words thoughtlessly; but these things rest in the depths of our being. When language pours forth from us, then we indeed experience ancient times on Earth. From the time we wake up until we fall asleep, we experience, spiritually, ancient times on Earth, even while sleeping; and from the time we fall asleep until we wake up, we experience those events which point the way into earthly life for descending souls.

These, you see, are realities. These realities must be absorbed by modern humanity if it does not want to become acquainted only with the forces of decline, but also with ascending forces. It would be much better if a large number of people would do something different before going to sleep at night, than what they do nowadays. Just think what the last thing is for many people when they go to sleep at night. For today's humanity, it would be right to say: I want to go into that world in which there are ascending forces, in which those forces can be experienced which lead souls down here into the earthly world, in which these forces can be experienced spiritually. Today the human being experiences forces for the future between falling asleep and waking up. And that is why he should develop a kind of craving for those teachings which speak of the spiritual world, which develop a consciousness of what is experienced consciously by those souls who are in a similar condition to souls between falling sleep and waking up. From there, from that world, must come that which gives the great impulses for moving civilization forward, for healing civilization. From there must come the spiritual, political, and social-economic impulses which must develop as the healing forces of our civilization. For, in our time, we must again attain the possibility of understanding the Mystery of Golgotha spiritually.

What, then, is the essential thing—or, let us say, *one* essential thing, for naturally there are countless—about the Mystery of Golgotha? A God, a supra-earthly being came down, resided in Jesus of Nazareth. A characteristic of such beings is that they cannot die. All the beings you find described in my *Occult Science* as beings of the higher hierarchies, the Angels, Archangels, and so on, up to the highest, the Seraphim, Cherubim, and so forth, they do not die in the same way; you can read about this, about the destiny of their lives; they do not die the way human beings die. What did Christ, who arose out of these higher hierarchies, take upon himself? He dies in a human body. That, you see, is his most significant transition toward effective activity within earthly humanity. He died in a human body. He has gone through the experience of dying, which other gods who are connected to the Earth do not experience. This was more or less understood until 333 AD; we must learn to understand this once again. We must learn to understand again that one divine being experienced death as a deed and thereby was immersed in Earth development, lives with us in Earth development. But we must, of course, develop great modesty so as to recognize that this being naturally stands far above that which the human soul-constitution can experience. This being descended from worlds where death is unknown. Who are the beings who serve this Christ-being? Not all achieved the same sacrifice; not all descended to the earth and died. Beings, starting with the hierarchy of the Angels up to the higher hierarchies, serve the Christ who united Himself with Earth development. But we do not discover them if we do not raise ourselves up to divine knowledge of the higher hierarchies. What leads to the Christ must be sought in knowledge of spiritual worlds. First, we need spiritual knowledge, so that we can, once again, arrive at Christ-knowledge. For the Christ is on the earth, but what surrounds him exists in the world of the higher hierarchies. And the great temptation for humanity in modern times was that it underwent the great triumphs of the newer natural sciences, that it learned to recognize mere outer natural forces. But spiritual beings live behind these natural forces. What the newer natural sciences claim is indeed accurate, but behind these forces of nature live guiding and leading spiritual beings; they serve the Christ. Christ is in all of Earth development. Heavenly beings serve him, but heavenly beings are recognized only by spiritual science. That is why spiritual science has a boundlessly meaningful task vis-à-vis the renewal of Christianity. From this you can see that today we cannot carry out spiritual science as if it were merely a personal matter. Today this spiritual science is a matter for the whole of civilized humanity. And that is why it was an absolute inner necessity from the beginning of the group that bears the name "Anthroposophical Society" to carry out spiritual science in a manner different from how it was carried out in the Theosophical Society. The Theosophical Society had, from the very beginning, something of a sectarian nature in its entire constitution, something that reckoned with the egoism of recent times. To anthroposophy fell the task of reckoning with modern consciousness, of reckoning with what is otherwise considered the external culture of humanity, and of carrying into it the results of spiritual observation. In this context, all the small conflicts and cat fights are simply negligible. The essential aspect was that I had to make sure that the spiritual movement which reckons with all of modern science was kept pure. In so doing, it does not matter to me whether one or the other recognizes this or that. Even if the whole world were yet to scold, even if the whole world were to criticize only negatively what I have represented as spiritual science, it would be of no account; instead, what matters is that in reality what is represented by me as spiritual science exists in full accord with modern scientific attitudes and the modern moral conscience.

First, I had to present *The Philosophy of Freedom*, the declaration of karma. I often had to listen, in deep sorrow, in the circle of theosophists, when they said: "If one or the other person suffers, or if one or the other is a socially afflicted being of a lower class or caste, then that is simply his karma, he earned it." That was an interpretation of the idea of karma that was needed by the egotistical people of the nineteenth or twentieth centuries. Such people did not consider that we do not live only in this present Earth life, but rather that we will also live in the future. And today we should not always look back at what we had in previous lives, but rather we should also consider that in future lives we will look back first of all at what we now experience. Freedom is in full accord with the idea of karma, only that everything that appears in life's ledger stands in a karmic context.

If I calculate life's destiny according to debits and credits and find the difference, then I acquire a life-balance, but that does not mean that individual numbers are not subject to natural necessity, just as individual numbers in a business ledger depend on industriousness and a balance must of necessity be the result. In this way, within the karma of life, freedom is absolutely compatible with the idea of karma. We should not give ourselves over to the convenience of fatalism if we put forward the idea of karma as fully justified. Similarly, spiritual science must exist in full harmony with the moral convictions of modern humanity. And that is why the necessity of being effective through spiritual science in a larger context arose at the time in which, so to speak, the catastrophe occurred for everything that soul, spiritual, and physical egoism caused for modern humanity. Would it have been honest and straightforward to preach that spiritual science exists to help humanity, and then have no social views at the time when social demands have become as urgent as they are today? Should we just stick with the clichéd declamations about human love? Shouldn't we, instead, progress toward real social impulses? Consider this progression toward real social impulses as a result of basic tenets of spiritual science, as a result of what I told you today about waking and sleeping, about being asleep while awake and the awakening out of sleep through spiritual science; consider it as a result of the knowledge that tells you: the spirits who serve the Christ only become evident for us when we look up into the spiritual world, and also—through spiritual science—the Mystery of Golgotha first becomes clear in a manner appropriate for today's humanity; consider it as a result of the fact that spiritual science should not remain stuck in any sort of sectarian lodges or branches, but that we must carry it out into the world, as well as we can, each according to what he can do in his sphere. In Dornach, the intent was not to create a merely sectarian site but rather a place where all science, the entirety of active life, social life, the life of art could be fructified. Anthroposophically oriented spiritual science must become a matter for the broad masses of humanity, even though its most important element, that which is closest to our hearts and gives us inner strength, is indeed conducted in the narrower circles of our branches. That is where we should collect the strength to foster aspects of higher knowledge which we first take up in our branches. But this knowledge must be fostered. For today we live in an age in which people actually don't know what they want because they sleep through the most important things in life, although they all want to recognize the spirit. This is what we must feel as pioneers, I might say, of spiritual renewal, as anthroposophists, in the deepest depths of our hearts.

That is why I wish with all my heart that there be, within the branches, also in Holland, such an earnest, diligent, and assiduous study of what can be given as knowledge from spiritual worlds in our movement. I wish for truly diligent studying within the branches. But I wish that it not just remain as an activity within the branches, but that what happens in the branches be just the beginning of carrying it out among all human beings, each in his own way, so that the yearning which today lives in all humanity may be satisfied by the anthroposophically oriented view of the spirit. This is also why we ought to understand what these yearnings of modern humanity consist of. Let us not believe that we will become materialistic by spiritualizing matter. Let us be clear that a great calamity awaits humanity if one does not recognize it properly, so as to avert it.

The Eighth Ecumenical Council of 869 eradicated from humanity the view of the spirit. Those who are rather materialistically disposed would like to prepare the next stage; they would like to prepare to abolish the soul as well, and to make it part of a widespread dogmatic view of contemporary and future life that the human being is only a body. And certain diabolically initiated individuals seek means—not through influencing the soul, but through ingredients, through certain liquids which can be found in nature—to educate toward materialism, to prepare the human being materialistically as a body. More with other principles than those of the Waldorf School—which are spiritual protests against modern materialism—other people devise experimental psychology, which today conducts all sorts of experiments to test capacities. That is merely the prelude of what one actually wants. One wants to educate children without addressing the soul, but instead through outer material means, so that capacities develop in relation to physicality. We approach the automation of the human being if we don't realize in time that the path toward eradicating the soul along with the spirit may not be allowed to be taken, but that instead the path in the opposite direction of the one taken by the Eighth Ecumenical Council must be taken; the path that must be taken is the one toward finding the spirit again, and to the extent that it can be found again in humanity, it must be cultivated in all branches of human, practical life.

This is what I would like to place into your dear souls, into your hearts, now that we have been able to see one another again after a longer time. Cultivate spiritual science as a matter of the heart first of all, just as the individual human being must cultivate it today so as to make progress himself. Cultivate what you have absorbed individually by carrying it out into humanity in all realms of life. Then you will gradually find the way toward doing the right thing, each in his place, in the midst of modern humanity's difficult, earnest time of trial.

Lecture Fourteen

DORNACH, MARCH 11, 1921

SINCE THE LAST time we saw each other here, our anthroposophical movement has made some important progress. We had prepared a longer series of lectures in Stuttgart after I left here, which were first to be held within Germany. My activity in mid-February was designated as preparation time for these lectures. And then, after mid-February, a somewhat more widespread lecturing activity began in the most important cities of Germany; it was prompted by a larger number of our friends, led by the Waldorf teachers and the colleagues in Stuttgart, but also by younger friends who had only recently joined the anthroposophical movement. This series of lectures will not be completed until the Stuttgart university course starts on May 12.

This lecturing activity arose, after all, through insight into the necessity of doing something drastic for the anthroposophical movement and all that is—or at least should be—its results and everything connected to it. Of course, it is exceptionally difficult to have reasonably full halls in those cities in which only small groups of our friends are active on our behalf. Nevertheless, in these difficult times, everything even remotely possible must be done.

The content of these lectures was meant to show how, on the one hand, anthroposophical spiritual science is to position itself within the great contemporary questions of culture and civilization, and then, from that, to show what consequences for social life result from this basic anthroposophical view. The tenor of the lectures which have just been held, and will still be held in many German cities, went in just this direction. Dr. Boos† contributed to this lecture series with his activity and will continue to contribute in various German cities, and we will see whether this strong advance which we thereby attempted to make is met with understanding in our present time, with the understanding that is so necessary today.

After the preparatory lectures for this lecturing activity had been completed on February 17, I was able to go to Holland so as to provide a series of lectures there on behalf of anthroposophical spiritual science. The lectures I gave there were essentially intended to show how anthroposophical spiritual science emerges from all the challenges of contemporary civilization, and how anthroposophical spiritual science can be something essential and important for precisely those souls of the present day who are truly, earnestly seeking. In a number of Dutch cities, I gave lectures on two themes: first, "The being of anthroposophical spiritual science and its relationship to the great questions of civilization today," and then, "Education, teaching, and practical life questions from the perspective of anthroposophically oriented spiritual science."

I spoke on these topics in Amsterdam on the nineteenth of February, in Hilversum on the twentieth, and in Utrecht on the twenty-first. On the afternoon of the twenty-second of February, I was then able to give a lecture with slides about our building in Dornach. On the twenty-third, I gave a lecture in the Hague, on the twenty-fourth again in Utrecht; on the twenty-fifth, I gave a lecture at the Technical College in Delft on economic organization as influenced by the threefold division of the social organism. The lecture scheduled for the twenty-sixth was cancelled because I needed to take care of my voice, because on the twenty-seventh I had to give a lecture at a branch meeting in the Hague for our university friends and that evening again in the Hague, a public lecture on questions of education and teaching from the perspective of spiritual science. On the afternoon of the twenty-eighth, I gave a lecture with slides about our building in Dornach, and that same evening I gave the second public lecture in Amsterdam. On March 1, I gave a lecture in the university auditorium in Amsterdam on the theme of "Anthroposophy and Philosophy." On March 2, I gave a public lecture in Rotterdam. On March 3, I gave a public lecture in Hengelo† in Holland. That place is particularly interesting because it is, I might say, fundamentally an artificially created place. In the 60s and 70s of the last century, industrialists first created welfare institutions, and Hengelo was eventually formed, based on actually true industrial-social thinking. That becomes especially clear when one visits the early childhood center there. Of course, I had very little time, but I visited the lesson, and there it became quite especially apparent that these small children were different from other small children, such as those one finds today starting in, say, the first grade of a Waldorf school, who simply appear from the folk in the manner in which today's civilization has formed them. That is different in Hengelo. In Hengelo, certain welfare institutions of an industrial nature had first been set up, and the people who settled there worked there in the 70s of the last century; their children now work in the wide-spread, local establishments, and the children of these working people, meaning the second generation, these were then the ones in the early childhood center. One could really see this very clearly; they are not just children who came off the street, but rather, if I may put it like this, have been artificially nurtured through several generations by a civilization that, in a certain sense, emerged from the way of thinking of the time, of course, to their advantage, but nurtured quite artificially, and bear the character of an artificial civilization. Naturally, it is difficult to meet the prejudice so prevalent in the world today, precisely when, if I may put it like this, one enters into such a milieu. In various lectures, I indicated how, right as the last third of the nineteenth century began, we had a wave of liberalism, a wave of free spirituality, which if it had been able to find continuation on the spiritual side probably would have achieved something of exceptional significance. Instead of that, we were driven back into reaction, because we had a materialistically scientific spirit which was not in keeping with the liberal intentions of that time. It is strange how karmic things play out.

For example, now—meaning, in recent days—I gave this lecture in Hengelo for the local industrialists there, the people who are involved in industry, and saw how that which was broken off at its peak, which only lacks a spiritual continuation, actually still works into the present. Returning here, I happened to reach for a book on my shelf which is of some interest in relation to these things. This book, which is not particularly significant—it is a book dealing with philosophical questions†—was written by the former Bonn University philosopher, Jürgen Bona Meyer; but this copy belonged to the well-known materialist, Arnold Dodel, who was active in Zürich. In this copy, you can see how much of the book he had read. There are, let's say, 460 pages; up to page, I believe, 114, there are pencil markings with his comments everywhere. And from these comments one can see how materialism fought in an almost "bull-like" way against what still wanted to assert itself from the old philosophy, albeit in the clumsy manner of the Bonn University philosopher Bona Meyer; how materialism fights there, how materialism bickers there, how materialism, apart from all that, also appears with incredible arrogance. That, you see, my dear friends, that is what took the wind out of a better intention back then, and what can show how absolutely necessary a deepening into a spiritual life is if we want civilization to progress; if we don't want to rush into the decline, the decline which is clearly perceptible especially in the economic realm, and, I might say, bursts into view everywhere. For the fact that the 60s and 70s did not allow any spiritual life to arise, that is what actually caused all the misfortune of recent times.

In addition to the lectures that I gave in various places, we then also had eurythmy performances, specifically on February 20 in Hilversum, on February 22 in Amsterdam, on the February 26 in Rotterdam, on February 27 in the Hague. Thus, on February 27 in the Hague, there were three events: in the morning a branch meeting, in the afternoon a eurythmy performance, and in the evening the public lecture. Then there was another eurythmy performance on March 2 in Amsterdam, for which Mr. Stuten† provided the introductory words; I could not attend because I had to give a lecture in Rotterdam on that day.

What has to be said is simply that, indeed, it is clearly evident how everywhere among the people there is a kind of yearning for soul nourishment, for whatever can bring the soul forward. Eurythmy performances were subsequently organized and in part already accomplished in Cologne and in Essen, and will be given in Mannheim, Karlsruhe, Freiburg, and Stuttgart. I would like to mention other things which have often needed to be discussed here, which accompany our movement like a shadow; the more our movement proves how inwardly needed it is, the greater the opposition grows. What characterizes this opposition is that the more widespread it becomes, as it gets bigger, it becomes, at the same time, ever fouler and baser. Thus, for example, on February 28 in Amsterdam, when I got to the concert hall, a man was standing there distributing leaflets† which, in a rather slimy way, said about the same things as are also spread here through Reverend Kully's leaflet† and other similar ones.

So, you see, these things are not localized but spread throughout the world, and everything is done to spread them. The opposition is—I need to mention this ever and again—much better organized, much more active than the Anthroposophical Society in this direction, and also much better organized in its actions. On the contrary, if an activity is undertaken here or there, then there are countless friends of ours who don't agree with it, who want us to allow ourselves to be flogged and to carry our bruises around without in any way defending ourselves.

One can find charming things if, for example, one considers the, one might say, comically distinguished "School of Wisdom" in Darmstadt led by Count Hermann Keyserling. It has published something like a brochure, though a rather thick one, entitled "Der Weg zur Vollendung" [The path to perfection],† which appeared with the well-known so-called "Bauchbinde," which carries book announcements, and there advertisements proclaimed that my attacks would be "ended": "Ending Steiner's Attacks." This piece really is extraordinarily funny. What someone who read some of it said to me the other day is almost true, namely, that the gist of it is: Whoever has not stepped foot on the parquet floors of the School of Wisdom in Darmstadt is an idiot! That really is the approximate content of "The Road to Perfection."

But there is something else that is really quite charming. As you know, in my public lecture in Stuttgart,† I quite deliberately called

Count Hermann Keyserling a liar because he really did lie, and he resented this; while he says that other assessments I made of his philosophy may be justified—he allows them to be justified!—he contests this accusation, and with an extraordinarily important justification: He says that if I had simply said† that what he asserted was incorrect, then he could have understood that; but, after all, he hadn't had much time for special Steiner research, and, therefore, one had to understand that he might also say inaccurate things. Well, you see, that is characteristic for all these ignoramuses of today, who, in addition to being ignorant are also lazy, are terribly lazy, and in their laziness even claim a certain right not to know certain things. Then, if one accuses them of lying, they say they don't have the time to carry out Steiner research, meaning, they don't have the time to convince themselves of the things they claim. Of course, they need not carry out Steiner research, but then they should—I want to be polite—keep their mouths shut. If they keep their mouths shut, no one will accuse them of anything; but if they trumpet untrue things out into the world and then say they don't have the time to get to know these things properly, then it is absolutely a symptom of the terrible moral and intellectual rottenness of our contemporary so-called spiritual people, notably such a parquet-spiritualist as Count Hermann Keyserling.

Actually, the most notable aspect is that one sees very clearly, already today, that these people cannot, after all, do anything scientific; they can do nothing scientific because they are too comfortable to deal seriously with spiritual science at all, insofar as they hold any scientific or literary positions. This is the case especially with people like professor Fuchs† in Göttingen. Because these people cannot get anywhere with spiritual science, they reach for other methods, and these methods consist of using any kind of questionable means to destroy the movement. When I returned to Stuttgart from Holland, I was, for instance, surprised by the article in the *Frankfurter Zeitung*,† which in the meantime had, of course, been more widely distributed, and which, because of our activities in regard to the question of Upper Silesia, is entitled "Verräter am Deutschtum" [Traitor to Germanness] and speaks of national treason and all sorts of other things. It is really very characteristic that one uses these things to enter through the back door in order to destroy this matter.

Well, these things are only evidence for the kind of base means to which the representatives of our current spiritual life stoop, and from these things you can see that really not a word that was spoken here was unjustified, that I was obliged to characterize our educational institutions, namely our universities, accordingly. What must be seen ever more clearly is that what is needed here is a thorough metamorphosis, a thorough re-structuring especially of our colleges. And from this point of view, the gathering of a small circle of university students working to bring anthroposophically oriented spiritual science into the university realm in spite of the opposition raging from the other side, is welcomed with real joy. This becomes apparent in the preparation of such undertakings as the upcoming university course in Stuttgart, as well as in the university course which will be held here again beginning April 3.

This, my dear friends, is what I wanted to present to you so as to give you a picture of the activity of the last few weeks.

Today I would like to discuss with you a kind of summary of truths that we are already familiar with from this or that perspective but that must come before our souls again and again if we want to form impulses out of the whole depth of spiritual-scientific knowledge, impulses necessary for human activity in the present time.

I have, indeed, often spoken to you about how different streams work together to form the entirety of the world into which the human being is placed, and about the terms luciferic, ahrimanic, and that which is, in a way, the state of equilibrium of these two streams, and which can be best expressed when we speak of the Christ-stream. As you are aware, the central Group† of our building is meant to express this very secret of the trinity: Lucifer – Ahriman – Christ.

In considering the human being, who is, ultimately, the confluence of cosmic forces, we can see exactly how these three, as I might say, streams work through him. We know that we should clearly delineate what is mainly—you know how this is to be understood—the organization of the head, which is essentially also the bearer of the nerve-sense system. We know that we can then delineate the rhythmic system, which includes the rhythm of breathing and the circulation of the blood as its most significant aspects, meaning, everything which proceeds rhythmically, and that then, as the third member of the external human being, the metabolic system is to be observed, and this is intimately connected with the development of the limb system. But we also know that we can grasp this trinity of the human being from a soul perspective. For the nerve-sense organization, the organization of the head, is essentially the bearer of everything connected with conceptualization, with the life of thought. The rhythmic organization is the bearer of everything related to the life of feeling; and the metabolic system is the bearer of the life of will.

Now let us be clear about the following: Only through our nerve-sense system, out of which the life of concepts develops, do we have true day-consciousness, a day-consciousness penetrated by full light. The rhythmic system, which we can also call the chest system, is the bearer of the life of feeling. There, in the middle part of the soul, the feelings develop. And it is the rhythmic system where the feelings have their bodily counterpart. This life of feeling, as we have often discussed, is not permeated by clear, lucid consciousness in the same way as the life of concepts. If we consider the human soul without prejudice, we cannot say anything other than that the life of feeling has no greater light of consciousness than our dreams. Dreams, which do indeed take place in pictures, and the life of feelings are equally conscious and unconscious. They just look different because the life of feeling is not experienced in pictures but in soul-essence that does not take on picture form. Dreams exist in pictures. That is the difference between the life of feeling and dream life. But in relationship to the intensity of their consciousness, these two are indistinguishable. The life of will, then, which has its physical counterpart in the metabolic-limb system, is entirely sheathed in unconsciousness just as the human being is when he sleeps, from falling asleep to waking up. As regards the life of will, the human being is, while being awake, a sleeping being. While willing, the human being actually sees only what he accomplishes through his will; then he imagines it as he imagines other things as well. But what is actually active in the will, the inner life of soul in willing, is actually slept through, just as the life of feeling is dreamed.

Now, however, let us look at this sleeping life of will or its physical counterpart, this sleeping life of metabolism and limbs. The human being does not exist only in his physical, natural environment, he also exists in a spiritual world. No matter what his level of consciousness is, he exists with his entire being in the spiritual cosmos. Let us now consider the will. We might put it like this: If this is the spiritual cosmos (see Plate Six in the appendix, lighter part), which for now I don't want to characterize any further—you know, "spiritual cosmos" is really very universal, one can ever only take one part at a time—then this here (red) would be a certain part of the spiritual cosmos, namely, that part which belongs primarily to our will, respectively our metabolic-limb system. So that then, if you think of the life of will as soul, and the life of metabolism and limbs as physical, and think of these as separated from the human being, and then ask yourself, How is this embedded in the spiritual cosmos? then this entire relationship to a spiritual cosmos is depicted by this drawing. And for us the question arises: What is the white part here? We know that the red part is the human life of will, seen as soul, or the human life of metabolism and limbs, seen physically; but what is it to which, so to speak, this life belongs? Let me express myself in yet other words. If you observe one or another part of the human organism, let's say, for example, the liver, then you will say to yourself: This liver belongs to the entire organism and it has meaning within the entire organism. Similarly, we can regard the entire human metabolic-limb system, the system of will, as a member of a great organism, of a world-organism, which is here represented in white. And then the question arises: What is the great cosmic organism in which the human experience of will and of the metabolic-limb system is embedded?

You see, that element in which the human being is embedded with respect to his third member is the cosmic life of the spiritual beings that the Bible calls the Elohim.† Indeed, just as we live in outer nature, which we see through our senses, so, too, do we co-exist with the life of the Elohim through a part of our being whose activity we actually sleep through.

Now, let us discuss these things more precisely; to begin with, I just want to characterize them. Let us consider the life of these Elohim within all of cosmic evolution. If you take a look in my *Occult Science*, you will find that these are the Spirits of Form; they ascend from earlier stages of development. If we go back, we come to the earlier developmental stage of cosmic Moon existence. There, these Spirits of Form were Archai, Primal Forces, Primal Beginnings. If we go back to the time of Sun existence, there they were Archangels; if we go back to the time of Saturn existence, there they were Angels. Thus, since that time, they have ascended and arrived at the existence of Elohim, the existence of the Spirits of Form.

When we observe our human development, we have to say to ourselves: We also evolve; when will we have reached the height that these spirits have now attained? We will be at that height when we have passed through the time of Jupiter, Venus, and Vulcan, and are within what comes then. If you add together what I presented in my *Occult Science*, then you have seven successive phases of development, one could also call them developmental spheres (see Plate 5 in the appendix). And the Spirits of Form, the Elohim, have entered the eighth sphere of development.

Saturn existence		1	5
Sun existence		2	6
Moon existence		3	7
Earth existence	(human)	4	8 (Elohim)
Jupiter existence		5	
Venus existence		6	
Vulcan existence		7	
	(human)	8	

This is what characterizes the circumstance of the Elohim. When the Earth was created, they were at the stage which will characterize us human beings on Vulcan. They will ascend into the eighth sphere. Now the great question, the great cosmic question was: How is it, or how was it, for the human being during this Earth existence? You see, the human being was able to remain a member in the development of the Elohim, just as he had been before. The Elohim developed through Saturn, Sun, and Moon existence as far as the stage I have now described for you. There, they carried, in a way, the human being in their womb, as you will find described in my *Occult Science*. But everything I described there was dormant in the womb of the Elohim. It is, indeed, described as if I were to describe the liver in its development. If one describes its stages, then it rests in the womb of the human being. So the entire development of the human being that I described rested in the womb of the Elohim.

When the Earth then came into existence, there was the question: Will human beings simply remain a dependent part of the great organism that ascended to its eighth sphere, in the great cosmic organism of the Elohim, or will they develop themselves toward freedom, will they become independent? This question, Will human beings become independent? was decided through a very specific cosmic deed. As regards our will system on the soul level, and our metabolic-limb system on the physical level, we are, indeed, parts of the Elohim; there we are asleep. There we are not separated out. We are separated out as regards our head organization.

And how did this separation occur? This separation occurred through the fact that certain spiritual beings, who, had they developed normally, would also have become Elohim, did not become Elohim, but instead remained back at the level of Archai or Archangeloi. So we can say that these are beings who, had they developed normally, would have been able to be Elohim. But they did not stride forward normally; they remained behind. If we regard them today from an occult perspective, they belong to the same sphere as the Angels or the Archangels or the Archai; but they are not of the same nature as the Angels or the Archangels or the Archai; rather, they are actually of the same nature as the Elohim, as the Spirits of Form, only they remained behind in their development and thus joined the host of Angels and Archangels, making themselves known in that same sphere, and therefore their effectiveness had to limit itself to work not on the entire human being, on what the human being had to achieve primarily on the earth, that is, the metabolic-limb system, but instead they work on the head organization of the human being. So that we can say: With regard to the head organization of the human being—if I draw this here as the opposite pole of the will system, of the metabolic-limb system (see Plate 6 in the appendix, pink)—there the great cosmic organism of the Elohim is not at work; instead, what is at work are the Elohim that remained behind, which I will draw like this (yellow). Inside of this sphere, the Angeloi, Archangeloi, and Archai are at work. These beings, these Elohim that remained behind are actually the opponents of the other Elohim. The other Elohim cut the human being off from themselves; but they could not have given him his freedom, because they influenced the entire human being. In comparison, those Spirits of Form who remained behind limited themselves to the head, and thereby they gave the human being reason, understanding. These are, essentially, the luciferic spirits. They are, as you can now see in this image, providers of will at a lower level. The Elohim give will to the entire human being; the luciferic spirits, on the other hand, give the head its will. Otherwise, the head would be permeated only by ideas without will. Ideas become rational only because they are permeated by will and gain the capacity for judgment. This stems from these spirits.

Perhaps you can see from this depiction, again from a certain perspective, how one ought not to apply Philistine concepts when considering cosmic polarities. One should not merely look at the luciferic beings with disdain, if I may put it like this; rather, one must be clear: these are spirits of a much higher order than human beings. Fundamentally, they are not adversaries of the human being, they are adversaries of the Elohim because they remained behind and they limit themselves to the human head. That is what we must take into account here.

If you now imagine what these spirits would accomplish if they had free reign over human evolution, then you will arrive at the following: You will say to yourself: Indeed, when the earth came into being, the Elohim ascended to their grandeur, the others remained behind at an earlier level of development; they are the bearers of what is primarily impressed upon the human being from the past, from Saturn, Sun, and Moon existence, the bearers of what is to be placed into the human being from the sublime past, which we underwent in the three previous metamorphoses of evolution.

Because they remained behind, opposing what the Elohim intended for human beings of the Earth, we can also characterize them in relation to the human being by saying: These spirits, who are actually Spirits of Form, but who meet us in the spiritual world among the host of Angels, Archangels, and Archai, these spirits impress upon the human being everything which would like to prevent him from descending into full Earth existence. They want to keep him above the realm of the minerals. More than anything, they would like to have the human being experience only what exists in sprouting plant life, in animal life, in human life itself. But they do not want to let him descend to the dead mineral world. And, most especially, these spirits have no inclination whatsoever to convey to humanity anything related to our technology. They are, in a way, angry at it. They want to keep the human being in a spiritual sphere, they do not want to allow the human being to descend to the earthly. That is why they are also opponents of the Elohim, because the Elohim, who solidified the human being out of the dust of the earth, as the Bible puts it, pulled him down into the mineral realm. To that he admittedly owes his freedom. But freedom, freedom which the human being should experience in the earthly world, is of no concern whatsoever for the spirits who wanted to keep the human being free from the earthly.

Now, human beings have, in a sense, been placed into the earthly mineral world by the Elohim. But thereby, other spirits in turn received access. Now pay attention to the difference between the spirits I just spoke of and the spirits I shall now speak about. Those about whom I just spoke are in the sphere where the Angels, Archangels, Archai exist. We find them among the host of these spirits, and it is they who bear mobility into the human head, bear mobile rationality, activity of fantasy, artistic activity, and so forth. But because the human being had been pushed down into the mineral realm, the Elohim gave him an independence, but an independence which was not a full independence—for he experiences it while asleep in his will and in his metabolic-limb system, thereby other spirits gained access. These other spirits sneak, so to speak, into evolution. The spirits of which I spoke were present during evolution, they remained behind; they were unable to participate in it, but are Elohim who remained behind; they were with the Elohim in the cosmos and only do not want to let the human being descend entirely to the Earth. But he did descend through the Elohim. Now other spirits come from elsewhere. We find them when we direct our occult sight at the host of Cherubim, Seraphim, and Thrones. Among the spirits who actually belong to this rank, there were also certain ones who remained behind. They did not enter into this host but became Spirits of Wisdom. These spiritual beings show themselves in a way which can be described like this: they actually want to start an entirely new creation on the Earth; they would really like to conserve the human being. In the same way that he is incarnated in the mineral realm because of the Elohim, they would like to take him as a beginning and lead evolution forward from this beginning. They want to extinguish the entire past: Never mind the past—they say—that's none of our business; there was a time when the human being descended into the mineral realm, well—let's tear him away from the Elohim, the Elohim don't need him; let's tear him away from the Elohim and let's start a new evolution. Let's have him be the starting point so that he lives on and on!

These are the ahrimanic beings. These ahrimanic beings want to extinguish the entire past and want to allot to human beings only that which he achieved directly on the Earth.

You see how the Elohim exist in the middle. The Elohim would like to connect the past with the future. The spirits I depicted earlier want to penetrate the human being and his lofty past. The other spirits would like to extinguish the entire past, to take away from the Elohim what man is as a being created from the dust of the earth and to make a new beginning, to make evolution begin with the Earth. Away with this "balloon" of the cosmos, with Saturn, Sun, and Moon; none of that is to have any meaning for the human being. A new evolution is to start with the Earth; it should be a new Saturn, then comes the Sun, and so forth. That is the ideal of these other beings. They storm into the subconscious of human beings, into the life of will, the life of the metabolic-limb system, there they storm in. Among spiritual beings, it is they who want to teach human beings a special interest in the mineral-material element, who want to teach human beings an interest for all that is, for example, externally machine-like, mechanical. Most of all they would like to destroy what the Earth retained from Old Moon, would like for the animal world to disappear, for the physical human world to disappear, for the plant world to disappear, for only the *physical* laws of the mineral world to remain, and, especially, for human beings to be removed from the Earth; and they would like to create a new Saturn out of machines, a new world made of all sorts of machines. That is how the world is to continue. This is actually their ideal. It is their ideal to turn everything in the realm of external science into matter, to mechanize everything. In the realm of religion, we can detect these two opposites.

In past ages—you know this from other lectures[†] which I also presented here—human beings were more vulnerable to the first group of spirits, which affect the head. Thus, you still find in Plato[†] that when speaking of the eternal aspect of the human soul, one spoke of the *pre-birth* existence, of what the human being actually remembered of the previous existence. This ceases to be the case the further we get into the Middle Ages, until the Church entirely forbids the belief in pre-existence; and today the belief in the pre-existence of the human being is considered heretical by the Church. Thus, there is, on the one hand, the inclination to the knowledge of pre-existence; on the other hand, the ahrimanized Church, which sees the life of the human being as continuing after death, and then lets it be merely the result of what the human being is here on Earth.

There you have it as a creed: The human being will carry whatever he experiences here in the physical body onward through death. His soul will ever and again look back upon that. All of subsequent life is only the continuation of what was here between birth and death. That is exactly what the ahrimanic spirits want. These are precisely the important questions facing contemporary humanity: Will the ahrimanic belief continue to proliferate, as if there were only one life after death, or will the consciousness of pre-existence awaken again, and will pre-existence and post-existence then be connected by that which is the intermediate balance?

This is what spiritual science must seek, this Christ-principle, the equilibrium, the balance between the luciferic and the ahrimanic—on the one hand, pre-existence, and, on the other, post-existence. These are the important questions of the present time—that now, after the period in which humanity submitted to the ahrimanic belief in post-existence only, we once again include the consciousness, the realization of pre-existence, in order to arrive at a understanding of full humanity.

Lecture Fifteen

DORNACH, MARCH 13, 1921

FROM THE WHOLE depiction of anthroposophical spiritual science you can see the importance of understanding how different spiritual beings involve themselves—guiding, strengthening—in the various realms of existence. It is essential that, in the present time, humanity find its way to the recognition of how various realms of existence are guided, directed, and so forth, by individual spiritual beings. For, in recent times, our civilization has blurred this consciousness of concrete spirituality in existence. One talks easily about divinity pervading everything in general. But by speaking in generalities about the divine, one does not achieve the kind of understanding of the world that can then also be a proper foundation for life.

It is certainly correct that ultimately everything one perceives spiritually must tend toward unity. However, if one looks for unification, shall I say, too soon, then all true insights into the course of world events are blurred. That is why it is essential that the generalized, abstract talk about the divine be left behind and that one get to know the specific guiding beings in nature and history and so forth, as we have done often in the course of time. And from this point of view, I would like to draw your attention today to very important, meaningful foundations of our world constitution.

The day before yesterday I drew attention to how certain beings gather together in the world as if battling, as it were, for the formation, the whole enlivening of the human being. We again placed before our souls the truth, which for us is fundamentally an old truth, about the opposition between the luciferic and ahrimanic spiritual forces. Now, today we will look at the matter again from a different perspective.

Particularly characteristic of recent civilization, which is now stuck in such a catastrophic condition, which reveals such forces of decline, is the spread of rational thinking to all humanity. One really must gain some kind of insight into the entirely different soul state of humanity, also beyond civilized Europe, seven or eight centuries ago. What sets the tone today, what pervades the entire soul life of human beings today, and what will, from a certain perspective, increasingly pervade it, is rational thinking. Well, it is perhaps a matter of also connecting such an inward concept with something more externally concrete. For it is certainly good if one really grasps and penetrates external material existence from the perspective of the spirit also. At the foundation of our thinking are the purely mineral processes in this organism. Please understand me correctly:

The processes in us that actually denote humanity, the processes we have in common with animal nature, processes we share with plant nature, all this is indirectly, not directly, connected with the fact that in a more modern sense of human development, we are rationally thinking human beings. The fact that we also have within ourselves a solid mineral constitution enables us to think rationally.

When we look at the kingdoms of nature in the universe, we have to say that they are out there and they are also in us. Let us look first at the realm of warmth phenomena, meaning, the warmth ether.[†] We bear the effect of this warmth ether within ourselves. We bear it within our blood. The effectiveness of our blood consists essentially in our conducting warmth processes, by means of the blood as bearer of warmth processes, into our entire organism. Rational thinking is not based on all that takes place in the realm of warmth in this way. So when we look out at the warmth processes in the cosmos, we can say: These warmth processes also take place within our skin; but what meets us through the warmth processes of the cosmos, what most especially meets someone who observes the cosmos in the condition during which it initially shows only warmth processes, all that exists out there during the Saturn condition, this represents in the cosmos nothing of which we can say, it stimulates rational thinking in us.

Nor does our rational thinking depend on what happens in us when we breathe, when we process the air in our organism. If we consider the realm of the air, then we find that there are also processes in this realm which continue in our breathing process. But everything, too, which we find represented in the realm of the air, all this also has nothing directly to do with our rational thinking.

For the third realm, we can look at that of the appearance of water. We see the processes of the liquid realm out in the cosmos. These, too, continue their activity in our metabolism, insofar as it is active in liquid form. Out in nature we see circulation of liquids; in ourselves, we also see a sort of circulation of liquids. All this, which takes place in us in this way, again has nothing to do with our intellectual thinking. But if we look out into the cosmos and see that water densifies into ice, that certain mineral substances are deposited as sediments, that rocks are formed, that crystals are formed, in short, when we consider the mineral processes of the solids out in the cosmos in their correspondence within the boundaries of our organism, then, what takes place there as mineral processes is related to what ultimately peaks, culminates in our rational thinking.

Thus, as human beings we are integrated into the cosmos in these different realms. But if we were merely integrated into these different realms without being taken up to a greater extent by the mineral realm, by those forces which we see before us out in the world in crystallization, in the depositing of salt and so forth, then we would not be the thinking beings we have been since the middle of the fifteenth century. That, after all, is a fact, that since the middle of the fifteenth century, this working of the mineral forces in the human organism has become decisive, dominant. Before that, other forces, forces of water, forces of air, and so forth, were the dominant element at work in man. But that is also why rational thinking was not the especially significant element in human activity.

Now, in everything which surrounds us in the various realms in which we live, the solid earthly realm, the watery-fluid realm, the airy realm, the realm of warmth—for now, we will refrain from considering the higher kinds of ether—in all these, divine spiritual beings are also at work. These realms do not consist only of what we call material world forces, material world entities; rather, all these realms are permeated by various spiritual beings. Let us then make a schematic drawing of something that can illustrate an important fact about our connection to the world.

Let us imagine that here I would schematically draw the realm of the mineral-earthly (see Plate 7 in the appendix, light); then here I would characterize the watery realm (red); here I would characterize the airy realm (blue), and then the realm of the warmth ether (red-violet).

Now the peculiar thing is that all the spiritual beings which the pre-Christian time, mainly pre-Christian Judaism, imagined as existing under the guidance of Yahweh, or Jehovah, in other words, everything which was seen by the Hebrew initiates as belonging to the realm of Yahweh or Jehovah, essentially spread its dominion across the first three realms—also across others, but of these four, across the first three. So that if I were to draw the realms which through the rule of Yahweh spanned the world, I would have to say, it is this realm (the upper three in the drawing). It really is so that the rule of Yahweh spans all that is in the realm of nature which we have enumerated, with the exception of the mineral-physical realm. Thus, you must be clear, when God is mentioned in the ancient Jewish scriptures, then mention is always made only of the Yahweh-realm itself in relation to the warmth ether, the being of air, the being of water; and this fundamental truth was indicated—it was a profound truth of initiation in the pre-Christian era—in a very spiritual way already in the story of creation. It is brought to expression clearly, one only need understand the meaning of the Bible correctly; Yahweh went, in a manner of speaking, to the earth and created the human being out of the dust of the earth. He took that which was not his own realm to create the outer form of the human being. The Bible actually expresses this clearly. As already mentioned, in pre-Christian Jewish initiation science, this was an initiation truth, that Yahweh did not form the outer human being out of the realms he ruled over; instead, he went to the earth and out of the dust of the earth, which was foreign to him, he formed the human sheath, which could not come out of his realm. Then he breathed what he gave of himself, the animalistic soul, the *Nephesch.*[†] That is what he gave of himself, that came out of the three realms he ruled over. It is certainly the case that superficial Bible researchers actually don't usually understand what is in the Bible. The Bible—one who understands it will see this—speaks with great precision, and one really has to take its sentences very precisely. Yahweh created the human being out of the dust of the earth, meaning, out of the mineral realm which was foreign to him, and he gave him the breath of the soul out of his own realm. Thus, what lives in the human being as the outpouring of Yahweh is indicated by Yahweh's breathing the living breath into the human being.

Now, the human being continued to develop, and he developed an element foreign to Yahweh by continuing to develop with the mineral realm, which then, in more recent times, meaning since the fifth post-Atlantean epoch, gave rise to that realm which has become particularly dominant because it formed the basis for his rational culture. Thus, we can say: As long as rational culture did not dominate human beings, they could still be ruled over by a reign such as Yahweh's. But then, from the time of the founding of Christianity until the beginning of the fifth post-Atlantean epoch, the mineral nature asserted itself. Then humanity had to be helped, in a way, from a different side. And then you can also see how necessary the Christ-impulse became for humanity at the time when mineral nature became essential. The old Yahweh-, or Jehovah-impulse, was not sufficient anymore.

Now hold what I have just told you side by side with certain facts. Consider the fact that the human being would not think rationally if he were only subject to Yahweh-nature, which has no influence on his mineral nature. That is why, if we want to give preference to Yahweh's activity in the human being, we cannot look at what exists in our rational culture, but rather, we ought to go only up to that which expresses itself in our dreams. The content of our dreams, that which does not reach the comprehension of our soul life in sharply contoured rational concepts, that is the life of Yahweh in us. Everything which moves in the liquid element, including what is more phantasy-filled, which could be compared externally with the influence of the moon on the human being, this is Yahweh-nature within the human being. What opposes Yahweh-nature is sharp thinking. But for that, the human being can thank the deposits of salt which work as mineral activity in him.

Now, consider that basically historical development shows that the old Yahweh religion lost its meaning with the Mystery of Golgotha. For one thing, its meaning was lost because the human being entered into a phase of development in which his mineral nature became dominant. When the Mystery of Golgotha then took place, enough of the ancient dream wisdom remained so that the Mystery of Golgotha could be understood through this ancient dream wisdom. And those who transcended this ancient dream wisdom, who already had attained something of intellectual culture through all manner of initiations, as Saul-Paul had, they needed a particular influence, such as met Paul through the event of Damascus, in order to understand the Mystery of Golgotha. The Christian tradition tells of how Saul-Paul, who in a certain sense had been initiated into the Hebrew mysteries before the Mystery of Golgotha, had to be moved by knowledge that did not work by means of the sharp contours of the intellect, but rather one that flourished in the blurred elements of dreaminess. There Paul experienced the certainty that the Christ had been present in Jesus through the Mystery of Golgotha. With the ancient dream wisdom, one could definitely still understand something of the Event of Golgotha, and by being subject to a particular influence and transported into that region, as was the case with Paul, one could understand the Event of Golgotha.

Well, the ancient dream wisdom diminished more and more. It remained only in human dreams and is to be found there in full decadence. And when the fifteenth century arrived, European civilization became ever more dependent on intellectual culture, and under the influence of this intellectual culture, modern science emerged.

Now, please consider the following: The old Yahweh religion must not only be understood in terms of the outer words; that would be a materialistic conception of religion; one must understand it in its inner spirit. It appears to us historically in such a way that the Yahweh-God is the God of one Folk. Beyond the border of the Jewish folk, the Yahweh-God is no longer the Yahweh-God. And this is the essence of the Yahweh-God, that he does not embrace all of humanity, but rather he embraces a part of humanity. Fundamentally, this perception of God has remained until our time, and during the World War one could especially see how again each folk spoke of how divine providence, or some even said the Christ, helped them. In a way, each folk wanted to march against the others under the leadership of Christ. But by calling something "Christ," the Christ is not yet met; rather, the Christ is met only if one approaches in one's whole feeling that being which has the Christ-nature. One can say a thousand times: I want to fight in the name of Christ—if one fights only for one nation, then one simply gives the being of which one speaks a false name; one says Christ and means the Yahweh-God. And within this catastrophe of war, all nations fell back into the Yahweh-Religion. But so many Yahwehs were present. Each nation honored a God who, in character, was actually Yahweh. The Christ actually disappeared completely from the consciousness of the people. One could see, in these catastrophic events, how the Christ disappeared completely from the consciousness of the people.

But we can also see this in other ways. The entire scientific culture has now indeed arisen. How far does this modern scientific culture extend? Fundamentally, only up to the mineral-physical. Just think of how extremely uncomfortable modern scientists become if one expects them to talk of something other than the mineral-physical. As soon as there is talk about anything that includes a principle of life, modern scientists demand that one should just explain the mineral, chemical processes within what lives; one simply does not consider actual life itself, not to speak of the soul and so forth. Thus, this modern science developed entirely within what was not embraced in the Yahweh religion. This modern science developed entirely within the element of the mineral-physical life which was an element alien to Yahweh. To become an element in civilization, this science is entirely dependent on receiving divine spirituality from a different side.

Within ancient Judaism, when people mentioned any kind of insight, it was a dreamy insight. The prophets, who had the highest insights, are presented to you as bearers of prophetic dreams. That is all connected to the matter at hand. Out of this dream wisdom, one was also still able to understand the Mystery of Golgotha. But the dream wisdom waned. The Mystery of Golgotha was, indeed, still handed down historically; it was talked about in traditional church communities, but actual understanding could not be found there. In contrast, modern science arose in an essentially godless, spiritless element, in the element alien to Yahweh, and—because comprehension did not yet spread over the Christ-element—in the mineral-physical element alien to the spirit.

This science must first be permeated again by spirituality right down into its individual particles. It is spiritless. It is spiritless because it can no longer be Yahweh-like. External culture attempted to continue with something religious by giving Yahweh the name of Christ during the catastrophe of war. It was continued, however, through a kind of religious counterfeiting. But science turned away entirely from spirit; it gives only descriptions of the physical-sensory because one hasn't yet attained to an understanding of the Christ, and one holds up the ancient Yahweh understanding most when one rages against the other, as happened during the catastrophe of war, but not when examining nature. There we have a spiritless science, an intellectually spiritless science. Thus, we are surrounded by a realm in which what is Yahweh-like or Jehovah-like reigns. That permeates us. But we don't realize it anymore because it permeates us mainly in conditions which are conditions of sleep. If we were to enter into the element of sleep and suddenly awaken outside of our body, then we would perceive the spirit-nature under Yahweh's guidance very clearly; then, in a way, dreams would appear to us surging on the Yahweh-ocean, from out of the element of Yahweh.

Also in our will, in relation to which, as I have often explained to you, we sleep while awake, Yahweh-nature reigns. Yahweh-nature reigns in the entire human metabolism. Insofar as feelings rise up out of metabolism to infiltrate the rhythmic system, waves arise out of the Yahweh-ocean, just as dreams, on the other side, arouse certain feelings.[†] However, there where we live in the realm which becomes understandable for us only through the intellect, through reason, Yahweh is not involved. When the moon slowly bathes everything in a uniformly dreamy light and this dreamy light floods out over everything, then one could say that the human being has spread the

Yahweh-character across the realms of the world. When the sun shines brightly upon the rocks, when it touches upon the various objects and gives them sharp contours so that we are inclined to grasp them with our reason, then it is the sun-nature, which is not Yahweh-nature, expressing itself. We can only spiritualize the world if we can impart the Christ-being to it, if we can see into this world such that we can see the Christ-being in it. Modern science did not have an eye for this Christ-being and observed whatever is not Yahweh-like, what is instead understood only as shining in the sun and comprehensible in sharp intellectual contours, without spirit.

That is the deeper connection. And what sort of a realm is it that faces us in this mineral realm? I spoke about it the day before yesterday, that, on the one hand, the luciferic beings appeared within the Yahweh-realm because they are stuck at a previous stage of development. If we are present in Yahweh's realm, for example, in sleep, then the luciferic beings become noticeable in our feelings, in our will impulses. The realm which we are to master with our intellect is expanded around us as the mineral realm. That is the realm that is alien to Yahweh, that is the realm into which those beings which belong to the ahrimanic realm penetrated. But the ahrimanic beings, they penetrated because Yahweh could not, so to speak, keep them away (see Plate 7 in the appendix, green). And by expanding our view to include this realm, we are in danger, every minute, of being surprised and confused in this realm by the ahrimanic beings. These ahrimanic beings—I did try to capture this image in the Group Statue which is to stand in our Goetheanum eventually—can only be at home in realms surrounding us within the mineral world. These ahrimanic beings are mainly intellectually gifted beings. The Mephistophelian figure which you see under the wooden Group, this Mephistophelian-ahrimanic figure is profoundly clever, entirely saturated by intellect, but with something that is actually Yahweh-like, something that usually exists in the human metabolism insofar as it does not deposit salt nor is at all mineral, but exists rather as liquid nature, in the exchange of liquids, in the metamorphosis of liquids, with everything that exists in our breathing, in our warmth condition—with all this the ahrimanic has no direct relationship.

However, it strives to enter into it. The human being was created out of the dust of the earth. What is of a mineral nature there is actually part of ahriman's realm. That is where Ahriman can enter, where he feels well. And he also feels well when he can penetrate us in relation to all that is mineral. You secrete salt, which is actually how you can think; through this secretion of salt, in fact through everything which asserts itself as mineral process in you, that is what enables you to be a thinking being. Into this realm Ahriman wants to enter.

But he actually has a real relationship only to this mineral realm. And that is why he battles for also acquiring his share of the blood, the breathing, metabolism. This he can do only by cultivating certain characteristics in the human soul, by cultivating, for example, a very particular tendency toward dry intellect that wants to be absorbed in materialism, toward that aspect of the intellect which mocks any truths imbued with feeling, where he can thus cultivate in the human soul the arrogance of the intellect. Then he appropriates human blood, human breathing, human metabolism for himself, and he can, in a way, scurry out of the salty, mineral element into the blood, into breathing.

That is the battle fought by Ahriman in the world through the human being. In that Yahweh went to the earth and created the human being out of the earth, in order to advance the human being further than he would have been able to in his own realm, he created him out of an element alien to himself and only blew in, injected, his own element. But thereby Yahweh took as aid something to which the ahrimanic beings had access. Thereby Yahweh became intertwined in this battle in Earth development against the ahrimanic element which, with the aid of the human being, wants, by means of the detour through the mineral process, to acquire the world for itself.

Fundamentally, the ahrimanic beings accomplished much in this area. For when the human being is born or received into physical existence, he comes down, descends out of spirit-soul worlds, surrounds himself with physical matter. But the way civilization currently exists in accordance with the habits of traditional confessions, one would like to forget this pre-birth existence in the spirit-soul realm. One would not like to admit this; one would, in a way, like to eliminate pre-birth being from human existence. Pre-existence was, more and more, declared heretical by traditional confessions. One wants to limit oneself to having the human being begin with physical birth or conception, and then to connect to it whatever lies beyond death. If this belief in only a post-mortem condition, only an after-death condition, were never pushed back, if it were to take hold of humanity exclusively, then the ahrimanic beings would have won. For, if the human being were only to consider what he experiences of his earthly nature between birth and death, and only appreciate a continuation of life after death without looking at a past life prior to birth, then the ahrimanic aspect of the mineral process would actually, gradually seize what is human. Everything of a Yahweh-nature, which came over from Saturn, Sun, and Moon, would be thrown away from earthly development, and a new creation, one which would, however, deny all that preceded it, would begin with the Earth.

That is why it is so important that this view which denies pre-existence is fought as energetically as possible. The human being must recognize that he was before he was born or conceived in physical existence. He must—in reverence and devotion—receive what the divine spiritual world imparted to him before this physical-earthly existence. By adding recognition of pre-birth to his belief in the afterlife, he prepares his soul so that it cannot be gnawed at by Ahriman.

Thus it is necessary—this follows from these discussions—and I have already indicated this, that we do gradually include in language a word which we do not have. Just as we speak of immortality when we think of the end of our physical existence, so we must also learn to speak of unbornness. For just as we are immortal, we are also, in reality, unborn as human beings. But just search in civilized languages for a viable word meaning "unborn"! "Immortal" you will find everywhere, but "unborn" you will not find. We need the word "unborn." It must be just as viable in civilized languages as the word "immortal," which these languages already have. That is how the ahrimanization of modern civilization is revealed. Our not having a word for not-yet-born is one of the most important symptoms for the ahrimanization of modern civilization. For we perish from the earth at death just as little as we only originate at birth or conception. We need a word that clearly indicates pre-existence. One may on no account underestimate the meaning that lies in the word.

You may think ever so much, ever so cleverly, there is something in you which simply is intellectual in the human being. At the moment when thought imprints itself into word, even if the word as such is only thought, as in meditation, at that moment the word is imprinted into the ether of the world. The thought as such does not imprint itself into the world ether, or we would never be able to become free beings through pure thinking. For we are bound at the very moment that something is imprinted. It is not through the word that we are free but through pure thinking—you can find more about this in my *Philosophy of Freedom*—but the word imprints itself into the world ether.

Now consider: for initiation science, it is simply a fact today that thereby, because the civilized languages have no viable word for unbornness, this unbornness, which is of such importance for humanity, does not in any way imprint itself on any part of the world ether. Everything, however, related to the important words concerning the human being in his childhood, his youth, which is imprinted on the world ether, signifies a dreadful fright for the ahrimanic powers. Immortality, imprinted in the world ether, can actually be tolerated quite well by the ahrimanic powers, for immortality means that they begin a new creation and want to go forth with the human being. The ahrimanic beings, continually whizzing through the ether so as to play their games with the human being, are not irritated if all manner of announcements about immortality are made from the pulpits to be inscribed in the world ether. That makes the ahrimanic beings feel good. But it is a dreadful fright for them when they find the word "unbornness" imprinted on the world ether. Then the light within which they move is entirely snuffed out. Then they can't continue, they lose their orientation, they feel as if they're in an abyss, as if they've lost their grounding. And from that you can see that it is an ahrimanic endeavor to prevent humanity from speaking of unbornness. No matter how paradoxical it may appear to modern humanity to speak of such things, modern civilization needs to speak about them. Just as the meteorologist describes the wind, or as one describes the gulf stream in describing the earth, in the same way there must be descriptions of what happens spiritually, the way the ahrimanic beings traverse our environment, how they feel good in the presence of everything concerning death and dying, even if dying is negated; and how they are shocked into the terror of darkness when they come upon anything to do with unbornness, with growth and thriving. And we must learn to speak of these things scientifically, the way that modern science speaks of the mineral-physical realm which has been abandoned by Jehovah.

At bottom, we ourselves must take up nothing less than the battle against the ahrimanic powers. And, in the end, whether people know it or not, the extensive arguments against anthroposophically oriented spiritual science are, at the same time, Ahriman's battle against that which humanity needs and which must be stressed more and more intensively by anthroposophically oriented spiritual science.

If one experiences something like the most recent attacks, then one sees palpably: these people don't touch on spiritual science itself. I have spoken to you about the particularly ugly, nefarious attack now taking place again in Germany, wherein the "noble" *Frankfurter Zeitung* behaves in an especially shameful manner. To be sure, it did accept our rejoinder after having made its disgusting attack, but only in order to attach its own stupid remarks in an entire column. Such things can be traced back to those people who absolutely want the science of anthroposophy to disappear but are too lazy or too incapable to actually examine it.

Such people then resort to such attacks as are now surfacing in Germany, so as to cast doubt on whatever they cannot refute. If you connect these matters with the ahrimanic beings, then you will be able to see through things somewhat. Many people today who seem to be able to think very well have positions in scientific establishments. But why? Ahriman is invading the mineral world, so don't be surprised when these people develop quite a lot of intellect. It is Ahriman in them; and it is more comfortable to let Ahriman think in you than to think yourself. You can certainly also pass your exams more easily if you let Ahriman think in you. You can more easily become an assistant professor or university professor if you let Ahriman do the thinking at the podium instead of thinking yourself. And because so many people let Ahriman think in them, attacks naturally come from the ahrimanic side. Therefore, these matters certainly do have an inner spiritual connection which one must see through. That is why one ought not to be so foolish as to lay blame when we are compelled, again and again, to strike with quite sharp blows against that which wants to annihilate spiritual science down to its foundations.

Yesterday the course of lectures already began in Stuttgart; I myself will probably be speaking in Stuttgart, starting on the sixteenth, on a scientific theme,† namely mathematics, scientific experimental observation, and scientific results. These lectures, as well as those which will be given here starting April 3,† are meant to show how spiritual science can fructify science today. And it is precisely since we have been working in this direction that we find ever more attacks. But I hope that understanding will also grow for the need to prepare against what arises there; for this preparation also means, at the same time, a certain strengthening in the direction of anthroposophically oriented spiritual science. And this strengthening must happen. Within the world of our declining forces, all of this contributes to the ascending forces.

Lecture Sixteen

DORNACH, MARCH 27, 1921

A SIGNIFICANT CONTRAST exists between the Christmas thought and the Easter thought; and whoever is able to juxtapose the two thoughts, of which we have often spoken in our context, whoever is able to connect them with each other appropriately, so as to find an inwardly enlivening interaction—an interaction between the Christmas thought and the Easter thought—will be directed toward an inner experience which, in a certain sense, circumscribes the riddles of humanity in a comprehensive way.

The Christmas thought does, of course, point us toward birth. We know how through birth the eternal in the human being enters into the world from which the visible, sensory, bodily being of man has been taken. And if we approach the Christmas thought with this view, then it will appear to us as the thought which connects us to the suprasensory. Then it appears, in addition to everything else it conveys to us, in such a way that it points, so to speak, to the one pole of our being where we are related as sensory-physical beings to the spiritual-suprasensory. That is why the birth of the human being will never become comprehensible out of a science which only relies on observation of the sense-perceptible, physical world for its assumptions.

At the other pole of human experience lies the thought which underlies the festival of Easter, a thought which, in the course of Western development, increasingly became a thought that prepared the materialistic conception of the West. The Easter thought can be grasped initially in a more abstract way if one is clear about how the eternal, the immortal in the human being, which cannot be born, how the spiritual suprasensory element which descends from the spiritual world clothes itself in the human physical body. From the beginning of this physical existence—as I have explained here from various perspectives—this activity of the spirit in the physical body actually leads the physical body toward death, and with the thought of birth, the thought of death is simultaneously given.

I have indicated how the organization of man's head can only be understood if one knows: Fundamentally, there is a continual dying in the head; it can be fought only by the life forces in the rest of the human organism. And the moment the death forces, which are always present in the human being in the head and determine his thinking nature, gain the upper hand over man's transitory being—at that moment death sets in.

Thus, the thought of death is, in truth, only the other side of the thought of birth, and therefore the thought of death cannot come to expression in the Easter thought. At the time when Christianity still found its first form out of an Oriental outlook, we see how Pauline Christianity, above all else, does not direct humanity toward the death of Christ Jesus, but rather toward the resurrection, as indicated by this form of Christianity in Paul's powerful words:† "But if Christ be not risen, your faith is dead."

The resurrection, the triumph over death, the overcoming of death, that, above all, is what was present as the Easter thought in the first form of Christianity, when it was still shaped by the wisdom of the East. But we can also see how, on the other side, pictures appear in which Christ Jesus is portrayed as the Good Shepherd, who watches, so to speak, over the eternal concerns of the human being asleep in his temporal existence. We see everywhere that, fundamentally, early Christianity is directed toward the words in the Gospel:† "He whom you seek is not here." You must seek him, we may add, in the spiritual world; you may not seek him in the physical-sensory world. If you seek him in the physical-sensory world, then the only thing that can be said to you is: He whom you seek as a physical-sensory being, he is not to be found anymore in the physical-sensory world.

The grand, comprehensive wisdom, which in the first Christian centuries still attempted to penetrate the Mystery of Golgotha and everything that belongs to it, then immersed itself in the materialism of the West. During the first centuries, this materialism hadn't yet achieved a full breakthrough. It prepared itself slowly. One might say that the first materialistic impulses were still very weak and hardly noticeable; only much later did they change into what became ever more materialistic and permeated Western civilization more and more. The oriental idea of religion merged with the emerging Western idea about the state. In the fourth century, Christianity became the state religion,† meaning that something penetrated Christianity which can no longer be called religion.

Julian the Apostate,† who was not a Christian but was a religious human being, was unable to say yes, above all, to what happened to Christianity through Constantine. And so we see how at first very weakly, but yet already somewhat noticeably in the mixing of Christianity with declining Romanism, the materialism of the West throws out its first rays. It was also under this influence that the image of Christ Jesus, which at first did not even exist, which is definitely not part of the origin of Christianity, came into being: the image of Christ Jesus as the crucified, suffering Man of Sorrows, the one who passes away in pain under the weight of the unspeakable suffering inflicted on him.

With this, a break came into the entire view of the Christian world; for this image, which thence passed through the centuries—the pain-drenched Christ hanging on the cross—this is the Christ who can no longer be grasped as a spiritual being, but only as a bodily, corporeal being. And the more that the stigmata were impressed upon the human body, that the art of different ages succeeded in perfectly impressing the stigmata on the Redeemer hanging on the cross, the more were the seeds of materialistic Christianity sown. The Crucifix is the expression of the transition to Christian materialism. It is not a contradiction to acknowledge that in a great and powerful way the pain of the Redeemer was incarnated through art in its full depth and significance. Nevertheless, the truth is that this image of the Redeemer succumbing to pain on the cross bids farewell to a truly spiritual conception of Christianity.

The view of Christ as cosmic judge was later mixed into this conception of the man of suffering; the cosmic judge, whom we can see so magnificently in the Sixteen Chapel in Rome, is actually only another expression for Yahweh or Jehovah, for the Yahweh or Jehovah who has been transformed into the juridical element. The same spirit who caused the triumphant spirit, the victor over death to disappear from the picture of the grave out of which the Redeemer rises, over which the Redeemer triumphs—this same spirit declared, at the Eighth General Ecumenical Council of 869 in Constantinople, that the spirit was something one was not allowed to believe in, decreed that the human being was to be considered as consisting only of body and soul and that the spirit consisted of only a few characteristics which the soul bears.

As we watch spirituality being wafted away from the crucifix, as we feel in the physicality which represents only the pain-infused soul, without the spirit of the one who triumphs, without the spirit as the one who bears and also, at the same time, cares for humanity, we see how the Council's decision also struck the spirit from the human being.

And Good Friday and the Festival of Resurrection, Easter, were pushed together. In the days when people were not yet so dry and sober and meager in comprehension, the Good Friday festival became, in a certain sense, a festival in which the Easter thought was transformed in a thoroughly egotistical way. Wallowing in pain, immersing one's own soul lustfully in pain, feeling the bliss of pain, that was the Good Friday thought throughout the ages; it was, in a way, meant merely to provide the background for an Easter thought, a thought which humanity became less and less able to grasp in its true form. The self-same humanity that elevated to an article of faith the principle which states that man consists only of body and soul, that very same humanity demanded for its feeling only the dying Redeemer, demanded the counter-image of its own physical pain, so that it could have a background—though only in an external transition—in order to feel what was originally felt in an elemental way as the consciousness that the living spirit must always be victorious over everything that takes place in the physical body. One first needed the image of death by martyrdom in order to feel the actual Easter thought as a contrast.

One will have to feel ever more deeply how in this way the actual spirit vision and spirit perception disappeared from Western culture; and one will certainly look with wonder—and at the same time with the feeling of witnessing a certain tragedy—at all the artistic attempts to represent the Man of Sorrows on the cross. It is not enough to attempt to raise oneself up with a few hastily formed thoughts or with some interspersed perceptions to what our time needs. One must fully see through all that has been on a downward trajectory for a long time as regards spirituality in Western culture.

It is necessary today for that which belongs to the greatest in one field to be felt, at the same time, as something above which humanity must raise itself. But we need the Easter thought within our entire Western culture. In other words, we need to rise to the spirit again. What once emerged magnificently as the holy mystery of birth, the mystery of Christmas, eventually sank into those sentimentalities which were merely the opposite pole of materialistic development, into those sentimentalities which wallowed and wallowed in all sorts of songs about the little baby Jesus. It was a voluptuous wallowing in the sensation of the little child. Instead of perceiving the grand, mighty mystery of the penetration of a super-earthly spirit in the mystery of Christmas, the dry Philistine songs of the "baby Jesus" eventually prevailed and set the tone.

Characteristic of that development of Christianity which runs purely along the lines of reason—which up to this day has enabled certain representatives to say that the Son doesn't belong in the Gospels at all,[†] but only the Father belongs in the Gospels—is that this development retains the resurrection thought insofar as this thought is still intertwined with the thought of death, also for this Christianity. But characteristic is how in the form which I have just described the Good Friday thought moved into the foreground of modern development, and how the resurrection thought, the true Easter thought, gradually receded.

The Easter thought must be emphasized particularly in an age which ought to indicate that the human being must experience the resurrection of his being through the spirit. We need the Easter thought; we need a complete understanding of the Easter thought.

But for that, we must be clear that the Man of Sorrows is an expression for the Western advance of materialism, as is the merely judicial Judge of the World, on the other side. We need the Christ as a suprasensory being, as a being whose nature is beyond the earthly yet has been pulled into earthly development. We must penetrate with all human thinking to this Sun thought.

Just as we must see that the Christmas thought became something that, shall I say, dragged the greatest mystery into the trivial feeling of sentimentality, in just the same way, we must see how necessary it is to emphasize the Easter thought, so that something enters into human development which is not understandable based on earthly conditions, but becomes understandable on the basis of spiritual knowledge, of spiritual cognition.

Spiritual cognition must find its first great support in the resurrection thought, must also recognize in the human being that his eternal spirituality is unaffected by the bodily-physical nature, must see in the Pauline words, "But if Christ be not risen, your faith is dead," an affirmation—which in more recent times has to be gained by other more conscious means—an affirmation of what fundamentally constitutes the actual being of the Christ.

This is how we must again remember the Easter thought today. This is how the days during which we remember the Easter thought must again become an inner festival, a festival in which we celebrate, for ourselves, the victory of the spirit over corporeality. We must keep in view Jesus suffering on the cross, because we ought not be unhistorical; but, above the cross, the Victor who remains untouched by either birth or death, and who alone can direct our gaze upward to the eternal realms of the spiritual life, must appear to us. Only in this way will we approach the true essence of the Christ again.

Western humanity has drawn the Christ down to itself: drawn him down as a small child, drawn him down as the one who is preferably felt in death, in pain. I have often pointed out that an equal length of time exists *before* the Mystery of Golgotha from the time that Buddha uttered the words that death is evil and *after* the Mystery of Golgotha when the crucifix, the crucified one, appears and the gaze is directed toward death, which is perceived not as being evil, but rather as something which in reality has no existence.

But this perception, which still partakes of an oriental wisdom deeper than Buddhism, this perception underlies the other, which clings to the view of the Suffering One. We must rise not only in our thoughts—for they are miserly—but with the whole breadth of our feelings to the destiny of human conceptions of the Mystery of Golgotha in the course of the centuries. It must become clear to us that we must return to a pure, authentic understanding of the Mystery of Golgotha. We must bear in mind how even in ancient Judaism, Yahweh was not thought of as the universal judge in the judicial sense. The greatest dramatic representation of the religious feeling of ancient Judaism, the Book of Job, which represents Job's suffering, basically excludes any feeling of an external righteousness. Job is the suffering human being, the human being who sees what happens to him in the external world as destiny. Only gradually does the judicial concept of retribution move into the world order. But in a certain way, what we have as image in the altar of the Sistine Chapel by Michelangelo is indeed a revival of the Yahweh principle.

We, however, need the Christ, whom we can seek inwardly because when we seek him, he appears at once. We need the Christ, who moves into our will, who warms and fires our will, so that this will becomes strong for those deeds which are demanded of us for the evolution of humanity. We need that Christ whom we see not as the one who suffers, but the one who hovers above the cross and looks upon that which ends insubstantially on the cross. We need the strong consciousness of the eternity of the spirit.

We do not gain the strong consciousness of the eternity of the spirit if we lose ourselves in the image only of the crucifix. And when we see how the image of the crucifix eventually became increasingly the suffering one, the pained one, then we will see what kind of force this particular direction of human perception has gained. It is the aversion of humanity's gaze from actual spirituality and the turning toward the merely earthly-physical element. This is sometimes expressed in magnificent ways; but for those who, like Goethe, for example, have already felt something of the necessity of our civilization's penetration back to the spirit, for such people it always seemed like something with which they would actually not go along. Goethe did indeed express often enough[†] that the crucified Redeemer basically does not express what he feels about Christianity: the elevation of man to the spiritual.

It is necessary for the mood of both Good Friday and of Easter to be transformed, for the Good Friday mood to be formed into something which bears in itself the looking at the perishing Jesus and therewith feels fundamentally: this is only the other side of being born. Whoever does not see in being born at the same time what is dying, does not see completely. Whoever is able to feel in what appears in the mood of death on Good Friday that there he is given only one side of what it means to be human, which is the other pole of what is given through the arrival of the child at birth, will prepare himself properly for the actual mood of Easter, for that mood which can only consist in man's knowing: And whatever my human sheath, which is born, may be—the actual human being is unborn, just as he is eternal.

The actual human being must connect with what entered the world as the Christ, who cannot die, who sees something other than himself when he sees the Man of Sorrow on the cross. A feeling must arise about what actually happened since the end of the first century when the idea of the spirit was gradually lost to Western civilization. And it will be the universal Easter thought when a large enough number of people feel that the spirit must once again arise within modern civilization.

Outwardly, one will have to express this in such a way that man will not only want to investigate what is imposed on him, will not seek laws of nature or laws of history that are similar to laws of nature, but will desire knowledge of his own will, knowledge of his own freedom, will desire to feel the actual nature of his will, which carries him through the gates of death, but which must be looked at spiritually so that it can be seen in its true form.

How is the human being to gain the strength for the Whitsun thought, for the outpouring of the spirit, after the Eighth General Ecumenical Council in Constantinople dogmatically declared the

Whitsun thought to be a mere phrase? How is the human being to gain the strength for this Whitsun thought if he cannot penetrate to the Easter thought, to the true Easter thought, to the thought of the resurrection of the spirit! The human being must not be dazed by the image of the dying, suffering Savior. The human being must get to know the connection of pain with material existence.

That was a fundamental principle of the ancient wisdom which still came out of the instinctive foundations of human knowledge. We must once again strive to attain this knowledge through conscious cognition. But this was a fundamental principle, that the origin of pain is its connection to matter, that suffering comes from the connection of man with matter. It would be absurd, however, to believe that the Christ, because he passed through death as a divine-spiritual being, did not suffer pain. To explain the pain of the Mystery of Golgotha as mere semblance of pain would be unreal thinking. It must be thought of as real in the most significant sense, but it must not be thought of as its counter-image. Something of what we see when we place the Mystery of Golgotha before us as we survey the entire evolution of humanity must again be won.

When the image of the freest human being was to be presented to the ancient neophytes, when these neophytes had gone through various preliminary stages, when they had gone through all the exercises through which they could gain certain insights and which were presented to them dramatically in image form, then they were finally led before the image of man suffering completely in his physical body, in the red violet robe with the crown of thorns on his head, before the image of the Chrestos. And in contemplating this Chrestos, the soul was to gain those forces which make the human being into an actual human being. And the drops of blood on all the most important places of that old Chrestos came to meet the gaze of the neophyte and were meant to be there to eliminate the powerlessness and the human weakness and to raise the triumphant spirit out of the inner human being.

Contemplation of pain was to signify the resurrection of the spiritual being. The human being was to face, in the deepest sense, what can be expressed in simple words as: "You may owe your wants to various aspects of your life; but if you have attained insight into the spiritual connections, you owe that to your suffering, your pain. You owe it to the circumstance that you did not perish in your suffering and pain, but instead had the strength to lift yourself out of them." That is why, in the ancient mysteries, the image of the suffering Chrestos was replaced by the other image of the triumphant Christus, who gazes down upon the suffering Chrestos as on that which has been overcome.

The possibility of having the triumphant spiritual Christ before and in the soul, and especially in the will, must be found again. That is what we must face in the present and especially in what we want to do in this present time to bring about a wholesome, human future. But we will never be able to grasp this Easter thought, this true Easter thought, if we are not able to understand that we must look beyond the merely earthly into the cosmic if we want to speak of the Christ at all.

Recent thinking has turned the cosmos into a corpse for us. Today we behold the stars and the course of the stars and calculate all this. That is, we calculate something about the corpse of the world—and we don't see how the intentions of the cosmic spirit live in the life of the stars, in the course of the stars. The Christ descended into humanity so as to connect the human soul with the cosmic spirit. And only one who indicates that what appears as physical-sensory nature in the sun is the outer expression for the spirit of our world, the resurrected spirit of our world, can be a true herald of the Gospel of Christ Himself.

There must come to life something like the unity of the reflection of that which is world-spirit in the moon and that which this world-spirit itself is in the sun. The placing of the Easter Festival in the spring through the relationship of sun and moon must become alive again. We must be able to connect with that which the Easter Festival has determined for Earth evolution out of the cosmos itself. We must know that it was the most protective and the most awake spirits of the cosmos who, from this world clock whose hands for earthly existence are the sun and the moon, have made comprehensible the great, meaningful hour in world and human evolution in which the Resurrection is to be placed. We must learn from the spirit to feel the course of these two hands of sun and moon clock, just as we learn to understand the course of the hands of the clock for our physical affairs. We must connect the physical, earthly with the supra-physical, supra-earthly.

The Easter thought tolerates only interpretation stemming from the supra-earthly. For what happened at the Mystery of Golgotha, insofar as it is the mystery of Resurrection, was something which is distinct from the rest of human affairs. The other affairs of mankind take place on the earth very differently from what happened at the Mystery of Golgotha. The earth absorbed cosmic forces, and from what it then itself became, human forces of will sprout in human metabolism. But when the Mystery of Golgotha had taken place, a new confluence of the will penetrated into earthly events. Something that was a cosmic event took place on the earth, something for which the earth was merely the stage. The human being was once again connected to the cosmos. That is what has to be understood, and this understanding begins to provide the Easter thought its full scope. Man was again connected with the cosmos.

This is what must be understood, and only the understanding of it gives the Easter thought its full scope. That is why not only the image of the crucifix must stand before our souls. And if art had produced the most beautiful, the greatest, the most meaningful, the most sublime image of the crucifix—the thought must arise: "The One Whom you seek, He is not here." The one who must appear to you above the cross is the one who is now here, and out of the spirit, for the spirit, awakening the spirit, he speaks to you.

This is what must enter into the evolution of humanity as the Easter thought; the human heart and human understanding must raise themselves to this. We, in our time, are not merely called upon to admire antiquity. We are called upon not only to be able to enter more deeply, to immerse ourselves, into what was created. We must become new creators. Even if the cross itself has been made beautiful by what the artists have done with it, we ought not to leave it at that. We must hear the words of the spiritual beings who call to us when we seek them in death and suffering: The One Whom you seek, He is no longer here! – And so we must seek the one who is here.

We must understand how to turn at Easter toward the spirit which alone can be given us in the image of the Resurrection. Then we will be able to progress in the right way from the mood of the suffering of Good Friday to the spiritual mood of Easter Day. Then, too, we will be able to find in this mood of Easter Day that which our will must receive so that, in the face of the forces of decline, we become active through mankind's forces of resurrection. And we need such forces as can participate in this. And at the moment when we understand the resurrection thought of Easter in the right way, the Easter thought will become warm and illuminating, and will kindle the force in us which we need for the future evolution of mankind.

Lecture Seventeen

DORNACH, MARCH 28, 1921

Today, it is of special importance to seek out the viewpoints of the various ancient spiritual seekers, not only because malicious and amateurish enemies of spiritual science, as it is represented here, charge us with simply having adopted all manner of things from ancient times, but, above all, because recognition of what can presently be discovered from original spiritual sources becomes comprehensible if one associates it with the forces humanity possessed inwardly in ancient times, with the different means of seeking spiritual knowledge in more ancient, instinctive ages of human evolution. And in order to draw your attention to something like this, I would like to talk today about a certain mix-up that has frequently taken place in relation to Christ Jesus and one of his contemporaries, Apollonius of Tyana.[†] In a certain way, the two have been mixed up, and there are even attempts to compare in an unhistorical way the life of Apollonius of Tyana with the life of Christ Jesus. When one compares Apollonius of Tyana with Christ Jesus, many external similarities in their biographies do indeed appear. Above all, we know that narratives about Christ Jesus in the Gospels relate events which today fall under the category of miracles, and that biographers of Apollonius of Tyana also relate all sorts of stories about miracles accomplished by this Apollonius. The manner in which such things are related today indicates nothing other than that people have a completely amateurish understanding of the development of humanity. What is related there as the healing of illnesses and other similar things, which in the Gospels are called signs, simply corresponds to a completely different stage of humanity's development from the one in which we live today. In the course of time, the psychic influence of one human being on another—indeed, even the psychic influence of the human being on his inanimate environment—retreated for ordinary consciousness. And if, then, such things relating to the time before the beginning of our Christian era are described for us, whoever has real inner knowledge of such things knows that what someone experienced in those times was different from what can happen in a similar way today. Today, it is necessary to start with different pre-conditions, pre-conditions which are to be created again through spiritual-scientific knowledge. And if we want to understand the Gospels properly, then we definitely should not consider stories about miracles as the main aspect, but we must be clear that stories about miracles were natural for a person of high moral standing in the times in question here. One simply did not assume that this would be different in a person such as, say, Jesus of Nazareth, in whom the Christ lived, or a person such as Apollonius of Tyana.

Let us understand each other well in this; what I want to say is that in relation to such a man one speaks of what one calls miracles; this is self-evident. Nothing unusual is meant by such stories. And when contemporary theology strives to infer the divinity of Christ Jesus most especially from the fact that he wrought miracles, then this theology simple shows nothing other than that it does not stand on a Christian standpoint, not to mention the fact that such a view is unhistorical. In the case of Christ Jesus, it is never a matter of accomplishing miracles, but always a matter of what is explained in relation to the description of the miracles. It is always the case that attention is drawn to how Christ Jesus worked specifically out of the strength of his I, whereas earlier humanity, when it wanted to accomplish great deeds, worked with a lesser strength of the I. In the same way, we would not understand the Lord's Prayer if we were to explain it by claiming that we find its individual sentences among an earlier humanity and that, therefore, it must be ancient. Whoever compares the earlier form of these sentences in the Lord's Prayer with the Lord's Prayer itself will realize that the Lord's Prayer was everywhere intended to carry over what in earlier times was never said with a direction toward the I, to then say it with a direction toward the I.

Thus, we should not somehow search for similarities which occur in relation to this biographical moment for Christ Jesus. It is, after all, also natural that, in a certain way, similar descriptions will then surface when it is a matter of carrying out miracles, that is, what one *now* calls miracles. We must look at something quite different if we want to be clear about how a figure like Apollonius of Tyana relates to Christ Jesus. The following must then be mentioned.

Indeed, it is related about Apollonius of Tyana how already in childhood, he showed great facility, how he grew up with this great facility, how he took part in the most excellent teachings which could be given at that time, such as, for example, the teachings that grew out of the School of Pythagoras. Then, however, it is also described how Apollonius of Tyana, specifically in order to gain knowledge, undertook great journeys, and about his travels we are told that, at first, they did not take him far, but then came the long journey he made to the sages of India. We are told how he learned to revere and admire the Indian sages, how through them he penetrated to certain sources of knowledge. We are then told how he returned, how, inspired by what he had seen among these Indian sages, he then taught again in southern Europe in the most manifold ways. But we are also then told how he went to Egypt, at first to northern Egypt, where he absorbed what he could absorb there, and how this seemed poor, very poor in comparison to the wonderful sagacity he had found amongst the Indians. Then we are told how he travelled up the Nile to its source, but also to the site of the so-called Gymnosophists;† this was a community of those sages who had the greatest reputation in that time, apart from the Brahmins, the Indian sages. Then, however, it is also related that Apollonius of Tyana was already so saturated with Indian wisdom that he could distinguish between it and the lesser Egyptian Gymnosophists. And then we are told how he once again returned, how he then made his various wonderful journeys to Rome, where he was persecuted and imprisoned, and so forth.

What is interesting for us is mainly the fact that these long journeys are attributed to Apollonius of Tyana, and that the steady deepening of his own wisdom is definitely credited to these journeys. Apollonius becomes ever wiser because he meets the wisest people in his world at that time. He wanders, so to speak, from one place to the next. He seeks those people who possess the greatest wisdom of the age.

In this way he differentiates himself from Christ Jesus, who spends his days upon the earth in a relatively small area, who conveys to humanity what he has to say entirely from within, who need not speak about what can be found across the face of the earth itself, but rather has to relate to humanity what he has brought from extraterrestrial worlds to the earth. Indeed, attempts have been made to ascribe to Christ Jesus all manner of journeys to India, but that is the purest dilettantism. What is significant here is that in the same age, two beings faced one another; on the one hand, Christ Jesus, who speaks entirely from supra-earthly realms, and, on the other hand, Apollonius of Tyana, who gathers all that is to be found on earth, when he is capable through his own great facility of taking it up into his own soul. This is the main difference, the significant difference, and whoever cannot see this is simply unable to recognize what is communicated to later ages through the existence of these two personalities.

However, what is associated with the person of Apollonius of Tyana is indicative of certain characteristics of earlier times. I mean times long before the Mystery, in other words, very ancient days of humanity. Some aspects of this remained in a later humanity, and we will see how Apollonius of Tyana encountered what had been preserved among the Brahmins as well as among the Gymnosophists of Egypt. However, if one goes back into ancient times using spiritual-scientific historical research, one recognizes very clearly what is involved; and Apollonius of Tyana himself indicates—according to his biographer[†]—in strong language what matters here. He indicates how the sheer, immeasurable wisdom which he encountered amongst the Indians is bound to the extraterrestrial influences which streamed in toward humanity at a particular spot on Earth. We are informed that the human being is not exposed to earthly influences alone. It is easy to study these earthly influences, even though today, in the face of other influences, they do retreat from the human being. Certain lower organic creatures acquire the coloration of what they enjoy, purely according to their metabolism. Among certain lower organic creatures, we can see exactly how what they absorb as metabolic products gives them their coloration or other characteristics. I have pointed out to you how Vincenz Knauer,† my old friend from the Benedictine Order—which does not mean that I was in that order but that he was in it—indicated that what lies within the spiritual content of a concept is something real in the face of the mere sensory existence of matter. Indeed, he said, in the sense of the Scholastics: If one could lock up a wolf and feed him only lamb for a long time, the wolf would still not become a lamb, even though he would then consist primarily of lamb. For Vincenz Knauer, this attests to the fact that in the wolf, in the form, the configuration of the wolf, in that which is encompassed by the concept Wolf, there is something else besides the material aspect, for according to the merely material aspect, the wolf would be a lamb if he had always eaten only lamb. But he does not become one. This is already somewhat different among the higher animals than among the very low organic creatures; these do indeed show, right down to their color, the influences of their metabolism. Of course, for human beings it is the case to an even greater extent than for the wolf that they do not show the effects of metabolism; for, otherwise, in those regions which enjoy a lot of paprika, there would have to be only yellow people, and we know that when people enjoy certain things, it is at most conditions like jaundice that appear. The human being is even now, to a high degree, independent of earthly metabolic effects. But today, in this materialistic age—which has not merely a theoretical but also a very real foundation—he is also less affected by the influences of the extraterrestrial world, the cosmos, than was the case earlier. And the ancient Indian wisdom can essentially be traced back—to express it in summary—to the particular incidence of the sun's rays in Indian regions. There, the sun's rays fall at a different angle than elsewhere. That means that the extraterrestrial, cosmic influences on human beings are different than elsewhere. And if such an ancient Indian had spoken in full consciousness, he would have said, had he even known what Europe is and so forth, something like the following: "Oh, over there in Europe, people can never attain to any kind of wisdom, for the sun does not shine on them in such a way that they can attain to any kind of wisdom; they can only be bound to whatever their metabolism cooks up from the earthly element. There can be no talk of any wisdom over there in Europe. Over there, there are only humans of a lesser sort; these are half animals, for they do not have the sort of sunlight that is necessary if one wants to become a wise person." That is how an ancient Indian would have spoken, if he had spoken about these things at all. Because of his special relationship to the sun's rays, his way of speaking about what was human in Europe would have hardly differed from the way people today talk about their pets. It wasn't as if he didn't love these humans of a lower order; people can, after all, love their pets a lot, but he would not have considered them equal in their spiritual capacity.

I simply wanted to point out that what belonged to the human being as ancient wisdom was dependent on one's location on the earth. This is, of course, also related to something else. In more ancient times of Earth evolution, human beings in general differentiated themselves much more according to this dependence than was the case later on. This differentiation became immediately apparent when settled people left the location of their settlements and moved to other areas. They changed in their souls, even physically they became different. This, indeed, relates to the differentiation across the earth. Thus, it was essentially what the ancient human being possessed from the cosmic surroundings of the earth, what he presented again when he took in these influences from the cosmic surroundings of the earth in a corresponding way. So we can say: in olden times, a true sage was he who lived in that place on earth where one can actually become wise. For that reason, however, these ancients turned their gaze toward such a place with some justification. If today one were to believe, somewhat in the same way, that wisdom is confined to some place in Asia, then one would simply be providing proof that one is not living in one's time, that is, in the present. There are certainly odd people who even today speak of such especially propitious places on the earth's surface; but these things, in a higher sense, in the sense of a true spiritual knowledge, must be called thoroughly dilettantish. However, if we go back to the most ancient times, we must think of the wise person as being connected with his location.

What sort of a person, then, is Apollonius of Tyana? Apollonius of Tyana wants to become wise on the earth even though he does not live near a place where one could become outstandingly wise—such a place as the region near the source of the Nile where the Gymnosophists lived. He simply had the inner desire to become wise in such a way. Therefore, he set out on his journey, in the same way as Pythagoras once did.

Thus, we see how Apollonius of Tyana is, in a certain sense, a person who seeks in the breadth of the earth, that which ought to fill the human being with inner satisfaction, which enables him to achieve inner spirituality. For Apollonius of Tyana lived at a time which was more or less an echo of the times during which what I just said about the connection of a person to a particular place was especially true. In India, there remained something of what had once been, and that is what Apollonius of Tyana came to know. But he already represented a later age in which someone was obliged to seek what was, in the highest sense, human wisdom at every place on earth. Except that he was obliged to seek it on long journeys.

Here, a determining direction presents itself to us through the Mystery of Golgotha, so that we may say: Because the Christ lived in Jesus of Nazareth, Jesus of Nazareth became simultaneously that being on the earth who set the tone for this seeking, regardless of the particular location on the earth. Thereby, Apollonius of Tyana and Christ Jesus are the greatest of opposites. Apollonius of Tyana is, in a certain way, that contemporary of Christ Jesus whose constitution was already of a later time, and he no longer lives in the old world but already in a new world. But in this new time, one can live only with the Christ-impulse. The Christ-impulse comes from Jesus of Nazareth. Jesus of Nazareth and Apollonius of Tyana are the two poles of humanity from the beginning of our Christian era.

And it is precisely through this that our attention is directed to what entered humanity through Christ Jesus. It is especially important for us to grasp what I mentioned yesterday, namely, that above all what entered humanity comes to expression in the resurrection thought. The resurrection thought tells us that the human being need not perish through what binds him to the earth but can, instead, find something in himself which raises itself above his boundedness to the earth if he takes up the Christ-impulse. Everything that weighs on, that torments the Man of Sorrows hanging on the cross ultimately emanates from forces of Earth existence that are implanted in the human body and thus in the human being in general. Let us look up to the crucifix with the face submerged in suffering, with the body ransacked by pain, and we find the deepest expression of that which Earth existence can imprint on the human being. If then, however, we look up to that which I alluded to yesterday, where we then should glimpse above the cross the Risen One, then we become aware of that in the human being which can always rise, which can raise itself out of what only contains Earth forces, and which shows us how the human being is a cosmic being, how the Earth only imprints its forces on part of him, yet how out of these forces can rise that which constitutes the cosmic ingredient of the human being.

These are the things that must be seen in connection with the resurrection thought, and these are the things which, especially in our time, when we are striving for the resurrection of spirit knowledge, must be recognized. What we must grasp, above all, in the resurrection thought is that instinctive wisdom did, indeed, exist in former times. What existed there was something grand, something that was certainly related to the eternal being of man. But when we go back into those former times, this wisdom was, at the same time, something suggestive, something that came over the human being, something within which the human being no longer lived in freedom. In former times, man's will nature was less expressed. It is the will nature of human beings which had to develop itself especially in that age of Earth evolution following the Mystery of Golgotha. With respect to his will, ancient man definitely existed in a dull condition. But the will must be penetrated by wisdom, by the strength of ideas, by spirituality. That is what counts. That is why it is necessary, above all, that the Christ-impulse enter the will of the human being. But this must be understood rightly. The cultivation of the will from the present into the future is especially important. In relation to his will, the human being must become ever more conscious. In today's common, civilized life, we experience only the reaction that results from the comfortable clinging to old prejudices, the reaction against the cultivation of the will. Today, one would really just like to avoid cultivating the will. One really hates to cultivate the will. How does the human being act in this regard?

When he is challenged to be a complete human being, a full human being whose wisdom also takes hold of his will, then he says: "I won't get involved in that; let the church guide my will. The church has its ancient commandments; the church will tell me how I am to proceed with my will." Or if he doesn't say that, then today the human being says something different; he says: "Oh, why should I give my will a direction, I have the state. The state has its laws, the state has its institutions, the state does everything. The state takes over the care of the child. It now takes over care of the child when it is already past the greatest difficulties. A time will come when the state manages to take over the care of the child already at that stage of life when these difficulties still involve all sorts of things. But why shouldn't there be courtiers to change diapers and a Ministry of Diapering! This would certainly open up all sorts of interesting possibilities for the appointment of public authorities.

But then, at a later age, when things are no longer so difficult, when they are simpler with respect to childrearing, then the state no longer trusts anyone to have their own opinion, and, on the whole, people are entirely satisfied with this. They need not think, for example, about what their children revere, for although the state doesn't really think about this correctly either, people believe that it does at least think about it. Well now, I could go on for a long time with such observations. Where the human being ought to be striving to transform his will into activity, to saturate it with wisdom, that is where today the human being actually becomes the being who appeals to something else that certainly is not located in the center of his will, to radiate some light there. But that is exactly what is at stake, that the will take up the light-filled impulses, and that is precisely what lies in the properly understood Christ-thought.

Christ is that being who never takes ownership of groups in any way, who never becomes involved with any groups. It is the greatest absurdity to speak of a Christ who is German, or French, or Scandinavian, or Dutch, or Montenegrin, or to speak of a Christ from, let's say, Morocco, because the Christ is that being who knows no groups, but knows only single individuals, and whoever believes that there is any connection with the groups from the Christ-being misunderstands the Christ-being.

But this understanding of Christ must come first; it must come with the understanding of the human individuality. For when this happens, the resurrection thought will also again come into being, for the spirit can arise only in the single human individuality. The spirit can only be resurrected when the possibility of development is given to the individual. Of course, that can only happen if one removes the control of spiritual life from the organization of the state, as is proposed in the threefolding of the social organism. Today, it may appear, shall I say, barbaric to many people to relate the resurrection thought with something like the threefold thought. But whoever has a sense for and an understanding of the unity of human civilization will also grasp how what is conceived for the social life must definitely arise out of a comprehension which strives for the highest that is accessible to the human being. The resurrection thought has to be grasped spiritually. That can only happen when one relies not merely on observation, meaning on the intellect, but when one attempts to understand in the right way how the human will must be taken hold of.

And spiritual science, as it is meant here, is definitely something which passes into the human will. Spiritual science, as it is meant here, does not understand all the other talk. Take everything entailed in our literature. If people only consider intellectually the concepts and ideas in our literature, to what will it lead? Only to lame discussions! They will be able to engage in all sorts of profane discussions about what spiritual science says. But what is entailed in spiritual science by way of thoughts and ideas, this wants to be taken up by the will, this wants to occupy the entire human being. Thus, the cultivation of will, with respect to spiritual science, begins at the level of comprehension.

Let me say that this ought to enter the entire being of those who engage with what is here called the spiritual-scientific movement. This spiritual science, this anthroposophical movement, had, after all, to turn toward all manner of practicalities out of its relationship to the evolution of time. It is not to cause offense in my characterization—that is far from my intention at this moment—but to bring attention to certain things, which tend in one direction or another, that I append the following.

You see, we have recently created all kinds of practical institutions. For these practical institutions we need people, we have to employ people in them. Obviously, we employ those who understand something of the intentions within the anthroposophical movement, or at least ought to understand something. Now it was presumed—this might be one way of viewing things, I merely want to present some possibilities—that anthroposophists would now come into practical positions out of the whole fire of anthroposophy and become active in these positions, saying to themselves: "Now, to accomplish practical things, it is necessary to work out of different foundations; I am now, as I stand, truly as an anthroposophist within the whole thing, and it is not important to me to do much more than is usual in the present age. I am at one with what is willed through these practical matters." That would be one possible perspective. The other possible view would be the following: "Well, yes, there are all sorts of practical institutions; there is the possibility now to also be active as an anthroposophist. But I am an anthroposophist; therefore, I do not want to be treated in the way that was customary for the old positions. Indeed, one had to arrive punctually and leave punctually in those old positions—that is no longer the case; I will arrive when I wish and depart when I wish; occasionally, I won't show up at all, or I will do something other than what should be done, for in anthroposophy things have to be different than they were in the old philistine world." That would be an extreme version of the other perspective. I simply want to present possibilities, because already today one may draw attention to such possibilities; for what we are engaged in is certainly much too earnest for us to continue with what, for self-evident reasons, some circles of anthroposophists who enjoy the old sectarian spirit are spreading further. These circles occasionally find it most natural to say: "Well, people have been drinking tea for so many years, and have talked while drinking tea—so let us avoid whatever people have talked about while drinking tea or coffee, or after drinking black coffee in the afternoon! But why should one avoid talking about Saturn, Sun, Moon while drinking tea or coffee, why not about reincarnation, why not speculate about what this or that person might have been in a previous incarnation! In other words, why not carry on a kind of salon-like anthroposophy or something of the kind?"

We are certainly past such things. This won't do anymore. We can no longer focus on that. Today, the only thing we can focus on are the two other possibilities. I merely mean to characterize; and I am certainly not now saying that I'm stating something that already exists, but rather I'm merely drawing attention to the fact that with one of these two possibilities we could progress well, that with the other, which is just where anthroposophists want something quite special, a new tone, so that they no longer show up, say, at eight o'clock, but rather at half past ten because they perhaps had to meditate until then, and so forth, that a proper culture of will, as was just characterized, will actually not be able to connect itself with this possibility. The times are too earnest to omit looking at these polar opposite ways of dealing with things. I don't want to make statements about this, but I advise you to look around, to see whether these two possibilities exist, and then to form an opinion, and then, depending on that opinion, act accordingly. It is very nice to call oneself an anthroposophist; but for our time it is not enough. Our time demands of the human being that which touches the will, which also intervenes in human development absolutely supportively.

It is certainly extraordinarily uplifting to say: "Here or there, somewhere hidden and remote, sits this or that 'Master.'" Such a place was once, in fact, from a certain quarter, disclosed in Hungary, and several naïve citizens of Budapest then investigated police records but did not find this Master's location at the relevant spot! When one is then told such a thing, that the great spiritual powers of the earth were sought in this way, one really can do nothing but smile, for it was naïve on the part of those who pursued the matter in this way, who sought for a postal address of the spiritual leaders of humanity; it was naïve of those who indicated such things in this way, as if one could seek postal addresses. But I would prefer not to take this any further.

Admittedly, different people have different views about these things. For example, there was one who carried on among us, a certain—what did he call himself again at that time? In his books he called himself Max Heindel,† but here he had a different name; he called himself Grashof. This man had first absorbed everything he could absorb from public lectures and books. From that he made, somewhat mystically, a book called *Rosicrucian Cosmo Conception*, and then, in a second edition, he also took up what is in the lecture cycles and whatever else he could copy. Then he told his people over in America that he had indeed taken up the first level here, but that in order to achieve the second, he wandered deep into Hungary, to a Master. Then he claimed to have received from him what had actually been copied from all the lecture cycles he had received, and in particular from all the lectures he had obtained and copied, which was nothing but plagiarism! Some of you will know that this had a hugely comical result, namely, that everything was translated back into German† with the remark that one could indeed have something like this in Europe, but that it was better to get it in the form in which it could emerge under the free sun of America.

Humanity really likes to be given what it can take up without exerting the will. Will culture, if it is really practiced, certainly makes such a thing impossible. When the will remains weak, then it simply becomes weaker and weaker when faced with the possibility of judging whatever comes to meet it from the external world. We must learn to connect what we experience in everyday life with the highest. We cannot be permitted to carry out a kind of double-entry bookkeeping. We must be clear that when we take hold of the spirit, we then also go beyond the superficial assessment of ordinary life. And if we proffer one thing or another feelingly, then, strange as it may seem when put in this way, we approach the element of the resurrection faith, which is just what we need today. We need the first element, I might say, the very first beginning, which consists in our taking up in our will what can come from spiritual science. Then the path which we are pursuing leads in the direction we are shown, the path to the true resurrection faith. Today we must come to an expansion of the Easter thought. We must bring together what anthroposophy ought to be for us as human beings with what, for the broadest circles of humanity, is actually only a word that no longer has any content. And such a word is, for the broadest circles of humanity, the word Resurrection, the word Easter. Meaning must once again be connected with such things. Within the human being we must attain knowledge, knowledge of humanity's evolution, and we must again learn to understand, in the full light of human consciousness, the meaning of the Pauline words:[†] "If Christ be not risen, your faith is in vain." Also in vain is all knowledge—and all human striving—if it cannot take up the true Easter thought of resurrection into the innermost realm of the human soul.

Lecture Eighteen

DORNACH, APRIL 1, 1921

If we look at what we have often regarded as the object of esoteric observation, what we find in my *Theosophy*, in my *Occult Science*, and in other books as the organization of the human being, if we look at it more from the outside and in the form of an outline, then we can look, on the one hand, at everything we can call the powers of understanding, the faculties of understanding in the human being. Certainly, what we summarize there as faculties of understanding encompasses the most diverse aspects of what we have described as the members of the human being. It is precisely through such considerations, which look at the various concepts and ideas we have from different points of view, that we make progress in our discussions. Thus, on the one hand, we see activities more related to reason in human soul-spiritual life, and, on the other hand, we see activities more related to the capacity for desire, to activities of the will in human spirit and soul life. Today we want to look at these abilities from the point of view of mankind as a whole, that is, we want to ask ourselves: What is the significance of the more rational forces in the life of mankind as a whole, and what is the significance of the more volitional forces?

Undertaking such an approach can be fruitful only if one considers neither the human being nor all of humanity as isolated from the entire planet Earth, but rather as a part of the entire planet Earth. That one is justified in doing this you will see from tracing the discussions in, for example, *Occult Science* about the Saturn, Sun, and Moon evolution of our Earth.

If you recall what is said there about the evolution of Saturn, Sun, and Moon, then you will see that the matter is not seen the way today's geologists and natural scientists see it when they consider the Earth, on the one hand, geologically, as if the human being did not belong to it, and then again as if humanity consisted of a kind of isolated anthropology, as if this humanity were strolling around on alien ground. Therefore, this cannot lead to a truly fruitful way of looking at things. If you follow what is said about Saturn, Sun, and Moon evolution, you will see that the forces at play in humanity and the forces at play in the rest of the planet cannot be thought of as separated at all. It is a phase of evolution that has enabled humanity to attain a certain detachment from the planet and to be able to walk about on it independently; for our method of observation, it ought not to be exclusively authoritative. We must consider humanity in its connection with the whole Earth. And there we must say first of all: If we look at the capacity for reason and remember what was said about earlier metamorphoses, about Saturn, Sun, and Moon metamorphoses, then we will realize that this inwardness which we have in today's intellectually developed human being was not present in earlier metamorphoses of Earth evolution. What has been localized, as it were, in our heads as intellect was distributed as a general intellectuality, as a far-reaching, lawful intellectuality across the entire planet. One could say: Intellect was active in the facts of all of Earth evolution. The human being on the Moon—not to speak of Saturn and Sun—did not yet have conscious understanding, but rather a kind of dreaming consciousness. This dream-like consciousness looked out upon the manifestations of the world, and while having the dream-like consciousness, the human being did not say to himself: Out there, world manifestations are at work, and I grasp them with my intellect. Instead, the human being dreamed in pictures. He saw what we perceive today as intellect that is localized in our heads as things and facts spread about outwardly. We distinguish between the laws of nature and that in us which comprehends these laws of nature, and we call the latter our intellect. The human being of the past lived consciously through his soul only in pictures, and this was still the case for the older parts of our Earth evolution, and he did not differentiate between the outer laws of nature and his intellect; rather, nature itself had the intellect; nature itself gave itself its laws. Intellect worked out there. It is a phase of evolution in a humanity that has become independent to say: "We bear the intellect within us, and out there are the laws of nature." For the human being of ancient times, the sum of these laws of nature was the intellect.

Now we, as earthly humanity, have indeed already developed, to some degree, the consciousness that the intellect is present within us, and that the laws of nature, which we comprehend only with our intellect, are present outside of us. By pointing out this fact, we are touching upon an important developmental impulse of humanity. But we must be conscious of how this important developmental impulse of humanity must be comprehended more and more and developed more and more. Fundamentally, it is not yet fully developed today. True, we tell ourselves that we have the intellect within us, and that out there the laws of nature prevail; but we do not yet make this intellect entirely our own. We, as humanity, have stopped halfway with regard to taking the intellect, reason, the lawfulness of nature into ourselves. And it is precisely in our time that one has to look the most at the things I just mentioned, especially from the spiritual-scientific point of view. Today we are still extraordinarily proud when, with respect to everything connected with the intellect, everything we recognize as human knowledge, we have something in common with our fellow human beings. Today it is still considered extraordinarily incisive in the whole of human natural evolution that science is cultivated as something which, so to speak, hovers above all of humanity, and that by devoting themselves to science, people should, so to speak, sacrifice their individuality, should think just as "everyone" thinks. That is the ideal especially of our public educational institutions—to educate and make something of science which is entirely impersonal, which is entirely unindividual, in the face of which one says "I" as little as possible and "one" as much as possible: *one* has found this or that, *one* must consider this or that to be true! And the ideal of the official representatives of science today would indeed be this: that one would actually no longer be able to distinguish the individual lecturers—or at most with regard to temperament—when one travels from one university to another far-off university. It would be considered an ideal if, let's say, one could listen to a lecture on botany somewhere in the north, then quickly fly south in a balloon to hear the continuation of that lecture, which would correspond completely with what "one" knows in the field of botany! In this field, one considers what is impersonal or unindividual as correct, and one has a terrible fear that somehow something personal could make its way into this science, into this effort of human understanding. It is just in this field that the leveling of all human culture applies most of all. One is proud of avoiding any departure from what has been formulated in a certain way once and for all. Thus, one wants to separate science from the human being. After all, it is also separated from people in other respects. Examples of this can be cited. Just consider for a moment how today most people who take part in scientific life write their dissertations, their private lecturers' books, their professorship candidacy books, and so forth. They are engaged as little as possible and they reckon as little as possible with having these books read generally. They are written; but those who are meant to examine them in the relevant department hardly read them; rather, at most, a single person is obliged to read them and then to tell the others what they are to make of them. For science is, after all, something about which "one" thinks, not personally; and then these books are stored in libraries. Then, when someone else writes something similar, he takes a look at the library catalogue and tries to find anything similar that he must take into account, and this then is again stored with attempts to avoid what is individual or personal. After all, it is all separated. Untold stuff of personal interest to no one abounds in libraries. This is, basically, a terrible state of affairs. But even more terrible is that the people involved don't even notice this; they feel entirely calm about not needing to know anything, for after all, one can find everything in the library if only one can look up the relevant keyword in the catalogues. That is how things stand. But people walk side by side with this generalized science. This science would certainly look different if people were to store it in their heads and not on library shelves.

This gives one a glimpse, shall I say, through a chink or two—for one could cite much in this direction—about how the general intellectual culture is still unindividual, impersonal in humanity today, how people want it to be like something of a cloud existence passing over them. However, what people create doesn't belong only to them, but to the whole universe. That is why I said: in order to arrive at a fruitful consideration, we must consider the human being in connection with his planet, and then again the planet in connection with the whole universe.

Thus, the human being can deal with what he creates, to which he applies his intellect, in two ways. On the one hand, he can make an effort with this intellect to form sciences, which then all flow into the "one thinks," "one knows," "one has achieved such and such progress"; then one writes this in books, which one stores, and then this is the science upon which the generations grow; and human beings can dry up with this sort of use of their intellect. They can manage to look for what actually interests them in various other things, but not in what is, without this interest, untruth, objective untruth untouched by anything personal, stored objectively in libraries; they can do it in such a way that they avoid touching it. There have been gatherings of scholars who in their terminology used shop talk. It was considered somewhat off-putting if after the official speeches, one conversed in small groups about individual aspects of science. There one spoke about all sorts of nonsense that was far removed from the scientific matters at hand. And those who were so weak as to be enthused by their science and who then started, let's say, to talk about this or that philological or other question over tea or coffee were then just "talking shop," were the ones who were not to be taken seriously, who lacked a worldly spirit.

I once encountered this impersonal approach to science in a unique way. I was at a gathering at which Helmholtz gave a lecture.[†] At this lecture, which was read verbatim by Helmholtz, though it had already been in print for a long time, people listened, well, the way one listens at such a lecture. After the lecture a journalist approached me and said: "What was the point of that? That wasn't necessary at all. Anyone who wants to can read such a lecture when it is printed; why should it then also be read aloud? It would certainly make a lot more sense if Helmholtz simply walked about the auditorium and shook hands with everyone; that would be much better; much more would be accomplished that way." This is really an example of alienation with regard to what "flies about" as science in such an impersonal way. Of course, people dry up that way. That is one way to grasp intellectual culture.

The other way is this—that one is interested in all the details, that the mind catches fire and enlivens science, that it melts science down into living concepts, that everything we comprehend, everything we grasp is received by the inner life of soul. In this way, one can really imbue everything which science gives with inner fire; in this way, by comprehending the individual sciences, one can gradually penetrate into the whole existence of the world; in this way, one can form something which becomes an intrinsically personal matter for every human being who pursues it. That is the other thing. And everything that is being done from one side is impersonal, is basically separated from the human being. What people would love to do most of all is to invent automatons for scientific activity, so that they would have no need at all to think with their own heads; then, perhaps, without their heads, they would be productive. But what arises out of the fully heartfelt pursuit of science are not merely matters concerning humanity, they are matters concerning the whole planet and therefore the whole universe. For what the human being does when he thinks, when he forms anything intellectually in his head, this is an event just as much as when water flows from a spring down a stream to the sea, or when it evaporates, or when it rains. What happens externally, materially in rain, or when the plant sprouts, and so on, these are events of one kind. What happens through the human being are events of another kind. It is not only an event but an event concerning the whole planet. And precisely this is the task of the human being in his evolution on the earth: to take this intellect which was formerly spread over the planet, into himself, to unite with it. Thus, it is a developmental impulse of the human being to make knowledge into a personal matter which he can imbue with enthusiasm, so that it can become one with him, so that it can be grasped by his heartfelt fire. And if the latter does not happen, if he only stores knowledge in an impersonal manner, then something that is to happen for the sake of Earth evolution will not take place. The heart (*Gemüt*) of mankind will not be taken hold of by intellectual culture. Intellectual culture develops, so to speak, only in the head and hovers too far above the surface of the earth, merely in people's heads; it develops only in people's heads and ought to descend into the heart. But the luciferic spirits are waiting for what is not grasped by hearts; in other words, for what is not taken hold of by the human heart (*Gemüt*). And that which the luciferic spirits are so waiting for, they can receive when it hovers impersonally above the earth in this way. For the only possible way to wrest the world of the intellect from the luciferic spirits is to imbue it with heart (*Gemüt*), to turn it into a personal affair. And what is happening in our time, what has been happening for a long time and what must be changed, is just this, that we allow our earthly existence to become prey to the luciferic world by way of the cold, sober dryness of the intellect. That causes Earth to be held back in its evolution; that causes Earth to be held back at an earlier stage. It will not reach its end. And if human beings continue to carry on with the impersonal aspects of so-called science for a long, long time, then the consequence will be that human beings will lose their soulfulness altogether. This impersonal science is the murderer of human soulfulness and spirituality; it dries out the human being, it desiccates him. In the end, it will turn Earth into something one could call a dead planet populated with automaton-like human beings who lose their soul-spiritual nature by this means. Here, too, one must say: these things really have to be taken seriously. Merely observing this cosmic murder through the abstract, impersonal pursuit of knowledge cannot be allowed to happen. That is the one thing.

The other is the human capacity for desire. This is connected with the will aspect in the human being. What is connected with the will aspect in the human being can go either of two ways: The one way is that this will aspect can subordinate itself to commandments and state laws and so forth, and adhere to general lawfulness so that there is general lawfulness and alongside it only people's purely instinctive desire.

The other way is that the capacity for desire which is mirrored in the human being and present as capacity for will, gradually raises itself to pure thinking, expresses itself in individual freedom, so that it pours itself into social life as love. This is the expression of will and the capacity for desire as I described it in *The Philosophy of Freedom*. There I showed how general human lawfulness must originate in every human individuality and that when this element which originates in every human individuality raises itself to pure thinking, then, through the harmonizing of what people do, social order emerges. People fear all social orders which are constituted by having each person find his direction individually. They want to organize what it is that people should want. They want to put the "categorical imperative" in place of the love working out of every human being. However, because such abstract commandments exist—be they commandments according to the style of the Decalogue or of some kind of centralized state—because of the existence of such commandments, only the instinctive desires, those desires which we see living especially today and which have basically become the only social ingredients of the present time, are asserted out of the individual element of the human being. Again, what happens in the human being when he does not form his will individually, does not raise it to pure thinking, this, again, is not something which concerns human beings alone, but the entire planet, and thus also the cosmos. And the ahrimanic spirits are greedily waiting for what happens when the human will cannot form itself individually. This they appropriate, these ahrimanic spirits, and they use everything which lives in the human being as desire that is not developed into love, that lives as will, they use it in such a way as to transfer it to individual demonic beings. Just as a more general state of being emerges from the intellectual activity hovering over humanity, so quite individually formed demonic beings emerge out of the capacity for desire, in single individualities, which has not been transformed into love. And if there were no striving for the individual forming of the free community in the social order, Earth would become filled with beings which would then be individual but which would lead an ahrimanic-spiritual existence and would deprive Earth of the possibility of transforming into the next planetary metamorphosis, into the Jupiter metamorphosis. Illustrated schematically, it would be something like this (see Plate 8 in the appendix): that the abstract intellectuality would shape our planet (see illustration, left), on the one hand, and would not allow it to attain completion; and that which emerges from the will which has not been transformed into love, that would, on the other hand (right), form all sorts of individual beings. Schematically, this illustrates what someone who sees into the beginnings of a civilization that undermines the rightful evolutionary process of the planet Earth can see today as what happens when those impulses which are now sprouting so strongly in the Western world continue unrestrained (see illustration, left); and what develops so strongly in the Eastern world (see illustration, right), what emerges there only from human subjectivity in the state culture that has fallen into decadence; that is actually the evolution of Earth desired by individual demons. What is developing in the West is that which wants to sail into a general intellectuality and to turn people gradually into automatons.

These things are clearly perceptible, even if only in the dispositions of those automatons which today are already partially present—I quite consciously say "partially," for they are certainly still something very individual. One can indeed already see this automatization in many things. But something very individual is still present in these automatons, namely, something which can still be noticed as a kind of appendage to each of these automatons, an appendage in which, even if these things aren't exactly converted into banknotes, there is the tinkling of gold and silver. But the general automatization would see to it that the individual wallets would become general communist wallets.

But this should not be considered with mere sympathy or antipathy, but rather with that view which sees through world events, which can consider what is happening among people in relation to cosmic events. If one looks at things in this way, then one will say to oneself: It is given to human beings to advance the planet in its evolution wisely. This particular way of being, as it is here indicated schematically, threatens humanity if humanity does not attempt to transform knowledge into wisdom, which can only happen if the human being is personally committed, so that he takes it up personally and connects it once again with that which, by way of love, changes the individual capacity for desire into a universal matter for all of humanity. With a strong impulse of inner understanding, one can take these things up through spiritual science. Basically, this is indicated today by what has become, so to speak, fixed as a cosmic symbol in the Moon.

When the Moon is in its first or last quarter, then, in what it shows us in its crescent shape, we have an image of what Earth could become; on the darker side, it shows—to one who can see supersensibly—these small demonic forms which move in an abominable way into the concave bend of the crescent. So that one actually speaks very truly when one says: The human being must, by means of what I just described, preserve the Earth from Moon existence. The Moon shows, in a cosmic image which is placed before us, what Earth can become. And so we do have to become accustomed also in this way to penetrating with inner sense what we see outside in the cosmos. We must look at the Moon in such a way that we say: It points out to us something which is set, by means of cosmic evolution, like the caricature of Earth existence, like something which Earth existence can become if the human being does not learn to make impersonal knowledge into a personal matter, to forge individual desire into love, by which it becomes something that can be a universal matter in the associative social life of all humanity. One can better understand what happens in the cosmos if one looks at what takes place in the human being; and, conversely, one can see the task of humanity properly if one can see through the conditions of the cosmos in a meaningful way. Then it will, indeed, turn to that which ought to live in humanity as morality, as ethicality.

The things one says about Lucifer and Ahriman are truly not meant to be cause for theorizing about them, so that one should speak of them only to say: Ahriman is this, Lucifer is that. Rather, one should now take up these concepts in such a way that, basically, in everything taking place around oneself, one sees the effect of luciferic spirits, which want to keep the Earth at an earlier stage, and that one sees in everything that is Ahriman what wants to keep the Earth stuck so that it cannot progress into future phases. But one must see through these things in detail. One must, I would say, be able to evaluate morality according to natural law and natural law according to morality. If this happens, then the great bridge between the moral worldview and the theoretical worldview—a bridge I have often spoken of here—will be built.

It is from this perspective that the things taking place today must also be considered. For only when the free will of the human being intervenes in these world events can what I have here briefly presented to you be applied. The further evolution of the Earth is absolutely the task of human beings and humanity. This must not be overlooked. And those who only want to theorize, who, for example, only want to see or hear, "In so and so many centuries or millennia, this will happen," such people do not take into account that we already live in an age when it has been given to humanity to participate in the metamorphoses of Earth evolution, that the human heart and soul must take up what exists as universal world intellect, and that what lives individually in the human being as the capacity for desire must flow out of the human being in the form of universal human love, which, however, can be attained only in pure, free thinking.

In this way I have placed before the soul's eye two cultural streams which are important above all others, and I have in this way tried to show, again from a certain perspective, what the task of spiritual science is when it is taken seriously. The task lies along such lines. It really does not consist of a few people feeling good about knowing this or that; rather, it consists—the task of this spiritual science when it is taken seriously—of intervening in the evolution of humanity in such a way that world events form themselves in the right way from out of humanity.

My dear friends,† now I would just like to say a few more words about something different, something quite different. I have heard that a certain anxiety prevails—in those circles which bear responsibility for the matter—a certain anxiety about that part of the program for our course in which we anticipate many serious conversations for the evenings, about social matters and other topics, and there is talk about "little piquancies." I was somewhat surprised by this anxiety in view of how often it has been said here that only through the inner collaboration from soul to soul of all those who count themselves part of the anthroposophical movement can the salvation of this movement come about. I was surprised because I believed—as this has been emphasized so often here—that at least with regard to this custom of allowing fiery speech, each person, from everything he carries in his soul as spiritual richness, had long since made soul preparation; and I actually thought that we would not be able to find an end to these evenings in which what has been stored up by individual souls as spiritual richness over a long period of time is expressed in veritable firestorms of piquancies—piquancies in the nobler sense!

This is still my hope, but I just want to point out that this cannot consist of sending one speaker after another up to the podium so that he can let loose his piquancies! In my opinion, this would not be the right thing for this part of the program. Rather, everyone ought to be modest enough to let loose such fire perhaps only to a small circle in his vicinity which he happens to meet just at that moment, so that these others then must see how fiery they can be. Much can be said with laughter, but much can also be said with other feelings that arise as a necessary consequence. Piquancies need not be merely matters for merriment, they can also be other things. And so I imagined that this would really develop from one person to the next. Last time, during the course,[†] there was so little of what happens in personal exchanges between one another that one might think: Much has been accumulated in silence, which should now be released. But I imagine it to be somewhat like this: in these few days—for really there are only two more—everyone will take counsel with himself and look into the depth of his soul to discover what he carries in his soul of such possible piquancies, so that he can then go about from one group to the next and that the events each evening can be extraordinarily stimulating. It will not be amiss for a certain social life to develop in this way. It is not necessary for us always to sit in our seats and want to listen to something; for if everyone did that—just think what would then happen to us! That really won't do, will it! It would make no sense then to speak of a "Society" if something didn't arise socially in this way.

Thus, as already mentioned, I don't want to follow the suggestions to give some kind of guidance in this matter, but I would just like to express my opinion that it only need be said that one should not hold back with such things; then, hopefully, they will indeed develop. So let's hope that we'll see the very best also in this regard in the next ten days.

EDITORIAL AND REFERENCE NOTES

On this edition

Textual basis: Stenographic transcript of the lectures by Rudolf Steiner: for the lectures given in Stuttgart and The Hague: Mrs. Hedda Hummel of Cologne; for the lectures given in Dornach: the official Dornach stenographer Helene Finckh (1883–1960). Production of the plain text by the stenographers. For the 1978 edition, only individual passages were compared again with the original stenography, insofar as these are available (only from the Dornach lectures).

The *title of the volume* was chosen by the editor of the 1st German edition (1953), Carlo Septimus Picht.

On the blackboard drawings: Beginning in 1919, Rudolf Steiner's blackboard drawings, which he often made during his lectures, were recorded using sheets of black paper that were then rolled up and saved. Roughly 1,100 such drawings were preserved in this way. The blackboard drawings from the present lectures are reproduced in reduced size at the end of this volume.

A considerable part of the references, especially the documentation of the oppositional articles cited by Rudolf Steiner, can be traced back to the first editor of these lectures, Carlo Septimus Picht (1887–1954).

Notes on the text

Works by Rudolf Steiner within the Collected Works (CW) are indicated in the notes with the bibliographic number. See also the overview at the end of the volume.

5 Euclid
Euclid (c. 300 BC). His *Elements* offers the basic teachings of all mathematics.

Varuna
A Vedic god. The hymns to him are among the most sublime in the *Rigveda*, the oldest part of the *Veda*. See the corresponding text in Rudolf Steiner's lecture of December 26, 1920, in *Universal Spirituality and Human Physicality* (CW 202).

6 Soma juice
The juice of the soma plant, a species of sacrostemma, was a ritual drink with a powerfully intoxicating effect. Its inspiring power was worshipped as the god "Soma"—comparable to the Greek Dionysus. On the occult meaning of "Soma," see H. P. Blavatsky, *The Secret Doctrine*, Volumes I and II.

the philosopher's stone
See the lecture of September 29, 1905, in *Foundations of Esotericism* (CW 93a): depiction of the carbon process from exhalation via the assimilation of plants to coal and diamond. "Coal is the philosopher's stone."

6 Novalis
"He who does not grasp a mathematical book with devotion and read it like the word of God does not understand it" (*Mathematical Fragments*).

Kant
Prolegomena, 1783, § 6 ff. "How Is Pure Mathematics Possible?" "Mathematics and physics are the two theoretical cognitions of reason that are to determine their objects *a priori*. . ." (from the preface to the 2nd edition of the *Critique of Pure Reason*, 1787).

10 schools of wisdom in Darmstadt
Count Hermann Keyserling (1880–1946), philosopher of culture and history, founded a "School of Wisdom" in Darmstadt in 1920 that also acted as an opponent of anthroposophy.

11 fact of the Mystery of Golgotha
Rudolf Steiner, *Christianity as Mystical Fact and the Mysteries of Antiquity* (CW 8).

13 The Christmas tree began only in the nineteenth century
See Rudolf Steiner, "The Christmas Tree as a Symbol," lecture of December 21, 1909, in *Deeper Secrets of Human Evolution in Light of the Gospels* (CW 117).

14 Proclamation
Luke 2:14

15 a certain missionary preacher by the name of Frohnmeyer
D. L. Johannes Frohnmeyer (1850–1921). The passage can be found in: *Die theosophische Bewegung, ihre Geschichte, Darstellung und Beurteilung* [The theosophical movement, its history, presentation and assessment], (Stuttgart and Basel, 1920), p. 107: "A 9 m high statue of the ideal man is currently being sculpted in Dornach: at the top with 'luciferic' features, at the bottom with animal features." (This statement was omitted in the 2nd edition.) Frohnmeyer took this completely inaccurate statement from an article by the pastor Heinrich Nidekker-Roos ("Christlicher Volksbote aus Basel" [Christian folk-messenger from Basel], 1920, year 88, no. 23, June 9, p. 178f.) without checking it, without citing the source, as if it were his own statement, instead of traveling from nearby Basel to look at the sculptural group himself. See also the lectures of January 16, 1921, and February 6, 1921, in the present volume.

20 such a catastrophe
This refers to the First World War and its consequences.

I have often pointed out
See the lecture of December 14, 1920, in *Universal Spirituality and Human Physicality* (CW 202).

23 Rabindranath Tagore
Rabindranath Tagore (1861–1945), Indian poet, philosopher, and freedom fighter.

26 what I also presented on Thursday in a public lecture
Public lecture of January 4, 1921, in *Die Anthroposophie und ihre Gegner* [Anthroposophy and its opponents] (GA 255b).

a scientist from Zürich
See *Neue Zürcher Zeitung*, 1920, no. 2158, 1st morning paper (Dec. 29): "Anthroposophische Geisteswissenschaft" [Anthroposophical spiritual science], signed. M. Sz. [Dr. Mieczyslaw Sztern], discussion of Rudolf Steiner's two lectures on December 6 and 8, 1920, Zürich. – The two above-mentioned quotations, which apply to the lecture of December 6, "Anthroposophical Spiritual Science, Its Results and Its Scientific Justification," read verbatim in Sztern:

> Steiner began his characterization of anthroposophical spiritual science by relating it most closely to the most certain of the sciences, mathematics. . . . This analogy, somewhat striking at first glance, is immediately perceived in its flimsiness as soon as one later learns which authority it is that Steiner ultimately relies on and invokes for the certainty of anthroposophical knowledge: it is "experience," "intuitive comprehension," "supersensible seeing." Mathematical truths, however, do not derive their certainty from "intuition" or "experience"; it is rather the purely intellectual insight into the seamlessly closed chain of logical deductions that gives the mathematical "proof" its excellent certainty value. . . . The "mathematical point," the "straight line," the "n-dimensional space," "the differential," in short, all the basic concepts and axioms of mathematics are no more "true," no more certain than the basic concepts of natural science, as "atom," energy," "force," etc. . . . The axioms are . . . not "absolutely," but only "relatively true. . . ."
>
> Dr. Sztern then gave a lecture against anthroposophy on May 28, 1921, under the title "Plato, Goethe, und die Anthroposophie" (see *Neue Zürcher Zeitung*, 1921, no. 805 (June 2): "Plato, Goethe und die Anthroposophie" [Referat], gez. n. [Sztern?]).

27 our Waldorf School
Founded in 1919 by Rudolf Steiner and Emil Molt as a school for the children of the workers and employees of the Waldorf Astoria cigarette factory in Stuttgart.

28 the preacher and professor Traub
The passage mentioned can be found in Prof. Dr. Friedrich Traub, "Rudolf Steiner als Philosoph und Theosoph" (Tübingen, 1919), p. 34:

> Those truths which one accepts in everyday life on good faith are details

of knowledge with limited value. In theosophy, we are dealing with the last and highest values of the worldview. If authoritative truthfulness is sufficient there, this does not mean that it is also appropriate here. On the contrary, we must demand that in questions of worldview, the individual stands on his own and does not simply accept what others tell him. If I were ever to find myself in the position of having to venture something great on one of those truths we are told in school, such as that Alexander the Great destroyed the Persian Empire or that Hannibal crossed the Alps—if I were to come to the complete conviction that life and happiness depend on such a truth, then I would no longer be content with accepting external authority, but would do everything in my power to attain an independent certainty of those things.

34 Darwinism
Charles Darwin (1809–1882), English naturalist, founder of Darwinism, i.e., the theory of descent and natural selection (theory of descent and natural selection among living beings through the struggle for existence).

Adam Smith
Adam Smith (1723–1790), English philosopher and sociologist.

37 Fichte, Schelling, Hegel

Johann Gottlieb Fichte (1762–1814).

Friedrich Wilhelm Joseph von Schelling (1775–1854).

Georg Wilhelm Friedrich Hegel (1770–1831).

close to gradually giving birth to something
This refers to Schelling's late works, *Philosophy of Mythology* and *Philosophy of Revelation.*

38 Schiller's *Letters on the Aesthetic Education of Man*
Addressed to Duke Friedrich Christian of Schleswig-Holstein-Sonderburg-Augustenburg after November 1791, lost in the fire at Christiansburg Castle in Copenhagen in February 1794, restored by Schiller in an extended reworking and published in 1795.

Ralph Waldo Trine
Ralph Waldo Trine (1866–1958), American philosophical writer. This refers primarily to his widely distributed work, *In Tune with the Infinite* (New York, 1897).

39 *Bhagavad Gita*
Bhagavad Gita (Sanskrit: "The Song of the Diving") is a religious-philosophical poem that forms an episode of the Indian epic poem the *Mahabharata.*

Christian Science
A religious movement founded in New England by Mary Baker Eddy in 1879.

40 the Traubs

See note to page 23. As authors of similar counter-writings, there are the other theologians: Repke, Gennrich, Bachmann, Frohnmeyer, Gogarten, Niebergall, Zimmermann S. J., Laun, etc. See also Louis Werbeck, "Die christlichen Gegner Rudolf Steiners und der Anthroposophie durch sie selbst widerlegt. Eine Gegnerschaft als Kultur-Verfallserscheinung" [The Christian opponents of Rudolf Steiner and anthroposophy refuted by themselves. An opposition as a phenomenon of cultural decay] (Stuttgart, 1924).

41 "Schools of Wisdom"

See note to page 10 [schools of wisdom in Darmstadt]. Tagore also founded a "School of Wisdom" and was a guest speaker in Darmstadt in 1921.

45 Our considerations during my time here

This includes not only the preceding lectures but a total of thirty-seven lectures, speeches, etc., including "Das Verhältnis der verschiedennaturwissenschaftlichen Gebiete zur Astronomie," GA 323, and a course for academics with four lectures, in the period from January 1-18, 1921, the entire duration of the stay in Stuttgart at that time (GA 73a in preparation).

49 Basilius Valentinus

An alchemist, allegedly from the fifteenth century, about whom there is no reliable external information. According to Rudolf Steiner, he was a Benedictine monk from the early Middle Ages who carried out tremendously important medical and alchemical investigations and whose teachings were recorded by his students; see lecture of April 26, 1924, in *Karmic Relationships, Volume II* (CW 236). In the lecture of May 14, 1920, in Dornach (CW 201), the "already quite falsified, but still approximately readable writings of Basilius Valentinus" are mentioned.

51 "Law of Conservation of Mass"

Formulated in 1789 by Antoine Laurent Lavoisier (1743–1794), French chemist and founder of modern chemistry.

"Law of Conservation of Energy"

Formulated in 1842 by the physician and natural scientist Julius Robert Mayer (1814–1878), although it should be noted that "the matter did not pass into the human soul in the subtle manner in which it is treated by Mayer, but in a much coarser way" (Joule, Helmholtz), Rudolf Steiner, lecture of April 16, 1918, in *Dying Earth and Living Cosmos* (CW 181).

52 the lectures given as recently as last week

This refers to the four lectures given for the academics in Stuttgart on January 11, 12, 14, and 15, 1921.

53 in a public lecture

Stuttgart, January 4, 1921, *Anthroposophy and the Natural Sciences* (CW 75).

53 Frohnmeyer
See note to page 15.

54 the gentlemen . . . who were gathered in Geneva
This is the First Assembly of the League of Nations held in Geneva from November 15 to December 18, 1920, under the chairmanship of the Belgian politician Paul Hymans.

60 Our considerations before I left
The lecturer had been in Stuttgart from January 1–18, 1921, for a wide range of lecturing activities.

61 Wallace
Alfred Russel Wallace (1823–1913), British zoologist. *The Wonderful Century: Its Successes and Its Failures* (New York, 1898). The quotation is not verbatim, but a summary of thoughts from this book.

62 Moon, Sun, and Saturn periods
Rudolf Steiner, *An Outline of Occult Science* (CW 13).

66 the real truth lies between two opposite assertions
See Aristotle, *Nicomachean Ethics*, LT/8.

67 A lovely little story
This concerns the celebration of the twenty-fifth anniversary of the Dental Institute of the University of Zürich on January 14, 1921, in the auditorium of the university, where Dr. Alfred Gysi gave a lecture on "Dental caries, its prevention and the consequences of its neglect" [focal infection of granulomas in dead teeth] (see *Universität Zürich. Rektoratsrede und Jahresbericht 1920/21*, Zürich n.d. [1921], p. 29f. and *Schweizerische Vierteljahresschrift für Zahnheilkunde*, 1921, vol. XXXI, no. 1, p. 1ff.). Anthroposophy was not touched on in this lecture, nor was there a discussion afterwards. However, at the subsequent banquet in the Blacksmith's Guild House, professor Dr. Oskar Römer, Director of the Dental Institute of the University of Leipzig, gave a speech on behalf of the Institute to the highly deserving director of the Zürich Institute, Dr. A. Gysi, referring to his anthroposophical studies. The remark mentioned by Rudolf Steiner was probably made in connection with this speech. For his part, professor Römer gave a lecture on April 6, 1921, at a university course at the Goetheanum, entitled "On dental caries or tooth decay with reference to the results of Rudolf Steiner's spiritual research" (Stuttgart, 1921). The quote, "No creative spirit penetrates into Nature's interior," comes from a poem by the Swiss physician, botanist and poet Albrecht von Haller (1708–1777) and is rejected by Goethe in a protest poem: "True Enough. To the Physicist" (1820).

68 A very learned economist

Fritz Terhalle, *Freie oder gebundene Preisbildung? Ein Beitrag zu unserer Preispolitik seit Beginn des Weltkrieges* [Free or fixed pricing? A contribution to our pricing policy since the beginning of the World War] (Jena, 1920), p. 121, where Terhalle quotes the following passage from Ludwig Pohle, *Die gegenwärtige Krisis in der Deutschen Volkswirtschaftslehre. Betrachtungen über das Verhältnis zwischen Politik und nationalökonomischer Wissenschaft* (Leipzig, 1911), p. 114: "They [the coercive measures] are intended to satisfy public opinion, which is agitated by the discovery of certain phenomena perceived as 'abuses,' by making sure that countermeasures are taken by the government. Public opinion, which, according to the apt words of G. Brandes [Georg Brandes (1842–1927), Danish literary historian], is guided far more by the imagination than by reason, does not ask and is unable to judge whether the measures that have been taken are really able to improve anything significantly, even if the reform that has been introduced perhaps only offers the appearance of reality and basically leaves everything as it was." – Terhalle comments: "For the future of peace, too, there would of course be the important task of cultivating a greater awareness of economic necessities among the broad sections of the population and educating them to think economically."

69 Pantheism is a favorite objection

See Otto Zimmermann S.J., "Anthroposophische Irrlehren" [Anthroposophical heresies] in *Stimmen der Zeit*, 95th volume, 4th issue, p. 335ff: "Anthroposophy, insofar as it has come to light in printed publications, is pantheistic. It is at most unclear what kind of pantheism it prefers. . . ."

70 something that recently appeared in a Swiss newspaper

This is probably the report of a lecture by the pastor Friedrich Gogarten on "The Supersensible World of Anthroposophy," which he also gave in Nuremberg on February 9, 1921, and which contained the sentence: "The spirit can never be perceived" (see *Christentum und Gegenwart*, no. 4, April, Nuremberg, 1921, p. 58).

71 essentials of the social question

See *Towards Social Renewal* (CW 23).

77 Kommende Tag and Futurum

Der Kommende Tag: Aktiengesellschaft zur Förderungwirtschaftlicher und geistiger Werte [The coming day: Joint-stock company for the promotion of economic and spiritual values], founded March 13, 1920, in Stuttgart; see founding prospectus of A.-G. Der Kommende Tag from March 1920; see also Emil Leinhas, "Die Idee des 'Kommende Tages'" [The idea of the "Coming Day"] (Stuttgart, 1921).

Futurum A.-G., Ökonomische Gesellschaft zur internationalen Förderung wirtschaftlicher und geistiger Werte [Futurum A.-G. (joint-stock company):

Economic society for the international promotion of economic and spiritual values], founded June 16, 1920, in Dornach/Solothurn; see founding prospectus from October 1920; see also Dr. Emil Oeschen, "Von der Futurum A.-G." in *Das Goetheanum*, weekly, no. 11, 13, 20 (Dornach, 1921). With regard to the attacks mentioned by Steiner, the critical trade journal reports in the *Frankfurter Zeitung* in 1921 (Jan. 1 and Feb. 22) were decisive, especially for the German and foreign press. Futurum was discussed in more detail in the *Basler Nachrichten* (Nov. 26, 1920), the *National-Zeitung*, (Dec. 3, 1920), etc. Articles in response to the fundamental objections raised therein can be found in the weekly journal *Dreigliederung des sozialen Organismus* (Stuttgart 1920/21).

74 in Vienna in 1914
Rudolf Steiner, *The Inner Nature of Man and Our Life between Death and Rebirth* (CW 153).

77 this attack that rages at us from all corners
The erroneous propaganda that the Waldorf School is a "worldview school" was spread by opponents soon after its foundation.

79 I have given you examples
See the Dornach lectures of October 24 and 29, 1920, in *The New Spirituality and the Christ Experience of the Twentieth Century* (CW 200).

80 the effect of a gold standard on free trade
Rudolf Steiner presumably remembered the parliamentary discussions on this subject, which he himself had witnessed in Austria and which naturally also dealt with similar processes in other countries. Austria did not adopt a gold standard until 1892, while England had had it since 1816. Germany introduced it in 1871 and 1873 respectively, Sweden and Denmark followed in 1872–1875. The shift from the free trade efforts of the sixties and seventies in Germany to a protective tariff policy took place in 1879. In Austria, the protective tariff system was tightened in 1882 and 1887.

83 papal encyclicals
This refers to Pius X's encyclical of September 8, 1907. See the Dornach lecture of June 6, 1920, in *Healing the Social Organism* (CW 198).

84 as I recently said in Stuttgart
See the lecture of January 16, 1921, in the present volume.

87 This document originates in Switzerland
This lithograph commemorating the Swiss Sonderbund War was in all likelihood issued on the occasion of the commemorative ceremony on December 4, 1847, at which General Dufour was celebrated as the victor and received the thanks of the people of Bern (speech, serenade, torchlight procession); see *Berner Zeitung*, no. 291 (Dec. 5, 1847). The commemorative leaf, deco-

rated with oak leaves and two groups of flags, shows the eye of God at the top with the inscription: *Des wahren Schweizers Hort und Zuversicht!* [The true Swiss stronghold and assurance]. To the right and left are two laurel wreath vignettes, one with the inscription: Ehre und Dank den XII liberalen Ständen [Honor and thanks to the XII liberal states], the other with a crown above the monogram WHD [Wilhelm Heinrich Dufour] and the caption: Dem Verdienst seine Krone [To the credit of his crown]. In the center of the upper part stands the Swiss coat of arms between two oak branches. The omission in the quotation concerns the battle locations that Rudolf Steiner did not mention here.

90 Years ago, I explained
See the Berlin lecture of February 4, 1913, in *Zur Geschichte der Deutschen Sektion der Theosophischen Gesellschaft 1902–1913* [On the history of the German Section of the Theosophical Society 1902–1913] (GA 250).

91 I was, for a period of eight years, an educator
This is how it stands in the shorthand. Rudolf Steiner worked from 1884 to 1890, that is, for six years, in the house of the cotton importer Ladislaus Specht in Vienna as the educator of his four sons.

92 Goethe's "The Fairy Tale of the Green Snake and the Beautiful Lily"
Published in 1795. Translated into English by Thomas Carlyle in 1832.

The Portal of Initiation
The Portal of Initiation: A Rosicrucian Mystery, in *Four Mystery Dramas* (CW 14).

the great crisis of the year 1873
The world economic crisis of 1873, which started at the Vienna Stock Exchange and spread to all major branches of world trade and industry, was caused by changes in technology (the mechanization of businesses), which led to increased world trade, fixed capital, and overproduction.

a man named Bontoux
Eugene Bontoux (1820–1904), French financier, general director of the Austrian Southern Railway, then manufacturer and railroad builder (in Hungary, Serbia, etc.), founder of the *Union générale*, Paris, with funds from the Legitimists and clericals, which collapsed in 1882.

93 Paris Bourse crash
The stock market crisis that broke out in France at the beginning of 1882, which was linked to stock market speculation and a number of Bontoux institutions, in particular the *Union générale* and the Banque de Lyon et de la Loire.

95 Lenins and Trotskys

Leon Trotsky (1879–1940), Marxist theorist and politician. With Vladimir Ilyich Lenin, b. Ulyanov (1870–1924), leader of the Bolshevik Revolution.

96 About Steiner's Goetheanum in Dornach
The following six quotations were read aloud by Rudolf Steiner from the book *Ein Blick in die Zukunft? Den Freunden der wissenschaftlichen Astrologie* [A glimpse into the future? To the friends of scientific astrology] by Elsbeth Ebertin. The first, third, and sixth quotations are taken from an essay entitled "Der Tempel in Dornach" in the magazine *Der Leuchtturm* (Lorch [Württemberg], October 1920). The second, fourth, and fifth quotations are in the original text by Elsbeth Ebertin.

the efforts of this little group
Presumably, this refers to the appearance of Rudolf Steiner's horoscope, which was first published by Alan Leo in his *The Art of Synthesis* (already in its second edition in 1908) and has gone through several reprints.

97 with particularly influential generals
This refers to the grotesque exploitation of Steiner's personal friendship with the Chief of the General Staff Helmuth von Moltke by opponents who made the absurd claim that Steiner was partly to blame for the loss of the Battle of the Marne in 1914.

counselors of commerce
Reference to Emil Molt, the founder of the first Waldorf School in Stuttgart.

that I was a particularly dangerous Freemason
There is no known documentary evidence of this rumor. See *Autobiography* (CW 28), Chapter XXXVI. The claim that Rudolf Steiner was a Jesuit (later "Jesuit apprentice") appeared as early as 1901. In the lecture of May 24, 1920, in *The Redemption of Thinking: A Study in the Philosophy of Thomas Aquinas* (CW 74):

> At that time I wrote my book *Views of the World and of Life in the Nineteenth Century* [later retitled *The Riddles of Philosophy*, CW 18]. In it you will find the following sentence on page 172: "These thinkers were really able to move in the world of ideas without embodying this world in a coarse, sensory form." Thus I spoke of the Scholastics, and then I spoke of the Catholic thinkers who at that time took up the study of Scholasticism again: and the Catholic thinkers who today endeavor to renew this art of thought are in this respect quite worthy of consideration. What one of them, the Jesuit priest Joseph Kleutgen, says in his book *Die Philosophie der Vorzeit* [The philosophy of prehistoric times] (Innsbruck, 1878) will always be valid. . . . But this had the consequence that at that time it was said that I myself was a Jesuit in disguise.

C.S. Picht reports that in Munich, at the end of the first decade of the century, the rumor was spread that Rudolf Steiner had been educated in the

Jesuit monastery of Kalksburg near Vienna; then it was said that he had been seen in the Moravian Jesuit college of Bojkowitz, east of Brünn; finally, the theosophist Franz Hartmann expressed to Annie Besant, the president of the Theosophical Society, that he considered Dr. Steiner a Jesuit, which Besant passed on to Dr. Steiner in 1909, adding, to confirm how amused she was by such an assertion, that Hartmann himself had already taken her for a Jesuit. Despite this, Annie Besant publicly called Rudolf Steiner a "pupil of the Jesuits" at the General Assembly of her Society in Adyar in 1912, which prompted Rudolf Steiner to refute this claim with a sketch of his life in the form of a lecture (given on February 4, 1913, in GA 250).

99 It is really necessary to take some care
At that time, the colleagues at the Goetheanum organized their own fire department as a precautionary measure. A permanent security service was also set up. Nevertheless, the Goetheanum burned to the ground on New Year's Eve 1922/23 in an act of arson. In the meantime, a new building in sculpted concrete was erected on the same site as a second Goetheanum, based on a model by Rudolf Steiner.

103 luciferic and ahrimanic beings
Regarding the hierarchies, see Rudolf Steiner *The Spiritual Hierarchies and the Physical World* (CW 110). Regarding the powers of Lucifer and Ahriman working in the development of humanity, see Rudolf Steiner, *An Outline of Occult Science* (CW 13) and *Problems of Society, An Esoteric View: From Luciferic Past to Ahrimanic Future* (CW 193).

107 how Eastern culture has fallen into decadence
See the lecture of January 6, 1921, in the present volume.

109 Old Moon
See the lecture of January 21, 1921, in the present volume

Nirvana
Nirvana (Sanskrit, meaning "extinguishing") is a designation for the highest goal of human striving and the highest place that can be reached only by the elect through attainment of the highest knowledge and detachment from all earthly desire.

110 what I described last time
See the lecture of January 23, 1921, in the present volume.

117 the war which took place between China and Japan
This is the First Sino-Japanese War, which broke out between China and Japan in 1894 and ended in 1895 with the Treaty of Shimonoseki. After ceding land, China was obliged to pay an indemnity of 200 million taels to Japan in seven annual installments.

119 "the golden rule of modern. . ."

This is in reference to the golden rule of mechanics, which states that simple mechanisms do not change the amount of work that is needed, but rather trade force for distance. One loses as much in distance as one gains in force. For example, to reduce the force required to lift an object using a lever, one must extend the length of the lever's arm correspondingly.

120 that the brain secretes thoughts

See Carl Vogt, *Physiologische Briefe für Gebildete aller Stände* [Physiological letters for educated people of all classes], (Stuttgart and Tübingen, 1845), p. 206:

> Every natural scientist will, I think, through reasonably consistent thinking, come to the conclusion that all those faculties which we understand under the name of soul activities are only functions of the substance of the brain, or, to express myself somewhat crudely: that thoughts stand in the same relation to the brain as bile to the liver or urine to the kidneys. To assume there is a soul that uses the brain as an instrument with which it can work as it pleases is pure nonsense.

In the 2nd revised and expanded edition (Gießen, 1854), p. 323, this passage is repeated with the addition of a quotation from Jacob Moleschott, *Der Kreislauf des Lebens* (Mainz, 1852), p. 402: "The comparison [see above] is unassailable if one understands where Vogt places the point of comparison. The brain is just as indispensable for the production of thoughts as the liver is for the preparation of bile and the kidneys for the secretion of urine."

122 some kind of nebular conditions

This refers to the Kant-Laplace theory.

124 "Harnack-like"

Adolf Harnack, *What Is Christianity?* (London and New York, 1901).

127 Spengler

Oswald Spengler, *The Decline of the West: Form and Actuality*, vol 1 (1918). Volume 2, subtitled *Perspectives of World History*, was not published until 1922.

128 *Hochland*

Published by Karl Muth, Jos. Köselsche Buchhandlung, Munich and Kempten. Second issue 1920/21, 18th year.

128 Rabindranath Tagore

See note to page 23.

130 Copernicus

Nicolaus Copernicus (1473–1543), Polish astronomer, founder of the heliocentric view of the world.

133 Achilles
Greek hero in Homer's *Iliad.*

"Sing to me, O Muse"
Opening lines of Homer's *Iliad.*

Aeschylus
Aeschylus, (*c.* 525–*c.* 456 BC), Greek playwright, best known for the *Oresteia* (458 BC).

136 Haeckelian riddles of the universe
Ernst Haeckel, *The Riddle of the Universe* (originally published in German in 1899).

137 Kühnemann
Eugen Kühnemann (1868–1946), philosopher, author of *Deutschland und Amerika*, 1917.

138 Hans Ehrenberg
Hans Ehrenberg, *Die Heimkehr des Ketzers. Eine Wegweisung* [The homecoming of a heretic: A guide], from the collection, *Bücher vom Kreuzweg* [Books from the way of the cross], (Würzburg, 1920).

that there is, besides the Petrine Establishment, a Johannine Establishment
The relevant passage in the essay "Wege und Irrwege nach Rom" [True and false paths to Rome], by Fritz Fuchs reads: "Ehrenberg perpetuates heresy. 'For Jesus Christ himself created the heretic when he ruthlessly placed John next to Peter, whom he had appointed, and called out to Peter the dismissive words: If I will that he tarry till I come, what is that to thee?'" (John 21/22).

If there come any unto you
2 John 10.

Children, love one another
John 13:34.

140 St. Francis Xavier
Francis Xavier (1506–1552), co-founder of the Jesuit order, missionary in India and Japan. Canonized in 1622.

143 in the public lecture last Tuesday in Basel
Lecture of February 1, 1921, in *Das Innere der Natur und das Wesen der Menschenseele* [The inner aspect of nature and the being of the human soul] (GA 80b).

144 Aristarchus of Samos
Aristarchus of Samos (*c.* 320–250 BC), Greek astronomer.

144 Galileo's trial

Galileo Galilei (1564–1642), Italian astronomer and physicist. In the trial before the Inquisition Tribunal in Rome in 1632, Galileo had to renounce Copernicus' heliocentric view of the universe.

150 which designates Jesus as emperor

See also the lecture of October 5, 1911, in *From Jesus to Christ* (CW 131).

153 the French ambassador Paléologue

Maurice Paléologue (1859–1944), French ambassador in St. Petersburg (1914–1917).

in the presence of the President of the French Republic, Poincaré

From July 20 to 23, 1914, Poincaré, President of the Republic, and Viviani, Prime Minister of France, were in St. Petersburg.

The French ambassador provided a literal report

See Maurice Paléologue *An Ambassador's Memoirs*, trans. F. A. Holt, 2 vols.

156 *Evangelisches Missionsmagazin*

Both book reviews cited are by D. G. Heinzelmann. The pamphlet "Die Hetze gegen das Goetheanum" [The agitation against the Goetheanum] was published by the publishing house of Goetheanum (Dornach, 1920); it contains Rudolf Steiner's public lecture of June 5, 1920: "Die Wahrheit gegen das Goetheanum und deren Verteidigung gegen Unwahrheit" [The truth about anthroposophy and its defense against untruth] (pp. 1–53), as well as a "Aktenmäßige Darstellung der Hetze gegen das Goetheanum" [Documentary account of the agitation against the Goetheanum] by Dr. Roman Boos (pp. 54–104).

Dr. Steiner wanders into untruths against his better judgment

The passage from Heinzelmann's review reads verbatim: "Dr. Steiner sometimes falls into a dangerous sophistry (cf. p. 20 the completely new definition of 'knowing untruth' = an untruth that violates something that one *must* know (!); up until now, knowing untruth was an untruth against better knowledge)."

But this is what it says: "Dr. Boos . . ."

Quote from Rudolf Steiner's lecture of June 5, 1920. The "knowing untruth" in relation to the Akasha Chronicle refers to Max Kully (1878–1936), who was a parish priest in Arlesheim near Basel, close to the Goetheanum, and who wrote the lowest inflammatory articles against anthroposophy in the *Katholisches Sonntagsblatt*, Basel, under the pseudonym "Spektator," which were rejected even by official Catholic authorities. See his series: "Zur Aufklärung über alte und moderne 'Geisteswissenschaft' und ihre Ableger" [Towards enlightenment regarding ancient and modern "spiritual science" and its offshoots], May 16 and 30, 1920.

156 *Upanishads*
Ancient Indian, religious-philosophical texts.

Bhagavad Gita
See note to p. 39.

160 a feuilleton about Carlyle and Nietzsche in the *Neue Zürcher Zeitung*
"Nietzsche über Carlyle. Zum 5. Februar, dem 40. Todestage Carlyles" [Nietzsche on Carlyle. On February 5, the 40th anniversary of Carlyle's death], by Dr. Hans Hartmann, Solingen-Foche. *Neue Zürcher Zeitung*, Sunday, February 6, 1921. The relevant passage reads:

> Nietzsche, however, has only very few greats whom he did not dare to touch throughout his life, and among these Goethe stands at the top, far above Beethoven. One should therefore think that through the medium of Goethe, Carlyle and Nietzsche must also appear to be absolutely related (that does not mean identical). However, Goethe is not only claimed by Steiner, the Mazdaznan people, liberal Christianity, and a few other "thinkers," and not only they interpret him in their own way, but Carlyle and Nietzsche do as well.

162 Dornach February 8, 1921
This lecture made special demands on the stenographer. Undoubtedly, large parts were spoken very quickly, and the speech, especially in the second part, alternated rapidly between quoted material and commentary; there are most certainly gaps and inaccuracies in the transcript.

164 *Die Tat*
Die Tat, monthly magazine for the future of German culture, published by Eugen Diederichs in Jena. February 1921, "Anthroposophisches Sonderheft" [Anthroposophical special issue].

168 Max Dessoir
Max Dessoir (1867–1947), philosopher.

170 the Frohnmeyers and Gogartens and Bruhns and Leeses

D. L. Johannes Frohnmeyer (1850–1921).

Friedrich Gogarten (1887–1931), Protestant theologian. *Rudolf Steiners Geisteswissenschaft und das Christentum* [Rudolf Steiner's spiritual science and Christianity] (Stuttgart, 1920).

Wilhelm Bruhn, *Theosophierende Anthroposophie* [Theosophizing anthroposophy], *Aus Natur und Geisteswelt* [Of nature and the spiritual world], vol. 775. (Leipzig and Berlin, 1921).

Kurt Leese, *Moderne Theosophie, ein Beitrag zum Verständnis der geistigen Strömungen der Gegenwart* [Modern Theosophy, a contribution to the understanding of contemporary spiritual currents] (Berlin, 1921).

170 they are all, all honorable men
From the speech of Marcus Antonius at the funeral of Julius Caesar in Shakespeare's *Julius Caesar*, Act III, Scene 2.

172 my book *Riddles of the Soul*
In the second chapter of *Riddles of the Soul*, Rudolf Steiner discusses Max Dessoir's book, *Vom Jenseits der Seele, die Geheimwissenschaften in kritischer Betrachtung* [From beyond the soul, the secret sciences in critical review] (1917). The episode mentioned can be found on pp. 32ff. of Dessoir's book and is quoted by Rudolf Steiner in *Riddles of the Soul.*

There simply are reasons
From the fragmentary shorthand before this point, it can be seen that Rudolf Steiner describes an incident from a course of lectures held by Dessoir at the time when he was doing his psychophysical investigations, in which he fell into a complete confusion of thought without realizing it himself.

Max Scheler
Max Scheler (1874–1928), philosopher.

173 Wil Salewski
Wilhelm Johannes von Salewski (1889–1950), pastor, co-founder of the Christian Community.

177 What we are talking about is God's secret wisdom . . .
This is a paraphrase of 1 Corinthians 2:6–10:

> We do, however, speak a message of wisdom among the mature, but not the wisdom of this age or of the rulers of this age, who are coming to nothing. No, we declare God's wisdom, a mystery that has been hidden and that God destined for our glory before time began. None of the rulers of this age understood it, for if they had, they would not have crucified the Lord of glory. However, as it is written: . . . these are the things God has revealed to us by his Spirit. The Spirit searches all things, even the deep things of God.

178 this is, of course, a quote from Goethe
A line from the poem "Urworte. Orphisch" [Primal words. Orphic].

180 The well-known *Berliner Tageblatt* fabricates an article
This refers to a report by Christian Bouchholtz entitled "Das abergläubische Berlin. Okkulte Volksschulen und spiritistische Laboratorien" [Superstitious Berlin: Occult elementary schools and spiritualist laboratories] in issue no. 39 of the *Berliner Tageblatt* on Tuesday, January 25, 1921. An excerpt appeared in the English *Daily Telegraph* on January 26. Dr. Roman Boos then wrote a rebuttal entitled "Rudolf Steiner und das Goetheanum," which he tried to have published in the Swiss press.

181 to investigate his sources

This passage is concerned with the first two essays in the February issue of *Die Tat*: J.W. Hauer, "Anthroposophy as a Path to the Spirit" and Walter Johannes Stein, "Anthroposophy as Monism and as Theosophy." Rudolf Steiner said the following about this:

> I would also like to share with you something concerning the rebuttals from the most recent issue of *Die Tat*. Our dear friend, Dr. Stein, has written a very sensible and diligent essay refuting the nonsensical article by Hauer. But what does one achieve with such refutations? One achieves, for example, the following. You see, Hauer stated in earlier lectures that there are hair-raising contradictions between the first and second editions of *The Philosophy of Freedom*. He says this in connection with the dissertation of our friend Dr. Stein and accuses him of not taking into account that such a contradiction exists between the second and first editions of *The Philosophy of Freedom*. Now, Dr. Stein could of course respond by pointing out that he did not quote from the second edition at all, for the second edition, at the time when he was writing his dissertation, had not yet been published. So, you see how concerned the gentleman is with the truth. One accuses Dr. Stein of writing a work on the basis of the revised *Philosophy of Freedom*, when the new edition had not even been published yet. Dr. Stein quoted everything according to the unrevised first edition, and everything Dr. Stein says refers to the first edition, and naturally Dr. Stein brings this up in his essay. This J. W. Hauser, who is, I am told, also a teacher of young people, finds first the following. He says: "Anyone can check whether my view is correct by taking the trouble to read in its entirety Dr. Stein's essay on Büchner. Why does Dr. Stein say (on p. 831 of his essay, I am 'quoting him') that he based his book on the second edition of *The Philosophy of Freedom* and calls it 'untrue'? Usually, in the case of unintentional misunderstandings, one says 'incorrect.'"
>
> You see, under certain circumstances these gentlemen are even sensitive! "And is it malicious slander for me to make such an assertion, when Dr. Stein only gives the page numbers of the second edition in his quotations without a note? It is not customary scholarly practice to print the text of a first edition and then insert the page numbers of the second edition without noting this."
>
> Now you see what happened in reality. In reality, this man did the following pointless thing: Dr. Stein wrote his book only on the basis of the first edition of *The Philosophy of Freedom*. J.W. Hauer accuses Dr. Stein of not dealing with what is not yet anthroposophy in the first edition of *The Philosophy of Freedom* but that Dr. Stein unlawfully bases his book only on the second edition, whereby he is guilty of a small oversight: He only quoted from the first edition; it was only when Stein's book was finished and was to be printed that the second edition of *The Philosophy of Freedom* appeared, and there he inserted the page numbers of the second edition, but did not change anything in the quotations. Hauer did the

imprudent thing of accusing Dr. Stein, who inserted the page numbers according to the second edition which I am supposed to have altered, of having based his book on the second edition of *The Philosophy of Freedom*. Stein, however, quoted from the first edition, but forgot to note after the publication of the second edition that the quotations were taken from the first edition and only the page numbers from the second edition. But Hauer concludes from this oversight on Stein's part that he is this evil person who conceals the whole fact that I changed my entire worldview in the new edition of *The Philosophy of Freedom*, and who would imply to the readers that what is in the second edition is correct, not what is in the first edition. So what it comes down to is that such a muckraker doesn't go into that at all, but he wriggles out again with such an excuse. That's what you achieve with such a rebuttal. People like that can always make excuses, because of course things like that can always happen. You could waste your whole time with things like that. And what good would it do, for example, if I were to refute what is written at the end of the essay by this J.W. Hauer: "Dr. Steiner himself (*Denkschrift über die Abtrennung der anthroposophischen Gesellschaft von der theosophischen Gesellschaft*, published by Dr. Hübbe-Schleiden, Leipzig, 1913, p. 64) was admitted to the esoteric school of the Theosophical Society by Mrs. Besant on October 23, 1902." That this esoteric school was worth nothing and offered nothing could only be said by someone who had become acquainted with it! In order to discuss all these things, one would have to get involved in a lot of debates, which would lead to a tapeworm discussion.

181 placing the spiritual underpinnings . . . in the right light
Since the shorthand pad ended here, the transition to the end of the lecture is not seamless.

186 the middle of the fourth post-Atlantean epoch
According to Rudolf Steiner, the fourth, Greco-Latin cultural epoch lasted from 747 BC to 1413 AD. Thus the year 333 AD is the exact middle of this period.

192 Cimabue
Giovanni Cimabue (*c.* 1240–1302), Italian painter.

Giotto
Giotto di Bondone (c. 1267–1337), Italian painter.

193 Adolf Harnack
Adolf Harnack (1851–1930), Protestant theologian. See *What Is Christianity?* 8th lecture.

202 Dr. Boos
Dr. Roman Boos (1889–1952), social scientist, writer, and speaker.

203 a public lecture in Hengelo
A pamphlet entitled "Gebr. Stork & Co Maschinenfabrik Hengelo-Holland" can be found in Rudolf Steiner's library.

204 A book dealing with philosophical questions
Jürgen Bona Meyer (1829–1897), professor of philosophy in Bonn, *Philosophische Zeitfragen,* 2nd expanded and revised edition (Bonn, 1874). Arnold Dodel (1843–1908), author and professor of botany at the University of Zürich. The copy of the book mentioned by Steiner is in his library. Dodel worked through it up to page 114, underlining numerous passages and making—mostly sarcastic—notes in the margins. As Steiner describes them as symptomatic, some of them are recorded here: "pretty phrase?" – "Philosophers always take refuge in the almost inaccessible realm of the metaphysical when they come into conflict with the physical, clever?" – "Aberration?" – "The author has undoubtedly overlooked Darwin here!" – "Brazen, dear sir!" – "It smacks of sophism!" – "Certainly not to us materialists!" – "So the outside world does exist!" – "So no one among the materialists has thought deeply?" – "This guy talks like a pope!" – "I think some materialists have clearer heads than this dogmatizing and swearing professor of philosophy!" – "The author is talking nonsense!" – "Yes, my dear fellow!" – "Nonsense!" – "Fechner's flower souls! I dread it!" – "The author oracles!" – "Pretty presumption!" – "The philosophy professor wants to school us!" – "How this guy whines!???" – "How infallible the philosopher is!" – "Devil take these critics!" – "So, here's the philosopher pulling back his shirtsleeves, let's see!" – "This question, dear sir, you are incapable of answering." – "Bona, bona, pale envy has blinded you!" – "Hallelujah, critic! You will be long forgotten if Darwin's giant construction is still admired!" The review concludes on p. 114 with the note: "*Salut et bénédiction la-dessus!* We would have gladly done without it. Zürich, September 30, 1874. A.D."

204 Mr. Stuten
Jan Stuten (1890–1948), Dutch musician, sculptor, stage designer, and actor; among numerous other compositions, he created music for Goethe's *Faust* for performances at the Goetheanum in Dornach, Switzerland.

205 distributing leaflets
This is a leaflet by the Dutch scholar and opponent of anthroposophy Dr. H. K. E. De Jong, The Hague, partly reprinted in Max Kully's inflammatory pamphlet "Die Geheimnisse des Tempels von Dornach" [The secrets of the Dornach Temple], 2nd part (Basel, 1921), p. 4f.

Reverend Kully's leaflet
De Jong and Kully were in correspondence with each other.

"Der Weg zur Vollendung" [The path to perfection]
"Der Weg zur Vollendung. Mitteilungen der Gesellschaft für freie

Philosophie, Schule der Weisheit, Darmstadt [The path to perfection: Communications of the Society for Free Philosophy, School of Wisdom, Darmstadt]. Published by Count Hermann Keyserling, 1st issue, Darmstadt, 1920. The text of the "Bauchbinde" corresponds to the publisher's comment on the second cover page of this first issue in the sentence: "Thus Rudolf Steiner's attacks must also be dealt with in the first issue."

in my public lecture in Stuttgart
This is the lecture of November 16, 1920, in *Die Anthroposophie und ihre Gegner* [Anthroposophy and its opponents] (GA 225b). Keyserling had written of Rudolf Steiner in his book *Philosophie der Kunst* [Philosophy of art] (Darmstadt, 1920), p. 241, that "it is at any rate symbolic of his nature that his spiritual career in certain respects emanated from Haeckel." Rudolf Steiner took exception to this for good reason and said in the lecture mentioned above: "It is not true that I have sought any connection to Haeckel. Haeckel came of his own accord to me, to the kind of endeavors I have cultivated."

206 if I had simply said
Literally, ". . . instead of correcting any error on my part, which I would gladly put up with, for I have had no time for special Steiner source research . . . Steiner flatly accuses me of lying" (see "Der Weg zur Vollendung," p. 46ff. under "Bücherschau," described in the table of contents as: Erledigung der Angriffe Rudolf Steiners [Dealing with Rudolf Steiner's attacks]).

professor Fuchs
Prof. Dr. med. Hugo Fuchs, director of the Anatomical Institute in Göttingen. In the *Göttinger Tageblatt* in 1920 (May 26, 27), he had sought vehemently to discredit anthroposophically oriented spiritual science and the efforts of the "Bund für Dreigliederung des sozialen Organismus" (Federation for the Threefolding of the Social Organism), and also used his lectures to steer his listeners in this direction and to incite them to protest when the opportunity arose, for which an educational lecture organized by the Anthroposophical Society and the aforementioned Federation initially provided an opportunity. On February 25, 1921, a protest against the Bund was held in Göttingen in connection with professor Fuchs' agitation with reference to Upper Silesia. The counterprotest planned by the Bund was banned by the police chief—naturally under the influence of Göttingen (see the weekly journal *Dreigliederung des sozialen Organismus*, Stuttgart, 1920, no. 4, supplement, no. 5; 1921, no. 36 and no. 40).

206 article in the *Frankfurter Zeitung*
Frankfurter Zeitung, 1921, 65th year, no. 167 (March 4), 2nd morning page, p. 2: "Verräter am Deutschtum" [Traitor to Germanness]. For the reply of the "Federation for the Threefolding of the Social Organism" (together with the foolish addition of the editorial staff of the *Frankfurter Zeitung*)

see ibid., no. 188 (March 12), 1st morning page, p. 2: "Dreigliederung des sozialen Organismus und Oberschlesien" [Threefolding of the social organism and Upper Silesia]. In no. 196 (March 15), 2nd morning page, the criticism was qualified and the accusation of treason was dropped. At the beginning of 1921, in the run-up to the referendum on the division of the south eastern territories of Silesia between Germany and Poland, Silesian friends of Rudolf Steiner's threefolding idea campaigned for a neutral Upper Silesian state as a closed economic area, attracting protests from nationalist circles in particular.

207 the central Group
This refers to the nearly thirty-foot tall sculpture of the Representative of Humanity between Lucifer and Ahriman, carved in wood by Rudolf Steiner with the help of Edith Maryon, which survived the fire of the First Goetheanum and now stands in the Second Goetheanum in Dornach, Switzerland.

209 Elohim
This follows the Hebrew wording of *Genesis.*

215 from other lectures
See Rudolf Steiner, *Michael's Mission* (CW 194).

Thus, you still find in Plato
See especially Plato's *Phaidon*, as well as the chapter "Plato as Mystic" in Rudolf Steiner, *Christianity as Mystical Fact and the Mysteries of Antiquity* (CW 8).

218 warmth ether
There are four ethers: warmth ether, light ether, sound (chemical) ether, and life ether. See Rudolf Steiner, *Genesis: Secrets of Creation* (CW 122).

220 *Nephesch*
See the lecture of August 26, 1910, in *Genesis: Secrets of Creation* (CW 122) and the lecture of April 27, 1909, in *Disease, Karma, and Healing: Spiritual-scientific Enquiries into the Nature of the Human Being* (CW 107).

224 on the other side, arouse certain feelings
See the beginning of the previous lecture of March 11, 1921, in the present volume.

230 I myself will probably be speaking in Stuttgart . . . on a scientific theme
Lectures of March 16 to 23, 1921, in *Anthroposophy and Science: Observation, Experiment, Mathematics* (CW 324).

lectures . . . which will be given here starting April 3
These are the lectures of April 3–10, 1921, given at the second anthroposophical university course, published as *Die befruchtende Wirkung der*

Anthroposophie auf die Fachwissenschaften [The fertilizing effect of anthroposophy on the individual fields of science], (GA 76).

232 Paul's powerful words
1 Cor. 15:14.

the words in the Gospel
Matt. 28:5; Mark 16:6; Luke 24:6.

233 Christianity became the state religion
In 324 by Emperor Constantine I.

Julian the Apostate
Julian, Roman Emperor 361–363 A.D. See the lecture of April 19, 1917, in *Building Stones for an Understanding of the Mystery of Golgotha* (CW 175).

235 the Son doesn't belong in the Gospels at all
See Adolf Harnack (1851–1939), in *What Is Christianity?* (London and New York, 1901).

238 Goethe did indeed express often enough
For example, in *Wilhelm Meister's Apprenticeship*, book 2, chapter 2.

243 Apollonius of Tyana
Apollonius of Tyana, first century Greek philosopher and miracle worker.

245 Gymnosophists
Among the later Greeks, the name given to ancient Indian philosophers who practiced contemplation and the strictest asceticism. They disdained all clothing.

246 according to his biographer
Philostratus, Flavius, the Elder, Greek sophist and rhetorician (*c.* 170s–240s AD), wrote a biography of Apollonius of Tyana at the request of the Empress Julia, wife of the Roman Emperor Septimus Severus (193–211 AD).

247 Vincenz Knauer
Vincenz Knauer (1828–1894), philosopher, private lecturer in Vienna. See *Die Hauptprobleme der Philosophie* [The main problems of philosophy] (Vienna and Leipzig, 1892), p. 136f.

255 Max Heindel
Max Heindel (1865–1919), a Dane who called himself "Grashof" in Berlin. Author of occult writings such as *The Web of Destiny, Musical Scale in the Stream of Evolution*, as well as the book mentioned here by Rudolf Steiner: *Rosicrucian Cosmo-Conception or Christian Occult Science*, 1st

edition (Chicago, 1909), with a dedication to Dr. Steiner, reading: "To my valued friend, Dr. Rudolph Steiner, in grateful recognition of much valuable information received; and to my friend, Dr. Alma von Brandis, in heartfelt appreciation of the inestimable influence for soul-growth she has exercised in my life." See also the lecture of May 11, 1917, in *The Spiritual Background to the First World War* (CW 174b) and the lecture of June 10, 1917, in *Zur Geschichte der Anthroposophischen Gesellschaft 1913–1922* [On the history of the Anthroposophical Society 1913–1922] (GA 251).

that everything was translated back into German
Title of the German edition: *Die Weltanschauung der Rosenkreuzer oder Mystisches Christentum. Eine elementare Abhandlung über die vergangene Entwicklung, die gegenwärtige Zusammensetzung und die künftige Entfaltung der Menschheit von Max Heindel. Seine Botschaft und Bestimmung: Ein urteilsfähiger Intellekt. Ein fühlendes Herz. Ein gesunder Körper.* [The worldview of the Rosicrucians or mystical Christianity: An elementary treatise on the past development, the present composition, and the future unfolding of humanity by Max Heindel. Its message and purpose: A discerning intellect. A feeling heart. A healthy body]. Authorized translation by S. von der Wiesen. Theosophical Publishing House, Leipzig, Dr. Hugo Vollrath. Published as 10 teaching letters.

256 the meaning of the Pauline words
1 Corinthians 15:14.

261 at which Helmholtz gave a lecture
The lecture in question was given in Weimar in 1892 at the general assembly of the Goethe Society: "Goethes Vorahnungen kommender naturwissenschaftlicher Ideen" [Goethe's premonitions of coming scientific ideas]. The lecture was first published in the July issue of the *Deutsche Rundschau*, Berlin, and then appeared as a pamphlet (Berlin, 1892). – See also Rudolf Steiner, *Autobiography* (CW 28).

267 My dear friends
The remarks at the end of the lecture, which were not included in earlier editions, refer to the program of the forthcoming (second) anthroposophical university course, which took place from April 3 to 10, 1921, in Dornach (*Die befruchtende Wirkung der Anthroposophie auf die Fachwissenschaften* [The fertilizing effect of anthroposophy on the individual fields of science] [GA 76]). The program of the course announced "stimulating social-scientific-artistic disputations with a little piquancy in between," a formulation that caused some excitement and outrage.

268 Last time, during the course
This likely refers to the first university course in autumn 1920.

RUDOLF STEINER'S COLLECTED WORKS

The German Edition of Rudolf Steiner's Collected Works (the *Gesamtausgabe* [GA], published by Rudolf Steiner Verlag, Dornach, Switzerland) will be completed in the year 2025. The works are organized either by type of work (written, spoken, artistic creations), chronology, audience (public or other), or subject (education, art, etc.). For ease of comparison, the Collected Works in English (CW), listed below, follows the German organization and numbering.

The volumes that have so far been published in the English Collected Works edition appear *in italics with their published titles*; all other volumes, including those that have appeared in editions other than the CW, are set in Roman type with *literal translations* of the German titles. Published English titles are not necessarily the same as the German.

This list is current as of the date of this volume's publication.

A. Written Works

I. Writings 1884–1925

CW 1	Introductions and Selected Commentary on Goethe's Natural-scientific Writings
CW 1a–e	Goethe's Natural-scientific Writings
CW 1f	Editorial Afterwords to Goethe's Natural-scientific Writings in the Weimar Edition (1891–1896)
CW 2	*Goethe's Theory of Knowledge: An Outline of the Epistemology of His Worldview*
CW 3	Truth and Science
CW 4	The Philosophy of Freedom
CW 4a	Documents to "The Philosophy of Freedom"
CW 5	Friedrich Nietzsche, A Fighter against His Own Time
CW 6	Goethe's Worldview
CW 7	Mysticism at the Dawn of Modern Spiritual Life and Its Relationship with Modern Worldviews
CW 8	*Christianity as Mystical Fact and the Mysteries of Antiquity*
CW 9	Theosophy: An Introduction into Supersensible World Knowledge and Human Purpose
CW 10	How Does One Attain Knowledge of Higher Worlds?
CW 11	From the Akasha-Chronicle
CW 12	Levels of Higher Knowledge
CW 13	Occult Science in Outline
CW 14	*Four Modern Mystery Dramas*
CW 15	The Spiritual Guidance of the Individual and Humanity
CW 16/17	*A Way of Self-Knowledge & The Threshold of the Spiritual World*

CW 18 The Riddles of Philosophy in Their History, Presented as an Outline
CW 18a Views of the World and of Life in the Nineteenth Century
CW 19 Thoughts during the Time of War (1915) and Further Texts on the Events of the World War (1917–1921)
CW 20 The Riddles of the Human Being: Articulated and Unarticulated in the Thinking, Views and Opinions of a Series of German and Austrian Personalities
CW 21 The Riddles of the Soul
CW 22 Goethe's Spiritual Nature and Its Revelation in "Faust" and through the "Fairy Tale of the Snake and the Lily"
CW 23 The Central Points of the Social Question in the Necessities of Life in the Present and the Future
CW 24 Essays Concerning the Threefold Division of the Social Organism and the Period 1915–1921
CW 25 Three Steps of Anthroposophy. Philosophy – Cosmology – Religion
CW 26 Anthroposophical Leading Thoughts
CW 27 Fundamentals for Expansion of the Art of Healing according to Spiritual-Scientific Insights
CW 28 *Autobiography: Chapters in the Course of My Life: 1861–1907*

II. Collected Essays

CW 29 Collected Essays on Dramaturgy, 1889–1900
CW 30 Methodical Foundations of Anthroposophy: Collected Essays on Philosophy, Natural Science, Aesthetics and Psychology, 1884–1901
CW 31 Collected Essays on Culture and Current Events, 1887–1901
CW 32 Collected Essays on Literature, 1884–1902
CW 33 Biographies and Biographical Sketches, 1894–1905
CW 34 Lucifer-Gnosis: Foundational Essays on Anthroposophy and Reports from the Periodicals "Luzifer" and "Lucifer-Gnosis," 1903–1908
CW 35 Philosophy and Anthroposophy: Collected Essays, 1904–1923
CW 36 The Goetheanum-Idea in the Middle of the Cultural Crisis of the Present: Collected Essays from the Periodical "Das Goetheanum," 1921–1925
CW 37 Writings on the History of the Anthroposophical Movement and Society 1902–1925

III. Publications from the Literary Estate

CW 38/1 Complete Letters, Vol. 1: Weimar Period 1879–1890
CW 38/2 Complete Letters, Vol. 2: Weimar Period 1890–1897

CW 38/3	Complete Letters, Vol. 3: Early Berlin Period 1897–1905 [forthcoming]
CW 38/4	Complete Letters, Vol. 4: Activity within the Theosophical Society 1905–1912 [forthcoming]
CW 38/5	Complete Letters, Vol. 5: From the Founding of the Anthroposophical Society to the Opening of the Goetheanum 1913–1920 [forthcoming]
CW 38/6	Complete Letters, Vol. 6: The Last Years 1920–1925 [forthcoming]
CW 40	Truth-Wrought Words
CW 40a	Sayings, Poems and Mantras; Supplementary Volume
CW 41a	Translations and Free Renderings from the Old and New Testaments
CW 41b	Translations and Free Renderings of Various Works
CW 42	Stage Adaptations I: Dramas by Edouard Schuré
CW 43	Stage Adaptations II: The Oberufer Christmas Plays
CW 44	Sketches, Fragments and Paralipomena on the Four Mystery Dramas
CW 45	Anthroposophy: A Fragment from the Year 1910
CW 46	Posthumous Essays and Fragments 1879–1924
CW 47/48	Notebooks and Notepads (digital edition)
CW 49	Notes for and about Helmuth and Eliza von Moltke and Relatives, 1904–1924 [forthcoming]
CW 50	[Blank number]

B. Lectures

I. Public Lectures

CW 51	*On Philosophy, History, and Literature: Lectures at the Worker Education School and the Independent College, Berlin, 1901–1905*
CW 52	Spiritual Teachings Concerning the Soul and Observation of the World
CW 53	The Origin and Goal of the Human Being
CW 54	The Riddles of the World and Anthroposophy
CW 55	Knowledge of the Supersensible in Our Times and Its Meaning for Life Today
CW 56	Knowledge of the Soul and of the Spirit
CW 57	Where and How Does One Find the Spirit?
CW 58	The Metamorphoses of the Soul Life. Paths of Soul Experiences: Part One
CW 59	The Metamorphoses of the Soul Life. Paths of Soul Experiences: Part Two

CW 60	The Answers of Spiritual Science to the Biggest Questions of Existence
CW 61	Human History in the Light of Spiritual Research
CW 62	*Results of Spiritual Research*
CW 63	Spiritual Science as a Treasure for Life
CW 64	Out of Destiny-Burdened Times
CW 65	Out of Central European Spiritual Life
CW 66	Spirit and Matter, Life and Death
CW 67	The Eternal in the Human Soul. Immortality and Freedom
CW 68a	On the Being of Christianity
CW 68b	The Cycle of the Human Being within the Sense-, Soul-, and Spirit-World
CW 68c	Goethe and the Present
CW 68d	The Being of Man in the Light of Spiritual Science
CW 69a	Truths and Errors of Spiritual Research. Spiritual Science and the Future of Mankind
CW 69b	Knowledge and Immortality
CW 69c	New Christ-Experience
CW 69d	Death and Immortality in the Light of Spiritual Science
CW 69e	Spiritual Science and the Spiritual Goals of Our Time
CW 70a	Human Soul, Destiny and Death
CW 70b	Paths to the Knowledge of the Eternal Powers of the Human Soul
CW 71a	Soul Immortality [forthcoming]
CW 71b	The Human Being as a Soul and Spirit Being
CW 72	Freedom – Immortality – Social Life
CW 73	The Supplementing of the Modern Sciences through Anthroposophy
CW 73a	Specialized Fields of Knowledge and Anthroposophy
CW 74	The Philosophy of Thomas Aquinas
CW 75	*Anthroposophy and the Natural Sciences: Foundations and Methods*
CW 76	The Fructifying Effect of Anthroposophy on Specialized Fields
CW 77a	The Task of Anthroposophy in Relation to Science and Life: The Darmstadt College Course
CW 77b	Art and Anthroposophy. The Goetheanum-Impulse
CW 78	Anthroposophy, Its Roots of Knowledge and Fruits for Life
CW 79	The Reality of the Higher Worlds
CW 80a	The Being of Anthroposophy
CW 80b	The Inner Realm of Nature and the Being of the Human Soul
CW 80c	Anthroposophical Spiritual Science and the Great Civilizational Questions of the Present
CW 81	*Reimagining Academic Studies: Science, Philosophy, Education, Social Science, Theology, Theory of Language*

CW 82	*Becoming Fully Human: The Significance of Anthroposophy in Contemporary Spiritual Life*
CW 83	*The Tension between East and West*
CW 84	*The Aims of Anthroposophy and the Purpose of the Goetheanum*
CW 85	Supplementary Volume: Individual Public Lectures I [forthcoming]
CW 86	Supplementary Volume: Individual Public Lectures II [forthcoming]

II. Lectures to the Members of the Anthroposophical Society

CW 87	Ancient Mysteries and Christianity
CW 88	*Concerning the Astral World and Devachan*
CW 89	Consciousness – Life – Form. Fundamental Principles of a Spiritual-Scientific Cosmology
CW 90a	Self-knowledge and Knowledge of the Divine, Vol. I. Theosophy, Christology, and Mythology
CW 90b	Self-knowledge and Knowledge of the Divine, Vol. II. Theosophy, Christology, and Mythology
CW 90c	Theosophy and Occultism
CW 91	Cosmology and Human Evolution. Introduction to Theosophy – Theory of Colors
CW 92	*The Occult Truths of Myths and Legends: Greek and Germanic Mythology: Richard Wagner in the Light of Spiritual Science*
CW 93	The Temple Legend and the Golden Legend as a Symbolic Expression of Past and Future Secrets of Human Development. From the Contents of the Esoteric School
CW 93a	Fundamentals of Esotericism
CW 94	Cosmogony. Popular Occultism. The Gospel of John. Theosophy Based on the Gospel of John
CW 95	At the Gates of Theosophy
CW 96	Origin-Impulses of Spiritual Science. Christian Esotericism in the Light of New Spirit-knowledge
CW 97	The Christian Mystery
CW 98	*Nature Beings and Spirit Beings: Their Activity in Our Visible World*
CW 99	The Theosophy of the Rosicrucians
CW 100	*True Knowledge of the Christ: Theosophy and Rosicucianism—The Gospel of John*
CW 101	Myths and Legends. Occult Signs and Symbols
CW 102	*Good and Evil Spirits and Their Influence on Humanity*
CW 103	*The Gospel of John*
CW 104	The Apocalypse of John
CW 104a	From the Picture-Script of the Apocalypse of John
CW 105	*Universe, Earth, Human Being: Their Relationship to Egyptian Myths and Modern Civilization*

CW 106 Egyptian Myths and Mysteries in Relation to the Active Spiritual Forces of the Present
CW 107 *Disease, Karma, and Healing: Spiritual-scientific Enquiries into the Nature of the Human Being*
CW 108 Answering the Questions of Life and the World through Anthroposophy
CW 109 The Principle of Spiritual Economy in Connection with the Question of Reincarnation. An Aspect of the Spiritual Guidance of Humanity
CW 110 *The Spiritual Hierarchies and the Physical World: Zodiac, Planets, and Cosmos*
CW 111 Introduction to the Foundations of Theosophy
CW 112 The Gospel of John in Relation to the Three Other Gospels, Especially the Gospel of Luke
CW 113 The Orient in the Light of the Occident. The Children of Lucifer and the Brothers of Christ
CW 114 The Gospel of Luke
CW 115 Anthroposophy – Psychosophy – Pneumatosophy
CW 116 *The Christ-Impulse and the Development of Ego-Consciousness*
CW 117 *Deeper Secrets of Human Evolution in Light of the Gospels*
CW 117a The Gospel of John and the Three Other Gospels
CW 118 The Event of the Christ-Appearance in the Etheric World
CW 119 *Macrocosm and Microcosm: The Greater and the Lesser World: Questions Concerning the Soul, Life and the Spirit*
CW 120 The Revelations of Karma
CW 121 *The Mission of Folk Souls*
CW 122 The Secrets of the Biblical Creation-Story. The Six-Day Work in the First Book of Moses
CW 123 The Gospel of Matthew
CW 124 *Background to the Gospel of St. Mark*
CW 125 *Paths and Goals of the Spiritual Human Being: Life Questions in the Light of Spiritual Science*
CW 126 Occult History. Esoteric Observations of the Karmic Relationships of Personalities and Events of World History
CW 127 *The Mission of the New Spiritual Revelation: The Pivotal Nature of the Christ Event in Earth Evolution*
CW 128 An Occult Physiology
CW 129 *Wonders of the World: Trials of the Soul, Revelations of the Spirit*
CW 130 Esoteric Christianity and the Spiritual Guidance of Humanity
CW 131 *From Jesus to Christ*
CW 132 *Inner Experiences of Evolution*
CW 133 *Earthly and Cosmic Man*

CW 134 *The World of the Senses and the World of the Spirit*
CW 135 Reincarnation and Karma and Their Meaning for the Culture of the Present
CW 136 *Spiritual Beings in the Heavenly Bodies and in the Kingdoms of Nature*
CW 137 The Human Being in the Light of Occultism, Theosophy and Philosophy
CW 138 On Initiation. On Eternity and the Passing Moment. On the Light of the Spirit and the Darkness of Life
CW 139 The Gospel of Mark
CW 140 Occult Investigation into the Life between Death and New Birth. The Living Interaction between Life and Death
CW 141 *Between Death and Rebirth: In Relation to Cosmic Facts*
CW 142/46 *The Bhagavad Gita and the West: The Esoteric Significance of the Bhagavad Gita and Its Relation to the Epistles of Paul*
CW 143 *Three Paths to Christ: Experiencing the Supersensible*
CW 144 *The Mysteries of Initiation: From Isis to the Holy Grail*
CW 145 What Significance Does Occult Development of the Human Being Have for the Sheaths – Physical Body, Etheric Body, Astral Body, and Self?
CW 146 [See CW 142/46]
CW 147 The Secrets of the Threshold
CW 148 The Fifth Gospel
CW 149 *Christ and the Spiritual World: The Quest for the Holy Grail*
CW 150 *How the Spiritual World Projects into Physical Existence: The Influence of the Dead*
CW 151 *Human and Cosmic Thought*
CW 152 *Approaching the Mystery of Golgotha*
CW 153 The Inner Being of Man and Life Between Death and New Birth
CW 154 How Does One Gain an Understanding of the Spiritual World? The Flowing in of Spiritual Impulses from out of the World of the Deceased
CW 155 *Christ and the Human Soul: The Meaning of Life – The Spiritual Foundation of Morality – Anthroposophy and Christianity*
CW 156 *Inner Reading and Inner Hearing: And How to Achieve Existence in the World of Ideas*
CW 157 Human Destinies and the Destiny of Peoples
CW 157a The Formation of Destiny and the Life after Death
CW 158 *Our Connection with the Elemental World: Kalevala – Olaf Åsteson – the Russian People: The World as the Result of Balancing Influences*
CW 159 *The Mystery of Death: The Nature and Significance of Central Europe and the European Folk-Spirits*
CW 160 [Blank number]

CW 161 *Artistic Sensitivity as a Spiritual Approach to Knowing Life and the World*
CW 162 Questions of Art and Life in Light of Spiritual Science
CW 163 Coincidence, Necessity and Providence. Imaginative Knowledge and the Processes after Death
CW 164 *The Value of Thinking for a Cognition that Satisfies the Human Being: The Relationship between Spiritual Science and Natural Science*
CW 165 *Unifying Humanity Spiritually through the Christ Impulse*
CW 166 *Necessity and Freedom*
CW 167 *The Human Spirit Past and Present: Occult Fraternities and the Mystery of Golgotha*
CW 168 *The Connection between the Living and the Dead*
CW 169 World-being and Selfhood
CW 170 The Riddle of the Human Being. The Spiritual Background of Human History
CW 171 Inner Development-Impulses of Humanity. Goethe and the Crisis of the 19th Century.
CW 172 The Karma of the Vocation of the Human Being in Connection with Goethe's Life.
CW 173a Observations of Modern History, Vol. I: Paths to an Objective Judgment
CW 173b Observations of Modern History, Vol. II: The Karma of Untruthfulness
CW 173c Observations of Modern History, Vol. III: The Reality of Occult Impulses
CW 174a *Europe Between East and West in Cosmic and Human History*
CW 174b *The Spiritual Background to the First World War*
CW 175 *Building Stones for an Understanding of the Mystery of Golgotha: Human Life in a Cosmic Context*
CW 176 *The Karma of Materialism: Aspects of Human Evolution*
CW 177 *The Fall of the Spirits of Darkness: The Spiritual Background to the Outer World: Spiritual Beings and Their Effects*
CW 178 Individual Spiritual Beings and Their Influence in the Soul of the Human Being
CW 179 *The Influence of the Dead on Destiny*
CW 180 Mystery Truths and Christmas Impulses. Ancient Myths and their Meaning.
CW 181 *Dying Earth and Living Cosmos: The Living Gifts of Anthroposophy: The Need for New Forms of Consciousness*
CW 182 Death as Transformation of Life
CW 183 *Human Evolution: A Spiritual-Scientific Quest*
CW 184 *Eternal and Transient Elements in Human Life: The Cosmic Past of Humanity and the Mystery of Evil*

CW 185 Historical Symptomology
CW 185a Historical-Developmental Foundations for Forming a Social Judgment
CW 186 The Fundamental Social Demands of Our Time. In Changed Times
CW 187 How Can Humanity Find the Christ Again? The Threefold Shadow-Existence of our Time and the New Christ-Light
CW 188 *Goetheanism: An Impulse of Transformation and Resurrection*
CW 189 *Conscious Society: Anthroposophy and the Social Question*
CW 190 *Past and Future Impulses in Societal Events*
CW 191 *Understanding Society through Spiritual-Scientific Knowledge: Social Threefolding, Christ, Lucifer, and Ahriman*
CW 192 Spiritual-Scientific Treatment of Social and Pedagogical Questions
CW 193 *Problems of Society: An Esoteric View, from Luciferic Past to Ahrimanic Future*
CW 194 *Michael's Mission: Revealing the Essential Secrets of Human Nature*
CW 195 *Cosmic New Year: Thoughts for New Year 1920*
CW 196 *What Is Necessary in These Urgent Times*
CW 197 *Polarities in the Evolution of Humanity: West and East – Materialism and Mysticism – Knowledge and Belief*
CW 198 *Healing the Social Organism*
CW 199 Spiritual Science as Knowledge of the Foundational Impulses of Social Formation
CW 200 The New Spirituality and the Christ-Experience of the 20th Century
CW 201 The Correspondences Between Microcosm and Macrocosm. The Human Being – A Hieroglyph of the Universe.
CW 202 *Universal Spirituality and Human Physicality: Bridging the Divide: The Search for the New Isis and the Divine Sophia*
CW 203 *The Hour of Decision: Human Responsibility for World Evolution through Our Spiritual Connection with the Earth and the World of the Stars*
CW 204 Perspectives of the Development of Humanity. The Materialistic Knowledge-Impulse and the Task of Anthroposophy.
CW 205 Human Development, World-Soul, and World-Spirit. Part One: The Human Being as a Being of Body and Soul in Relationship to the World.
CW 206 Human Development, World-Soul, and World-Spirit. Part Two: The Human Being as a Spiritual Being in the Process of Historical Development
CW 207 Anthroposophy as Cosmosophy. Part One: Characteristic Features of the Human Being in the Earthly and the Cosmic Realms
CW 208 Anthroposophy as Cosmosophy. Part Two: The Forming of the Human Being as the Result of Cosmic Influence

CW 209 *The Language of the Cosmos: Cosmic Influences and the Spiritual Task of Northern Europe*
CW 210 Old and New Methods of Initiation. Drama and Poetry in the Change of Consciousness in the Modern Age
CW 211 *The Sun Mystery and the Mystery of Death and Resurrection: Exoteric and Esoteric Christianity*
CW 212 *Life of the Human Soul: And Its Relation to World Evolution*
CW 213 *Human Questions and Cosmic Answers*
CW 214 The Mystery of the Trinity: The Human Being in Relationship with the Spiritual World in the Course of Time
CW 215 Philosophy, Cosmology, and Religion in Anthroposophy
CW 216 *Supersensible Impulses in the Historical Development of Humanity*
CW 217 *Becoming the Archangel Michael's Companions: Rudolf Steiner's Challenge to the Younger Generation*
CW 217a *Youth and the Etheric Heart: Rudolf Steiner Speaks to the Younger Generation*
CW 218 *Spirit as Sculptor of the Human Organism*
CW 219 The Relationship of the World of the Stars to the Human Being, and of the Human Being to the World of the Stars. The Spiritual Communion of Humanity
CW 220 *Awake! For the Sake of the Future*
CW 221 Earth-Knowing and Heaven-Insight
CW 222 *The Driving Force of Spiritual Powers in World History*
CW 223 The Cycle of the Year as Breathing Process of the Earth and the Four Great Festival-Seasons. Anthroposophy and the Human Heart (*Gemüt*)
CW 224 The Human Soul and its Connection with Divine-Spiritual Individualities. The Internalization of the Festivals of the Year
CW 225 *Three Perspectives of Anthroposophy: Cultural Phenomena from the Point of View of Spiritual Science*
CW 226 Human Being, Human Destiny, and World Development
CW 227 Initiation-Knowledge
CW 228 *Initiation Science: And the Development of the Human Mind*
CW 229 The Experiencing of the Course of the Year in Four Cosmic Imaginations
CW 230 The Human Being as Harmony of the Creative, Building, and Formative World-Word
CW 231 The Supersensible Human Being, Understood Anthroposophically
CW 232 The Forming of the Mysteries
CW 233 *World History and the Mysteries in the Light of Anthroposophy*
CW 233a *Rosicrucianism and Modern Initiation: Mystery Centres of the Middle Ages: The Easter Festival and the History of the Mysteries*
CW 234 Anthroposophy. A Summary after 21 Years

CW 235 Esoteric Observations of Karmic Relationships in 6 Volumes, Vol. 1
CW 236 Esoteric Observations of Karmic Relationships in 6 Volumes, Vol. 2
CW 237 Esoteric Observations of Karmic Relationships in 6 Volumes, Vol. 3: The Karmic Relationships of the Anthroposophical Movement
CW 238 Esoteric Observations of Karmic Relationships in 6 Volumes, Vol. 4: The Spiritual Life of the Present in Relationship to the Anthroposophical Movement
CW 239 Esoteric Observations of Karmic Relationships in 6 Volumes, Vol. 5
CW 240 Esoteric Observations of Karmic Relationships in 6 Volumes, Vol. 6
CW 241 [Blank number]
CW 242 [Blank number]
CW 243 *True and False Paths of Spiritual Research*
CW 244 Answers to Questions, and Interviews
CW 245 [Blank number]
CW 246 Supplementary Volume I: Individual Members Lectures
CW 247 Supplementary Volume II: Individual Members Lectures
CW 248 [Blank number]
CW 249 [Blank number]
CW 250 On the History of the German Section of the Theosophical Society 1902–1913. Lectures, Speeches, Reports, and Minutes
CW 251 On the History of the Anthroposophical Society 1913–1922
CW 252 On the History of the Building Association and the Goetheanum Association 1911–1924
CW 253 *Sexuality, Inner Development, and Community Life: Ethical and Spiritual Dimensions of the Crisis in the Anthroposophical Society in Dornach, 1915*
CW 254 The Occult Movement in the 19th Century and Its Relationship to World Culture. Significant Points from the Exoteric Cultural Life around the Middle of the 19th Century
CW 255b Anthroposophy and Its Opponents
CW 256 [Blank number]
CW 257 Anthroposophical Community-Building
CW 258 *The Anthroposophic Movement: The History and Conditions of the Anthroposophical Movement in Relation to the Anthroposophical Society: An Encouragement for Self-Examination*
CW 259 The Year of Destiny 1923 in the History of the Anthroposophical Society. From the Burning of the Goetheanum to the Christmas Conference

CW 260 The Christmas Conference for the Founding of the General Anthroposophical Society 1923/24
CW 260a The Constitution of the General Anthroposophical Society and the School for Spiritual Science. The Rebuilding of the Goetheanum
CW 261 *Our Dead: Memorial, Funeral, and Cremation Addresses 1906–1924*
CW 262 Rudolf Steiner and Marie Steiner-von Sivers: Correspondence and Documents, 1901–1925
CW 263/1 Rudolf Steiner and Edith Maryon: Correspondence: Letters, Verses, Sketches, 1912–1924
CW 264 *From the History and Contents of the First Section of the Esoteric School: Letters, Documents, and Lectures: 1904–1914*
CW 265 *Freemasonry and Ritual Work: The Misraim Service*
CW 265a Teaching and Instruction Lessons for Members of the Knowledge-Cultic Section of the Esoteric School 1904–1914 [forthcoming]
CW 266/1 *From the Esoteric School: Esoteric Lessons 1904–1909*
CW 266/2 *From the Esoteric School: Esoteric Lessons 1910–1912*
CW 266/3 *From the Esoteric School: Esoteric Lessons 1913–1923*
CW 267 *Soul Exercises: Word and Symbol Meditations*
CW 268 *Mantric Sayings: Meditations 1903–1925*
CW 269 Ritual Texts for the Celebration of the Free Christian Religious Instruction. The Collected Verses for Teachers and Students of the Waldorf School
CW 270 Esoteric Instructions for the First Class of the School for Spiritual Science at the Goetheanum 1924, 4 Volumes

III. Lectures and Courses on Specific Realms of Life

Lectures on Art

CW 271 *Art and Theory of Art: Foundations of a New Aesthetics*
CW 272 *Anthroposophy in the Light of Goethe's* Faust*: Volume One of Spiritual-Scientific Commentaries on Goethe's* Faust
CW 273 *Goethe's* Faust *in the Light of Anthroposophy: Volume Two of Spiritual-Scientific Commentaries on Goethe's* Faust
CW 274 Addresses for the Christmas Plays from the Old Folk Traditions
CW 275 Art in the Light of Mystery Wisdom
CW 276 *The Arts and Their Mission*
CW 277a The Origin and Development of Eurythmy 1912–1918
CW 277b The Origin and Development of Eurythmy 1918–1920
CW 277c The Origin and Development of Eurythmy 1920–1922 [forthcoming]
CW 277d The Origin and Development of Eurythmy 1923–1924 [forthcoming]

CW 278 Eurythmy as Visible Song
CW 279 *Eurythmy as Speech Made Visible: Speech Eurythmy Course*
CW 280 The Method and Nature of Speech Formation
CW 281 The Art of Recitation and Declamation
CW 282 Speech Formation and Dramatic Art
CW 283 *The Inner Nature of Music and the Experience of Tone*
CW 284 *Rosicrucianism Renewed: The Unity of Art, Science & Religion: The Theosophical Congress of Whitsun 1907*
CW 285 [Blank number]
CW 286 Paths to a New Style of Architecture. "And the Building Becomes Man"
CW 287 *Architecture as Peacework: The First Goetheanum, Dornach, 1914*
CW 288 *Architecture, Sculpture, and Painting of the First Goetheanum*
CW 289 The Building-Idea of the Goetheanum: Lectures with Slides from the Years 1920–1921
CW 290 *Toward a New Theory of Architecture: The First Goetheanum in Pictures* [no longer in the German GA]
CW 291 The Being of Colors
CW 291a Knowledge of Colors. Supplementary Volume to "The Being of Colors"
CW 292 *Art History as a Reflection of Inner Spiritual Impulses*

Lectures on Education

CW 293 General Knowledge of the Human Being as the Foundation of Pedagogy
CW 294 The Art of Education: Methodology and Didactics
CW 295 The Art of Education: Seminar Discussions and Lectures on Lesson Planning
CW 296 The Question of Education as a Social Question
CW 297 The Idea and Practice of the Waldorf School
CW 297a Education for Life: Self-Education and the Practice of Pedagogy
CW 298 Rudolf Steiner in the Waldorf School
CW 299 Spiritual-Scientific Observations on Speech
CW 300a Conferences with the Teachers of the Free Waldorf School in Stuttgart, 1919 to 1924, in 3 Volumes, Vol. 1
CW 300b Conferences with the Teachers of the Free Waldorf School in Stuttgart, 1919 to 1924, in 3 Volumes, Vol. 2
CW 300c Conferences with the Teachers of the Free Waldorf School in Stuttgart, 1919 to 1924, in 3 Volumes, Vol. 3
CW 301 The Renewal of Pedagogical-Didactical Art through Spiritual Science
CW 302 Knowledge of the Human Being and the Forming of Class Lessons
CW 302a Education and Teaching from a Knowledge of the Human Being
CW 303 The Healthy Development of the Human Being

CW 304 Methods of Education and Teaching Based on Anthroposophy
CW 304a Anthroposophical Knowledge of the Human Being and Pedagogy
CW 305 The Soul-Spiritual Foundational Forces of the Art of Education. Spiritual Values in Education and Social Life
CW 306 Pedagogical Praxis from the Viewpoint of a Spiritual-Scientific Knowledge of the Human Being. The Education of the Child and Young Human Beings
CW 307 The Spiritual Life of the Present and Education
CW 308 The Method of Teaching and the Life-Requirements for Teaching
CW 309 Anthroposophical Pedagogy and Its Prerequisites
CW 310 The Pedagogical Value of a Knowledge of the Human Being and the Cultural Value of Pedagogy
CW 311 The Art of Education from an Understanding of the Being of Humanity

Lectures on Medicine

CW 312 *Introducing Anthroposophical Medicine*
CW 313 *Illness and Therapy: Spiritual-Scientific Aspects of Healing*
CW 314 *Physiology and Healing: Treatment, Therapy, and Hygiene*
CW 315 Curative Eurythmy
CW 316 *Understanding Healing: Meditative Reflections on Deepening Medicine through Spiritual Science*
CW 317 *Education for Special Needs: The Curative Education Course*
CW 318 The Working Together of Doctors and Pastors
CW 319 *The Healing Process: Spirit, Nature & Our Bodies*

Lectures on Natural Science

CW 320 Spiritual-Scientific Impulses for the Development of Physics 1: The First Natural-Scientific Course: Light, Color, Tone, Mass, Electricity, Magnetism
CW 321 Spiritual-Scientific Impulses for the Development of Physics 2: The Second Natural-Scientific Course: Warmth at the Border of Positive and Negative Materiality
CW 322 The Borders of the Knowledge of Nature
CW 323 *Interdisciplinary Astronomy: Third Scientific Course*
CW 324 Nature Observation, Mathematics, and Scientific Experimentation and Results from the Viewpoint of Anthroposophy
CW 324a The Fourth Dimension in Mathematics and Reality
CW 325 Natural Science and the World-Historical Development of Humanity since Ancient Times
CW 326 The Moment of the Coming Into Being of Natural Science in World History and Its Development Since Then

CW 327 *Agriculture: Spiritual-Scientific Foundations for Agricultural Renewal*

Lectures on Social Life and the Threefold Arrangement of the Social Organism

CW 328 The Social Question
CW 329 The Liberation of the Human Being as the Foundation for a New Social Form
CW 330 The Renewal of the Social Organism
CW 331 Work-Council and Socialization
CW 332a The Social Future
CW 332b Lectures and Speeches on Social and Economic Issues
CW 333 *Freedom of Thought and Societal Forces: Implementing the Demands of Modern Society*
CW 334 From the Unified State to the Threefold Social Organism
CW 335 The Crisis of the Present and the Path to Healthy Thinking
CW 336 The Great Questions of the Times and Anthroposophical Spiritual Knowledge
CW 337a Social Ideas, Social Realities, Social Practice, Vol. 1: Question-and-Answer Evenings and Study Evenings of the Alliance for the Threefold Social Organism in Stuttgart, 1919–1920
CW 337b Social Ideas, Social Realities, Social Practice, Vol. 2: Discussion Evenings of the Swiss Alliance for the Threefold Social Organism
CW 338 *Communicating Anthroposophy: The Course for Speakers to Promote the Idea of Threefolding*
CW 339 Anthroposophy, Threefold Social Organism, and the Art of Public Speaking
CW 340/41 *Rethinking Economics: Lectures and Seminars on World Economics*

Lectures and Courses on Christian Religious Work

CW 342 *First Steps in Christian Religious Renewal: Preparing the Ground for The Christian Community*
CW 343 Lectures and Courses on Christian Religious Work, Vol. 2: Spiritual Knowledge – Religious Feeling – Cultic Doing
CW 344 Lectures and Courses on Christian Religious Work, Vol. 3: Lectures at the Founding of the Christian Community
CW 345 Lectures and Courses on Christian Religious Work, Vol. 4: Concerning the Nature of the Working Word
CW 346 Lectures and Courses on Christian Religious Work, Vol. 5: The Apocalypse and the Work of the Priest

Lectures for Workers at the Goetheanum

CW 347 The Knowledge of the Nature of the Human Being According to Body, Soul and Spirit. On Earlier Conditions of the Earth

CW 348 On Health and Illness. Foundations of a Spiritual-Scientific Doctrine of the Senses
CW 349 On the Life of the Human Being and of the Earth. On the Nature of Christianity
CW 350 Rhythms in the Cosmos and in the Human Being. How Does One Come To See the Spiritual World?
CW 351 The Human Being and the World. The Influence of the Spirit in Nature. On the Nature of Bees
CW 352 Nature and the Human Being Observed Spiritual-Scientifically
CW 353 The History of Humanity and the World-Views of the Folk Cultures
CW 354 The Creation of the World and the Human Being. Life on Earth and the Influence of the Stars

C. Artistic Works

CW A 1–10; 57 The Architectural Work I: The Goetheanum and Its Predecessors
CW A 11 The Sculptural Work
CW A 12 The Goetheanum Windows. The Speech of Light. Sketches and Studies
CW A 13–16; 52–56 The Painting Work
CW A 14 Sketches for the Painting of the Small Dome of the First Goetheanum
CW A 27–43 The Architectural Work II: Commercial and Residential Buildings in Dornach and Other Places [forthcoming]
CW A 45 The Graphic Work
CW A 48 The Drawing Work
CW A 51 The Art of Jewelry as a Goethean Language of Form
CW A 54.0 A Path of Training in Painting. Pastel Sketches and Watercolors
CW A 54.1 Nature Moods. Nine Training Sketches for Painters

Eurythmy Figures

CW A 26 Skectches of the Eurythmy Figures
CW A 26a The Eurythmy Figures of Rudolf Steiner, Artistically Executed by Annemarie Bäschlin
CW A 26b Eurythmy Figures from the Time When They Were Created

Eurythmy Forms

CW A 23/1 Volume I: Eurythmy Forms for Poems by Rudolf Steiner
CW A 23/2 Volume II: Eurythmy Forms for the Calender of the Soul by Rudolf Steiner
CW A 23/3 Volume III: Euythmy Forms for Poems by J. W. von Goethe

CW A 23/4	Volume IV: Eurythmy Forms for Poems by Christian Morgenstern
CW A 23/5	Volume V: Eurythmy Forms for Poems by Albert Steffen
CW A 23/6	Volume VI: Eurythmy Forms for German Poems by Fercher von Steinwand, Hamerling, Hebbel, C. F. Meyer, Nietzsche, among others
CW A 23/7	Volume VII: Eurythmy Forms for English Poems
CW A 23/8	Volume VIII: Eurythmy Forms for French and Russian Poems
CW A 24	Volume IX: Eurythmy Forms for Tone Eurythmy

Blackboard Drawings from Lectures

CW A 58/1	Volume I: 20 Plates from Public Lectures 1920–1924 in CWs 73a, 74, 76, and 84
CW A 58/2	Volume II: 38 Plates from Lectures in 1919 in CWs 191 and 194
CW A 58/3	Volume III: 34 Plates from Lectures in 1920 in CWs 196 and 198
CW A 58/4	Volume IV: 33 Plates from Lectures in 1920 in CWs 199 and 200
CW A 58/5	Volume V: 31 Plates from Lectures in 1920 in CW 201
CW A 58/6	Volume VI: 46 Plates from Lectures 1920–1921 in CWs 202–204
CW A 58/7	Volume VII: 38 Plates from Lectures in 1921 in CWs 205 and 206
CW A 58/8	Volume VIII: 42 Plates from Lectures in 1921 in CWs 207–209
CW A 58/9	Volume IX: 40 Plates from Lectures in 1922 in CWs 210–212
CW A 58/10	Volume X: 35 Plates from Lectures in 1922 in CWs 213–215
CW A 58/11	Volume XI: 41 Plates from Lectures 1922–1923 in CWs 216, 218–220
CW A 58/12	Volume XII: 37 Plates from Lectures in 1923 in CWs 221–225
CW A 58/13	Volume XIII: 38 Plates from Lectures in 1923 in CWs 227–230
CW A 58/14	Volume XIV: 36 Plates from Lectures in 1923 in CWs 232 and 233
CW A 58/15	Volume XV: 37 Plates from Lectures in 1924 in CWs 233a, 234, and 243
CW A 58/16	Volume XVI: 56 Plates from the "Karma Lectures" in CWs 235–238 and 240
CW A 58/17	Volume XVII: 21 Plates from Lectures on the History of the Anthroposophical Society in CWs 257, 258, 260, and 260a
CW A 58/18	Volume XVIII: 33 Plates from Lectures on Art in CWs 271, 276, 283, 288–290, and 291
CW A 58/19	Volume XIX: 41 Plates from Lectures on Eurythmy in CWs 278, 279, and 315
CW A 58/20	Volume XX: 27 Plates from Lectures on Speech Formation in CWs 281 and 282
CW A 58/21	Volume XXI: 42 Plates from Lectures on Education in CWs 296, 303, 304, 306, and 311

CW A 58/22 Volume XXII: 46 Plates from Lectures on Medicine in CWs 312–315

CW A 58/23 Volume XXIII: 48 Plates from Lectures in 1924 in CWs 316–318

CW A 58/24 Volume XXIV: 39 Plates from Lectures on Natural Science and the Social Question in CWs 322, 326, 327, 339, and 340

CW A 58/25 Volume XXV: 33 Plates from the "Workers Lectures" (Volumes 1 and 2) in CWs 347 and 348

CW A 58/26 Volume XXVI: 51 Plates from the "Workers Lectures" (Volumes 3 and 4) in CWs 349 and 350

CW A 58/27 Volume XXVII: 35 Plates from the "Workers Lectures" (Volumes 5 and 6) in CWs 351 and 352

CW A 58/28 Volume XXVIII: 42 Plates from the "Workers Lectures" (Volumes 7 and 8) in CWs 353 and 354

CW A 58/29 Volume XXIX: 43 Plates from Lectures and Courses on Christian Religious Activity in CWs 342–344 and 346

CW A 58/30 Volume XXX: 27 Plates from CWs 255b, 324a, 337b, and 340, Corrigenda, Plates without CW Assignment, Copies

SIGNIFICANT EVENTS IN THE LIFE OF RUDOLF STEINER

1829: June 23: birth of Johann Steiner (1829–1910)—Rudolf Steiner's father—in Geras, Lower Austria.

1834: May 8: birth of Franciska Blie (1834–1918)—Rudolf Steiner's mother—in Horn, Lower Austria. "My father and mother were both children of the glorious Lower Austrian forest district north of the Danube."

1860: May 16: marriage of Johann Steiner and Franciska Blie.

1861: February 25: birth of *Rudolf Joseph Lorenz Steiner* in Kraljevec, Croatia, near the border with Hungary, where Johann Steiner works as a telegrapher for the South Austria Railroad. Rudolf Steiner is baptized two days later, February 27, the date usually given as his birthday.

1862: Summer: the family moves to Mödling, Lower Austria.

1863: The family moves to Pottschach, Lower Austria, near the Styrian border, where Johann Steiner becomes stationmaster. "The view stretched to the mountains...majestic peaks in the distance and the sweet charm of nature in the immediate surroundings."

1864: November 15: birth of Rudolf Steiner's sister, Leopoldine (d. November 1, 1927). She will become a seamstress and live with her parents for the rest of her life.

1866: July 28: birth of Rudolf Steiner's deaf-mute brother, Gustav (d. May 1, 1941).

1867: Rudolf Steiner enters the village school. Following a disagreement between his father and the schoolmaster, whose wife falsely accused the boy of causing a commotion, Rudolf Steiner is taken out of school and taught at home.

1868: A critical experience. Unknown to the family, an aunt dies in a distant town. Sitting in the station waiting room, Rudolf Steiner sees her "form," which speaks to him, asking for help. "Beginning with this experience, a new soul life began in the boy, one in which not only the outer trees and mountains spoke to him, but also the worlds that lay behind them. From this moment on, the boy began to live with the spirits of nature...."

1869: The family moves to the peaceful, rural village of Neudorfl, near Wiener-Neustadt in present-day Austria. Rudolf Steiner attends the village school. Because of the "unorthodoxy" of his writing and spelling, he has to do "extra lessons."

1870: Through a book lent to him by his tutor, he discovers geometry: "To grasp something purely in the spirit brought me inner happiness. I know that I first learned happiness through geometry." The same tutor allows him to draw, while other students still struggle with their reading and writing. "An artistic element" thus enters his education.

1871: Though his parents are not religious, Rudolf Steiner becomes a "church child," a favorite of the priest, who was "an exceptional character." "Up to the age of ten or eleven, among those I came to know, he was far and away the most significant." Among other things, he introduces Steiner to Copernican, heliocentric cosmology. As an altar boy, Rudolf Steiner serves at Masses, funerals, and Corpus Christi processions. At year's end, after an incident in which he escapes a thrashing, his father forbids him to go to church.

1872: Rudolf Steiner transfers to grammar school in Wiener-Neustadt, a five-mile walk from home, which must be done in all weathers.

1873–75: Through his teachers and on his own, Rudolf Steiner has many wonderful experiences with science and mathematics. Outside school, he teaches himself analytic geometry, trigonometry, differential equations, and calculus.

1876: Rudolf Steiner begins tutoring other students. He learns bookbinding from his father. He also teaches himself stenography.

1877: Rudolf Steiner discovers Kant's *Critique of Pure Reason*, which he reads and rereads. He also discovers and reads von Rotteck's *World History*.

1878: He studies extensively in contemporary psychology and philosophy.

1879: Rudolf Steiner graduates from high school with honors. His father is transferred to Inzersdorf, near Vienna. He uses his first visit to Vienna "to purchase a great number of philosophy books"—Kant, Fichte, Schelling, and Hegel, as well as numerous histories of philosophy. His aim: to find a path from the "I" to nature.

October 1879–1883: Rudolf Steiner attends the Technical College in Vienna—to study mathematics, chemistry, physics, mineralogy, botany, zoology, biology, geology, and mechanics—with a scholarship. He also attends lectures in history and literature, while avidly reading philosophy on his own. His two favorite professors are Karl Julius Schröer (German language and literature) and Edmund Reitlinger (physics). He also audits lectures by Robert Zimmerman on aesthetics and Franz Brentano on philosophy. During this year he begins his friendship with Moritz Zitter (1861–1921), who will help support him financially when he is in Berlin.

1880: Rudolf Steiner attends lectures on Schiller and Goethe by Karl Julius Schröer, who becomes his mentor. Also "through a remarkable combination of circumstances," he meets Felix Koguzki, an "herb gatherer" and healer, who could "see deeply into the secrets of nature." Rudolf Steiner will meet and study with this "emissary of the Master" throughout his time in Vienna.

1881: January: "... I didn't sleep a wink. I was busy with philosophical problems until about 12:30 a.m. Then, finally, I threw myself down on my couch. All my striving during the previous year had been to research whether the following statement by Schelling was true or not: *Within everyone dwells a secret, marvelous capacity to draw back from the stream of time—out of the self clothed in all that comes to us from outside—into our innermost being and there, in the immutable form of the Eternal, to look into ourselves*. I believe, and I am still quite certain of it, that I discovered this capacity in myself; I had long had an inkling of it. Now the whole of idealist philosophy stood before me in modified form. What's a sleepless night compared to that!"

Rudolf Steiner begins communicating with leading thinkers of the day, who send him books in return, which he reads eagerly.

July: "I am not one of those who dives into the day like an animal in human form. I pursue a quite specific goal, an idealistic aim—knowledge of the truth! This cannot be done offhandedly. It requires the greatest striving in the world, free of all egotism, and equally of all resignation."

August: Steiner puts down on paper for the first time thoughts for a "Philosophy of Freedom." "The striving for the absolute: this human yearning is freedom." He also seeks to outline a "peasant philosophy," describing what the worldview of a "peasant"—one who lives close to the earth and the old ways—really is.

1881–1882: Felix Koguzki, the herb gatherer, reveals himself to be the envoy of another, higher initiatory personality, who instructs Rudolf Steiner to penetrate Fichte's philosophy and to master modern scientific thinking as a preparation for right entry into the spirit. This "Master" also teaches him the double (evolutionary and involutionary) nature of time.

1882: Through the offices of Karl Julius Schröer, Rudolf Steiner is asked by Joseph Kurschner to edit Goethe's scientific writings for the *Deutschen National-Literatur* edition. He writes "A Possible Critique of Atomistic Concepts" and sends it to Friedrich Theodor Vischer.

1883: Rudolf Steiner completes his college studies and begins work on the Goethe project.

1884: First volume of Goethe's *Scientific Writings* (CW 1) appears (March). He lectures on Goethe and Lessing, and Goethe's approach to science. In July, he enters the household of Ladislaus and Pauline Specht as tutor to the four Specht boys. He will live there until 1890. At this time, he meets Josef Breuer (1842–1925), the coauthor with Sigmund Freud of *Studies in Hysteria*, who is the Specht family doctor.

1885: While continuing to edit Goethe's writings, Rudolf Steiner reads deeply in contemporary philosophy (Edouard von Hartmann, Johannes Volkelt, and Richard Wahle, among others).

1886: May: Rudolf Steiner sends Kurschner the manuscript of *Outlines of Goethe's Theory of Knowledge* (CW 2), which appears in October, and which he sends out widely. He also meets the poet Marie Eugenie Delle Grazie and writes "Nature and Our Ideals" for her. He attends her salon, where he meets many priests, theologians, and philosophers, who will become his friends. Meanwhile, the director of the Goethe Archive in Weimar requests his collaboration with the *Sophien* edition of Goethe's works, particularly the writings on color.

1887: At the beginning of the year, Rudolf Steiner is very sick. As the year progresses and his health improves, he becomes increasingly "a man of letters," lecturing, writing essays, and taking part in Austrian cultural life. In August–September, the second volume of Goethe's *Scientific Writings* appears.

1888: January–July: Rudolf Steiner assumes editorship of the "German Weekly" (*Deutsche Wochenschrift*). He begins lecturing more intensively, giving, for example, a lecture titled "Goethe as Father of a New Aesthetics." He meets and becomes soul friends with Friedrich Eckstein (1861–1939), a vegetarian, philosopher of symbolism, alchemist, and musician, who will introduce him to various spiritual currents (including Theosophy) and with whom he will meditate and interpret esoteric and alchemical texts.

1889: Rudolf Steiner first reads Nietzsche (*Beyond Good and Evil*). He encounters Theosophy again and learns of Madame Blavatsky in the Theosophical circle around Marie Lang (1858–1934). Here he also meets well-known figures of Austrian life, as well as esoteric figures like the occultist Franz Hartman and Karl Leinigen-Billigen (translator of C.G. Harrison's *The Transcendental Universe*). During this period, Steiner first reads A.P. Sinnett's *Esoteric Buddhism* and Mabel Collins's *Light on the Path*. He also begins traveling, visiting Budapest, Weimar, and Berlin (where he meets philosopher Edouard von Hartman).

1890: Rudolf Steiner finishes volume 3 of Goethe's scientific writings. He begins his doctoral dissertation, which will become *Truth and Science* (CW 3). He also meets the poet and feminist Rosa Mayreder (1858–1938), with whom he can exchange his most intimate thoughts. In September, Rudolf Steiner moves to Weimar to work in the Goethe-Schiller Archive.

1891: Volume 3 of the Kurschner edition of Goethe appears. Meanwhile, Rudolf Steiner edits Goethe's studies in mineralogy and scientific writings for the *Sophien* edition. He meets Ludwig Laistner of the Cotta Publishing Company, who asks for a book on the basic question of metaphysics. From this will result, ultimately, *The Philosophy of Freedom* (CW 4), which will be published not by Cotta but by Emil Felber. In October, Rudolf Steiner takes the oral exam for a doctorate in philosophy, mathematics, and mechanics at Rostock University, receiving his doctorate on the twenty-sixth. In November, he gives his first lecture on Goethe's "Fairy Tale" in Vienna.

1892: Rudolf Steiner continues work at the Goethe-Schiller Archive and on his *Philosophy of Freedom. Truth and Science*, his doctoral dissertation, is published. Steiner undertakes to write introductions to books on Schopenhauer and Jean Paul for Cotta. At year's end, he finds lodging with Anna Eunike, née Schulz (1853–1911), a widow with four daughters and a son. He also develops a friendship with Otto Erich Hartleben (1864–1905) with whom he shares literary interests.

1893: Rudolf Steiner begins his habit of producing many reviews and articles. In March, he gives a lecture titled "Hypnotism, with Reference to Spiritism." In September, volume 4 of the Kurschner edition is completed. In November, *The Philosophy of Freedom* appears. This year, too, he meets John Henry Mackay (1864–1933), the anarchist, and Max Stirner, a scholar and biographer.

1894: Rudolf Steiner meets Elisabeth Förster Nietzsche, the philosopher's sister, and begins to read Nietzsche in earnest, beginning with the as yet unpublished *Antichrist.* He also meets Ernst Haeckel (1834–1919). In the fall, he begins to write *Nietzsche, A Fighter against His Time* (CW 5).

1895: May: *Nietzsche, A Fighter against His Time* appears.

1896: January 22: Rudolf Steiner sees Friedrich Nietzsche for the first and only time. Moves between the Nietzsche and the Goethe-Schiller Archives, where he completes his work before year's end. He falls out with Elisabeth Förster Nietzsche, thus ending his association with the Nietzsche Archive.

1897: Rudolf Steiner finishes the manuscript of *Goethe's Worldview* (CW 6). He moves to Berlin with Anna Eunike and begins editorship of the *Magazin fur Literatur.* From now on, Steiner will write countless reviews, literary and philosophical articles, and so on. He begins lecturing at the "Free Literary Society." In September, he attends the Zionist Congress in Basel. He sides with Dreyfus in the Dreyfus affair.

1898: Rudolf Steiner is very active as an editor in the political, artistic, and theatrical life of Berlin. He becomes friendly with John Henry Mackay and poet Ludwig Jacobowski (1868–1900). He joins Jacobowski's circle of writers, artists, and scientists—"The Coming Ones" (*Die Kommenden*)—and contributes lectures to the group until 1903. He also lectures at the "League for College Pedagogy." He writes an article for Goethe's sesquicentennial, "Goethe's Secret Revelation," on the "Fairy Tale of the Green Snake and the Beautiful Lily."

1898–99: "This was a trying time for my soul as I looked at Christianity. . . . I was able to progress only by contemplating, by means of spiritual perception, the evolution of Christianity. . . . Conscious knowledge of real Christianity began to dawn in me around the turn of the century. This seed continued to develop. My soul trial occurred shortly before the beginning of the twentieth century. It was decisive for my soul's development that I stood spiritually before the Mystery of Golgotha in a deep and solemn celebration of knowledge."

1899: Rudolf Steiner begins teaching and giving lectures and lecture cycles at the Workers' College, founded by Wilhelm Liebknecht (1826–1900). He will continue to do so until 1904. Writes: *Literature and Spiritual Life in the Nineteenth Century; Individualism in Philosophy*; *Haeckel and His Opponents; Poetry in the Present;* and begins what will become (fifteen years later) *The Riddles of Philosophy* (CW 18). He also meets many artists and writers, including Käthe Kollwitz, Stefan Zweig, and Rainer Maria Rilke. On October 31, he marries Anna Eunike.

1900: "I thought that the turn of the century must bring humanity a new light. It seemed to me that the separation of human thinking and willing from the spirit had peaked. A turn or reversal of direction in human evolution seemed to me a necessity." Rudolf Steiner finishes *World and Life Views in the Nineteenth Century* (the second part of what will become *The Riddles of Philosophy*) and dedicates it to Ernst Haeckel.

It is published in March. He continues lecturing at *Die Kommenden*, whose leadership he assumes after the death of Jacobowski. Also, he gives the Gutenberg Jubilee lecture before 7,000 typesetters and printers. In September, Rudolf Steiner is invited by Count and Countess Brockdorff to lecture in the Theosophical Library. His first lecture is on Nietzsche. His second lecture is titled "Goethe's Secret Revelation." October 6, he begins a lecture cycle on the mystics that will become *Mystics after Modernism* (CW 7). November–December: "Marie von Sivers appears in the audience...." Also in November, Steiner gives his first lecture at the Giordano Bruno Bund (where he will continue to lecture until May, 1905). He speaks on Bruno and modern Rome, focusing on the importance of the philosophy of Thomas Aquinas as monism.

1901: In continual financial straits, Rudolf Steiner's early friends Moritz Zitter and Rosa Mayreder help support him. In October, he begins the lecture cycle *Christianity as Mystical Fact* (CW 8) at the Theosophical Library. In November, he gives his first "Theosophical lecture" on Goethe's "Fairy Tale" in Hamburg at the invitation of Wilhelm Hubbe-Schleiden. He also attends a tea to celebrate the founding of the Theosophical Society at Count and Countess Brockdorff's. He gives a lecture cycle, "From Buddha to Christ," for the circle of the *Kommenden*. November 17, Marie von Sivers asks Rudolf Steiner if Theosophy does not need a Western-Christian spiritual movement (to complement Theosophy's Eastern emphasis). "The question was posed. Now, following spiritual laws, I could begin to give an answer...." In December, Rudolf Steiner writes his first article for a Theosophical publication. At year's end, the Brockdorffs and possibly Wilhelm Hubbe-Schleiden ask Rudolf Steiner to join the Theosophical Society and undertake the leadership of the German section. Rudolf Steiner agrees, on the condition that Marie von Sivers (then in Italy) work with him.

1902: Beginning in January, Rudolf Steiner attends the opening of the Workers' School in Spandau with Rosa Luxemberg (1870–1919). January 17, Rudolf Steiner joins the Theosophical Society. In April, he is asked to become general secretary of the German Section of the Theosophical Society, and works on preparations for its founding. In July, he visits London for a Theosophical congress. He meets Bertram Keightly, G.R.S. Mead, A.P. Sinnett, and Annie Besant, among others. In September, *Christianity as Mystical Fact* appears. In October, Rudolf Steiner gives his first public lecture on Theosophy ("Monism and Theosophy") to about three hundred people at the Giordano Bruno Bund. From October 19–21, the German Section of the Theosophical Society has its first meeting; Rudolf Steiner is the general secretary, and Annie Besant attends. Steiner lectures on practical karma studies. On October 23, Annie Besant inducts Rudolf Steiner into the Esoteric School of the Theosophical Society. On October 25, Steiner begins a weekly series of lectures: "The Field of Theosophy." During this year, Rudolf Steiner also first meets Ita Wegman (1876–1943), who will become his close collaborator in his final years.

1903: Rudolf Steiner holds about 300 lectures and seminars. In May, the first issue of the periodical *Luzifer* appears. In June, Rudolf Steiner visits London for the first meeting of the Federation of the European Sections of the Theosophical Society, where he meets Colonel Olcott. He begins to write *Theosophy* (CW 9).

1904: Rudolf Steiner continues lecturing at the Workers' College and elsewhere (about 90 lectures), while lecturing intensively all over Germany among Theosophists (about 140 lectures). In February, he meets Carl Unger (1878–1929), who will become a member of the board of the Anthroposophical Society (1913). In March, he meets Michael Bauer (1871–1929), a Christian mystic, who will also be on the board. In May, *Theosophy* appears, with the dedication: "To the spirit of Giordano Bruno." Rudolf Steiner and Marie von Sivers visit London for meetings with Annie Besant. In June, Rudolf Steiner and Marie von Sivers attend the meeting of the Federation of European Sections of the Theosophical Society in Amsterdam. In July, Steiner begins the articles in *Lucifer-Gnosis* that will become *How to Know Higher Worlds* (CW 10) and *Cosmic Memory* (CW 11). In September, Annie Besant visits Germany. In December, Steiner lectures on Freemasonry. He mentions the High Grade Masonry derived from John Yarker and represented by Theodore Reuss and Karl Kellner as a blank slate "into which a good image could be placed."

1905: This year, Steiner ends his non-Theosophical lecturing activity. Supported by Marie von Sivers, his Theosophical lecturing—both in public and in the Theosophical Society—increases significantly: "The German Theosophical Movement is of exceptional importance." Steiner recommends reading, among others, Fichte, Jacob Boehme, and Angelus Silesius. He begins to introduce Christian themes into Theosophy. He also begins to work with doctors (Felix Peipers and Ludwig Noll). In July, he is in London for the Federation of European Sections, where he attends a lecture by Annie Besant: "I have seldom seen Mrs. Besant speak in so inward and heartfelt a manner...." "Through Mrs. Besant I have found the way to H. P. Blavatsky." September to October, he gives a course of thirty-one lectures for a small group of esoteric students. In October, the annual meeting of the German Section of the Theosophical Society, which still remains very small, takes place. Rudolf Steiner reports membership has risen from 121 to 377 members. In November, seeking to establish esoteric "continuity," Rudolf Steiner and Marie von Sivers participate in a "Memphis-Misraim" Masonic ceremony. They pay forty-five marks for membership. "Yesterday, you saw how little remains of former esoteric institutions." "We are dealing only with a 'framework'... for the present, nothing lies behind it. The occult powers have completely withdrawn."

1906: Expansion of Theosophical work. Rudolf Steiner gives about 245 lectures, only 44 of which take place in Berlin. Cycles are given in Paris, Leipzig, Stuttgart, and Munich. Esoteric work also intensifies. Rudolf Steiner begins writing *An Outline of Esoteric Science* (CW 13). In January, Rudolf Steiner receives permission (a patent) from the Great Orient of the Scottish A & A Thirty-Three Degree Rite of the Order of the Ancient Freemasons of the Memphis-Misraim Rite to direct a chapter under the name "Mystica Aeterna." This will become the "Cognitive Cultic Section" (also called "Misraim Service") of the Esoteric School. (See: *From the History and Contents of the Cognitive Cultic Section* [CW 264].) During this time, Steiner also meets Albert Schweitzer. In May, he is in Paris, where he visits Edouard Schuré. Many Russians attend his lectures (including Konstantin Balmont, Dimitri Mereszkovski, Zinaida Hippius, and Maximilian Woloshin). He attends the General Meeting of the European Federation of the Theosophical Society, at which Col. Olcott is present for the last time. He spends the year's end in Venice and Rome, where he writes and works on his translation of H. P. Blavatsky's *Key to Theosophy*.

1907: Further expansion of the German Theosophical Movement according to the Rosicrucian directive to "introduce spirit into the world"—in education, in social questions, in art, and in science. In February, Col. Olcott dies in Adyar. Before he dies, Olcott indicates that "the Masters" wish Annie Besant to succeed him: much politicking ensues. Rudolf Steiner supports Besant's candidacy. April–May: preparations for the Congress of the Federation of European Sections of the Theosophical Society—the great, watershed Whitsun "Munich Congress," attended by Annie Besant and others. Steiner decides to separate Eastern and Western (Christian-Rosicrucian) esoteric schools. He takes his esoteric school out of the Theosophical Society (Besant and Rudolf Steiner are "in harmony" on this). Steiner makes his first lecture tours to Austria and Hungary. That summer, he is in Italy. In September, he visits Edouard Schuré, who will write the introduction to the French edition of *Christianity as Mystical Fact* in Barr, Alsace. Rudolf Steiner writes the autobiographical statement known as the "Barr Document." In *Luzifer–Gnosis*, "The Education of the Child" appears.

1908: The movement grows (membership: 1150). Lecturing expands. Steiner makes his first extended lecture tour to Holland and Scandinavia, as well as visits to Naples and Sicily. Themes: St. John's Gospel, the Apocalypse, Egypt, science, philosophy, and logic. *Lucifer-Gnosis* ceases publication. In Berlin, Marie von Sivers (with Johanna Mücke [1864–1949]) forms the *Philosophisch-Theosophisch* (after 1915 *Philosophisch-Anthroposophisch*) *Verlag* to publish Steiner's work. Steiner gives lecture cycles titled *The Gospel of St. John* (CW 103) and *The Apocalypse* (104).

1909: *An Outline of Esoteric Science* appears. Lecturing and travel continue. Rudolf Steiner's spiritual research expands to include the polarity of Lucifer and Ahriman; the work of great individualities in history; the

Maitreya Buddha and the Bodhisattvas; spiritual economy (CW 109); the work of the spiritual hierarchies in heaven and on Earth (CW 110). He also deepens and intensifies his research into the Gospels, giving lectures on the Gospel of St. Luke (CW 114) with the first mention of two Jesus children. Meets and becomes friends with Christian Morgenstern (1871–1914). In April, he lays the foundation stone for the Malsch model—the building that will lead to the first Goetheanum. In May, the International Congress of the Federation of European Sections of the Theosophical Society takes place in Budapest. Rudolf Steiner receives the Subba Row medal for *How to Know Higher Worlds*. During this time, Charles W. Leadbeater discovers Jiddu Krishnamurti (1895–1986) and proclaims him the future "world teacher," the bearer of the Maitreya Buddha and the "reappearing Christ." In October, Steiner delivers seminal lectures on "anthroposophy," which he will try, unsuccessfully, to rework over the next years into the unfinished work, *Anthroposophy (A Fragment)* (CW 45).

1910: New themes: *The Reappearance of Christ in the Etheric* (CW 118); *The Fifth Gospel* (CW 148); *The Mission of Folk Souls* (CW 121); *Occult History* (CW 126); the evolving development of etheric cognitive capacities. Rudolf Steiner continues his Gospel research with *The Gospel of St. Matthew* (CW 123). In January, his father dies. In April, he takes a month-long trip to Italy, including Rome, Monte Cassino, and Sicily. He also visits Scandinavia again. July–August, he writes the first mystery drama, *The Portal of Initiation* (CW 14). In November, he gives "psychosophy" lectures. In December, he submits "On the Psychological Foundations and Epistemological Framework of Theosophy" to the International Philosophical Congress in Bologna.

1911: The crisis in the Theosophical Society deepens. In January, "The Order of the Rising Sun," which will soon become "The Order of the Star in the East," is founded for the coming world teacher, Krishnamurti. At the same time, Marie von Sivers, Rudolf Steiner's coworker, falls ill. Fewer lectures are given, but important new ground is broken. In Prague, in March, Steiner meets Franz Kafka (1883–1924) and Hugo Bergmann (1883–1975). In April, he delivers his paper to the Philosophical Congress. He writes the second mystery drama, *The Soul's Probation* (CW 14). Also, while Marie von Sivers is convalescing, Rudolf Steiner begins work on *Calendar 1912/1913*, which will contain the "Calendar of the Soul" meditations. On March 19, Anna (Eunike) Steiner dies. In September, Rudolf Steiner visits Einsiedeln, birthplace of Paracelsus. In December, Friedrich Rittelmeyer, future founder of the Christian Community, meets Rudolf Steiner. The *Johannes-Bauverein*, the "building committee," which would lead to the first Goetheanum (first planned for Munich), is also founded, and a preliminary committee for the founding of an independent association is created that, in the following year, will become the Anthroposophical Society. Important lecture cycles include *Occult Physiology* (CW 128);

Wonders of the World (CW 129); *From Jesus to Christ* (CW 131). Other themes: esoteric Christianity; Christian Rosenkreutz; the spiritual guidance of humanity; the sense world and the world of the spirit.

1912: Despite the ongoing, now increasing crisis in the Theosophical Society, much is accomplished: *Calendar 1912/1913* is published; eurythmy is created; both the third mystery drama, *The Guardian of the Threshold* (CW 14) and *A Way of Self-Knowledge* (CW 16) are written. New (or renewed) themes include life between death and rebirth and karma and reincarnation. Other lecture cycles: *Spiritual Beings in the Heavenly Bodies and the Kingdoms of Nature* (CW 136); *The Human Being in the Light of Occultism, Theosophy, and Philosophy* (CW 137); *The Gospel of St. Mark* (CW 139); and *The Bhagavad Gita and the Epistles of Paul* (CW 142). On May 8, Rudolf Steiner celebrates White Lotus Day, H. P. Blavatsky's death day, which he had faithfully observed for the past decade, for the last time. In August, Rudolf Steiner suggests the "independent association" be called the "Anthroposophical Society." In September, the first eurythmy course takes place. Also, with Marie von Sivers, he first visits Dornach, near Basel, Switzerland, and they stand on the hill where the Goetheanum will be. In November, a Theosophical Society lodge is opened by direct mandate from Adyar (Annie Besant). In December, a meeting of the German section occurs at which it is decided that belonging to the Order of the Star of the East is incompatible with membership in the Theosophical Society. December 28: informal founding of the Anthroposophical Society in Berlin.

1913: Expulsion of the German section from the Theosophical Society. February 2–3: Foundation meeting of the Anthroposophical Society. Board members include: Marie von Sivers, Michael Bauer, and Carl Unger. September 20: Laying of the foundation stone for the *Johannes Bau* (Goetheanum) in Dornach. Building begins immediately. The third mystery drama, *The Soul's Awakening* (CW 14), is completed. Also: *The Threshold of the Spiritual World* (CW 147). Lecture cycles include: *The Bhagavad Gita and the Epistles of Paul* and *The Esoteric Meaning of the Bhagavad Gita* (CW 146), which the Russian philosopher Nikolai Berdyaev attends; *The Mysteries of the East and of Christianity* (CW 144); *The Effects of Esoteric Development* (CW 145); and *The Fifth Gospel* (CW 148). In May, Rudolf Steiner is in London and Paris, where anthroposophical work continues.

1914: Building continues on the *Johannes Bau* (Goetheanum) in Dornach, with artists and coworkers from seventeen nations. The general assembly of the Anthroposophical Society takes place. In May, Rudolf Steiner visits Paris, as well as Chartres Cathedral. June 28: assassination in Sarajevo ("Now the catastrophe has happened!"). August 1: War is declared. Rudolf Steiner returns to Germany from Dornach—he will travel back and forth. He writes the last chapter of *The Riddles of Philosophy*. Lecture cycles include: *Human and Cosmic Thought* (CW 151); *Inner Being of*

Humanity between Death and a New Birth (CW 153); *Occult Reading and Occult Hearing* (CW 156). December 24: marriage of Rudolf Steiner and Marie von Sivers.

1915: Building continues. Life after death becomes a major theme, also art. Writes: *Thoughts during a Time of War* (CW 24). Lectures include: *The Secret of Death* (CW 159); *The Uniting of Humanity through the Christ Impulse* (CW 165).

1916: Rudolf Steiner begins work with Edith Maryon (1872–1924) on the sculpture "The Representative of Humanity" ("The Group"—Christ, Lucifer, and Ahriman). He also works with the alchemist Alexander von Bernus on the quarterly *Das Reich*. He writes *The Riddle of Humanity* (CW 20). Lectures include: *Necessity and Freedom in World History and Human Action* (CW 166); *Past and Present in the Human Spirit* (CW 167); *The Karma of Vocation* (CW 172); *The Karma of Untruthfulness* (CW 173).

1917: Russian Revolution. The U.S. enters the war. Building continues. Rudolf Steiner delineates the idea of the "threefold nature of the human being" (in a public lecture March 15) and the "threefold nature of the social organism" (hammered out in May–June with the help of Otto von Lerchenfeld and Ludwig Polzer-Hoditz in the form of two documents titled *Memoranda*, which were distributed in high places). August–September: Rudolf Steiner writes *The Riddles of the Soul* (CW 20). Also: commentary on "The Chemical Wedding of Christian Rosenkreutz" for Alexander Bernus (*Das Reich*). Lectures include: *The Karma of Materialism* (CW 176); *The Spiritual Background of the Outer World: The Fall of the Spirits of Darkness* (CW 177).

1918: March 18: peace treaty of Brest-Litovsk—"Now everything will truly enter chaos! What is needed is cultural renewal." June: Rudolf Steiner visits Karlstein (Grail) Castle outside Prague. Lecture cycle: *From Symptom to Reality in Modern History* (CW 185). In mid-November, Emil Molt, of the Waldorf-Astoria Cigarette Company, has the idea of founding a school for his workers' children.

1919: Focus on the threefold social organism: tireless travel, countless lectures, meetings, and publications. At the same time, a new public stage of Anthroposophy emerges as cultural renewal begins. The coming years will see initiatives in pedagogy, medicine, pharmacology, and agriculture. January 27: threefold meeting: " We must first of all, with the money we have, found free schools that can bring people what they need." February: first public eurythmy performance in Zurich. Also: "Appeal to the German People" (CW 24), circulated March 6 as a newspaper insert. In April, *Toward Social Renewal* (CW 23)—"perhaps the most widely read of all books on politics appearing since the war"—appears. Rudolf Steiner is asked to undertake the "direction and leadership" of the school founded by the Waldorf-Astoria Company. Rudolf Steiner begins to talk about the "renewal" of education. May 30: a building is selected and purchased for the future Waldorf School.

August–September: Rudolf Steiner gives a lecture course for Waldorf teachers, *The Foundations of Human Experience (Study of Man)* (CW 293). September 7: Opening of the first Waldorf School. December (into January): first science course, the *Light Course* (CW 320).

1920: The Waldorf School flourishes. New threefold initiatives. Founding of limited companies *Der Kommenden Tag* and *Futurum A.G.* to infuse spiritual values into the economic realm. Rudolf Steiner also focuses on the sciences. Lectures: *Introducing Anthroposophical Medicine* (CW 312); *The Warmth Course* (CW 321); *The Boundaries of Natural Science* (CW 322); *The Redemption of Thinking* (CW 74). February: Johannes Werner Klein—later a cofounder of the Christian Community—asks Rudolf Steiner about the possibility of a "religious renewal," a "Johannine church." In March, Rudolf Steiner gives the first course for doctors and medical students. In April, a divinity student asks Rudolf Steiner a second time about the possibility of religious renewal. September 27–October 16: anthroposophical "college course." December: lectures titled *The Search for the New Isis* (CW 202).

1921: Rudolf Steiner continues his intensive work on cultural renewal, including the uphill battle for the threefold social order. "College" arts, scientific, theological, and medical courses include: *The Astronomy Course* (CW 323); *Observation, Mathematics, and Scientific Experiment* (CW 324); the *Second Medical Course* (CW 313); *Color* (CW 291). In June and September–October, Rudolf Steiner also gives the first two "priests' courses" (CW 342 and 343). The "youth movement" gains momentum. Magazines are founded: *Die Drei* (January), and—under the editorship of Albert Steffen (1884–1963)—the weekly, *Das Goetheanum* (August). In February–March, Rudolf Steiner takes his first trip outside Germany since the war (Holland). On April 7, Steiner receives a letter regarding "religious renewal," and May 22–23, he agrees to address the question in a practical way. In June, the Clinical-Therapeutic Institute opens in Arlesheim under the direction of Dr. Ita Wegman. In August, the Chemical-Pharmaceutical Laboratory opens in Arlesheim (Oskar Schmiedel and Ita Wegman, directors). The Clinical-Therapeutic Institute is inaugurated in Stuttgart (Dr. Ludwig Noll, director); also the Research Laboratory in Dornach (Ehrenfried Pfeiffer and Gunther Wachsmuth, directors). In November–December, Rudolf Steiner visits Norway.

1922: The first half of the year involves very active public lecturing (thousands attend); in the second half, Rudolf Steiner begins to withdraw and turn toward the Society—"The Society is asleep." It is "too weak" to do what is asked of it. The businesses—*Die Kommenden Tag* and *Futura A.G.*—fail. In January, with the help of an agent, Steiner undertakes a twelve-city German tour, accompanied by eurythmy performances. In two weeks he speaks to more than 2,000 people. In April, he gives a "college course" in The Hague. He also visits England. In June, he is in Vienna for the East-West Congress. In August–September, he is back in England for the Oxford Conference on Education. Returning to Dornach, he gives the lectures *Philosophy, Cosmology, and Religion* (CW 215), and gives the third priest's course (CW 344). On September 16, The Christian Community is founded. In October–November, Steiner is in Holland and England. He also speaks to the youth: *The Youth Course* (CW 217). In December, Steiner gives lectures titled *The Origins of Natural Science* (CW 326), and *Humanity and the World of Stars: The Spiritual Communion of Humanity* (CW 219). December 31: Fire at the Goetheanum, which is destroyed.

1923: Despite the fire, Rudolf Steiner continues his work unabated. A very hard year. Internal dispersion, dissension, and apathy abound. There is conflict—between old and new visions—within the society. A wake-up call is needed, and Rudolf Steiner responds with renewed lecturing vitality. His focus: the spiritual context of human life; initiation science; the course of the year; and community building. As a foundation for an artistic school, he creates a series of pastel sketches. Lecture cycles: *The Anthroposophic Movement* (CW 258); *Initiation Science* (CW 227) (in England at the Penmaenmawr Summer School); *The Four Seasons and the Archangels* (CW 229); *Harmony of the Creative Word* (CW 230); *The Supersensible Human* (CW 231), given in Holland for the founding of the Dutch society. On November 10, in response to the failed Hitler-Ludendorf putsch in Munich, Steiner closes his Berlin residence and moves the *Philosophisch-Anthroposophisch Verlag* (Press) to Dornach. On December 9, Steiner begins the serialization of his *Autobiography: The Course of My Life* (CW 28) in *Das Goetheanum*. It will continue to appear weekly, without a break, until his death. Late December-early January: Rudolf Steiner refounds the Anthroposophical Society (about 12,000 members internationally) and takes over its leadership. The new board members are: Marie Steiner, Ita Wegman, Albert Steffen, Elizabeth Vreede, and Guenther Wachsmuth. (See *The Christmas Meeting for the Founding of the General Anthroposophical Society* [CW 260]. Accompanying lectures: *Mystery Knowledge and Mystery Centers* [CW 232]; *World History in the Light of Anthroposophy* [CW 233].) December 25: the Foundation Stone is laid (in the hearts of members) in the form of the "Foundation Stone Meditation."

1924: January 1: having founded the Anthroposophical Society and taken over its leadership, Rudolf Steiner has the task of "reforming" it. The process begins with a weekly newssheet ("What's Happening in the Anthroposophical Society") in which Rudolf Steiner's "Letters to Members" and "Anthroposophical Leading Thoughts" appear (CW 26). The next step is the creation of a new esoteric class, the "first class" of the "School for Spiritual Science" (which was to have been followed, had Rudolf Steiner lived longer, by two more advanced classes). Then comes a new language for anthroposophy—practical, phenomenological, and direct—and Rudolf Steiner creates the model for the second Goetheanum. He begins the series of extensive "karma lectures" (CW 235–40); and finally, responding to needs, he creates two new initiatives: biodynamic agriculture and curative education. After the middle of the year, rumors begin to circulate regarding Steiner's health. Lectures: January–February, *Anthroposophy* (CW 234); February: *Eurythmy as Visible Singing* (CW 278); June: *The Agriculture Course* (CW 327); June–July: *Eurythmy as Visible Speech* (CW 279); *Curative Education* (CW 317); August: (England, "Second International Summer School") *Initiation Consciousness: True and False Paths in Spiritual Investigation* (CW 243); September: *Pastoral Medicine* (CW 318). On September 26, for the first time, Rudolf Steiner cancels a lecture. On September 28, he gives his last lecture. On September 29, he withdraws to his studio in the carpenter's shop; now he is definitively ill. Cared for by Ita Wegman, he continues working, however, and writing the weekly installments of his *Autobiography* and *Letters to the Members/Leading Thoughts* (CW 26).

1925: Rudolf Steiner, while continuing to work, continues to weaken. He finishes *Extending Practical Medicine* (CW 27) with Ita Wegman.

On March 30, around ten in the morning, Rudolf Steiner dies.

INDEX

G

H

I

RUDOLF STEINER'S BLACKBOARD DRAWINGS

PLATE 1

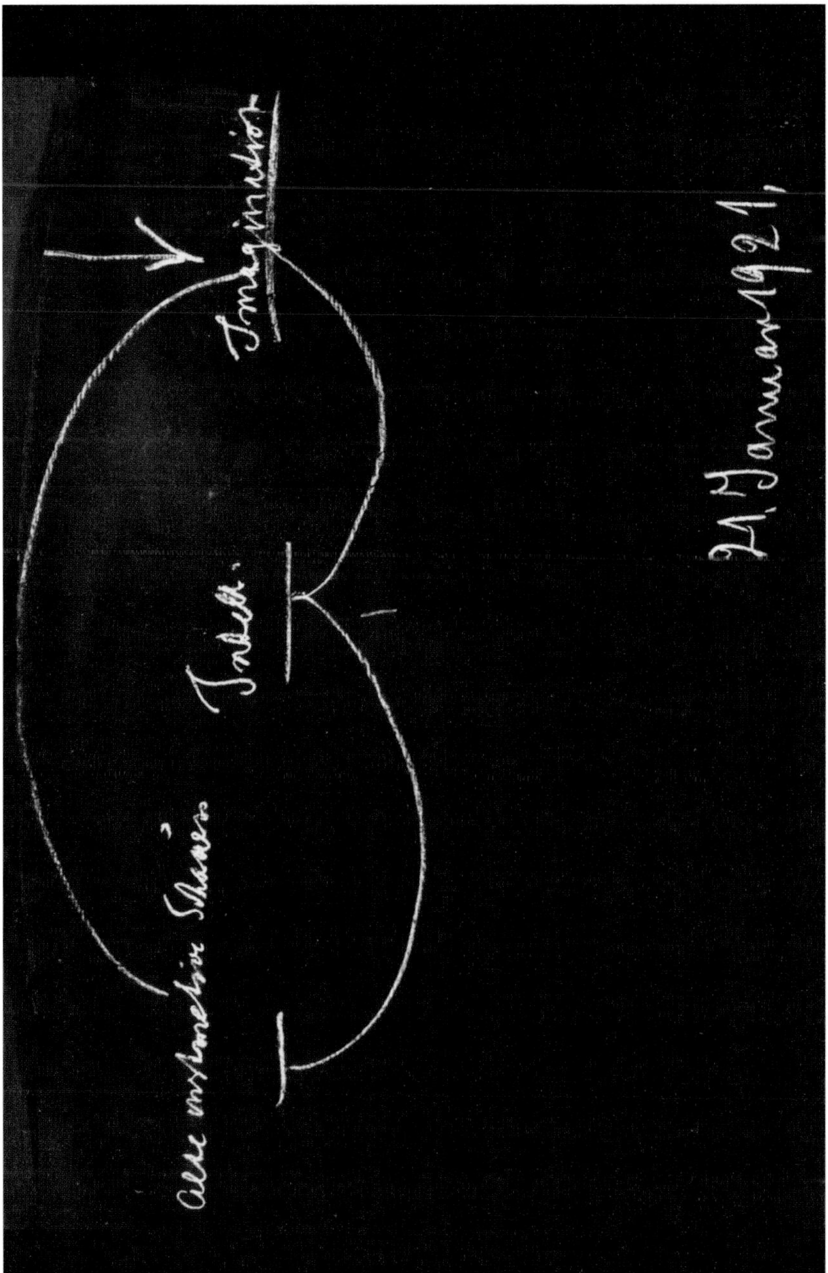

PLATE 2

PLATE 3

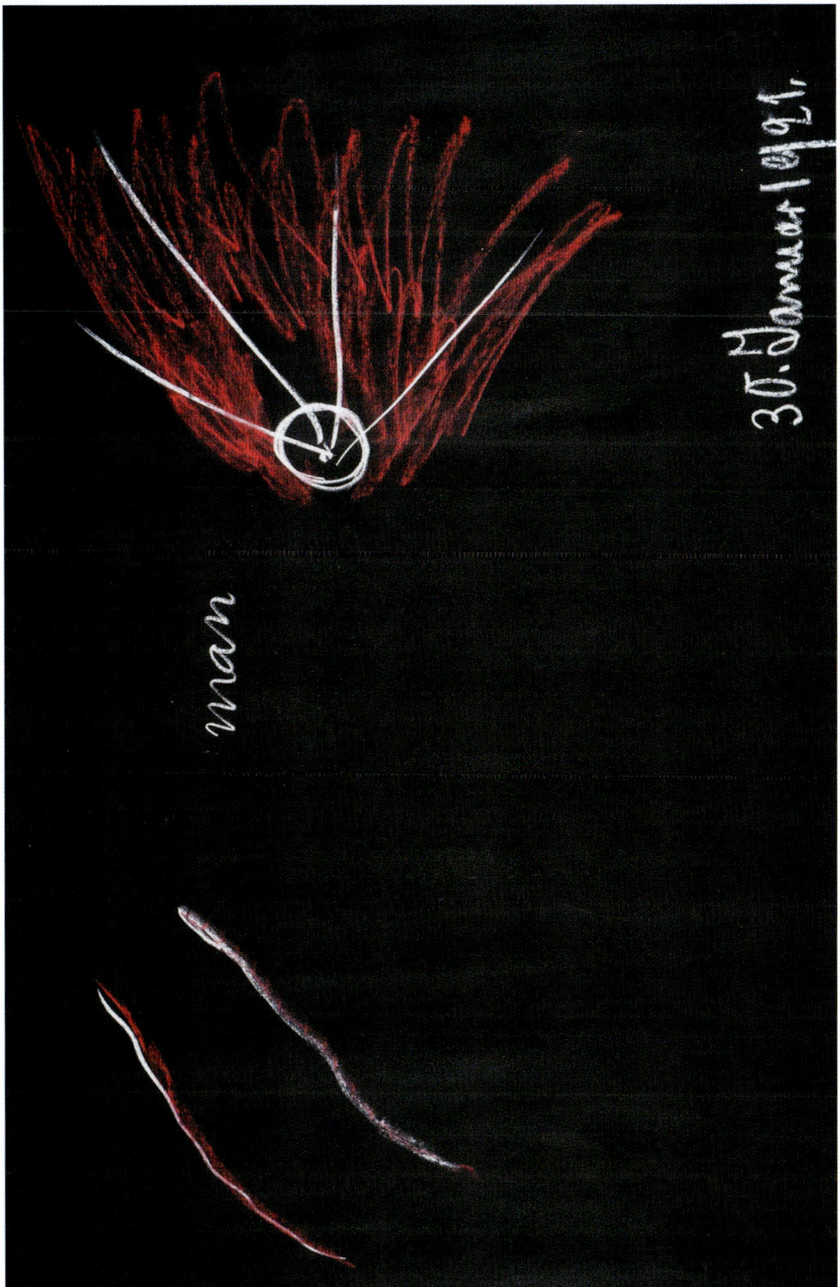

PLATE 4

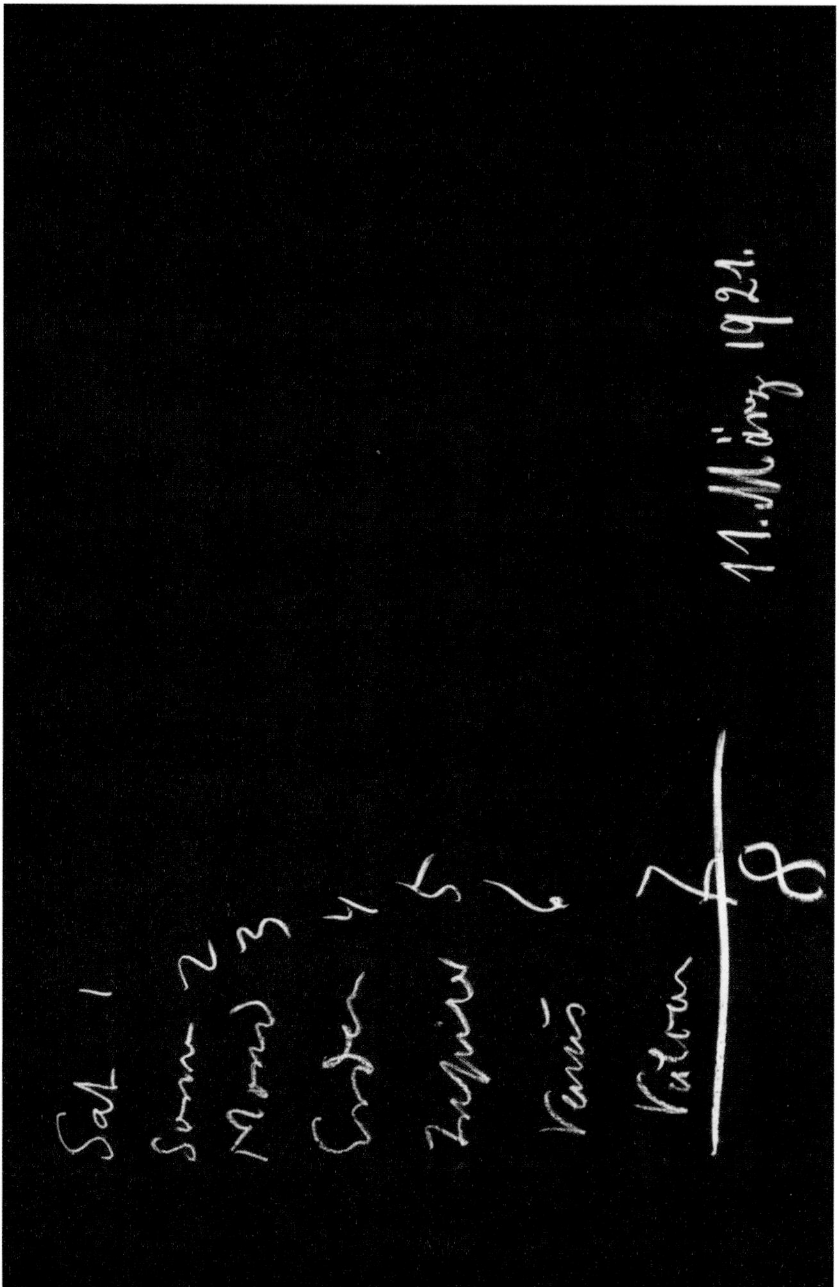

PLATE 5

PLATE 6

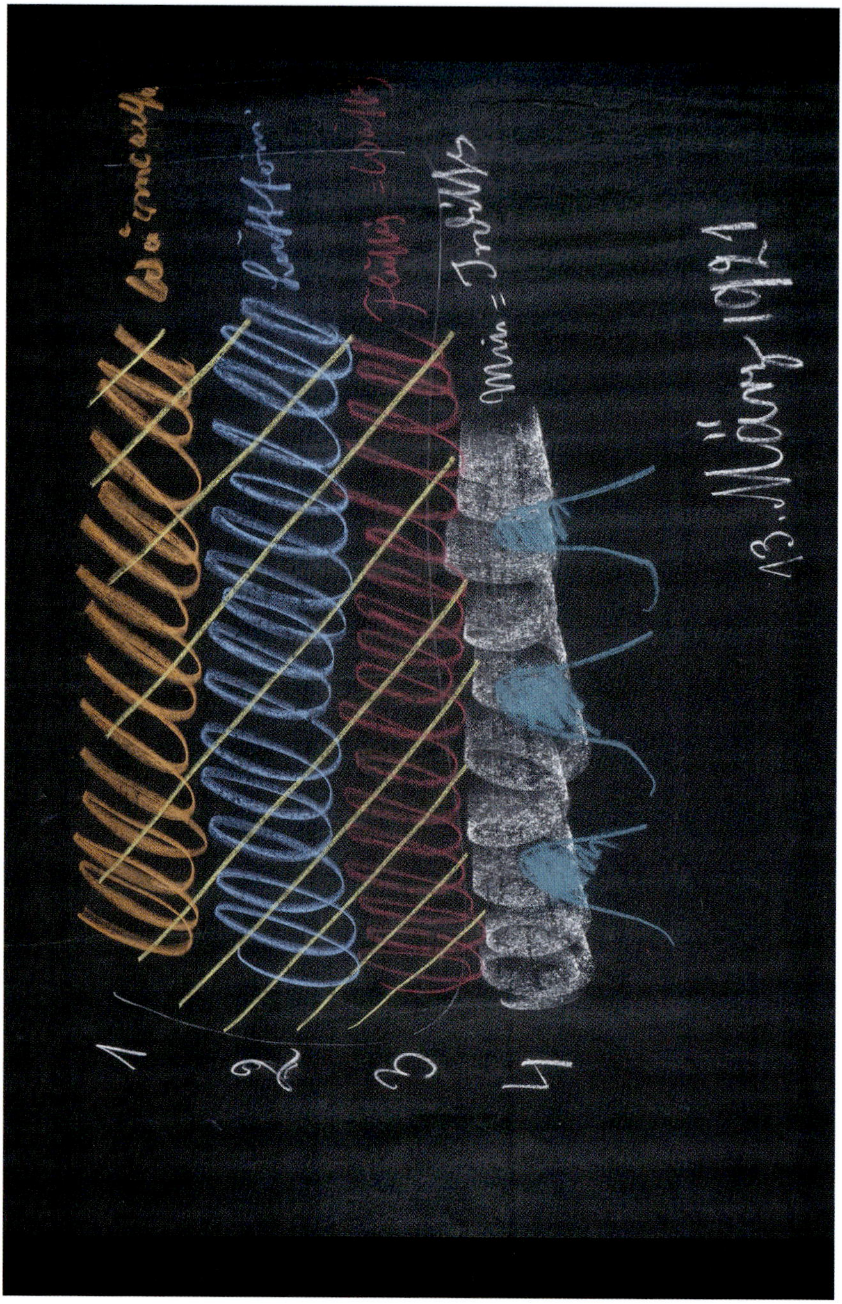

PLATE 7

PLATE 8

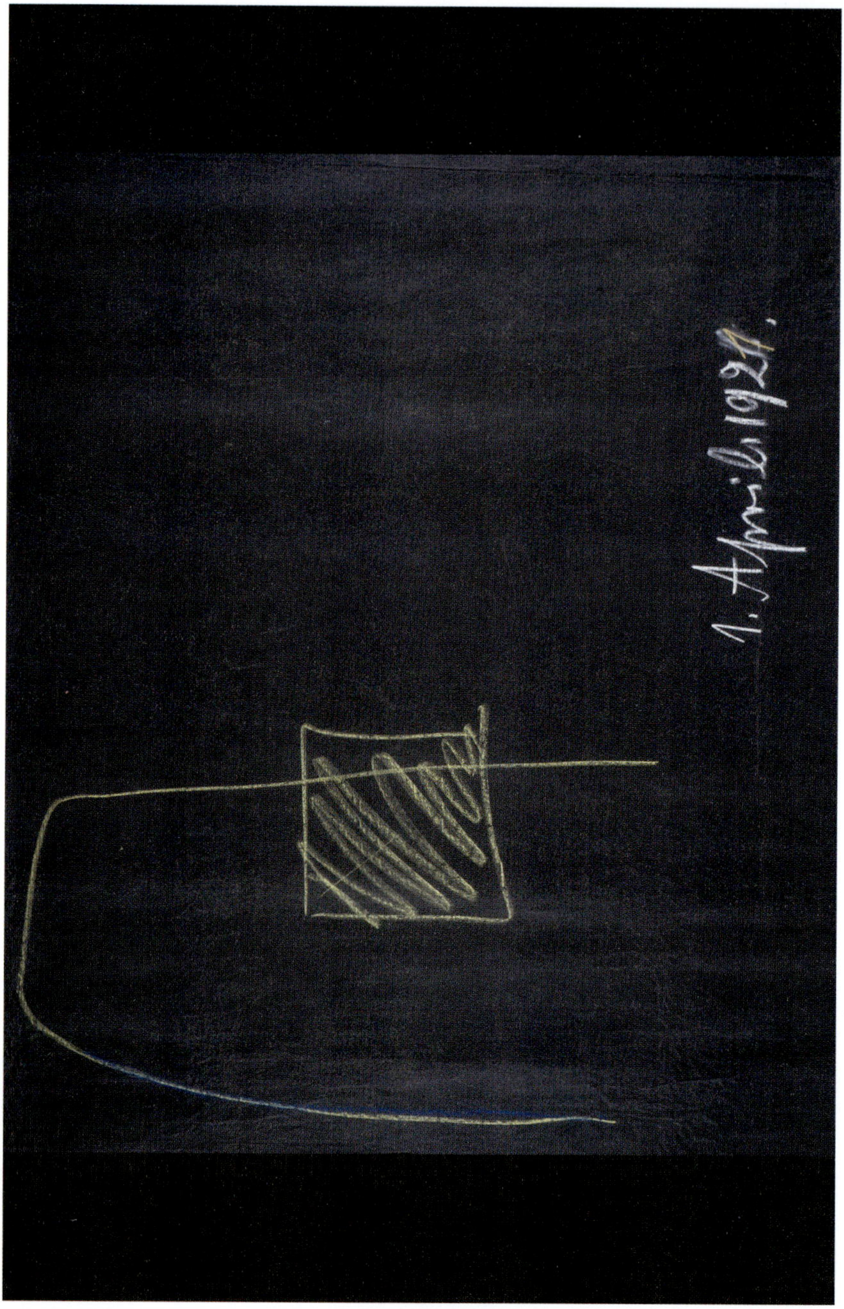

PLATE 9